VIRGIN KING

By the same author

Turning Japanese: The Fight for Industrial
Control of the New Europe

VIRGIN
KING

Inside Richard Branson's
Business Empire

Tim Jackson

HarperCollins*Publishers*

HarperCollins*Publishers*
77–85 Fulham Palace Road,
Hammersmith, London W6 8JB

Published by HarperCollins*Publishers* 1994

1 3 5 7 9 8 6 4 2

A catalogue record for this book is
available from the British Library

ISBN 0 00 224361 X

Photoset in Linotron Janson by
Rowland Phototypesetting Ltd
Bury St Edmunds, Suffolk

Printed and bound in Great Britain by
HarperCollinsManufacturing Glasgow

For Emily Marbach

CONTENTS

LIST OF ILLUSTRATIONS

(All photographs reproduced by kind permission of the Independent and Mirror Group Newspapers, unless stated otherwise.)

Section I

Tom Newman (*Tom Newman/Kate Simon*).
Mike Oldfield.
Nik Powell.
Shipton Manor, Oxfordshire.
Johnny Rotten (*Courtesy of Channel Four Television*).
Malcolm McLaren (*Courtesy of Channel Four Television*).
Boy George with Marilyn (*Pictorial Press, London*).
Richard Branson preparing to ski naked.
Branson letting off a fire extinguisher.
Ivana Trump being upturned by Richard Branson.
Steve Lewis.
Don Cruickshank.
Trevor Abbott.
Tony Elliot, publisher of *Time Out* magazine.
Randolph Fields.
Branson with Ted Toleman and Chay Blyth.
Challenger II on the River Thames.
Prime Minister Margaret Thatcher on *Challenger II* with Branson.
Branson's public-relations stunt during the stockmarket flotation of Virgin.
Roger Seelig.

Section II

Branson and Per Lindstrand, the Swedish balloonist.
Take-off from Japan.
The balloon's spectacular landing in the northern wastes of Canada.
Branson at the launch of his Mates condoms company.
Branson advertises the Barcelona megastore by waterskiing behind airship.
The compact-disc factory in the basement of the Oxford Street megastore.

Branson launches motorbike taxi service for Virgin's Upper Class passengers.
Branson launches Virgin computers.
Branson and Joan Templeman on their wedding day.
John Thornton.
Sir Colin Southgate.
Branson at the High Court after his victory against British Airways.
Lord King.
With Princess Diana at the launch of the first of Virgin's new fleet of Airbus A340 aircraft.
Branson with one of Virgin's new Airbus A340s.
The delivery of the application documents for Branson's bid to run the National Lottery.
The dejected Virgin chairman after the Lottery decision is announced.
The Range Rover in which the Virgin chairman and his family narrowly escaped death on the M40 motorway.
Richard Branson.

PROLOGUE: CONCEALING THE ART

RICHARD BRANSON is Britain's best-known entrepreneur, but it is not for his business activities that he is famous. Branson first achieved celebrity with his 1985 attempt on the Transatlantic sea speed record. Since then, he has ballooned across the Atlantic and the Pacific; spent an unhappy year at the helm of a Conservative government campaign to clean up the environment; launched a new brand of condoms in the hope of encouraging young people to have safer sex; and made a bid to run Britain's National Lottery, which was unsuccessful despite his promise to give away all his profits to charity.

Even when it is his business interests that bring him into the public eye, it is more often Branson the public-relations man than Branson the entrepreneur that is on display. If his picture is in the newspapers, it might be in order to announce a new plan to redevelop the old GLC County Hall on the south side of Westminster Bridge, and to drum up interest in the hotel and leisure complex that Branson hopes to build there; or to persuade the Radio Authority that Virgin 1215, Branson's medium-wave pop-music radio station, should be allowed to change to a more profitable frequency on FM. Or it could be to announce Virgin's participation in a consortium running trains between London and Paris through the new Channel Tunnel; or to win a £5m legal case against Lord King's British Airways. In every case, the coverage has a sound commercial reason behind it.

Only rarely does Richard Branson find his business activities under scrutiny against his will – and almost never does the public see this most public of entrepreneurs doing what he spends most of his time doing. But there should be no mistake: like most people who run companies of comparable size, Branson devotes most of his waking hours to his businesses – hiring staff, negotiating deals with other companies, conferring with lawyers and accountants, telephoning scores of his managers all over the world, answering letters from behind his desk. Few questions are asked about this side of his life; fewer still are answered.

This may be paradoxical, but it is not accidental. There are two Richard Bransons, one behind the other. The public man is informal, friendly, idealistic, happy-go-lucky, attached to his family, guided by strong principles, concerned to improve the society he lives in. The private man is a ruthlessly ambitious workaholic; a hard bargainer; an accountant with an instinctive feel for minimizing the losses on each new venture; a gambler who prefers to put his assets at risk every day rather than retire to a life of luxury on what he has already made. He is an empire-builder who keeps the inner workings of his businesses secret, and requires senior employees to sign binding confidentiality agreements before they come to work for him; a figure of great wealth and political influence who would not dream of breaking the law, but is equally determined not to pay a penny more in tax than he has to; an important customer for a number of top legal and accountancy firms, who knows the value of highly paid advice; and a business partner who may be informal and positive when he is being fairly treated, but will go to the High Court for a writ without a moment's hesitation when he believes he is not.

Most public figures would be hard put to maintain such a distance between their outer and inner selves. Yet there is nothing fraudulent about the way Richard Branson behaves. The key to understanding him is that his warm public persona is not a façade. It is every bit as real as the commercial steel underneath. But Branson has realized, instinctively if not consciously, that his business interests dictate which Richard Branson he should put first, and which the public should believe in. His motto ought to be *ars est celare artem* – art lies in concealing the art.

In many ways, Richard Branson is a model of what the socially responsible company chairman ought to be. A visit to his office provides the first clues. It is not an office at all, in fact, but a large white stucco house in Holland Park, a few miles to the west of

Marble Arch in central London. The house could hardly be described as modest – it is worth at least £5m – but less than a dozen people work inside, an astonishingly small number for the centre of a group of companies whose value is approaching £1bn. Branson himself keeps a desk in a sparsely decorated room on the first floor, but prefers to conduct his business from an apricot-coloured sofa in the sitting room that occupies the left half of the entire ground floor. To the right of the entrance hall, there is a large dining room for business lunches and dinners, with twenty or more chairs around its table. Branson's diary and his correspondence are dealt with by a personal assistant and two other secretaries; his press chief works in another room, with an assistant of his own. All the different Virgin Group businesses have their own headquarters, mostly in modest buildings scattered within a mile or two of the house. The nearest thing that the company has to a headquarters, apart from Holland Park, is in a three-storey building of brown brick around the corner in Campden Hill Road. That is where Trevor Abbott, the group's chief executive, keeps tabs on the money; that is the registered office of many of the hundred or so companies that make up Branson's empire.

'Small is beautiful' is evidently the guiding principle. Branson believes firmly that people work better in teams that are too compact to be impersonal. But separating the companies that make up the group into lots of small suburban houses and offices is not only more human than installing them in a single tower block in London's financial centre; it is also cheaper and more flexible. There have only ever been two exceptions to the rule: Branson's airline, Virgin Atlantic, which employs several hundred people in a couple of offices in the town of Crawley near Gatwick Airport; and the Virgin Music Group, which occupies a vast mansion set back from the Harrow Road. The reception area at Harrow Road boasts a stunning combination of Victorian cornices and minimalist art and furniture which was installed by a fashionable architect, and reputed to have cost £80,000. But this was not Branson's initiative; the man responsible for this act of corporate patronage was Simon Draper, who ran the Virgin Music Group until Branson sold it to Thorn-EMI in 1992.

While others make money from buying big companies that have

lost their way, cutting out the dead wood and returning them to profitability, Branson has made only a handful of acquisitions in his life, none of them costing more than £10m. Instead, his speciality is to build from scratch. In a business career spanning twenty-five years, he has used this approach to build an international retail chain, an airline, and a music business that includes records, music publishing and studios. The principle of starting from nothing applies to people as well as to businesses. Rather than hire in specialists from outside who will be expensive and may not be loyal, Branson prefers to offer big jobs to people who already work for him. This is by no means a rule: Trevor Abbott, the Virgin Group chief executive and Branson's most senior adviser, joined him when he had already been in business fifteen years; and one of the two managing directors of the airline was brought in only in 1990. Yet most of the leading players in the Virgin story are people who joined straight from school or university. One, Barbara Jeffries, first worked for Branson as a housekeeper at Shipton Manor in Oxfordshire; by 1992, she was managing director of all his studio businesses.

Since inexperienced staff necessarily make a few mistakes before acquiring expertise, it helps in such circumstances to take a long-term view. Luckily, Richard Branson has never evaluated his businesses on the basis of how much profit they make each year. When he signed musicians to the Virgin record label, he was often willing to pay advances that his competitors considered ruinously high – but in return, he would demand rights over a larger number of albums, and would want to keep control of the copyright over those albums for longer than other record companies. The record shops under the banner of Virgin Retail grew steadily in number for more than a decade, without ever making a proper return. But Branson ignored the advisers who told him time and again to close them down or sell them – and was proven right in 1988, when WH Smith, one of Britain's leading stationery chains, paid over £23m for the smaller and less successful stores, leaving him with a more closely focused chain of Virgin megastores. Branson has weathered equally stormy days at the airline, which took four years from its creation to turn in a reasonable profit. He kept his nerve during the 1991–2 recession in the air transport industry, emerging triumphantly at the beginning of 1994 with a daring deal that replaced his fleet of ageing Boeing 747s with more economical Airbus A340s.

This patience extends to his negotiating style, too. During the same recession, Branson was under huge pressure from his bankers to sell parts of the Virgin empire in order to reduce the mountain of debt he took on at the end of the 1980s. Yet he took more than a year to sell Virgin Music Group – and succeeded, like a carpet dealer in an Oriental bazaar, in persuading potential buyers that he neither needed nor especially wanted to sell. This strategy was rewarded in the astounding price that Thorn-EMI eventually paid in cash and assumed debt for the company: £560m, or almost $1bn at the prevailing exchange rate.

In the speeches that he is increasingly often asked to give, Branson is fond of pointing out that while conventional business analysis puts the interests of a company's shareholders first, followed by those of its customers and then its employees, he takes the opposite approach. For him, it is Virgin's employees who take top priority, particularly those who deal face to face with members of the public. If they are happy in their work, he hopes, then they will perform well – and in doing so they will satisfy his customers. Branson believes that the interests of Virgin's shareholders (which in effect means himself and his family) can be safely left behind, on the assumption that a company that pleases its customers will prosper itself.

Fame has brought Branson an array of rich and powerful friends, and an ability to arrange a meeting with almost anyone he wants in politics or business. When his libel action against British Airways was settled in the High Court, the Princess of Wales sent him a handwritten note of congratulation on a card headed 'Kensington Palace' bearing a monogram of a capital D with a coronet above it. 'Dear Richard,' it read. 'Hurray! Love from Diana. X.' The friendship was cemented a few months later, when Diana agreed to preside over the launching ceremony of the airline's first new Airbus. Her light-hearted appearance, which came only a few days after an announcement that she intended to retire from most of her public duties, put Branson and his company on the front page of newspapers all around the world.

Yet Branson himself is the opposite of elitist, and his company is one of the least hierarchical one could come across. To the annoyance of his senior managers, Branson seems to pay as much attention to a chat with a clerk in the airline's post-room as to a memorandum from his marketing director. Letters from his staff are always read first; when Branson travels on his own airline, he spends about half his hours on board talking to the cabin crew, and he travels into town at the other end not in a private limousine to a hotel at the city centre, but in the crew bus to the airport motel where those who will be flying back the following morning spend the night. Until he became an airline owner, and thus acquired the right to travel first-class for free on other airlines, Branson used always to fly economy class.

Richard Branson may work his secretaries hard, but he resists the temptation, to which many other company chairmen have succumbed, of ordering them around as if they were servants. He will ask for a mug of tea during a meeting at Holland Park as hesitantly as if he were a guest in someone else's house. Until recently, he used to dial his own telephone calls; he only stopped doing so when a growing number of people at the other end refused to talk to him because they thought he was only a practical joker pretending to be Richard Branson. (Given that Branson used to specialize in telephoning his friends and pretending to be other people, that is richly ironic.) It is no coincidence that Penni Pike, Branson's senior personal assistant, has worked for him in the same job since 1977.

He manages and motivates his staff by example. Branson is hugely energetic. He needs his eight hours' sleep a night, but is nevertheless able to put in very long hours without rest – keeping himself awake where necessary by snatching naps during the course of the day or en route between one meeting and the next. He travels by air on average once a week. Dozens of the present and former Virgin employees interviewed in the course of the research for this book have been influenced by his almost blind determination. Where others would try to put an idea into practice but then give up when obstacles appear to make it impossible, Branson takes it as an article of faith that there is a way around – if only it can be found. Sometimes, of course, he is wrong; but surprisingly often, the extra effort pays off with success – and others begin to imitate the Branson technique. The most extreme example of this approach was the establishment of Virgin Atlantic; by dint of extreme effort from a team of a dozen or so people, the airline was up and flying within four months of the day on which Branson first started discussing the idea.

While many businesses suffer from a 'Not Invented Here' syndrome – a resistance to ideas that come from other organizations – Branson has no shame in picking up suggestions wherever he finds them. All day long, he carries around with him a black A4 notebook – standard issue, bought from the Rymans stationery chain – into which he jots not merely ideas that might be put to use in his businesses, but also names and telephone numbers, notes on conversations, and lists of tasks to carry out. Richard Branson's daily to-do list usually contains thirty items or so; the idea is that by numbering them, he can attend to the most important first and thus make best use of his time. Such is the respect he is held in by his employees that many senior staff in the different Virgin companies now carry the same notebooks with them, and can be seen scribbling down thoughts and notes of conversations in exactly the same way. Like the rest of Branson's life, the notebook is resolutely low-tech. He neither types nor uses a computer; and he acquired a mobile phone for the first time only in late 1993.

As well as a second house in Holland Park, two doors down from the one that he uses as his office, Branson owns a villa in Minorca, a country house in Oxfordshire surrounded by fields and a large pond, and a private island in the Caribbean. There is a swimming-pool in the basement at Holland Park. The Oxfordshire house, his weekend retreat, has its own cricket pitch; Branson flew in a pair of Balinese craftsmen to build a cricket pavilion in the style of a traditional temple, complete with carved wooden doors and a roof of thatched rice straw. Necker Island, part of the British Virgin Islands, now belongs to the company rather than to Branson personally; it boasts a house large enough for twenty or more, a chef brought over from the Michelin-starred Manoir aux Quat'Saisons restaurant (in which Branson happens to own a controlling stake), and an extensive cellar that includes vintage clarets and burgundies as well as lighter whites suitable for quaffing on the beach.

Yet Branson seems oddly detached from the outward details of his life. It does not bother him that paint is flaking off the back of his house in Holland Park, or that the swimming-pool filter no longer works. He owns a Range Rover because he was given it by the buyer of the *Virgin Atlantic Challenger II*, the speedboat that broke the Atlantic speed record; but he is perfectly willing to allow his two children, both of primary-school age, to drive it around his fields in the country. He has always eschewed the ostentatiously high living of the music industry, particularly the chairman of one record company who makes a point of parking a spanking new Rolls-Royce or Bentley outside the front door of his offices. Since he married his second wife, Joan Templeman, Branson has supplemented his trademark collection of sweaters with more expensive casual jackets and shirts. Yet he often succeeds nevertheless in looking as though he picked the clothes he is wearing out of the cupboard at random in the dark – and he specializes in wearing brown shoes that look as though they were on special offer at Woolworths.

Nor does he have expensive gastronomic tastes. While many of his top managers have become connoisseurs of food and wine, Branson is the first to admit that he is unable to appreciate the finer points of the Quat'Saisons cuisine on his private island. He used to make it a rule never to spend more than £15 on a bottle, and was scandalized when colleagues wanted to spend company money tasting good vintages in restaurants.

Most rich men of Richard Branson's age start to collect things as a way of finding a use for the millions they have amassed. The pond in the grounds of his Oxfordshire house duly contains a number of rare species of duck and goose from around the world, their wings carefully clipped to prevent them from flying away. Branson takes pleasure in strolling around the pond pointing out the bright colours on the plumage of each one – but cannot quite remember which is which. He is fond of telling the story of how, when he used to live on a houseboat on the Regent's Canal, he and Joan once returned from a weekend away to find that the boat had flooded and sunk. Yet Branson had no regrets to discover that all his worldly goods had been lost – for he knew that his photograph album, which was more precious to him than anything that mere money could buy, was safely stored somewhere else. Proof of how little his attitude has changed can be seen in his decision to put the two houses in Holland Park on the market at the turn of 1994 with a price-tag of £15m, and to start looking for another houseboat so that his family could move back to the canal from which he started twenty years ago.

Indeed, most of Richard Branson's pleasures could be enjoyed just as easily without great riches. He loves tennis and swimming in the sea; underlying his boating and ballooning in the second half of the 1980s were great reserves of physical courage, which allowed him several times to face death without panic. He plays practical jokes that are more physical than intellectual – throwing people into swimming-pools, dressing up in bra and suspenders at parties for Virgin employees, pushing cakes into people's faces in the style of television cartoons. At an airline-industry awards ceremony, he once grabbed hold of Ivana Trump, the former wife of a leading American property billionaire, and turned her upside down in front of hundreds of astonished black-tie guests. It is this humour above all that makes Richard Branson such an object of affection among his employees. The ear-to-ear smile that he wears for so many hours every day conveys a simple message: business is fun.

Underneath this gregariousness is an insecurity. Richard Branson's lack of verbal fluency was intimately linked to his poor academic record at school, and his decision to leave rather than to go to university. For a man who has made his money in industries that are all about communication and people, Branson is sometimes astonishingly inarticulate. He will talk with passion when his interest is raised, but can be stumped by an utterly straightforward question. During one of the last interviews he gave for this book, Branson took a fifteen-minute break in order to record for a camera crew waiting in his sitting-room a short speech of welcome to a charity dinner that he could not attend. The speech was warm and friendly, conveying all the right points about the charity's work, and ending with a rousing demand to guests that he would never see to give generously to the appeal at the end of the evening. But its three minutes were punctuated with umms and aahs – hundreds of them, separating not just sentences and phrases but also single words. Despite the decade of practice he has had, and the hundreds of television interviews he has given, Branson remains clearly ill at ease with the spoken word. When he got up at the end of a chat-show interview in 1992 and poured a glass of water over the head of his host, the audience took his action as a joke, and laughed uproariously. They were probably wrong. Emptying the glass of water was more a sign of Richard Branson's frustration at being outmanoeuvred by the glib questions he had been asked.

If there is one respect in which Branson can fairly claim to have been valued by the public at less than his real worth, it is to do with his charitable activities. He is not a giver of huge sums to charity in the way that some businessmen are; nor does he have to his credit, as the Sainsbury family do, a gift to the cultural life of the nation on the scale of a new wing for the National Gallery. But Branson has been involved in three important projects in which he has attempted to give something back to the community from which he has made his riches. The first was the UK 2000 campaign, a scheme to bring together a number of different government and private initiatives to improve Britain's environment and to provide useful work experience for the young unemployed. From the very day Branson took on the chairmanship of the campaign, he was dogged with the tabloid misconception that it was nothing more than a litter-picking organisation; his departure from the job a year later, after acres of hostile press coverage, was a relief to himself as well as to his advisers at Virgin.

His second venture for the public good was the launch of Mates, a brand of cut-price condoms intended to shake up the monopoly in the British condom market that allowed the manufacturers of Durex not to advertise. The project was a commercial triumph: the new brand was easily established, and took more than a quarter of the market in less than two years. In terms of public health, however, the outcome was mixed; although condom advertisements were shown on British television for the first time, Mates did little to change the reluctance of young people to take elementary precautions against the spread of AIDS. Branson himself also came in for a good deal of criticism – despite the fact that he had risked large sums of his own money in a venture whose proceeds were intended only for charity.

Branson's bid to run the National Lottery suffered a similar fate. Once again, his intentions were altruistic; he would take no profits personally from the exercise, and the lottery and the money it raised would be administered by a foundation kept entirely independent of the Virgin empire. Branson was bitterly disappointed when the franchise was instead awarded to a business consortium; but he was angrier still to find himself criticised for his involvement in an exercise for the good of others. Somehow, despite the clear separation of the lottery from his business interests, Branson never quite managed to dispel the suspicion that he was hoping to benefit personally from running it.

Most public figures – politicians and sports stars as well as business people – would be less sensitive. They would expect their motives to be impugned, their failures exaggerated, their successes attacked, their physical characteristics made an object of fun. The very fact that Richard Branson can take such offence is proof of how unaccustomed he is to public criticism, and how he has come to take it for granted that a little effort and imagination in arranging what information is made public will inevitably result in positive coverage.

Achieving good press has been as important in Branson's business career as making sure that the books balance at the end of the year. From his first days as a magazine publisher and record retailer, Branson knew that descriptions of his ventures as successful and expansionary could become self-fulfilling. That is why he would arrange, when a newspaper journalist came to talk to him, for an employee to go to a nearby telephone box and ring in constantly during the interview in order to give an impression of activity; and why he similarly drafted in a couple of friends to pose as musicians signed to his record label for a television documentary when in fact Virgin Records had no artists at all on its roster. It took two factors, however, to turn Branson from a moderately well known and eccentric pop millionaire into a fully fledged celebrity. One was the launch of Virgin Atlantic, which gave him the opportunity to indulge his taste for dressing up in a series of outlandish outfits. (The apparent thirst for personal publicity which he then acquired had a great deal to do with the need to compete with British Airways on a shoestring advertising budget.) The other factor in his current fame was the danger involved in his record-breaking sea and balloon crossings of the Atlantic and Pacific. In public, Branson would talk about his thirst for adventure and his love of competition and the outdoors. In Virgin board meetings, he defended the spending of company money on these exercises by saying that they were the cheapest possible way of advertising group companies.

By the end of the 1980s, Branson's image as popular hero had become a bankable asset for his businesses, arguably even more valuable than the Virgin brand name itself. He would be wheeled out to meet rock stars signing contracts with Virgin Music, even though he had not been involved in the negotiations; and they, accustomed to receiving the adulation of fans themselves, would be awed as if they were in the presence of royalty. Four years after he sold Virgin Music, Branson took me on an impromptu tour of the company's recording studios at Shipton Manor in Oxfordshire. The woman who opened the front door was visibly delighted to see him, and reminded him as they kissed that she had worked for him a decade earlier. When we went into the studio itself, rich in the nostalgic smell of marijuana smoke, the band who were working there took their feet off the desks when he walked in.

One example of the commercial value that Branson squeezes from his own public persona and the strength of the Virgin brand was the air service that City Jet began to operate under the Virgin name between London's City Airport and Dublin in 1994. Another was the launch in 1993 of a Virgin personal computer, which was in reality being built entirely by a separate company that paid a royalty for use of the Virgin name. Even firms that have no dealings at all with Virgin want to cash in on the Branson name. American Express, Mercury and Fiat are only three of the companies that have used him in their advertisements. In the Mercury television advertisement, Virgin received a double benefit, for Branson's script required him to be an uncharacteristically fast-talking salesman of the attractions of Virgin Atlantic's service.

Lack of cash has been a constant theme throughout Virgin's history. Founded on a shoestring, the company was desperately undercapitalised throughout the 1970s, and narrowly avoided collapse in the recession that followed the election of Margaret Thatcher as Prime Minister in 1979. Even after it had established banking facilities suitable for a company of its size and had raised £25m from institutional investors, it still required great skill and assiduous chasing of debtors to make sure that none of the company's cheques bounced. Don Cruickshank, the management consultant brought in to take Virgin public, described the group during the time he worked for it as 'teetering on the edge of disaster, seven days a week'. In February 1985, after American aircraft had bombed Libya and passengers decided to avoid air travel, Cruickshank sat around a pub table with Branson and Trevor Abbott to discuss whether Virgin Atlantic should be closed down altogether. Once Virgin's shares were quoted on the Stock Exchange, there was more money about; but Branson's decision to take the company private in 1989 saddled it with a mountain of debt that was paid off only by giving up the 'crown jewels' of the business – the Virgin Music Group itself. Perhaps surprisingly, given his wish to reassure outsiders of the stability of Virgin's foundations, Branson himself describes his entire business career as a struggle for survival.

There is a tension at the heart of Branson's wooing of the media. Although he wishes himself and his businesses to be written about and filmed, he is less willing to make himself accountable to outsiders. When he decided to take Virgin public, one of the investment bankers who discussed the flotation with him (though not, interestingly, the one that was eventually chosen to handle it) warned Branson and his colleagues that life as a public company would be very different. The banker was right. Branson disliked having to pay dividends; he disliked having to explain to hostile analysts in the City why he had taken this or that decision; and although his small shareholders were always faithful, he disliked the thought that institutional investors might have the right to question business decisions that had hitherto been his sole prerogative to take. Branson was also uncomfortable with the need to win the approval of his fellow directors before spending the company's money – and on one occasion, which was successfully kept secret, had to find £700,000 from his own pocket when some shares he had bought on his own initiative lost value in the market crash of 1987. Branson's wish to be given back full control over Virgin was as important a factor as any other in the decision to take the company private. With the transaction now safely accomplished, he likes to tell the story of a Japanese businessman who was discussing the possibility of taking an equity stake in a Virgin business and trying to convince Branson of his own merits as a docile minority shareholder. 'Would you rather have Japanese wife or Western wife?' the businessman asked. The answer was, and is, quite clear: when the marriage in question is a commercial one, Branson would far rather have Japanese wife.

What makes the accountability issue particularly sensitive for Richard Branson is that he has always been a generator of ideas who needs someone else to follow behind him – attending to details, pruning back ventures that later prove mistaken and, where necessary, warning him against putting his wilder ideas into practice. Throughout his career, his relationship with the person who has performed this function has always been unstable. Branson's first partner was Nik Powell, a childhood friend to whom he gave a forty per cent shareholding in Virgin at the beginning of the 1970s. A decade later, dealings between the two had deteriorated sharply; Powell thought that Branson was taking foolhardy financial decisions, while Branson himself came to the conclusion that Powell was no longer contributing enough to the business to justify his position in it. It was more than two years after Powell's departure that Don Cruickshank, the managing director who took Virgin public, took on the responsibility. But this new pairing was not to last either. Five years later, after the two had clashed frequently, Branson's decision to take the company private again left his MD without a clear role. The gap was filled by Trevor Abbott, the group's more emollient finance director. Promoted to group managing director, Abbott has been more cautious than Cruickshank in saying no to his boss; five years into the job, he seems to have retained Branson's confidence without challenging his authority. Part of Abbott's secret is that he has no enthusiasm for the limelight that has so changed Branson's life. Although he wields considerable power both inside and outside the Virgin empire, Abbott passes almost unknown in public, save among a small number of suppliers, partners and customers, who hold him in high regard.

Each of these three men in turn has tried to devise a strategy to account in public for the essentially spontaneous decisions that Branson himself makes. Powell had grand ideas about vertical integration, believing that Virgin would make money from all the different activities involved in the production of music and film; but that notion was damaged fatally by the group's withdrawal from film production. Cruickshank preferred to cast Virgin as a music conglomerate whose core was the record company; but Branson had no compunction in selling it. Abbott has picked out Virgin's long-term cooperative ventures with other companies (notably in retailing and in the company's video-game business, but also in the airline itself) as the core of its vision. It is too early to offer a judgement on this, since Abbott's tenure in the group managing director job has only just reached five years. But by 1994, Virgin had already dissolved two of these strategic alliances (with Fujisankei in the record business, and with Seibu-Saison in the airline) – and the company was contemplating selling its video-game business to one of its minority American shareholders. Only months before, Branson had described that business as one that could grow to the same size as the airline within a decade.

These deals with other companies do illustrate, however, a skill that has become a Virgin hallmark. Richard Branson is a brilliant and ruthless negotiator. When the company was small and he was striking agreements on his own, Branson had enough cheek to demand far more than he ever hoped to win – but also enough patience to argue a deal point by tiny point if his adversary so demanded. He was highly skilful at hiding behind others, telling those he was negotiating with that it was the objections of his lawyers or his colleagues, rather than his own misgivings, that made him unable to agree to a proposal. To this day, he has an uncanny ability to portray a transaction in the terms that make it attractive to the person he is negotiating with, rather than allowing them to focus on what he intends to get out of it. He knows when to speak and when to stay silent; and he is capable of letting others leave a meeting under the impression that they have got what they want, even if they have not in fact done so. Finally, Branson is a masterful haggler: rather than accept an official fixed price when buying something, he will put in a lower (and often a significantly lower) offer. On many purchases – an aircraft, a house, an island, even the removal bill for a snooker-table – he will succeed. One of his friends jokes that if you ask Richard Branson to lend you a fiver, he will counter with an offer of £4.50.

It is this skill that has helped Branson to perform the most extraordinary feat of his business career. Most entrepreneurs who start businesses begin by owning all the company's shares, but find themselves forced to give away a growing proportion of equity to others as the need for new investment capital grows. Richard Branson's control over Virgin, however, has moved in the opposite direction. When *Tubular Bells* became a hit in 1973, Branson only owned 60 percent of the main Virgin holding company, and Nik Powell owned the remaining 40 per cent. At Powell's suggestion, others had been given 20 per cent holdings in subsidiary companies including the record company, the studios, and the Virgin management company. So Branson's effective holding over these companies was just under 50 per cent. Today, the various Virgin businesses are worth over £1bn – yet Branson and his family interests own more than 60 per cent of them.

Two policies allowed Branson to do this. First, he used the cash generated by the businesses themselves to make them grow. Second, he succeeded with great skill in easing out his minority shareholders. A shareholder in one of the subsidiaries departed the company in high dudgeon with Branson, leaving his shares behind him. Another subsidiary shareholder lost his stake when the company for which he worked was closed down altogether. Branson asked Nik Powell to go during the 1981 recession, giving him £1m cash, a cinema and some other assets in return for his 40 percent stake. (Within five years, that stake was to be worth almost £100m.) There was a similar pattern at Virgin Atlantic. When Randolph Fields brought Branson the idea of flying across the Atlantic, both men were originally to own half of the airline. During the negotiations before the airline's launch, Branson forced Fields to reduce his shareholding to 25 percent; later the same year, Fields was made to step down as the company's chairman; another year later, Branson bought out his remaining stake for £1m.

The one exception to this pattern was Simon Draper, Branson's South African cousin, who established the record label for him. Draper took the precaution of asking his older brother for advice, and demanded that his 20 percent shareholding in the record company should be converted into a less risky 15 percent holding in the parent company. As his position in the business strengthened, Draper demanded further safeguards – with the result that he became a millionaire many times over when the company went public in 1986. Draper was also unique in never negotiating directly with Branson. The arrangements would first be discussed by lawyers or other intermediaries; when Draper and Branson came to meet, the usual pattern was that Draper would make his demand and Branson would quickly accede to it. Yet Draper's craving to be financially independent from Branson, and immune from whatever decisions Branson might make inside Virgin, cost him dear. So keen was Draper to limit his risk on the airline that, after Virgin went private, he sold his ten percent stake in Virgin Atlantic back to Branson for £6m. As he signed the papers, Draper turned to the lawyer and smiled. 'I know this is probably the worst deal I will ever do in my life,' he said. It may yet prove to be; but Draper, who now runs a private publishing house and owns thirty-nine Aston Martin sports cars, has enough money not to care.

Richard Branson's wish to make sure he always does as well as possible from any business arrangement applies equally to his dealings with the Inland Revenue. He discovered early in his career the risks of breaking the law, when his botched attempt to evade purchase tax was detected by Her Majesty's Customs & Excise. Luckily, the Customs were willing to settle for the payment of a £53,000 penalty, so the young entrepreneur was spared the humiliation of a prosecution, and the risk of a gaol sentence that might have put an end to his ambitions. From that clumsy attempt at fraud he learned the distinction between tax avoidance (which consists of arranging matters so as to minimise the tax bill) and tax evasion (which is illegal); and he learned to make use of top-class advisers to ensure that every step he took was watertight and could be defended against challenge. But Branson's instinctive reluctance to see his hard-earned profits paid over to the Chancellor of the Exchequer never left him. In 1973, when Branson was not yet twenty-four years old, the first trademark of the Virgin record company was registered as the property of an offshore trust, thus legitimately placing beyond the taxman's reach part of the royalties that overseas companies paid to Virgin. Later in the 1970s, Branson made use of a number of carefully prepared tax-avoidance packages bought in from experts. Early in the 1980s, Don Cruickshank had to warn Branson that he might actually be wasting time and money with these convoluted schemes, since Virgin was growing so fast that the schemes could not keep up.

Before Virgin went public, Branson took the step that has saved him tens of millions in tax. He transferred ownership of many of his shares in the company to offshore trusts of which he and his family are beneficiaries — so that when the company went public, and when the music business was later sold in a transaction valued at £560m, the bulk of the capital gains could be free of tax. There the position still stands. The offshore trusts, resident in the Channel Islands, are the major shareholders in the holding companies of Branson's present businesses; and they are able, quite legally, to invest money in his ventures if the independent trustees believe it wise to do so. If Branson ever decides to retire, he will be quite at liberty to take a one-year tax holiday abroad and to come back to the UK several hundred million pounds richer without owing anything to the Inland Revenue. Hostile questions were asked in Parliament about these arrangements soon after the sale of Virgin Music Group; but the lawyers and accountants have done their jobs too well for there to be anything to criticise.

This book is an attempt to capture what makes Richard Branson distinctive as a businessman. It is therefore in part a biography, and in part a history of the Virgin empire that he has established. But it does not seek to do both jobs in full. There is little on these pages, for instance, about Branson's marriage to Joan Templeman, his second wife; and little about the companies in his empire with which he has so far had little to do – notably the communications businesses run by his brother-in-law Robert Devereux, and the Voyager hotel interests. In some cases, such as his participation in a consortium running train services through the Channel Tunnel, the projects are still at too early a stage for any serious conclusions to be drawn about them at all. Broadly, however, this book tells the story of Branson and his ventures one by one, starting from the mail-order record firm that was his very first serious venture at the end of the 1960s, and ending with his abortive attempt to run the National Lottery in 1994. Whether the reader will agree with the conclusions and predictions to be found in the epilogue, however, remains to be seen.

ONE

1969: Easy Work, Good Money

STEVE LEWIS, sixteen years old, knocked on the door. After a long pause, a bony youth with lank, black, greasy hair appeared. He had a prominent rip in the inside leg of his jeans. The brightness of the July sun highlighted the contrast between his pale, long fingers and the dark semicircles underneath his nails.

'Is this number forty-four Albion Street?' asked Lewis.

'Yes,' replied the boy, who looked eighteen or nineteen.

'I've come about the job which was advertised in the personal columns of *The Times*,' said Lewis. '"Record company and magazine looking for young people," it said. "Easy work, good money." This was the address to apply to.'

'The job's gone, But you can come and sell magazines for us if you want to.' Nik Powell, the boy on the doorstep, turned on his heel and led the way past piles of magazines wrapped in string and paper into the hall of the terraced house. 'Take that stack down to Hyde Park,' he said, pointing to one of the piles. 'You sell them for three shillings each, you keep one and six, and you bring the rest back here at the end of the day.'

Steve Lewis was just about to start studying for his A-levels at Christ's College in Finchley, and he wanted to earn some pocket money in the summer holidays. Music was his passion – everything from *Sergeant Pepper* to Jimi Hendrix, but the black American music of the Motown label in particular; that was why the advertisement had caught his eye. But he didn't want to hawk magazines in Hyde Park, he wasn't going to be intimidated into doing so by this unkempt, haughty teenager he had never met and he made his feelings clear.

Powell grudgingly identified himself and told Lewis that he would have to wait until Richard Branson was free. As he waited,

Lewis was struck by the glamour and buzz of the office. Phones were ringing; attractive women were coming and going. At the other end of the room, a young man with tousled light brown hair and a dazzling smile was talking very earnestly into the telephone.

When at last he finished his call and came over to see Steve Lewis, Richard Branson was a great deal more friendly than Nik Powell had been. His voice was mellifluous and rather posh. He explained that he had just set up a business to sell records by mail order, but admitted rather shamefacedly that he did not know much about music. Steve Lewis saw his opening. Within ten minutes he had dropped the names of enough obscure artists to convince the nineteen-year-old Richard Branson that he could provide the expertise that the business lacked. Branson, his interest rising, told Lewis that he had placed an advertisement in *Melody Maker*, the country's leading music magazine, offering a list of records at a discount. 'If the record you want is not listed here,' said the advertisement, 'write to Angie, and we'll give you a price.' The trouble was that Angie had left, yet the business was booming.

Branson had spotted a hole in the record market, and now it was all he could do to meet demand. Retail price maintenance – the system that allowed manufacturers of products to force shops to sell them at a minimum price – had been abolished by the government five years earlier, but neither record companies nor record shops had taken much notice. Rather than engage in a frenzy of discounting, the industry preferred to carry on much as it had done before, selling records at a standard price of thirty-nine shillings and elevenpence. Branson, therefore, had advertised his records at thirty-seven and six. A flood of customers had written in saying what they wanted, and enclosing postal orders and cheques. The records themselves had come in bulk from shops in Muswell Hill and the East End that were keen to unload excess stock. A group of girls had been recruited to type labels and to pack the records into envelopes. But without Angie, who could find the unusual titles that customers asked for? Who could distinguish the up-and-coming bands from the three-minute wonders?

Within half an hour, everything was agreed. Steve Lewis would become the new Angie. He would work for the business – Virgin Records, it was called – over the summer, at a wage of £10 a week.

When the autumn came, he would go back to school to start his A-levels. But he would come down to Albion Street every day after school at 5 PM, and work four hours for £1, of which six shillings would have to be spent in tube fares. Once the arrangements had been made, however, Lewis saw little more of Richard Branson. It was Nik Powell – the scruffy character who had opened the door, the junior member of the partnership – to whom he would report from day to day. To his relief, Steve Lewis found Powell increasingly friendly, and came to appreciate his idealism, his warmth and his dry wit.

The mail-order record business that began in 1969 was Richard Branson's first real commercial venture. But it was by no means the activity that he had intended to pursue. He had planned to start a national student magazine, and had first worked on it from the basement of a house belonging to the parents of a friend before moving his centre of operations to his parents' *pied-à-terre* in Albion Street, near Paddington Station. The house had been taken by Branson's parents on a short lease from the Church Commissioners for occasional nights in London, and he had been allowed to use part of it.

Student was an organizational, artistic and literary success. Its list of contributors and interview subjects read like a *Who's Who* of the counter-culture 1960s. John Le Carré, the diplomat-turned-spy writer whose novel *The Spy Who Came in from the Cold* had established him a powerful reputation, had provided a short story. There were articles about Vanessa Redgrave, the revolutionary actress; David Hockney, the fashionable pop artist; and Henry Moore, the sculptor. James Baldwin, an American novelist who was exploring the uncomfortable themes of homosexuality and race, appeared in print next to an extract from a notorious speech by Enoch Powell, a coldly brilliant classical scholar who had predicted a year earlier in Parliament that racial tension caused by immigration would make Britain run with 'rivers of blood'. Other names to be found in the magazine's pages were Alice Walker, Jean-Paul Sartre and Stephen Spender. Letters of support had been solicited from everyone from Peter Sellers to Lyndon B. Johnson, the President of the United States.

Richard Branson was not only the magazine's founder but also its editor-in-chief, interviewer-at-large, production manager and advertising director. With equal confidence, he telephoned famous people to ask for articles and businessmen to ask for advertisements. He boasted of the magazine's success to visiting newspaper journalists, but pleaded failure when there were printers' bills to pay. He had even once been promised a recording by John Lennon, to be distributed free as a plastic 45rpm single on the magazine's front cover.

When the Beatles' publicity man failed to honour his promise, the nineteen-year-old Branson had issued his very first writ – though Lennon had the last laugh by producing as his promised recording a tape-recording of the heartbeat of Yoko Ono's dying baby.

Despite these achievements, *Student* never made money. Not even Richard Branson's energy could produce new issues with the regularity that a proper magazine would have demanded. So the diversion of selling records by mail-order was something of a relief. What turned out to be the last edition of *Student* contained the first advertisement for Virgin Records – and by the time Steve Lewis appeared on the scene, there was little doubt about which venture would flourish and which would founder. The piles of undistributed magazines in the hall of 44 Albion Street, and the desperate attempts to find teenagers willing to break the by-laws by selling them in Hyde Park, were eloquent testimony to the greater commercial attraction of selling records.

It was no coincidence that Branson was the senior partner and Powell the junior. Richard Branson's air of confident assurance made him a natural leader. Had he not suffered a torn ligament on the football field, he might have been the sort of schoolboy who was captain of every sports team. As it was, he seemed by the age of nineteen to be more mature than the other inhabitants of the Albion Street house, from some of whom he collected a weekly rent of up to £10. Anyone who wanted to could hear the story about how he had lost his virginity at the age of fourteen to the daughter of his cram-school headmaster – and how, when he had been caught clambering through a lavatory window, he had faked a suicide attempt in order to avoid being expelled by his paramour's irate father.

The real story of Branson's first experience of sex was told less often, but was perhaps more revealing. His father, a typical product of public school, the upper middle class and the British army, had taken Branson to Soho one evening and arranged a ten-minute assignation for his son with a backstreet prostitute, while he waited dutifully downstairs.

Richard Branson's father Edward came from a distinguished county family. The family expectation had been that Edward Branson would follow his own father and grandfather before him into the law. But Edward had failed his Common Entrance exam, and instead of going to Eton had been sent to a very minor public school in Yorkshire. His stock had risen in value during the Second World War, when he served in the cavalry in Palestine, in tanks in the desert, and on the general staff in Germany. Once demobilized, however, the dashing Major Branson had been less fortunate when facing the cold realities of civilian life in late 1940s Britain. He studied to become a barrister, but failed to pass his exams.

Edward's father, Sir George Branson, who had received his knighthood as the traditional reward given to a High Court judge, was not amused at his son's apparent inability to measure up to the family's intellectual standards. His irritation was compounded by Edward's announcement that he had decided to marry a girl by the name of Evette Huntley-Flindt. Self-possessed, slim, beautiful and blue-eyed, Eve came from a respectable stockbroking background. But there were questions to be answered. Her father had retired to farm chickens in Devon; and Eve herself had worked as a dancer, an actress, and an air stewardess, serving drinks on the route between London and South America. Why, Sir George and his lady wanted to know, were Ted and Eve so keen to marry so quickly? After all, the two had only just met at a cocktail party; surely it would be prudent to wait a little.

The couple married on 14 October 1949. Eve gave birth to her first child, Richard Charles Nicholas Branson, on 18 July 1950 – precisely nine months and four days after the marriage. The child was born, according to his mother's account, three weeks overdue. By the time Richard arrived, his father had qualified as a barrister; and he had settled with his wife in a picturesque village called

Shamley Green, deep in the Surrey stockbroker belt in which people of their class and upbringing felt at home. But there was little money about – and the only home they could afford was Easteds, a condemned cottage which a 'dear old lady' was willing to let Eve Branson have for twelve shillings a week.

Richard inherited his easy charm, and his eye for a pretty woman, from his father. From his mother he inherited parsimony, enthusiasm, daring, an aptitude for sport, and a hyperactive tendency to pursue one madcap scheme after another until something succeeded. During Richard's childhood, Ted Branson would go dutifully to his London chambers by motorcycle every morning, picking up here and there the 'three-guinea briefs', often paid six months after the conclusion of the case, that were the sole means of support of a young and financially straitened criminal barrister. Meanwhile, Eve had gone into business at home with a helper in a little hut in the back garden, making and spray-painting objets d'art and 'fancy goods' – table mats, trays, tissue-box covers, decorative waste-paper baskets. At first her products were sold to local shops and taken up to Harrods in London. As the business grew larger, however, Eve would travel to fancy goods fairs in Blackpool or Bournemouth – on one occasion slipping three discs in her back when she picked up a heavy box and sneezed at the same time. Although he was willing to allow his wife to help support the family, Ted was in other respects an old-fashioned father. Only once did Eve venture to leave him with the baby; when she returned, Ted was at the window with the squalling Richard under one arm, and helplessly waving a nappy with his other hand. It was financial necessity that first prompted the couple to think of sending the young Richard to board at Scaitcliffe Preparatory School on the borders of Windsor Great Park; the school was run by a cousin of Ted's, who might have looked upon an occasional delay in paying the fees with more sympathy than a stranger.

As Richard grew up, his parents' finances became more comfortable. The owner of the cottage died, and generously stipulated in her will that the cottage should be offered to the Branson family for sale. 'As the people came from Somerset,' recalled Eve bluntly, 'the solicitors didn't know the value. We got that quite cheaply.' The family was later able to sell Easteds at a substantial profit, and to invest the proceeds in Tanyard Farm, a sixteenth-century farmhouse with its own orchard, dovecote and swimming-pool, on the other side of Shamley Green. But Richard had already learned from his mother. As a child, he pursued a number of unsuccessful moneymaking schemes, from growing Christmas trees to breeding budgerigars.

Eve had few expectations of Lindi and Vanessa, Richard's two younger sisters, other than that they should grow up healthy, happy and charming. But she had grand ideas for Richard, taking it almost for granted that he would some day become prime minister. 'I always aimed terribly high,' she remembered. 'You've got to get to the top. Nothing but the top was good enough.' There was only one difficulty. Richard showed little more aptitude for scholarship than his father had. He had scraped into Stowe only after his worried parents sent him to a crammer; once at public school, he had shown more interest in cricket than in Latin. He passed O-levels in scripture, English language, English literature, French, history and ancient history; but he failed elementary mathematics three times. By the age of seventeen, he was pressing his parents to move him from Stowe to a more 'useful' technical college. It soon became clear from the draft letters that he sent his father, urging him to copy them out in his own hand and send them back to the school, that Richard Branson had had enough of education. He saw no reason to take the regulation three A levels. He did not want to go to university. What he wanted to do was to work.

Steve Lewis did not have to spend long at Albion Street before he realized that the house was being used by Richard Branson as the centre not just for the mail-order record business and the magazine, but for two other activities as well. One was the Students' Advisory Centre, a voluntary organization set up by Branson to help answer teenagers' problems; the other was an employment agency which sought to match underemployed nurses with London families who wanted cleaners or babysitters. In his capacity as Angie, Lewis might therefore spend half his day chasing up obscure records to satisfy an order from a foreign collector. For the other half, he would be administering pregnancy tests to visiting teenage girls – reminding them to urinate in a bottle that was clean and had been rinsed very thoroughly to remove the last traces of soap – or referring worried young men with spots on their genitals to the relevant clinic at the nearby St Mary's Hospital.

The employment agency for nurses was a short-lived venture. Branson saw a business opportunity to capitalize on the public sympathy for the low pay of nurses; he contacted the *Daily Sketch*, which had been running a campaign to raise nurses' wages, and gave them an account of his plan with a philanthropic spin. DICK STARTS BABY-SIT PLAN TO HELP NURSES, read the paper's banner headline. The 'strap-line' above was more specific: 'Now a barrister's son joins battle for underpaid mercy girls'. In the article, Branson provided a plausible rebuttal to complaints by a nursing association that nurses who took in extra work would be too tired to do their normal hospital duties. 'Most of the nurses sit in front of a television at nights, watching babies, and are paid five shillings to seven and sixpence an hour for four hours.' The article described him helpfully as 'founder-editor' of *Student* magazine, and reported (without appearing to have taken any steps to verify the facts) his claim that Albion Street was getting calls 'every thirty seconds' for nurses to help out. In fact, the agency was far more casual and sporadic than the article suggested, especially since local families preferred to employ the same person to look after their children regularly than to invite into their houses an unknown member of an employment pool. But the coverage, which obviated the need to advertise for nurses, was an early example of Branson's ability to use the press to get his message across.

It was personal experience that had prompted Branson to set up the Students' Advisory Centre. According to the romantic account given to the *Sun* by the 'brilliant young editor', he had at the age of seventeen 'met a girl, made her pregnant, then spent three months of hell not knowing what to do or where to go ... Together, they set up an advice centre for young people.'

The Centre's most controversial activity was probably its discreet system of referring pregnant women to sympathetic doctors for abortions. But it was to be something far more mundane that brought it notoriety. Among the ills which the Centre's leaflets advertised help in curing was a reference to 'venereal disease'. In early 1970, the police told Branson that he was breaking the law by using the word 'venereal', and ordered him to remove it from his leaflets. When the young entrepreneur refused, he was promptly arrested and charged with two offences, one under the Venereal Diseases Act (1917), and the other under the Indecent Advertisements Act (1889). John Mortimer, a rising barrister who was later to achieve fame as a writer and playwright, offered to defend Branson at no charge. Despite Mortimer's eloquent denunciation of the archaic legislation that made it a crime to use a word that was in any case a euphemism, Branson was fined £7. But he won the wider argument; soon afterwards, the Venereal Diseases Act was repealed. The Students' Advisory Centre continues, with Branson's financial support, to give advice on venereal diseases to this day – though today they are known as 'sexually transmitted diseases', and the centre, based in Portobello Road, has changed its name to Help.

Lewis was happy with his work for the employment agency and the advisory service, but his work as Angie gave him cause for disquiet. The preprinted reply forms sent back to customers ended with the valediction 'Love and peace, Angie' – and some record buyers got the wrong end of the stick. It was not long before lovesick male students began writing to Lewis under his female pseudonym; when one said that he was coming to London and wanted to visit Angie in Albion Street, Lewis took fright. In future, his style of correspondence would be a little less friendly.

There was anyway little choice. While the other activities of the Albion Street gang withered, the record mail-order business, and hence Lewis's workload, continued to expand. When Lewis went into hospital with suspected meningitis, Nik Powell brought round the sack of correspondence for him to deal with in his bed. Thereafter, he would do most of his work at home, picking up the letters once a week. Lewis also became the compiler of the Virgin Records sale list, and as such the company's informal arbiter of musical taste.

Whatever arguments Richard Branson might offer, however, Steve Lewis had no intention of giving up the chance to go to university. The concession he was willing to make to Virgin was to apply to Brunel, in Uxbridge to the west of London, instead of to Manchester, so that he could be closer to Albion Street. Over the three years he spent at Brunel, Lewis was to combine his academic studies and his progression in the business with great success.

By his last year, when Lewis was ready to think about working for Virgin full-time, he was the only student at the university who already had a company car. There was undoubtedly something reassuring about working at Virgin. All the senior staff drew the same £50 a week, and all of them drove Volvos. In those days, the Swedish marque had no connotation of suburban solidity; rather, its image was raffish and slightly exotic – just like the company itself. It was only later, however, that Lewis began to reflect on the fact that although he and the other senior Virgin staff had the right to drive the Volvos, it was Richard Branson and his partner Nik Powell who owned them.

But Branson had bigger things on his mind. If he could profit from selling records, why should he not also profit from making them? The idea of opening a recording studio was put in Branson's mind by Newman, a guitarist and songwriter who had worked in Albion Street and had dabbled in amateur recording for a while. Once the record shops began to make money, it became a serious possibility. Newman was therefore duly sent off to buy some professional studio equipment. There was just one difficulty: the eight-track system he acquired was too large to fit in the crypt beneath the church across the road from the Albion Street house where the studio was to be installed. Another place would have to be found – and with London property prices what they were, it might as well be in the country.

Scouring the pages of *Country Life*, the glossy magazine of choice for those who wish to buy manor houses and estates, the two men made appointments to look at a number of possibilities between London and Wales, all of which proved disappointing on closer inspection. It was almost by chance that they dropped in at a seventeenth-century manor house at Shipton, a village on the Cherwell river twenty miles from Oxford. They arrived as the sun was setting, vaulted over the garden wall, and inspected the ruined mediaeval cloisters attached to the main Cotswold stone building.

On 11 January 1971, Steve Lewis discovered a kindred spirit. A fresh-faced young South African turned up at South Wharf Road, the new location of the Virgin offices, and announced himself as Richard Branson's cousin. Simon Draper had finished studying literature at a South African university, and had nine months to kill. London, as the centre of the musical world that absorbed all his energy and money, was a magnet to which Draper had been attracted in his search for an interesting job. He had heard through his uncle, who was Ted Branson's half-brother, that Richard was a fellow who couldn't pass his exams. Then Draper saw a copy of *Student*, and was impressed; and saw a Virgin mail-order advertisement in *Melody Maker*, and was enthused. He knew nothing whatever about business, but Simon Draper had pronounced tastes in music. Working with his young English cousin, he decided, might not be so bad after all.

Encouraged to confide in Draper by the family connection, Branson revealed to him over lunch that the Virgin empire was soon to become a great deal larger. A postal strike was threatened, which would if it took place immediately starve Branson of his mail-order financial lifeline. So Virgin would open a record shop as a substitute. But that was by no means the only plan up Branson's sleeve. He had already planned a fully fledged music empire, encompassing not only retailing but also an artistic agency, a chain of recording studios, a management company, a music publishing business – and a record label, for which a logo had already been designed. 'You can start my label,' said Branson.

Draper was at first tempted to be dismissive. The empire by the end of January 1971 would consist of a small and rather shabby shop in an upstairs room in Oxford Street, and a mail-order firm that was doing no business. His cousin's ambitions seemed a little fanciful, to say the least. But Draper's interest was tickled; he liked the look of the group of new friends whom he would meet if he came to South Wharf Road; and he loved the idea of turning the music that was his life's great enthusiasm into a way of making a living. He agreed to start the following day, but refused to commit himself on how long he would stay. It would never have crossed Simon Draper's mind that he would work for Richard Branson for more than twenty years.

Caroline Gold had required some persuading to work as Richard Branson's secretary. At twenty-one, she was a year older than him when she answered the ad in the *Evening Standard*. She had been to art school, and was married; and she had not been at all sure after her interview with this 'gauche, studenty type' that this was the right job. The crypt in which Branson had his desk was dark and damp; and the salary, at £12 a week, was significantly less than the £20 that her talents might have commanded elsewhere. But she had accepted the offer – intending, with the blithe confidence of someone brought up in an era free of mass unemployment, to find something else if this job did not work out. But Branson's mixture of simplicity and guile had charmed her, and the typing he had asked her to do on her first day at work was more interesting than she had expected. Instead of a stack of commercial correspondence about widgets and settlement dates, he dictated to her a string of letters to famous contributors to *Student*, thanking them for the articles they had sent in and apologizing for having been unable to use them. To her relief, she discovered that his dictation was so hesitant that she had no difficulty keeping up with shorthand. Then he took her across to the Albion Street house to meet the others. It was only when she knew and liked Richard Branson better, that Caroline Gold got around to wondering whether he had saved up some exciting letters just to impress her.

Branson surprised her with his ability to get things done. One example was the installation of new telephone lines when they were needed. In those days, ordering a new telephone was a major project that required correspondence with the General Post Office, and usually a delay of several months. But Richard Branson had found a shortcut. He had befriended a local telephone engineer, who made himself available around the clock to serve the needs of the growing business. Whether Branson paid anything for this service or not, Caroline Gold never discovered; but the middle-aged engineer once boasted to her that he was allowed to use Branson's houseboat on the canal at Little Venice for secret assignations with the women with whom he had affairs. He once approached her with the news that Branson had been forced to turn him down because of a prior engagement, and asked whether he might borrow the next-door boat where Caroline lived with her husband Rob. The answer was a polite no.

Branson had an uncanny knack for negotiation. On one occasion, a man telephoned to offer the nascent mail-order firm a load of bootlegged, or illegally copied, Jimi Hendrix records. The caller was told to come around to the Virgin offices in South Wharf Road, where Mr Zimmerman would discuss the transaction with him. At ten o'clock the following morning a shifty-looking character appeared, and duly asked for Mr Zimmerman. Branson explained that Mr Zimmerman was just around the corner, and would arrive in a minute. An hour later, Branson explained to the waiting caller that Mr Zimmerman was around the corner at the Riviera Café, and suggested that he should go and meet him there. When the angry bootlegger returned at twelve, complaining that there had been no Mr Zimmerman at the Riviera even though he had waited at least half an hour, Branson looked at him innocently.

'What did you want to see Mr Zimmerman about?'

The man opened the boot of his car, and replied that he was going to sell him some records.

Branson looked inside doubtfully. 'How much did you agree to sell them for?'

The man replied that he wanted £1 each for them.

'I'll give you 50p apiece,' said Branson. Within half an hour, the records had been stacked on the shelves inside South Wharf Road; within another few days, they had been sold by mail-order at £3 apiece to fans of Jimi Hendrix.

It was the purchase of the Manor, however, which made Caroline Gold and her husband realize that Branson was an entrepreneur whose powers of persuasion had to be taken seriously. He may have been only twenty-one at the time; he may have climbed over the wall of Shipton Manor with Tom Newman; but he was now beyond doubt the owner of a charming country house, complete with its own croquet lawn and swimming-pool. Including its attached cottages, the Manor had cost Branson £30,000. Some of that sum had been lent to the young entrepreneur by an aunt. The rest, however, came from Coutts Bank. Dressed in the pinstripe suit that Caroline Gold had taken him to buy, and in the black shoes with which she had advised him to replace his brown ones, Richard Branson had been given a mortgage of £22,500.

Soon after the purchase was complete, the sound of footsteps alerted Caroline and Rob Gold to the fact that they had a late-night visitor to their boat. It was Richard Branson, pale, shaken and extremely distressed, and he was in an appalling state. At first, he could say nothing but 'Oh no, oh no.' Only gradually did his story come out.

Rob Gold's younger sister was married at the time to a man called Andy, who owned a Transit van. Branson had received an order to send some records to Belgium, and had asked Andy to deliver his consignment in his van. Somehow, in the course of the deliveries, the two men had discovered a loophole in the customs procedures at Dover. When you passed the customs post, your papers would be stamped so that you would be able to prove that the records had been exported and thus reclaim the purchase tax you had already paid on them. But there seemed to be no proper arrangements for checking the records, or for making sure that they really had been exported.

Here, surely, was an opportunity for a young businessman. Instead of exporting the records that your documents showed you were carrying, why couldn't you fill in the paperwork and reclaim the tax as normal, but sell the 'exported' records in London and instead take to Belgium some old deleted records, picked up for a song from a company that was about to throw them away anyway? Come to think of it why bother to go to Belgium? The system at Dover seemed to be based entirely on trust; nobody was there to see if you simply drove around the docks and then came back to London without even getting on to the boat. Better still, there was no need even to go to the trouble of buying the old records; to a dozy Dover customs officer, a vanful of record sleeves with nothing in them would do just as well.

As Branson made trip after trip, revelling in the ease with which he was increasing the profits of his mail-order business, he never stopped to consider that the customs men might be less dim-witted than they seemed. But they were. The Transit van had been tailed; and the records he had been selling in London instead of exporting had been marked with an 'E' in fluorescent ink. An anonymous tip-off gave Branson a few hours in which to try to hide the evidence. But he was arrested at his houseboat, taken to Dover, and charged with producing fraudulent paperwork under the Customs & Excise Act 1952. The following morning, after a night in the cells, he was committed for trial. His mother, to whom the tearful

Branson had relayed the news over the telephone the previous evening, came up by the morning train and offered the family house as surety for his £30,000 bail.

To his enormous relief, Branson discovered over the course of the coming three months that dealing with Her Majesty's Customs & Excise was almost like a business negotiation. Although the maximum penalty for what he had done was two years' imprisonment, the investigators seemed to have no special desire to send Branson to gaol. True to their occupations as taxmen, what they wanted instead was money. Before the case came to trial, therefore, Branson and the customs settled their little dispute as follows: he would make an immediate down payment of £15,000, and would then pay taxes, duties and charges to the tune of another £38,000 over the next three years. Given the size of Virgin at the time, these were daunting sums of money to find. But he would have no criminal record, and he was free to go back to his mail-order business.

When they heard the story on the night after Branson's appearance in court at Dover, Caroline and Rob Gold were sympathetic. But they were hardly surprised. Some weeks earlier, Richard Branson had discovered that Caroline's father, Francis Rodgers, was a shipping agent who had just set up a containerized freight business. He had approached the older man with a request for advice and for a place to store some records. Caroline was not present at the conversation. But Francis Rodgers left her in no doubt: he had smelt a rat, and wanted nothing at all to do with the scheme. The customs scam was no adolescent mistake, as the investigators might have inferred from Branson's earnestness and youthful enthusiasm; it was a deliberate and quite knowing attempt to break the law and get away with it.

Luckily for Branson, his neighbours on the canal saw no reason to be judgemental on the matter. More luckily still, the Customs & Excise never found out about Branson's approach to Francis Rodgers. By the time they had begun to investigate the customs fraud, Caroline Gold had already given up her job to have children. She was no longer an employee of Richard Branson's, so nobody ever thought to interview her.

TWO

One Per Cent of Tubular Bells

'NIK AND RICHARD,' Simon Draper would later recall, 'had no particular feel for the music business. They found themselves in it by accident. They were public-school boys who had dropped out of education.'

While the two budding entrepreneurs did what they were good at – Richard sweet-talking the press and striking daring deals, the more introverted Nik reading his management magazines and trying to think of ways that Virgin could cut costs – they needed some real musical expertise. Steve Lewis, for all his encyclopaedic knowledge of Motown, was at first only a part-timer; he was also still at school. Tony Mellor, a former trade union official, had been in charge of buying stock for the mail-order company and the shops; but he soon disappeared to America, never to be seen again. So there was a vacuum for Draper to step into. After Branson's brush with the Customs, it had become clear that Branson's plan to start the record label would have to wait a little. In the meantime, Simon Draper would become the company's record buyer.

Over the next two years, Draper's work gave him an invaluable insight into the sort of music that would sell. Although the record shops and the mail-order business were not profitable, they were a goldmine of information about the likely future habits of the record-buying public, for the tastes of the Virgin clientele were more adventurous than those of the average teenager. For instance, the mail-order company received a growing number of requests for records by an obscure German band called Tangerine Dream, which Draper fulfilled by finding out where the records were produced and then buying a job lot of them. So it required no great insight to see that the band might be worth trying to acquire for the new Virgin label. 'When we signed Tangerine Dream in 1974,' said Draper, 'it looked like clever stuff. But we knew it was going to sell.' It did – by the million.

The great coup of Virgin's early years came via a different route. While the Manor was preparing for the first formal booking of its recording studio in 1971, an obscure band was allowed to come and rehearse there. During a quiet moment, one of its members produced from his pocket a demo tape that he had made and handed it over to Tom Newman, who was in charge of the studios. This was an occurrence that would become tiresomely familiar to anyone involved in the record business. But Newman listened to the tape, and he liked it; so did the other Virgin people he played it to. A few weeks later, he came back to the guitarist and told him that he should try and get a recording contract.

Simon Draper heard the tape later that year, by which time the young guitarist had been turned down by almost every record company in London, and pronounced it 'incredible'. He took a copy home to his flat, and played it time and again to anyone who would listen to it. The recording elicited an extraordinary reaction. When Virgin Records was ready to start its label, Draper decided, he would tell Richard to sign up Mike Oldfield.

Oldfield was an unlikely pop star. Son of an Essex doctor, born in Reading, he had an unhappy childhood; his mother drank too much and was prone to roller-coaster changes of mood. By the end of his teens, it was clear that Mike, too, was unable to face life as an independent adult. He was painfully shy, and was as lacking in self-confidence as Richard Branson was full of it. Women were attracted to him, not so much for the physical charms of his under-developed body and adolescent beard as for his air of vulnerability and for his bouts of depression from which only constant reassurance and attention could redeem him. Yet Oldfield was by no means an inadequate musician. He had been playing guitar professionally for five years, and had made two albums with the Whole World, Kevin Ayers's group. He had made the demo tape that he had given to Tom Newman entirely on his own, working painstakingly at home on a battered Akai tape-recorder that Ayers had lent him.

Oldfield arrived at the Manor at Draper's instigation, and spent a week in the recording studio there without even having a written

35

agreement with the Virgin record label. In the event, there was no hurry; it was to take months of work before the album was ready. Oldfield played more than twenty different instruments, laying each performance down on the tape on top of the mixture that was already there. This procedure, known as 'overdubbing', allowed him to build up a full-length instrumental album with only incidental help from others. It was a challenging use of the state-of-the-art recording equipment that Branson and Newman had agreed to buy. The machinery stood up to the punishment, but the tape did not. After being passed across the heads thousands of times, the master tape of *Tubular Bells* came dangerously close to wearing out. For Oldfield was not content to remake what was already on his demo tape, and to finish off the as yet uncomposed second half of the record. He wanted to polish and repolish; hence the weeks of work.

Richard Branson had been to a trade fair in the meantime, and had been warned that it would be commercial suicide to publish a record without any lyrics. Once persuaded, however, he set to work with gusto. By the time the album was complete, Branson had managed to learn a little about music industry contracts. He had asked Rob Gold, his houseboat neighbour, to explain to him how record companies worked – and the obliging Gold had put down the basics on a single sheet of yellow foolscap paper. 'He hardly knew what a record was,' Gold recalled. 'I told him that you go to a distributor to distribute your records, and that you get more if you're a production company that makes its own records. Your percentage is higher if you do your own marketing.' Crucially, Gold also told Branson what sort of figures he should be aiming at.

The deal that Branson struck with Oldfield was a standard record industry contract of the time. In fact, it was copied directly from an Island Records contract that Branson was given a copy of. Oldfield would give Virgin worldwide rights to *Tubular Bells* and to a fixed number of albums that he would make after that. In return, he would be paid a flat-rate royalty of five per cent of sales (but not on samples or records returned by retailers). He would also receive the equivalent of an annual salary of £1,000 a year, though this would be deducted from any future royalties he might earn.

This deal was no less attractive than the deals which hundreds of other aspiring rock stars had received; in fact it was more attractive, since Oldfield had failed to find a recording contract with a number of other labels before coming back to Virgin. But the seeds of ill-will were laid in that agreement. Oldfield had signed at the kitchen table of the Manor, negotiating directly with Branson. More important, the albums he was contracted to produce could easily be ten years' work; they would certainly tie him to Virgin for a period of time that was longer than the entire creative career of most rock musicians. And Richard Branson, the man with whom he would have to negotiate future changes to these arrangements, had made himself Oldfield's manager.

Branson's next job was to find a way of distributing *Tubular Bells*. Island Records, Britain's leading independent record label at the time, offered to license it from Virgin in return for a royalty. Branson refused: remembering the advice he had received from Rob Gold, he suggested instead that Island should do no more than press and distribute (P&D) the record on Virgin's behalf. David Betteridge, Island's managing director, told Branson he was mad. If it accepted a straightforward licensing deal, Virgin would be able to hand *Tubular Bells* over to Island and forget about it, but still pocket the difference between the royalty it was paying Oldfield and the much higher royalty it received from Island. By insisting on a P&D deal, Virgin would miss out on an advance from Island, and would itself have to carry the risk of financial failure. In any case, said Betteridge, Island did not do P&D deals; the other small companies for whom it distributed records were signed up on a full licensee basis. But Branson was adamant. In the end he got what he wanted.

Tubular Bells was released in May 1973 along with the three other albums that made up the beginning of the Virgin Records list. But it was on Oldfield's work that Virgin concentrated its attention, and where Branson's salesmanship came into its own. Having had the nerve to telephone businessmen he had never met before to ask them for advertising for a student magazine, the young entrepreneur had no hesitation in making a nuisance of himself in the offices of radio stations and music papers and magazines, trying to get air time or publicity for his new Oldfield album.

At first, the job of selling the record seemed daunting: albums were supposed to be made up of a dozen or so three-minute songs,

not of two long continuous instrumental compositions. But once
the record had received the honour of being broadcast in its entirety
on BBC Radio One by John Peel – a disc jockey of undisputed
authority and street credibility – its future was assured. Within a
matter of weeks, it was the number one selling album in the British
pop charts. Within a few weeks more, Branson had flown to the
United States, and sold a package of the four inaugural Virgin
albums to Atlantic Records for three-quarters of a million dollars.
Ahmet Ertegun, Atlantic's chief executive, sold Oldfield's record in
turn to the makers of a new film who were looking for a soundtrack.
The Exorcist, as the film was called, became a hit in America; so did
Tubular Bells. It reached third place in the US charts.

That single album, and to a lesser extent the Tangerine Dream
LP *Phaedra* released the following year, put Virgin on the map. It
also unleashed a torrent of money into the company's bank
accounts. The £38,000 that Branson had to finish paying to the
Customs, and the continuing dribble of losses from the shops and
the mail-order business, suddenly came to seem insignificant. Virgin Records was in business as an independent label; and Simon
Draper now had enough money to sign the bands that he wanted.

In July 1972, four days after his twenty-second birthday and while
Virgin Records was preparing its first albums for release, Richard
Branson married. His bride was Kristen Tomassi, a tall, slim blonde
New Yorker who had come to the Manor a year earlier on the
arm of an Australian boyfriend. Branson, struck instantly by her
high-cheeked, almost Scandinavian good looks and by his discovery
that her sense of fun matched his, decided instantly to make her
his own. Like him, Kristen loved friends, practical jokes, convivial
evenings with a bottle of wine and a joint or two, and sports. But
she was still a student when she visited the Manor, and had been
intending to go back to the university architecture course from
which she had been taking a summer break.

Branson won her with the same impulsive daring that had already
helped him to start a magazine and a mail-order business. On the
day that her two-week holiday in England was over, Kristen
received a telegram. A BOAT IS SINKING, it said, and asked her
to ring a telephone number. Kristen rang him from a call box to

thank him for the telegram, but insisted that she was going to leave all the same. When she went back to her packing, she was met by a friend of Branson's who had come around, on his orders, to take her baggage around to the houseboat. She followed in a taxi, to find Branson and Powell deep in a business discussion. Branson opened her case, upended it on the floor, and contined talking to Nik Powell as if this were the most natural thing in the world.

After a few weeks, Kristen began to fret about her half-finished architecture course, and (though she did not tell him this) the live-in boyfriend that she had left in America.

'You don't need to go to architecture school,' said Branson, with the unshakeable confidence of someone who knew that university could not have taught him anything he did not already know. 'You can do the architectural work on the Manor.' Before the summer was out, Kristen therefore found herself making regular visits to the Phillips auction rooms in nearby Bayswater, buying up huge pieces of cheap antique furniture for the Manor. Her best find was a second-hand billiard table, which cost £50 and required six people to manoeuvre it into position in the old house.

She soon found her own individuality being subsumed into a set of shared concerns about the business. Every aspect of Branson's life – from his dealings with colleagues at Virgin to his negotiations with the Inland Revenue – became part of hers. Kristen also found that she got on very well with Eve Branson, Richard's mother. Like her own mother, the head of the Branson household would tolerate no laziness or newspaper reading on Sunday mornings. Instead, guests at the Surrey farmhouse were required to swim, play croquet or feed the pigeons. Until they were married, Richard and Kristen were not allowed to sleep together in the family house, but they were invited to join his parents in their bed in the morning for sausage and eggs and strong tea.

The wedding took place at the village church of Shipton, and the party followed immediately afterwards at the Manor. It was an odd occasion; Branson's friends and colleagues dressed up in morning dress and grey top hats, their long hair splaying oddly from the sides. Branson's bank manager from Coutts, a guest of special importance given the cash-flow requirements of the business, was first on the receiving line. Kristen's father paid for the party.

When they returned to London after a suitably energetic holiday on a Greek island, Kristen began to prepare for the couple to move from the houseboat on the canal to a small terraced house in Denbigh Terrace, near Portobello Road. The bank manager justified his invitation to the wedding by providing them with a mortgage that allowed Branson to offer £80,000 for the house; in keeping with the gap between their means and aspirations, Kristen then devoted herself to decorating it in style on a shoestring, making the curtains herself and imbuing the house with a sense of style and proportion befitting a former architecture student. Their one extravagance was a huge, lavish sofa in which Branson would slump as he made endless telephone calls. Meanwhile, Kristen would cook – brilliantly, her friends told her – for the dinner parties whose frequency was matched only by the short notice at which she had to prepare them. In quieter moments, the two would stroll down to Holland Park and talk about their ambitions to live one day in one of the huge stucco houses there that were now so far beyond their financial reach.

As they settled into Denbigh Terrace, Kristen became used to seeing her husband deep in conversation at all hours with Nik Powell, Simon Draper and Ken Berry, a clerk whom Branson had plucked from the accounts department to become his personal assistant. It did not take her long to realize how important his work was to the man she had married. Any doubt that there might have been was dispelled by Branson's impulsive decision to give Mike Oldfield the Bentley that he and Kristen had received as a wedding present from Ted and Eve. The splendid car was given to Oldfield as a reward for agreeing to perform *Tubular Bells* at a concert at the Queen Elizabeth Hall. Kristen was given strict orders not to tell her mother-in-law, for fear of hurting her feelings – and it was in fact long, long afterwards that Eve discovered what had happened.

Kristen's first response to Branson's devotion to business was to try to behave like him: to throw herself into design decisions about the Manor, or to rush to and from the Virgin Rags clothes shops that were opening up inside the record stores, trying to make some order of the chaos that was the mark of Virgin's first and last venture into clothes retailing. She also worked hard as Branson's back-up in mollycoddling Virgin artists – spending a number of days, for instance, cheering up Mike Oldfield at an isolated country cottage, and at one point arranging to return a Mercedes roadster that the pop star had bought on the spur of the moment and then decided a week later that he did not like. But soon Kristen tired of trying to compete with her husband, and began instead a crusade to attract his attention. But he did not take the hint – not even when Kristen sent him a poem about the fact that they always seemed to meet in the hall at Denbigh Terrace, when Branson was rushing busily to his next oh-so-important meeting.

Kristen would afterwards declare that her decision to start sleeping with other people was a reaction to the fact that Richard had let his work get out of control. It was not a question of being unfaithful; even if she spent the entire night away from home, she never sought to be secretive about what she was doing. More, it was a cry for help. 'I wanted some private life for us, that's all I wanted,' she remembered. 'I just wanted half an hour a day.' Branson, meanwhile, suggested that the couple should have children. His wife could not resist responding with sarcasm, asking him how he intended to fit in another obligation into a life which left little enough room for her as it was.

Matters came to a head when Branson asked Kristen to help him entertain a rock star whom he wanted to sign to the record label. The artist's name was Kevin Ayers; it was he who had lent Mike Oldfield the tape machine on which he recorded his demo of *Tubular Bells*. He was older than Branson and Kristen, and he had all of her husband's self-assurance without the naïvety. The couple went to meet Ayers and his woman friend at the shop in Notting Hill Gate, drove the pair down the motorway to see the Manor, and then brought them back to the houseboat in the evening for dinner. Kristen cooked lobster while Richard told the jokes. Everyone drank too much; Ayers produced some cocaine, which the inexperienced Branson sniffed with him for the first time in his life – and the evening ended with Kristen in the arms of Kevin Ayers. She later claimed that Branson sought consolation from the woman that Ayers had brought with him; Branson denied that this was the case.

Although the spark of mutual attraction between his wife and Ayers was evident the following morning even to Branson, the marriage did not end immediately. Ayers pursued Kristen with flowers, presents, letters and telegrams. She went to Australia for a while to get away from everything and think, but Ayers found her there. She went to live with him briefly in France, returned to England for an attempted reconciliation with Branson – and then left again, this time for good. On the day she left, Branson was on the telephone at Denbigh Terrace, engrossed in a long negotiation to sign the Boomtown Rats to Virgin Records. The echo of his voice, raising the offer minute by minute, resounded in her ears as she slammed the door of the house for the last time. Months later, when she was living in a house in France without electricity and utterly cut off from the outside world, Kristen would imagine as she walked in the fields that she could hear the sound of the ringing telephone that had helped to destroy her life with Richard Branson. What almost broke her heart was the fact that Branson later offered to change his entire life in order to bring her back. He was willing to give up work, go and live in the country, make another life – and he told her so in letter after pleading letter. But it was too late. They divorced, citing Kevin Ayers as the co-respondent.

The irony was that Kristen's relationship with Kevin Ayers was doomed not to last. After bearing his baby, she began to feel that he had laid siege to her mostly because it was a challenge to steal from Richard Branson his most prized possession. She was only to find happiness in marriage many years later. But as the wounds healed, Branson and his former wife were able to restore some of the old brother-sister relationship that they had had in the earliest days. Kristen and her German husband Axel Ball would be invited to spend holidays with their family on Branson's private island. By the end of the 1980s, the two families were even in business together: Branson bought a controlling interest in a luxury hotel that they had opened in Majorca, and a new hotel was being planned in Hydra for which Kristen and her second husband would provide the architectural and managerial talent, and her first husband the money.

A matter of months after Richard Branson married Kristen Tomassi, his business partner Nik Powell married Kristen's younger sister Merrill. A matter of months after the failure of

Richard and Kristen's marriage, the marriage of Nik and Merrill failed also.

But the twin marriages, at which Richard and Nik served as each other's best man, said as much about the two founders of Virgin as about their wives. Nicholas Powell had been Branson's earliest real friend; they had met at the local private school at Shamley Green at the age of four. They were, as the closest of friends can sometimes be, almost opposites. Richard was fair-haired, gregarious and rudely healthy. Nik was dark, shy and epileptic. Richard was an indifferent student; Nik was more academic. When Richard went to Stowe, whose foundation in 1923 made it a parvenu among public schools, Nik was sent north to Yorkshire to be educated in the gloomy tradition of Ampleforth College, founded by Benedictine monks before the Reformation. Richard was the leader, Nik the follower; it was not clear who needed whom more.

Powell had lived at Albion Street in the gap between school and university, and had helped out on *Student*. But it was only when he gave up his place at Sussex, returning to London to become Branson's partner in the mail-order business, that the structure of their relationship was formalized in a business agreement. Powell was given 40 per cent of Virgin. As the venture grew, the two slipped into complementary roles. Powell would produce financial figures for the bank; Branson would take the figures to the meeting and persuade the bank manager to lend another few tens of thousands of pounds. Branson would decide suddenly that Virgin needed to open more record shops, and would galvanize everyone with the enthusiasm necessary to get the job done swiftly; Powell would do the stocktaking. Branson would rush off on one implausible scheme after another; Powell would provide the voice, sometimes gentle and sometimes not so gentle, telling him not to be such a damned fool. It was Branson whose gusto for life persuaded people that working for Virgin would be fun; it was Powell who stopped the biscuits in the coffee cupboard when times became hard. One did not need to know about the 60–40 split to know which was the senior partner and which the junior.

But there were other junior partners, too, who were given shares in the businesses they worked for because Powell thought that equity was the best possible incentive for hard work. One was Simon

Draper, who was given a 20 per cent stake in the record company. Another was Tom Newman, who had 20 per cent of the studio business. A third was Steve Lewis, who received 20 per cent of Virgin's management company. In common with the share split between Branson and Powell, these minority holdings were not negotiated. None of the three was asked to pay a penny for their shareholdings, nor to accept any financial risk on their own heads. Branson was prepared to take all the risks and to find all the money; the shareholdings were simply a reward, an expression of confidence in the future and a gesture of thanks for useful advice already given and work already done.

At first, this approach threw up no problems. In common with almost everybody else working for Virgin, Draper, Lewis and Newman were not much bothered by money. They were young and without responsibilities. Their salaries were perfectly adequate to cover the cost of renting a flat in London, going out for meals with friends, buying tickets to the movies, and, if they wished, smoking the occasional joint. Many of their living costs were paid by the company in any case. At the big communal dinners they all went out to, Richard would slip away and pay the bill before anyone had even noticed that he had gone. The fleet of company Volvos provided free transport for the trusted insiders. Perhaps most important of all, all three of the minority shareholders were doing what they wanted to do. Music was the passion of their lives; to be able to spend their days doing something they enjoyed, when many of their contemporaries were dressing up in drab suits and doing dull jobs in old-fashioned offices, seemed the greatest privilege of all. Who would be ungracious enough to start quibbling about equity?

Simon Draper was the first. In 1975 he went back to South Africa for a holiday and had a long chat about his work at Virgin with his older brother. He explained the way Virgin was structured. There was a holding company at the top, of which Branson owned 60 per cent and Powell 40. That company did business through a number of subsidiaries that it owned, covering records, studios, retail, mail-order and management. When someone at Virgin had been given a minority shareholding, it was always a shareholding in the subsidiary company. So Branson and Powell together owned 80 per cent of the subsidiary, and the rest belonged to the individual minority shareholder.

Draper's brother told him that since Virgin's shares were not quoted on any stock exchange, the value of a stake in the Virgin holding company was not clear until it was actually sold. But a minority shareholding in one of the subsidiary companies – which was what Draper himself possessed – was worse still; it was fundamentally unsafe. There was simply too much scope for Branson and Powell to change matters to their own advantage: if, for instance, they decided to dismiss Draper outright, he would be able to claim only the par value of his shares, not their real value as assets. Under company law, Draper's 20 per cent of the record company was not a large enough stake to give him a veto over decisions that might become important later; and the presence of the holding company above it could allow profits from the record company to be used to finance other companies in the group. The advice from Older Brother was simple: Simon Draper should try to swap his stake in the record company for a stake in the holding company – and if that were not possible, he should at the very least obtain some safeguards to protect his position.

Branson and Powell would not agree to the first option. But Draper extracted from them an agreement on what he would be paid if he were ever to sell out his 20 per cent of the record company. He would still be required to offer Branson and Powell first refusal on his shares; but they would be obliged to buy him out not just at any arbitrarily agreed price, but at a 'fair value' or £100,000 – whichever was the less.

The matter became more complicated in the 1980s, because Draper saw the financial transactions between the record company and other group companies being arranged in such a way as to reduce the record company's profits and liberate money for spending on the expansion of other companies in the group. Draper therefore insisted that the accounts should contain a note recording that for the purposes of valuing his shares, the record company's profits should be considered higher.

Steve Lewis was less hard-nosed about the matter. His 20 per cent stake was in a management company, whose job was to represent musicians, extracting the best possible terms from record companies and music publishing companies, in return for a commission on the musicians' earnings. Elsewhere in the music business, the relationship between managers and record companies was seen as inevitably hostile – for although a good manager could provide good ideas to promote a musician, and could smooth the dealings between the two sides, the unalterable fact was that it was in the manager's interest to extract for his client as attractive terms as possible from the record company, and in the record company's interest to resist.

At Virgin, however, Steve Lewis was expected to represent musicians who were signed to the record label and the publishing company, while simultaneously answering to an employer who owned the record company. The financial arrangements were also unusual. Most managers demand an advance for their client from the record company, and use it to pay wages to the band after extracting their own commission (usually 20 per cent). At Virgin, however, the management company that Lewis ran borrowed money from the record company, using that money to pay salaries to the musicians it represented. Matters were not helped by the fact that the management side was less successful than the record business itself. But the unusual relationship between the management company and the rest of the empire helped to make sure that the management company of which Steve Lewis owned 20 per cent never made any money. Four years after he had been given his shareholding, Lewis realized that it was not worth anything. The firm was later closed down.

Tom Newman's 20 per cent was in the studio business, which started at the Manor but soon encompassed a mobile studio and another site in London. He had never asked for a shareholding; Richard Branson had written him a letter, unprompted, offering him a stake in the studio business as a reward for the work he had done over the previous two years. Newman, who thought of himself as a songwriter, singer and guitarist rather than as a businessman, was delighted. He had put huge efforts into installing the studio at the Manor and into helping Mike Oldfield make his bestselling album. Here, it seemed, was recognition from a grateful employer.

It was not until more than four years later, when he was sitting in a pub with another Virgin employee, that Newman heard a story that made his blood run cold. His drinking partner, who had been asked by Nik Powell to carry out one of the periodic reorganizations of the Virgin empire, reported to Newman that he had noticed that Newman's shareholding was not in the main operating company that ran the studios, but in another company that was not trading at all.

The following day, Newman stormed into Branson's office at South Wharf Road, and confronted him.

'You bastard!' he yelled. 'The company's worthless!'

Branson was taken aback. He began to mumble some answer, but Newman merely became more angry. After abusing his employer further, Newman walked out of the office and slammed the door. He left Virgin the same day, and did not speak to Branson for the next four years. Newman's hot temper gave Branson no chance to defend himself; more significantly, Branson claimed afterwards that Newman had never explained his grievance to him.

The irony was that Newman was quite mistaken in believing he had been betrayed over his shares. Had he toubled to check the accounts at Companies House, he would have discovered that Caroline Studios, the company of which he had owned 20 per cent, was still in operation as the trading company for the studios business. After the reason for his abrupt departure had become clear, Branson and Powell might easily have explained the situation and brought him back. But they saw Newman more as a musician than a business type; and they were beginning to realize the risks involved in giving employees subsidiary stakes in the companies.

'My stupidity was such that instead of going straight to a lawyer, I was full of hurt pride. I thought Richard and I were partners; I was enjoying the situation,' Newman recalled.

The gap in the management structure was filled promptly. Soon after Newman left, Branson appointed Phil Newell, who had formerly worked as the Manor's maintenance engineer, to replace him.

Newman's sense of outrage was compounded when he looked at the royalty statements he received from Virgin for *Fine Old Tom*, an album that he had made himself at the Manor. The record had taken three weeks to make, and Newman had arranged to do it at times when the studios were not needed by other artists. Yet his statement from Virgin after the record was released showed a deduction of £11,000 for the cost of studio time – a figure reflecting Simon Draper's determination that studio time should be allocated to artists at its full price. But the album's recording costs altogether were so high for this modest piece of work that it would inevitably take years for the royalties earned by his record to cover that deduction. 'I'm not even sure that I came out positive in the end,' Newman recalled.

It was only after Tom Newman had left Virgin that his friend Mike Oldfield began to look again at the contract he had signed with Richard Branson. Talking to other artists, Oldfield discovered that the five per cent royalty, standard though it had been at the time of signature, was by now hardly fitting to his enhanced status. Double that figure would have been more commensurate with how commercially important an artist he had become; and some artists in the same position might even have had the gall to demand a royalty of 17 or 20 per cent, on the grounds that Oldfield was in the habit of delivering finished master tapes to Virgin, thus saving the record company all the time and expense of mixing and editing his work. Even the modest five per cent he was receiving, however, was not what it seemed, for Branson was deducting a fifth of it as commission for his services as Oldfield's manager.

Oldfield telephoned Tom Newman one day, miserably depressed, and asked the former studio manager to come around to his house. When Newman arrived, he heard the whole story; and, to compound the dilemma, Oldfield also told him that he felt in a weak moral position to complain, since Branson had taken on *Tubular Bells* when almost every other record company in the country had turned it down. Newman reminded Oldfield abruptly that it was not only Branson who had shown faith in him. He had done the same himself; so had Simon Draper. Oldfield should not therefore consider the debt to Branson so great that it ruled out any change in their business dealings. In any case, his contract with Virgin was now up for negotiation. 'If you don't do it now,' he said, 'it'll never happen.'

A few weeks later, Oldfield bit the bullet. He hired a new lawyer to renegotiate the terms of his contract with Virgin, and came out at a royalty rate of almost 12 per cent. As a gesture of thanks to the friend who had helped him summon up the courage to face Richard Branson across the table, Oldfield gave Tom Newman from that day onwards a share of his royalties equivalent to one percentage point. By 1994, more than twenty years after its first release, *Tubular Bells* was still selling so well that Newman's one per cent brought in almost £10,000 a year. Had Oldfield dared to demand a higher royalty earlier on, however, he might have been well over £1m richer.

THREE

Broken Bottles

BY 1975, when Mike Oldfield's third album reached number four in the charts, Virgin Records had become the hottest company to work for in the music business. In common with other small and avant-garde record labels, Virgin could claim to have 'integrity' in its choice of artists for its roster; like those of the giants of the industry, its choices seemed always to make money. There was only one other company that could make a similar claim: Island Records, the label founded by the Jamaican-born public schoolboy Chris Blackwell, which brought to stardom many of the world's most famous Caribbean artists, most notably Bob Marley in 1972.

'I was doctrinaire,' remembered Simon Draper. 'I wanted to sign original and worthwhile talent.' His philosophy was that Virgin should be trying to produce great records that happened also to be commercially successful. This brought him into occasional conflict with Richard Branson, who was keen to sign musicians who would make money for him, but less interested in the sort of music they played. When faced with a potentially profitable addition to the roster that he knew would be unacceptable to the trend-setters of the industry and the music press, Draper had to explain to Branson why an act that might make money could nevertheless not be the sort of act that Virgin Records should sign.

Uncommercial it may have seemed; but this attitude helped to attract to Virgin, and to keep in its ranks, a group of young and fashionably talented employees. An extraordinary number of the company's staff of the time recall that period as the most exciting of their working lives. One reason for this was that Virgin was willing to hire people who had enthusiasm and a love for music, but no formal experience in other record companies. Once inside, they would find themselves given important jobs to do – and left to get on with them. Unsupervised, they would put in long hours and great effort, and in the end would achieve far more than they had believed themselves capable of.

The days of equal pay for all at Virgin had long gone. Yet it was routine for members of the record company's staff to turn down offers of double their current salaries or even more from other companies. There were few complaints about the cramped and unpleasant working conditions in the Vernon Yard offices to which the company had by now moved. Perhaps this was because life at Virgin was fun. Everyone seemed to be friends. And although people took their jobs seriously, they did so as they would take seriously a game of tennis that they passionately wanted to win, rather than as a career. Pensions were not a matter that was often discussed.

John Varnom served for a while as the public face of the company – writing its press releases, drafting its advertisements in *Melody Maker*, and answering questions from journalists. He set the tone by telling a series of whoppers to anyone who telephoned that were so outrageous that they were impossible to believe. Branson, meanwhile, indulged his love of practical jokes to the full; he had a brilliant knack for mimicking voices, and would often call his colleagues at the office and engage them in long, increasingly implausible conversations before they realized who was speaking.

But it was the company's weekends abroad that did most to cement its team spirit. Starting on a Friday and ending on a Sunday night, the entire staff of the record company, publishing company and studio management team would decamp to a country house hotel. Attendance was in theory optional, but those who did not come were told jokingly that they were expected to spend the weekend working in the office. At the hotel, other record companies might fill the days with talk of sales targets or new products. At Virgin, business was banned. Instead, the guests would spend the weekend playing tennis or golf, swimming and sunning themselves, eating and drinking with great gusto, and taking a few drugs and sleeping with each other in the evenings.

Men who worked at Virgin looked back on those weekends as idyllic. The corporate women – who certainly had better opportunities to do well at Virgin than they would have had in other record companies – were a little more cynical. 'Open marriages were fashionable,' said one. 'You were uncool if you didn't have lots of partners. Men were getting what they'd always wanted, to get to screw lots of women apart from their wives. Women were getting screwed by lots of men, and were not very happy about it.' But even those who disapproved of the weekend atmosphere conceded that they had thought of Virgin almost as a feminist company in the early days. It was only later that the cynical thought crossed their minds that Branson might actually have been so keen to employ women because they were cheaper than men and worked twice as hard. 'It was manipulative, but with Richard it was instinctive,' said another ex-employee of Branson's uncanny ability to motivate people to work hard for him. 'He had an instinctive way of handling people that got this reaction from them.'

The core element in Virgin's successful mixture was the talent of Simon Draper. As an 'A&R' man, a specialist in artists and repertoire who decided which new acts the record company ought to sign, he was beyond compare. Draper seemed to have an uncanny touch for artists who were not yet famous but would soon become so; and it was on this touch that the Virgin Records empire was built. Branson never claimed to have any musical discernment; when he tried to hide his ignorance, the results were apt to be embarrassing. On one occasion, when Simon Draper was trying to sign Elvis Costello and the Attractions, Branson opened the conversation over a negotiating lunch on his boat by saying how much he had loved their last album. The band's manager, who was intensely suspicious of Branson and was trying to persuade the band that it would be better to sign with a record company which made no pretence of being young and fashionable, saw his chance.

'Name me your two favourite tracks,' he said.

Branson was embarrassed to have his ignorance exposed, and stayed silent. Dessert was not served.

But there was more to Virgin's success than Simon Draper's ears. Only slightly less important was the quiet talent of Ken Berry, the clerk whom Branson had plucked from the accounts department above the Notting Hill Gate shop to sit in an office next to him at Vernon Yard. 'Kenny', as Draper and Branson called him, had won his promotion because Branson noticed that whenever he or Nik

Powell telephoned the department for a piece of information, it was always Berry who provided the answer – and Berry's answers were always right. A pattern soon emerged in which Draper would make the artistic decisions about which acts to sign, Branson would knock out the broad agreement in his office up a flight of spiral stairs from Draper; and then Berry would be left to tie up the details in a formal contract. Later on, as Branson was to withdraw from daily involvement in the label, it would be Berry himself who carried out the negotiations in all but the biggest deals.

In the mid-1970s, Virgin was just one of a number of fashionable independent labels that had succeeded in reaching the general record-buying public. It was still smaller than Island Records, and roughly the same size as companies such as Chrysalis and Charisma. Branson's talent, without which Virgin might have stayed a small but politically correct name under the leadership of Simon Draper, was to put in place the policies that would turn Virgin into one of the 'majors'.

His approach had two prongs. One was to take breathtaking risks that others shrank from. When Draper told him that the rock group 10cc were going to be big, for instance, Branson was willing to bet a huge sum on a group that would have sunk Virgin if its next record had not been a hit. The group had already had a couple of light but successful pop singles when Simon Draper was played a tape of *The Original Soundtrack*, their latest album. Branson flew to New York and struck a provision deal on American rights to the record with Ahmet Ertegun at Atlantic (who had bought the *Tubular Bells* package for $750,000).

In the event, the £350,000 offer that Branson then made for the group was insufficient; their manager, Harvey Lisberg, signed the group to a rival label while the two members who were most keen to sign with Virgin were on their way to a holiday in the Caribbean. But the story got around the British music business, and demonstrated just how serious a competitor Branson was. Richard Williams, who was Island's A&R man at the time, was dumbstruck. 'At Island, we weren't dealing in big sums,' he remembered. 'We'd sign people for £20,000. I remember being in competition with Simon and Richard [for 10cc], and realizing that they were prepared to pay major-label money for this act. That was quite a shock: to realize that Richard, who was on a level with us and perhaps slightly junior, was prepared to compete with the EMIs and the Phonograms and the Warner Brothers.' The point became still clearer a year later, when Branson just failed to sign the Rolling Stones for $3.5m.

But it was not only by offering larger sums than he could afford that Richard Branson succeeded in raising the profile of his record label. He also paid attention to an aspect of the business that most of the other British independents had neglected: foreign distribution. While A&M Records were modestly established in America, almost all Virgin's other competitors were entirely domestic companies. When they had records to sell abroad, they relied on licensing deals. Branson was not happy with that idea. He knew that licensing a record to another record company overseas brought with it an advance, and required no managerial effort. But in the long term, a record company that relied on foreign licensees was putting itself in a similar position to the musician: instead of making the bulk of the profits on a successful record, it was taking only a modest commission.

Richard Branson therefore devoted much of his time from the end of the 1970s onwards to establishing a network of record companies across continental Europe. On every trip to France, Italy or Germany, he would have his eyes open not only for licensing deals, but for the key people whom he would be able to hire in future to run a Virgin company in that territory. At first it took time to win over Ken Berry and Simon Draper to the idea. But by the end of the decade, the structure was in place and the strategy was agreed. With Luigi Mantovani in Rome, Patrick Zelnik in Paris, and Udo Lange in Frankfurt, Virgin was now able to sign up artists and guarantee them not only good distribution in Britain, but also entry into the most important European markets. This made Virgin a more attractive business prospect to top-ranking musicians than the other independent labels. Despite the combined efforts of Branson, Draper and Berry, however, one thing was holding the record label back. Having failed to win 10cc, there was now no really exciting new act for Virgin to acquire. That was to change in 1977, when Richard Branson signed the Sex Pistols.

*   *   *

Malcolm McLaren, the eccentric and unstable talent who was responsible for the Sex Pistols, never liked Richard Branson. In fact that was an understatement; he hated him, with a loathing that was incomprehensible to others. Years after the Pistols had broken up, he would paint a series of fascinating but wildly improbably stream-of-consciousness pictures of his dealings with Virgin. The first concerned how he had taken his demo tape of the Pistols to Virgin's offices in Vernon Yard early in 1976, and had rudely refused when Simon Draper suggested that he leave it for Branson to listen to. 'No,' said McLaren. 'He either listens to it now or forget it.'

'I didn't trust Richard,' said McLaren. 'I looked into his eyes and didn't even want to leave without my demo cassette with me. I was thinking: this is a guy who could bootleg me tomorrow morning and have it on a stall in the Portobello Road . . . I didn't like the feel of the place. The chairs were so uncomfortable . . . I was asking for £15,000 for a couple of singles, and see how we go . . . I thought creative accountancy is definitely going to be a problem with this company.'

McLaren was by no means a professional manager. He had spent eight years at different art schools before opening a shop in the King's Road selling rubber and leather bondage gear. His principal experience of the record business was of managing an unsuccessful New York rock group in 1974; and the package that he brought to Simon Draper that day in 1976 was hardly the sort to appeal to an A&R man known for the sensitivity of his ears.

The Sex Pistols were, to put it bluntly, a band of yobs. Their sole musical talent, Glen Matlock, had been dropped as bass guitarist in favour of the more startlingly thuggish Sid Vicious. Johnny Rotten, a misanthropic teenager whose complexion and posture had been ruined by a bout of childhood meningitis, was the lead singer. The prime talent for which the band's other two members were famous, and which they had displayed to disastrous effect at pubs across London, was to belch, spit and swear at their audiences.

Simon Draper hated the music. 'It was all style and all aggression,' he recalled. 'To me, coming from a musical perspective, it just seemed like a great big noise. I went to see them at the 100 Club. [When we] came back after the gig, it was very exciting. There was such an air; it was so aggressive.' In the car on the way home, Draper commented that they couldn't sing – and then remembered, with a sinking realization, that people had made the same complaint of Mick Jagger when they had first heard the Rolling Stones. One magazine had described Jagger's voice as being like broken bottles. With the Pistols, however, the shards of glass was a literal rather than a metaphorical part of the act.

Rejected by Virgin, McLaren signed the band he was managing to EMI. Their first single, 'Anarchy in the UK', convinced Draper as soon as he heard it that he had been wrong. There was an energy and a directness in the Sex Pistols' music that was lacking in any other pop music of the time. More importantly, the group were packaged brilliantly. Jamie Reid, an art school friend of McLaren's, produced album-cover designs that were revolutionary in their mixture of passport-sized photographs and letters cut from tabloid newspapers, in the style of an anonymous letter.

McLaren himself, meanwhile, contrived a series of incidents that were designed in equal measure to offend the old and the middle class, and to attract the young, disgruntled and unemployed. The greatest of them was to have the Pistols invited to appear on 'Today', Bill Grundy's afternoon magazine programme on Thames Television. A few 'fucks' and 'shits' from the boys in spiked haircuts and ripped jeans, and punk rock was promoted from something unpleasant that happened in private music clubs to a national controversy.

Branson did not need to be alerted by Draper to the commercial possibilities of the Pistols' ability to shock. The very day of their appearance on Grundy's show, he had telephoned the managing director of EMI to offer to take this turbulent band off his hands. Since the EMI executive would not take his call, Branson left a message; the following morning, he was called to a meeting at EMI's offices.

Branson was ready to make a deal there and then; McLaren was determined to play cat and mouse. He shook hands on a deal with Branson that day, earning £50,000 in compensation from EMI for the record company's decision to assuage public anger by pulling the single from record shops. But McLaren then signed the Pistols to A&M Records, in a public ceremony outside the gates of Buckingham Palace. A&M paid £200,000 for the group, but had second thoughts when the group trashed its offices after a signing party. It took several more months, and five telephone calls a day from Richard Branson himself, before McLaren would condescend to accept a second compensation payment, this time from A&M, and sign his boys with Virgin Records.

Virgin entered into the spirit of things with enthusiasm. The group's next single, 'God Save The Queen', was given a loudspeaker performance from a boat on the Thames just outside the Houses of Parliament during the week of Queen Elizabeth II's Silver Jubilee. The police and the popular press obediently played their parts in the publicity stunt: McLaren was arrested, and the name of the group was all over the papers for a week. The record reached number two in the charts (some saying that only chart manipulation denied it the triumph of becoming number one), and sold over 100,000 copies in that week. Further success followed with the predictable controversy surrounding the Pistols' album, *Never Mind the Bollocks*, and the unsuccessful prosecution for obscenity that followed its release.

By the end of 1978, however, the phenomenon of the Sex Pistols had worked itself out. McLaren had made a revolutionary film about the group and its handling, *The Great Rock 'n' Roll Swindle*. He had briefly appointed Ronnie Biggs, a former train robber resident in Brazil, as the group's lead singer; and the group itself had begun to fall apart. Sid Vicious died two months later of a drugs overdose, before he could be tried for stabbing his girlfriend to death with a knife. And Johnny Rotten, reverting to the name of John Lydon with which he had been born, repudiated McLaren as a manager and began an action in the High Court to have his company's assets liquidated.

For Branson, Sid's death was a disaster, but Virgin managed to salvage some return on the contract. There was now no longer any hope that the group would become a serious money-spinner for Virgin; but the label still had the rights to the records the Pistols had already made. Draper also went on to release a posthumous album of Sid Vicious songs. More important, however, its association with the Sex Pistols and with punk rock had once again made Virgin a label that young artists would be willing to sign to. Richard Branson had been looking for a hit act that would 'put Virgin on the map'. Now he had found one. The five years after the end of the Sex Pistols would prove to be the record label's most creatively successful period. In that single half-decade, Virgin would break and develop into stardom such acts as Phil Collins, Culture Club, Simple Minds, Human League, Heaven 17, China Crisis and Japan – a set of achievements that few independent labels could equal over their entire lifetimes.

While Virgin's credibility among the professionals of the music industry was rising, however, wider trends outside were pointing worryingly downwards. Inflation, which had been falling under James Callaghan's Labour government, began once again to look threatening. Economic growth slowed down, and the government suffered a bruising succession of confrontations with the trade unions. Matters came to a head in the 'winter of discontent' at the end of 1978, which saw strikes and power cuts. The record industry, as a supplier of a non-essential product, was particularly hard hit. Album sales in Britain dropped by more than 15 per cent in the course of 1978; the industry as a whole began to turn from profit into deep loss.

Virgin, which now had a disparate rag-bag of interests ranging from the record label, management and studios to retail, restaurants and a private island, was forced to look for economies. A quarter of the record label's fifty-strong staff were sacked, starting with Arnold Frollows, the firm's respected head of A&R. It was Virgin's first ever round of compulsory redundancies. The artists' roster was purged of acts that were making insufficient money. Valuers were sent around the various properties owned by the company – ranging from the Manor in Oxfordshire to the houses dotted around Notting Hill Gate in which the company directors were living – in an attempt to add some extra weight to the group's balance sheet. An ambitious attempt to build on Virgin's European success by opening up shops in the United States was abandoned: Ken Berry, originally sent out to build an empire in America, was asked to wind down gracefully the company's interests there and come home.

The election of a Conservative government in the summer of 1979 made little immediate difference. Margaret Thatcher, the new prime minister, saw her first priority as conquering Labour's inflationary legacy. It was more than a year before she could begin to claim success, for inflation actually rose from just over 13 per cent in 1979 to 18 per cent in 1980; but the price of lower inflation was sharp cuts in public spending, a rise in interest rates, and a sudden increase in the number of unemployed. The Tories owed their election victory in part to a powerful series of posters, showing hundreds of ostensibly unemployed people queuing up above the slogan 'Labour isn't working'. That now became a bitter joke. The only consolation for Virgin was that as times became tougher, other companies were in worse straits.

The task for Branson and Powell in 1980 was to prune back the unwieldy plant they had created. At one point they even resorted to the expedient of inviting in a firm of management consultants to advise them on what to do. None of these reforms, however, had any significant effect on Coutts & Co, the company's blue-blooded bankers. Coutts flatly refused to increase the company's overdraft; and Virgin's bank manager began to ask instead when he could expect to be repaid some of what he had already lent.

It was fortunate, therefore, that a significant nest-egg had been set aside in case of bad times. Seven years ealier, before the record label had even been established, Branson and Powell had registered the trademark that would appear on its first few albums – a drawing of a pair of women – in the name of an offshore trust. When overseas record companies or subsidiaries later paid for the rights to Virgin albums, the royalties they were charged could therefore be split into two: a royalty for the record itself, which could be sent to Virgin in Britain; and a fee for the use of the Virgin trade-mark, which went directly to the trust overseas without incurring the attention of the UK taxman. Branson took advice from Har-bottle & Lewis, the company lawyers, so that the trust was set up correctly. Apart from that firm, no outsiders – either companies or people – were consulted on the trust òr its affairs.

Such an arrangement might have raised eyebrows at the Inland Revenue, particularly when put into effect by a pair of young businessmen who were still both under twenty-three at the time that the trust was established, and one of whom had already admitted to attempting to defraud the Customs & Excise. Yet this kind of trust arrangement was expressly allowed under British tax law; without it, Britain's high income and capital gains taxes were too much of a disincentive to foreign entities who were considering doing business in Britain.

There was, however, a proviso. In order to avoid any liability to tax, it was important that the trust's beneficiaries should all live overseas. Under UK tax laws, beneficiaries who lived in Britain could be taxed on their share of any capital gains that the trust made – even if they received no money from the trust. Their status as a potential or a future beneficiary could land them with a thumping tax bill. So the trust had to be set up either so that Branson and Powell and their families were not its beneficiaries, or so that no capital gains were actually made. The first of these conditions was hard to achieve, since the two men wanted to benefit from whatever financial success Virgin might achieve. The second condition was easier: as long as the trust simply held on to the income from the trademark it already owned, and did nothing that would 'crystallize' its capital gains, it could remain legally safe from tax.

The trust had discreetly accumulated substantial sums of money between the 1973 launch of the record company and the later decision to change Virgin's trade mark from the twins to the handwritten logo with the big capital 'V' that the group uses to this day. When Coutts pulled the plug on Virgin, therefore, Branson suddenly suggested to one of the company's financial people that they should approach the Bank of Nova Scotia. BNS, he said, held deposits in the Cayman Islands which Branson himself controlled. The bank would be willing to allow the company in London to borrow over £1m using those overseas deposits as security. That loan helped Virgin survive the recession.

FOUR

Media Mogul

BY THE SPRING OF 1981 it was almost ten years since Richard Branson had closed down *Student* magazine to concentrate on selling records by mail-order. A great deal had happened since then. Virgin had established a record label, a studio business, a chain of shops, a music publishing house; and although 1980 had been a miserably difficult year, the company was clearly beginning to prosper. Yet Branson had never conquered his early ambition to be a newspaper proprietor. For a man whose attention span was as short as his, there was something alluringly immediate about a business whose product was made one day, sold the day after, and discarded the next. The newspaper industry had a further attraction, too: newspaper proprietors had influence and respectability that would always be denied to the owner of a mere record company.

Branson would not have described himself as a friend of Tony Elliott, the founder and publisher of *Time Out*, the London listings magazine. But the two men were roughly contemporaries, and came from the same public school. They had the same unconventional approach to business, the same ability to guide and motivate young people, the same roots in the counterculture of the 1960s. Elliott had once even approached Branson, suggesting that the two should collaborate to launch a new magazine in New York. But the discussions had come to nothing when Branson realized that Elliott was trying to do to him what he himself had done to so many others: the publisher had no money, but was trying to persuade Branson that the two companies should establish a fifty-fifty joint venture.

By the turn of the 1980s, Elliott's magazine had clearly become a successful and thriving business. Despite the handicap of a palpable left-wing militancy among its journalists, *Time Out* was the information source of choice for young, fashionable Londoners who wanted to know which films to see, where to eat, where to shop, and which exhibitions to visit. Its classified section was the place to look for meditation classes, for friendly people to sand the floors of your house, and for cheap flights to south-east Asia. The magazine also did a roaring trade in gay lonely hearts.

The idea of owning a listings magazine with a pronounced political bent would never have occurred to Branson had it not been for the strike that hit the magazine in May 1981. Like his counterpart at Virgin, Tony Elliott had soon learned to distinguish between the political ideals of his staff and the practicalities of running a business. But Elliott had made a damaging error in 1973, when his magazine was still small enough for a minor negotiating concession to seem unimportant. At that time, most of his staff were paid £25 a week; the editors of the sections received £30. When the local chapel of the National Union of Journalists demanded an increase in the rank-and-file wages to £35, Elliott had conceded the principle of a weekly wage of £32.50 – equal pay for all his staff, no matter what jobs they did. As *Time Out* continued to grow, the system became untenable; the standard company wage was at once too high for Elliott to be able to diversify into other publishing ventures, and too low for him to be able to attract talented writers into the magazine from outside. By the end of the 1970s, Elliott had made a firm decision: cost what it may, he would win back the right to pay some staff more than others. 'I was pretty confident that we would in the end have either a Pyrrhic victory, in which the whole business would disappear,' he recalled later, 'or we would win.'

Initially, the former outcome seemed more likely. As soon as Elliott had insisted on changing the company's wage structures, the staff struck in protest. The management locked them out, with the help of a court order; and some dismissed *Time Out* employees established a picket line outside the magazine's Covent Garden offices. But the magazine itself had to cease publication.

A week after the publication of the last pre-strike *Time Out*, Branson telephoned Elliott at home.

'Look,' he said. 'I've been thinking about your problem. What would you say to the following scenario?' And Branson then outlined a plan that he would set up a new magazine called *Stepping*

Out, or something like it, and would get it established quickly as a successor to the old *Time Out*. That would give Elliott the time he needed to outlast the patience of the pickets outside his office door. 'Then,' said Branson, 'when you've sorted that situation out to the satisfactory conclusion that you want, I'll close down *Stepping Out* and we'll become the joint owners of the new *Time Out*.'

Elliott was no fool. He realized how much power such a plan would give Branson over him, and how little room for manoeuvre he would have once a magazine with a similar name was on the streets with his ostensible approval. But he swallowed his suspicions, and accepted Branson's invitation to come down to the Manor on a Saturday afternoon with his girlfriend and two other people.

At Branson's suggestion, he and Elliott went off for a walk at three o'clock, leaving their respective girlfriends behind. They returned several hours later, to the barely disguised irritation of Elliott's girlfriend, and Branson insisted that they stay for dinner. The dinner – which the more sophisticated Elliott later dismissed as 'school food', citing it as evidence of Branson's lack of attention to detail – proved to be a social disaster. Talk turned to the subject of the Social Democratic Party, the recent breakaway from the Labour Party led by a group of four senior politicians; and Branson, rarely someone to talk with interest about politics, became embroiled in a flaming row with Elliott's girlfriend.

Elliott and his girlfriend left immediately after dinner. By the time they reached London, the *Time Out* proprietor had arrived at two conclusions. First, he wanted to solve the problem of the strike on his own, rather than admitting an outsider to his life on what might well prove a permanent basis. Second, he wanted nothing more to do with Richard Branson. Whatever the reason – whether perhaps he drank too much and became aggressive, or whether simply the personal chemistry had been wrong – Branson's charm offensive had failed totally. Elliott turned down the proposal.

But Richard Branson's interest had been tickled, and it was too late to go back. If Elliott would not start *Stepping Out* in partnership with him, then he was quite entitled to do it on his own. And thus it was that Branson set to work hiring an editorial staff for a new London listings magazine to fill the gap left by the old *Time Out*. The team was assembled in three months, and the first edition of the magazine – which Branson decided to call *Event* – appeared in September.

There was just one problem. A week earlier, Elliott's former employees had established *City Limits*, their own listings magazine. A week before that, Elliott himself had come back with a new *Time Out*, staffed by a fresh corps of journalists but in many respects identical to the old. To make matters worse, Elliott had put some subtle changes into effect during the months that his magazine was off the streets. 'Agitprop' became less strident, and was renamed 'Politics'; a gay section, previously vetoed by the staff on the grounds that it was 'ghettoist', brought together the clubs and events of most interest to homosexuals; the 'Sell Out' department provided more pages of consumer and shopping news than before; and a much-overdue section on nightlife covered a subject that the magazine's former staff had dismissed as trivial and politically incorrect. The new *Time Out*'s first cover story, symbolizing the nascent metropolitan affluence appearing under Margaret Thatcher, was about all-night London.

Elliott knew that he would face competition, for Branson had poached Pearce Marchbank, *Time Out*'s design guru, to co-edit *Event* with Al Clark. But *Event* proved to be a damp squib. Its editorial approach was just a little too middlebrow; it went in for slightly tacky competitions; and it committed a fundamental error by printing the listings – for many readers, the magazine's principal attraction – in a point size so small that it was barely legible. The staff were at each other's throats.

Despite the undoubted literary and artistic talents of the team that Branson had assembled, the magazine soon began to go downhill. The real competition to Elliott's new *Time Out* was not *Event*, but *City Limits*. As the months rolled on, *Time Out*'s circulation began to rise above 60,000; *City Limits* stayed put at around 30,000; and *Event* declined, equally immune to changes of personnel and of style, to below 20,000 by the turn of the year. Tina Brown, later to become editor of the *Tatler*, *Vanity Fair* and the *New Yorker*, described Branson's venture with scathing accuracy as 'a triumph of managerial incompetence over editorial flair'.

Proof of the fall in the magazine's morale could be seen in its in-house magazine. As if it was not enough of a struggle to put the next issue of *Event* together, a group of mischievous members of the magazine's staff decided to start an underground gossip sheet, entirely for internal consumption, that would chronicle its lurching progress from issue to issue. The sheet was called *Non-Event*; Rod Vickery, usually one of Branson's most faithful lieutenants, did the artwork, while another couple of employees wrote the stories and a fourth ran off a copy for the desk of each member of staff. Terry Baughan, the man in charge of the Virgin Group's finances at the time, was at first speechless with fury. 'I'd love to get my hands on the people who did that,' he said. Vickery, kept safe from suspicion by virtue not only of his long service but also of his seniority in the company, said nothing.

The tough decisions forced on Branson by the tottering fortunes of his magazine turned *Event*'s journalists against him. Jonathan Meades, one of the later editors he appointed, recalled that Branson had disputed a £30 expense claim submitted by the magazine's film critic. 'But he also had three phones going at the same time, and on one of them he was trying to sign the Stranglers for £300,000,' Meades remembered. The experience of working for Branson also left him with a jaded impression of the young entrepreneur. 'He's impossible to conduct a conversation with because he is inarticulate ... Branson's very good at making money, but the rest of him hasn't kept up. It's like a form of autism.'

But Branson was never one to give up. With creditable bravado, he telephoned Elliott six months later. Brushing aside Elliott's questions about the restyles and the firings at *Event*, Branson came straight to the point.

'Look,' he said. 'We've had a really good run with the Human League. We've done really well, and I've got at least three-quarters of a million pounds sitting in the bank. I can either put it into *Event*, or I could put it into *Time Out*.'

Elliott, who was a little drunk at the time, took a deep breath before he responded.

'Richard,' he said. 'There's one thing you don't realize. You should stop this mission to acquire all or part of *Time Out*. At the end of the day, my readers don't respect you. They see you as an opportunist, as someone without genuine cultural integrity.'

Cultural integrity he may have lacked; but Richard Branson had an almost unlimited capacity to swallow failures and humiliations. 'Business opportunities are like buses,' he liked to say. 'There's always another coming along.' And so with barely a pause for self-doubt, Branson plunged back into the daily concerns of his record business, his ability to sniff out a good deal heightened by the awareness that Virgin's losses on *Event* had brought it perilously close to insolvency. It was not to be long, however, before Branson's thoughts had returned to publishing. If he was not cut out to be a magazine proprietor, why should he not own a film company? A video production business? A cable television company? A radio station? The thought may even have crossed his mind, albeit briefly, of owning a newspaper.

Unfortunately, the early omens were not good. Branson already owned one publishing business, known as Virgin Books, and it was not going well. He had received an approach in 1979 from a man called Maxim Jakubofki, whose main area of expertise was in the food industry but who fancied himself as a publisher of books. Jakubofki had even more gall than Branson himself. Before making an approach to the record entrepreneur, he had taken the precaution of registering a company in the name of Virgin Books so that if Branson turned down his suggestion to start a new book publishing subsidiary, he could hold in reserve the threat that he might go ahead and start Virgin Books independently. But Jakubofki was not as successful a publisher as he was a negotiator; and in less than two years, it had become clear that Virgin Books was in trouble. Among the weird ideas he had put into practice was a series of short novels written by rock stars; at one stage he even wanted to publish a book about chickens that had appeared in the movies. But the company's core problem under his stewardship was that it was trying to do too many things. Unable to choose even between fiction and non-fiction, Virgin Books was a small and not very successful publisher. In an ill-advised interview with the *Financial Times*, Branson had boasted that the company would publish books by undiscovered young talents, and would be looking for the literary equivalent of Mike Oldfield. It never found it.

As relations with Jakubofki deteriorated, Branson realized that he needed to bring someone into the publishing company whom he could trust. He knew exactly whom to ask for advice: his younger sister Vanessa's boyfriend, Robert Devereux, who worked at Macmillan, one of the grander names in British publishing. Devereux was twenty-five years old, and very bright indeed. He also had the tactical advantage of having beaten Branson regularly at chess. A lunch was arranged on the houseboat to which Devereux brought with him Rob Shreeve, his boss at Macmillan. Branson put his proposal: the two men should come to Virgin and sort out its books business. Shreeve, older and perhaps a little wiser than Devereux, wanted to know just how committed Branson was to his book publishing division. How much money did he think he would be able to invest in it? How many titles might it expect to bring out over the coming year? Whatever the answers were, it became clear that Devereux would join Virgin; Shreeve, though grateful for the lunch, would politely decline.

Devereux moved fast on his arrival at Virgin Books. He fired some of the staff, and frightened others into working harder. He threw out Jakubofki's strategy, and tried to decide how the small publishing company he was now in charge of should seek to compete against the corporate giants. Devereux's first major decision was to stop publishing fiction. Instead, he ruled that the firm should concentrate on quick, preferably cheap, books that would appeal to young people. While the rest of the publishing world was going collectively mad, paying huge advances to a small number of star authors that could never be recouped in royalties, Devereux preferred to think small. He was successful. Virgin Books stopped losing money; over the coming few years it began to acquire a reputation as a serviceable publisher of books about rock, sport and video games.

But Devereux could not satisfy his ambitions by staying the managing director of a small publishing house. He wanted more responsibilities inside the Virgin Group, and with the help of Richard Branson, who had become his brother-in-law when he married Vanessa Branson, that was what he got. Branson's closest advisers, Simon Draper and Ken Berry, viewed Devereux with polite suspicion when, still under the age of thirty, he joined the board of the Virgin Group. 'We all liked him and were very impressed by him,' recalled Draper, looking back on his feelings during the 1980s. But Devereux seemed to be trying to out-Branson Branson. 'He thought, "I can play bridge better than Richard, I can play sport better than Richard, I can *be* Richard."' To Draper's mind, Devereux's self-appraisal was wrong. What Devereux lacked, for all his cerebral qualities, were his brother-in-law's uncanny ability to inspire not merely great loyalty but also enormous effort among those who were working for him.

Those who were sceptical of Devereux's abilities felt they had been proved right when he persuaded the board to take a 20 per cent shareholding in W. H. Allen, a publishing company that had lost its market edge. Having merged Virgin's publishing interests into the firm, and then invested substantial Virgin funds in Allen, Devereux then allowed the existing management to carry on running it – and it was not long before Virgin was required to take a controlling stake in the company, cut out most of its unsuccessful operations, and write off substantial losses.

The company's forays into film-making were only marginally more successful. Robert Devereux and Al Clark, the company's erstwhile press officer and *Events* editor, made a little money for Virgin by topping up the finance of a couple of low-budget films, one called *Secret Places* and the other *Loose Connections*. They went on to put £4m into *Electric Dreams*, a high-tech love story directed by Steve Barron, a maker of pop videos. The film, whose soundtrack included a number one hit from the Human League's vocalist Phil Oakley, produced a modest return for Virgin, made more attractive by the fact that under specially favourable tax treatment for investing in British films, the Inland Revenue allowed Virgin to deduct its entire investment in the film from its taxable income for the year. But Virgin seemed somehow unable to leave this small but successful division where it was. The next project, brought to Virgin by Simon Perry, the producer of *Loose Connections*, was to turn George Orwell's novel of Stalinist totalitarianism, *Nineteen Eighty-Four*, into a film. It was not the first time a film of the book had been made; thirty years earlier, in the optimism of a fast-growing postwar society, a sanitized version with a happy ending had been put out. But there would be special resonance to releasing the film of

Nineteen Eighty-Four in 1984. It would cost just under £2m, and the director would be Michael Radford, Perry's partner.

When the proposal was brought to him, Branson agreed to back the film. John Hurt and Richard Burton were lined up to star in it. Before shooting could commence, however, Virgin received a piece of bad news: the film was going to be a little more expensive than its makers had expected. Instead of £2m, Virgin should now expect to stump up £2.5m. So convinced was Branson that Perry and Radford were going to pull off a masterpiece that he was bid up to £3.7m, and then, as the film continued astonishingly to over-run its shooting schedule and its budget with equal abandon, to £5.5m. The meeting at which that figure was first mentioned in Branson's hearing was a difficult one.

Still Virgin and its chairman appeared to be dazzled by the glamour of the movie business. Instead of doing what most investors would have done – sacking the producer and director, and replacing them with a pair of placemen who could be relied on to get the film in the can and then distributed with as small a loss to the backers as possible – he allowed Perry and Radford to finish off the project. But the greatest disagreement was still to come. In the hope of making the film a commercial success, Branson had arranged for the Eurythmics to produce a soundtrack. The music they came up with, assembled with breathtaking speed in a Caribbean studio while the band were serving out their required number of days of tax exile, was an impressive piece of soundtrack, but it seemed to have little connection with the movie. Perry and Radford insisted that they should use a soundtrack already written by Dominic Muldownie, which they considered far more suitable. If Branson did not agree, they said, he was welcome to distribute the film with whatever soundtrack he liked; but they could not be expected to talk of it as their own.

Faced with this threat, Branson looked for a compromise. The Muldownie soundtrack was used for the reviewers and the premiere; once the film was on general release, however, it would be replaced by the work of the Eurythmics – provided market research supported the view that audiences did not actually object to the more commercial rock soundtrack. In November 1984, a month after the film's release, Radford took the opportunity of giving an acceptance speech for an award for best British film of the year to attack Branson's company for having 'foisted' the Eurythmics soundtrack on him. That was embarrassing enough; Perry them compounded the sin by giving an interview to a gossip column in the *Daily Express*, in which he blamed Branson's inability to sell the film in the United States on his 'inexperience', and threw in an accusation of lying for good measure. Branson threatened to sue for libel.

The small satisfaction was that Perry and the newspaper caved in quickly, apologizing and withdrawing the allegations, agreeing to pay Branson's costs as well as their own, and making a donation to charity. But for Branson, the losses he made on the film came with an important lesson. Never again would he be tempted to set aside his own commercial interests for the sake of backing a director who wanted to make a masterpiece. In media businesses – whether records, books, films or magazines – the proprietor had to stay a little aloof from the product. Once he became too swept up in the creator's enthusiasm, his financier's judgement was sure to suffer.

FIVE

Do You Really Want to Hurt Me?

IN PRINCIPLE, there was no dispute between Richard Branson and Nik Powell about how they should respond to the harsh economic conditions of 1980. But the two men had different pet projects. In 1978, Branson bought a private island in the British Virgin Islands for $300,000 from a cash-strapped English aristocrat. He then spent nearly £1m buying two clubs: the Roof Gardens in Kensington, and Heaven, a nightclub near Charing Cross that was the largest gay club in Europe. Powell, by contrast, had been the leading light behind a plan to spend a similar sum on converting a cinema in Victoria into The Venue, a combination of restaurant, bar and concert place.

These two interests were a source of conflict: Powell complained that the island was an indulgence, and feared (incorrectly as it turned out) that the two clubs Branson had acquired might not make money. For his part, Branson felt that the Venue made demands on their time that were disproportionate to its importance to the Virgin Group. Everything there seemed to be a problem. Planning permission came only at the last minute, and Branson himself was forced to intervene to get even trusted members of staff to sell tickets for performances there. The waiting staff were paid very low salaries, and had to be placated at Christmas for the absence of an expected bonus with individual presents wrapped up by Nik Powell and Barbara Jeffries, the Venue's manager at the time. The working conditions there brought bad publicity to the group when *Private Eye* began to run articles claiming that the Venue's waiting staff and the bands who performed there were being exploited, and that recipients of free tickets were being denied entrance when the club finally began to fill up. And as if these problems were not enough, it was realized in late 1980 that no proper arrangements had been made for paying tax on staff salaries. Chris Craib, one of the group's senior accounting staff, had to make an impromptu return to the Inland Revenue, estimating the tax that he believed should have been paid over recent months but had not.

Beneath the blazing rows that Branson and Powell had over these difficulties, there was an underlying issue of far greater importance. Nik Powell's influence in the group had been waning over the past five years. The retail businesses in which he took greatest interest had proven to be indifferently managed and barely profitable; the record label, with which he had little to do, was the engine of Virgin's growth. Richard Branson had begun to confide more in Simon Draper and in Ken Berry than he did in Nik Powell. Branson had come to believe that for all Powell's talents, there was no longer an important job for him to do at Virgin.

The recession of 1980 made matters far worse. For while the triumvirate at the top of the music businesses still felt that he was not pulling his creative weight, Powell's ability to block decisions he disagreed with suddenly became much greater. No longer was Virgin expanding so rapidly that his concerns could be dismissed; instead, Powell himself was the butcher who was making the cuts, and Virgin was shrinking. As a 40 per cent shareholder in the Virgin holding company, Powell could stop Richard Branson from taking steps he did not approve of. And Branson, who had resisted all attempts to control him – at school, at home, and in his marriage to Kristen – did not like being subjected to this veto.

Branson would later say that it had taken him two years to summon up the courage to write the letter. Nik Powell, after all, was his childhood friend; the man who had dropped out of university to join him in Albion Street; the junior partner in the relationship that they both referred to as a 'marriage'. But in the end there was no choice. Branson wrote to Powell, telling him that he thought the two should separate.

The weakness in Powell's position was that although he had a 40 per cent shareholding, his contract with Branson was far from powerful. The key point in the agreement was the calculation that would be used to work out how much Powell's shares were worth if he decided to sell them back to Branson. Branson would later recall that the calculation was based on the company's net assets. With the help of his South African brother, Draper had been far more canny; he had insisted on a valuation based on a multiple of pre-tax earnings over earlier years. But the price of Powell's shareholding was based on Virgin's net assets as recorded in the company balance sheet. This may have included buildings and cars, tables and chairs. But it excluded the intangible asset that was a decade later to allow Branson to sell the Virgin music businesses for £560m: the Virgin catalogue. The contracts that Branson had signed with the artists – specifying the number of records that each one would have to deliver to Virgin in the future, and the length of time for which Virgin would be able to collect copyright fees on the work that the artist had already done – were the real jewel in the Virgin crown. Yet they were not reflected in the company's balance sheet; nor, therefore, were they reflected in the sum of money that Powell received when he and Branson parted company.

Neither Branson nor Powell would discuss the settlement in detail publicly. But Powell probably received £1m in cash, plus three assets he wanted to take with him: the Scala cinema, the video editing facilities that Virgin had invested in – and Steve Woolley, a man who knew backwards the film industry in which Powell thought he saw his future.

One million pounds must have seemed a fantastic sum to Powell in 1981. But he could not escape the fact that he had sold out to Branson when Virgin's fortunes, and hence its value, were at a nadir. Within a couple of years, the new acts that the record label had already taken on, such as Phil Collins and the Human League, would make the group highly profitable once again. Within five years, the 40 per cent that he had sold back to Branson would be worth £96m. Although Powell publicly pronounced himself quite satisfied with the deal, he would have been forgiven for having regrets.

Powell's friends admired his equanimity: he had become a Buddhist, and managed to curtail his frustration at the increasing friction with Branson during the dying months of their partnership by chanting regularly. But they were convinced that he had lost out all the same. 'It seemed to me to be an unrealistically small settlement for 40 per cent of such a vast, thriving company,' wrote

Sandie Shaw, a chart-topping singer who later became his wife, 'but Nik, who considered Virgin to be his "baby", was highly emotionally charged about leaving it, and was not capable of making rational decisions.'

'After Nik's departure,' Shaw continued in her autobiography, 'his existence and role within Virgin was systematically written out of its history. The impression given, if any, was that Nik had been some kind of managerial employee.'

Branson defended himself furiously against the allegation that he had treated his boyhood friend unfairly. 'I can see how it could be said that I eased Nik out at a time when the business was down, so it was easier to make him look bad and [to set a] lower price to buy him out . . . It was obviously very difficult because of our friendship . . . The money he received fairly reflected the input he had made. It was difficult for him to find a role to contribute. With Simon and Kenny and others there was really no role for him. He had no particular skills to contribute to the company as it was at that stage.'

Branson also claimed that the subsequent rise in the value of the record company was hard to predict. He pointed out that a few years later, Virgin bought Charisma Records, an independent label that had a fat catalogue including work by Genesis, Peter Gabriel and Monty Python, for only a few million pounds: 'The contract that I gave Nik originally gave him his shares for nothing but stipulated that when they were sold they were to reflect a minority stake in a private company . . . he was not selling control. Therefore I believe the price paid at the time was a fair one. I had also agreed to leave him with a small profit share for the future which he decided not to take and to swap for something else.'

After a decade in which the two men spent hours of every day in each other's company, the separation was very sudden. Nik Powell went off to found Palace Pictures with Steve Woolley, and was responsible for a number of successful films during the 1980s, including *Company of Wolves*, *Mona Lisa*, and latterly *The Crying Game*. Almost exactly ten years after his departure, however, Palace ran into financial difficulties and Powell came back to Branson, cap in hand. Virgin invested some money in the company, allowing it to continue in business for a few crucial months. When Powell returned a second time, however, Branson turned him down in the friendliest possible way: he asked him to go and see Robert Devereux, his brother-in-law, who was by then responsible for Virgin's film and other media interests. Devereux took a hard look at the Palace books and decided not to invest. Branson consoled himself with the thought that Polygram, the large European record company, were about to take a substantial stake in Palace. But Polygram were interested only in the company's production arm. By May 1992, Palace had gone into administration, and Powell was forced to start again for the second time in his career. 'I don't think we realized how close he was [to going under] at the last minute,' said Richard Branson afterwards.

'I gather,' said the headmaster sternly, looking down his nose through his spectacles at the school's morning assembly, 'that some of you are not entirely happy with the musical selections that we've been playing. So today we have a slight change in the usual programme. Instead of classical music, I have decided to offer you something a little different.'

The headmaster stepped to one side. A powerful spotlight picked out a circle in the centre of the curtains behind him. The curtains opened. And eight hundred primary school pupils, aged from five to twelve, jumped out of their seats in astonishment and began to scream. Not in their wildest dreams had they expected Boy George himself to perform a number-one hit song, at their school assembly.

Behind the scenes, Steve Lewis gave a smile of quiet satisfaction. He had been at the school since seven o'clock in the morning, helping to supervise as the roadies and technicians assembled the loudspeaker system, and watching as curious teachers peeked into the classroom where George, his make-up already applied, was ironing the shirt that he was about to wear. The 'concert', if that was the right word for a performance of a single song at a school in Finchley, was an outstanding success.

It had been set up for a television programme – 'Jim'll Fix It' – and filmed by hidden cameras. Two girls from the school had written in to Jimmy Savile, complaining about the miserable diet of Schubert and Shostakovitch to which their miserable headmaster subjected them at every morning assembly. Long after the girls had given up on their request, the programme's producer at the BBC had telephoned Virgin Records, just on the off-chance that the world's most famous pop star might be willing to co-operate in bringing the girls' fantasy to fruition. He was; the idea tickled his fancy, and his manager and his record company recognized that although he would receive no fee for his performance, the exposure to a television audience of millions of children and adults would help to sell records. The faces of the astonished children – most notably the two who had sent in the letter, who had been identified for the cameraman from school photographs so that viewers could see their disbelief as their dream came true – turned the concert into brilliant television. The only irony was that Boy George, a consummate professional performer who had played all over the world, sometimes to audiences of tens of thousands of people, was more nervous about playing in front of a school assembly than he had ever been before. Only when the curtains opened did the star begin to enjoy himself.

Not even the most skilful A&R person could have guessed in 1980 that George O'Dowd would within three years be topping the charts in seventeen different countries. A former window-dresser and model, who had worked for the Royal Shakespeare Company as a make-up artist, George had almost joined a band under the influence of Malcolm McLaren. By 1980, he was delivering stylishly polished performances in gay nightclubs in London, and had been signed as a songwriter to Virgin Music Publishers – but he had no recording contract. His manager, Tony Gordon, had contacted Simon Draper and offered to provide a fleet of limousines to take Draper and his colleagues down to a rehearsal room where Culture Club, George's new band, was performing an odd mixture of soul, pop and reggae. Danny Goodwyn, a Virgin talent scout, was one of his most enthusiastic fans. 'He was an extraordinary creature,' remembered Steve Lewis. 'What I liked about it was that there were some really classic pop songs – "I'll Tumble For Ya", which I thought was great, and "Do You Really Want To Hurt Me?", which was brilliant.' Back at Virgin's offices in Vernon Yard, however, there were doubts about whether such a clearly gay artist could attract a straight following.

Those doubts were soon laid to rest. Under intense pressure from Gordon – who had agreed with George and his fellow-members of Culture Club that he would either get them a place in the top thirty on one of their first three singles, or lose the right to manage them – Virgin assigned Lewis, who was by then deputy managing director of the record company, to look after the artist personally. There was little that Lewis needed to do. As well as an ability to write elegant songs in a number of different styles, George also knew exactly how he wanted the band to look. The artwork on record sleeves, the T-shirts – all the ideas came from him. An album had been recorded, and two singles from it had already been released in order to drum up public interest. But there was not yet a Top Thirty single. And Tony Gordon was getting worried.

It was the promotion department that solved the problem. A message was passed to Lewis that the song which the disc jockeys at the radio stations would be willing to play was 'Do You Really Want To Hurt Me?'. At a meeting with George, Lewis reported this. 'George freaked,' he recalled. 'He was convinced that it wouldn't be a hit.'

'People will think we're a white reggae band,' said the singer. 'It'll ruin our career.'

'Right now, George,' said Lewis, 'you don't have a career.' George allowed himself to be persuaded; the song duly went to number one.

But Culture Club just grew bigger and bigger. By 1983, with the launch of *Colour By Numbers*, the album containing the 'Karma Chameleon' hit single, George was the world's most successful musician for more than a decade. Virgin employees, sometimes unable to reach their offices because of the crowds of fans who had assembled outside in the hope of catching a glimpse of Boy George, began to understand what it must have been like to be at the centre of Beatlemania. The sums that flowed into Virgin's London bank accounts made the Oldfield millions of eight and nine years earlier seem almost paltry. Not for nothing was it later said that Boy George paid for Richard Branson's airline. There would be trouble later, as George became a heroin addict and attracted the wrath of the tabloid press. But for the moment, he and Virgin Records could do no wrong.

Long before George's popularity reached its height, Richard Branson had withdrawn from daily control over the record company. In no sense had he lost his touch as manager and deal-maker; only recently he had faced down an attempt to form a staff union by appearing uninvited at the meeting at which the staff were intending to prepare their demands, and shedding genuine tears at the idea. 'We're all one family,' he had said, prompting the plotters to melt away, shamefaced at the realization that they had hurt his feelings so much. But Branson had left the creative decisions to Simon Draper, and the contractual and managerial matters to Ken Berry, since 1978. Branson's role consisted of two activities: talking to both his lieutenants on the telephone, often several times a day; and appearing at the record company's new offices on the Harrow Road whenever his presence was required to elicit the signature of an especially big or important star. Even the overseas distribution deals could be left to them; thankfully, Branson was no longer responsible for climbing aboard an aircraft with a suitcase full of cassettes and carrying it exhaustedly from one office block in New York to the other, trying to sell the work of Virgin artists in Britain for distribution in the United States. Draper managed the company by means of informal weekly meetings, first at Branson's house, then in the coffee shop of the Hilton hotel at Shepherd's Bush, then at his own house. Steve Lewis, who had become deputy MD of the record company in 1979 after Virgin had withdrawn from the business of managing artists, was responsible for the weekly meetings at which the pop charts would be analysed and strategies for sales and marketing decided.

Simon Draper, taking advantage of Nik Powell's departure, had raised with Branson the question of his shareholding in Virgin. Pointing out that the record company was overwhelmingly the most profitable business in the Virgin Group, and that its profits were for years being reallocated to other areas for expansion, Draper suggested to Branson that his shareholding in the subsidiary record company should be converted into an identical shareholding in the parent. For until he owned part of the Virgin Group, Draper knew that he would never be financially secure. 'I used to get terribly anxious about the profits,' he remembered, 'because they were always massaging them. I remember having secreted away in a drawer a note from the auditors saying, "For the purposes of valuing your shares, the profits should have been x." '

Branson immediately saw the justice of Draper's case. But he was far too practised a negotiator to agree immediately to such a suggestion. In return for Draper's 20 per cent shareholding in the record company, he at first offered only 10 per cent of the group. It required a number of painful meetings between the lawyers for Branson to raise his offer to 15 per cent, and to accept Draper's demand for a payment of £100,000 in cash and for a watertight agreement on profits which guaranteed Draper's share of the money that the music group would make, but protected him from losses presided over by Branson elsewhere in the group. Draper's lawyer, who appeared not to recognize that it was the record company that was making the vast majority of the group's profits, was horrified. After all, Draper seemed to be parlaying a fifth of the record business for an only slightly smaller share of what seemed to be a much larger business – including retailing, films, clubs and a number of other interests. 'He didn't realize what a strong position I was in,' recalled Draper. 'He didn't realize how valuable the record company was in relation to the record shops . . . I should have asked for £300,000.'

Given Branson's normal business methods, the negotiation was conducted in a strange way. 'We hardly ever spoke face to face,' said Draper. 'Neither of us enjoy it. [When we did meet] I'd just say that's what I want, and he, very tightlipped, would always agree.' For Branson knew that Draper had too often seen behind the façade that worked so well with outsiders. His cousin, his most trusted business partner, preferred to negotiate with Branson by letter and through lawyers.

Perhaps for this reason, the deal turned out to be satisfactory to both sides. Draper no longer felt so anxious about the precarious-ness of his financial position. Part of the agreement was that Branson, as before, would have the obligation to buy Draper's shares in the event that he decided to sell them. But since Draper now owned almost a sixth of the whole Virgin group, it no longer made sense for the price at which Branson would buy him out to be based on profits. Instead, the two cousins agreed that the price would be set at 'fair value' – a phrase whose meaning would be determined by a firm of independent auditors, with an appeals process written into the agreement in case Branson and Draper could not agree on the auditors' conclusions.

SIX

Dear Randolph

THE FOUNDER OF Virgin Atlantic Airways, the company that was to change Richard Branson's life, was a barrister named Randolph Fields. Three years younger than Branson, he had been born in the United States to English parents, but moved to Britain at the age of nine. Like Branson, he had a chequered school career and showed early signs of entrepreneurial and negotiating flair. The two shared a taste for teenage politics, too: but by the time Branson was marching on the US embassy, Fields had already become more conventional. He took up the study of law at a London polytechnic, where he stood out from the majority of student activists. A newspaper later described him as having been a 'political leper'. Fields sued for libel but was awarded only nominal damages.

While Branson was as energetic and unkempt as ever in his beard and woolly jumpers, Fields favoured sober double-breasted suits and was beginning to run to fat. And while Branson had acquired a dubious reputation with Her Majesty's Customs and Excise, Fields had taken the bar examinations that entitled him to argue cases in both English and Californian courts. His growing practice in Los Angeles specialized in defending American insurance companies against asbestos claims. In less than two years, Fields had amassed savings of more than £200,000.

But life in California was dull, and the devil of adventure still gnawed at his soul. So Fields was in a receptive frame of mind when he heard on his kitchen radio during breakfast on 5 February 1982 that Sir Freddie Laker, the entrepreneur whose Skytrain service had brought the cost of flying across the Atlantic down to £49, had gone bust. Where the radio commentators saw only failure, Fields saw a business opportunity.

Four months later he was sitting in an armchair at the Gatwick

Airport Hilton Hotel, where Sir Freddie had sat up until the early hours of the morning trying to save part of his business from the receivers. Facing Fields, a handful of men who had been Laker's most senior employees listened with growing astonishment as he outlined a scheme for a new airline. It must have made an extraordinary scene: a handful of grizzled veterans, their cynicism of the airline business intensified by the Laker collapse that they had just witnessed, being lectured on the lessons of their own failure by a self-confident barrister of 29 whose experience of aircraft was limited to a few dozen flights back and forth across the Atlantic. Yet, miraculously, they were convinced. Within a few weeks, Fields had firm commitments from two valuable Laker managers: David Tait, who ran Sir Freddie's US sales operation; and Roy Gardner, an engineer trained by the Royal Air Force and British Caledonian Airways, who had been the entrepreneur's technical manager. Soon after that, Fields bought an off-the-shelf public company called Ritter PLC, and agreed with Tait and Gardner that the new airline would trade as British Atlantic Airways.

The young barrister had realized that Laker's demise left a gap in the lucrative but highly regulated market for air travel between London and New York. His idea was to scoop up Laker's licence, and to use it to fly a single jet between Heathrow and John F. Kennedy – either a McDonnell-Douglas DC-10 or a larger Boeing 747 – exclusively for business class travellers. He would offer the commercial customer a more comfortable, pampered passage than the existing airlines did. 'At the time, business class consisted of putting a curtain across the front of the economy cabin, and giving out free drinks,' Fields recalled. 'It was a joke.'

In most other industries, anyone who wished to set up in business was free to do so. But the Civil Aviation Authority, set up in 1971 by Edward Heath's Conservative government, saw itself as the guardian not of competition between carriers, but of safety standards – which might be put at risk if existing airlines were undercut by a newcomer. British civil servants had concluded that the best way to achieve this objective without ignoring the interests of the consumer altogether was for Britain to have two international airlines, British Airways and British Caledonian. The arrival of Laker had upset this careful planning, and it was therefore with little regret that some civil servants mourned his passing.

President Jimmy Carter's decision to deregulate the American airline industry made this policy harder to sustain. He appointed to the Federal Aviation Authority an economics professor from Cornell University who thought the purpose of the free market was 'to let people do crazy things', and who saw a succession of airline start-ups and bankruptcies as proof that the market was working. For the CAA, by contrast, an airline collapse of the Laker kind was evidence of a policy failure – since an airline that failed either never should have been allowed to start or should have been closed down by the regulators before it ran into trouble. It was no surprise, therefore, that when Fields applied for a transatlantic licence the CAA delayed as long as it could, and then turned him down.

Not to be put off, Fields appealed against the Authority's decision directly to the Secretary of State for Transport. In September 1983 the CAA was told to reconsider. The officials at its Kingsway head-quarters began to realize that Fields would never leave them in peace until he was awarded a route. They would never risk a repeat of the Laker fiasco by allowing him to fly a scheduled service between the main London and New York airports. But he could, if he wished, have the route between Gatwick, London's second airport, and Newark, New York's third. To deliver this message informally, Ray Colegate, the Authority's head of economic regulation, made an appointment to have lunch with Fields at an Italian restaurant in Covent Garden.

As soon as he got wind of the CAA's intentions, Fields realized that his original plan for an all-business service would have to be torn up. A minority of business travellers might be persuaded to trek out to more distant airports if offered free transport and a better service on board. But British Atlantic, Fields's new airline, could no longer rely on business traffic for its bread and butter. Instead, it must join the fight for budget travellers – and its first opponent would be People Express, the lowest-cost airline in the history of aviation.

Founded by a Wall Street analyst named Donald Burr, People Express was a firm whose name struck fear into the hearts of airline executives everywhere. It cut all the corners it could, except for those that might compromise passengers' safety. Its staff were paid less than those in other airlines, and had no effective union to represent them. No advance reservations were allowed; passengers had to turn up at the airport and pay for their passage before boarding the aircraft. The ticket price covered only the cost of a seat and the right to visit the lavatory on board; food, drink and entertainment were extra. As a result, People Express could afford to undercut all the other airlines that plied the Atlantic crossing.

The colour brochure that Fields had prepared for potential investors in 1982, expatiating upon the delights of his proposed business class service, therefore had to be jettisoned. But Fields was determined that his new airline should be no clone of People Express. Where Burr had painted his cabins dark, Fields's would be light. Where only cold snacks were sold aboard People Express, the meals given away on British Atlantic would be hot. Reservations would be taken; business class travellers would be carried; baggage, instead of being charged for, would be carried free up to thirty kilograms. To enable its passengers to enjoy the in-flight movie, British Atlantic would provide them with high-quality electrical headphones. (This was not quite the extravagance that it seemed, however. In the course of his researches, Fields had discovered that the acoustic headphones rented out by most airlines to economy class passengers, which worked on the same principle as an ear-trumpet, were in fact more expensive to provide. 'I discovered that the airlines were intentionally selling discomfort,' said Fields.)

Fields also began to consider a still more radical way to make his service stand out. Instead of offering a single feature film and a handful of music channels, he resolved to turn in-flight entertainment into the most important selling point of his airline. Flying was to be not merely glamorous, but also *fun*. If the American studio MGM could combine entertainment, hotel-keeping and gambling in the same Las Vegas establishment, why should he not perform similar alchemy 37,000 feet above the ground?

As he sat down to antipasti with Ray Colegate in the Italian restaurant where they had agreed to meet on 11 December, Fields therefore showed no surprise when Colegate announced that Gatwick–Newark might be his for the asking. The barrister already knew that he would have to argue his case at a public hearing if another carrier objected to the granting of his licence. He would also have to show that British Atlantic Airways had enough capital behind it to ensure that it would not leave passengers stranded on the wrong side of the ocean if it were to suffer the same fate as Laker. Confident that he could surmount both of these hurdles, Fields drew from his pocket an already completed application for the route, and handed it across the table to the astonished civil servant with a flourish.

Unfortunately, the profits of Fields's California law practice, augmented by modest loans from his mother and his sister's American husband, were not enough to turn the paper British Atlantic into an airline with craft, crew and reservations department. Fields knew that he had to find at least another £1m – and since the public hearing was called for 1 March, he needed it within three months. But with memories of the Laker collapse so fresh in bankers' memories, raising the necessary funding was to be no easy task. One after another, potential backers looked at his business plan with polite interest, promised to call back, and never did.

Trying hard not to sound desperate, Fields telephoned Richard Branson on 13 February 1984, the day before Valentine's Day. He explained his idea to Branson briefly, and sent around two copies of his business plan: one for Branson himself, the other for Terry Baughan, the nearest thing Virgin then had to a finance director. Two days later, after Branson and Baughan had been through the plan, the three men met on Branson's houseboat *Duende* to talk it over.

Branson realized at once that this deal was different from the scores of strange suggestions that filled his postbag every month. Fields's proposal was not only ambitious. It was also well researched, and supported with some analysis of the kind of traffic that the airline might hope to attract, how many seats it would have to fill to break even, and how its expected revenues would divide between business and economy class. And there was a second attraction: Virgin could afford to carry modest losses for a while, since they would help to reduce the tax bill on the fat profits that the record label was making at the time.

But it was hard to see what relevant experience Virgin had that qualified it to try its luck in the air travel industry. The group had certainly dipped its finger in many different pies: it had in its time published magazines, sold clothes and mail-order records, delivered sandwiches to offices, and dabbled in pubs and restaurants. But its diversifications had generally been modest, and had also generally been confined to businesses in which the company had some expertise that might be helpful. Nobody in the Virgin Group knew the first thing about airlines.

Branson's most loyal lieutenants were flatly opposed to the idea. Simon Draper was characteristically forthright.

'It'll be a total disaster,' he said to himself as Branson explained his plans over the telephone. But he tried to dissuade his friend diplomatically. He explained that although it might be a good idea, they should hold back nevertheless. 'You'll bankrupt the rest of Virgin,' he said, and added for good measure that if Branson was serious about going ahead with the idea, he should realize that this would be the beginning of the end of their relationship.

Ken Berry, always more quietly spoken, contented himself with the dry observation that the similarities between this proposed new venture and Virgin's existing businesses were 'not exactly obvious'. But he left Branson in no doubt that he too believed it would be a mistake to go into business with Fields. If Virgin was looking for new ventures to start whose losses could be offset against the tax that the group would have to pay on the millions it was earning from Boy George and its other moneyspinners, why not stick to ventures in the record business?

Branson could see that there was money to be made in flying the Atlantic. After spending a weekend vainly trying to call the People Express reservations line in London, he had concluded that People was either badly managed or so popular that it could not keep up with customer demand – or both. Either way, there seemed to be an opportunity there. But air travel was still a highly regulated industry in which a newcomer might have to fight with any number of state-owned monoliths, with monopoly profits from their home markets, subsidies from their countries' taxpayers, and suspiciously friendly relations with politicians and with the regulators who set the rules of the competitive game.

And yet . . . the world was changing. Laker might have gone

bust, but he had not done so quietly. The $1bn legal action he had launched in the British and American courts against the airlines that he claimed had conspired to bring him down was still before the courts, so the big carriers would have to be more subtle in their tactics against any new entrants. The safety and technical issues that had obsessed airline managers and regulators until the 1970s were disappearing, as aircraft had become more reliable and easier to maintain to a high standard. People who had never before imagined that they would travel between continents had begun to do so. In the airline business of the 1980s and 1990s, the skills that would matter would be marketing, good service, and the use of computerized reservations systems to fill the highest possible proportion of the seats on each flight. If People Express could be run by a Wall Street analyst, and British Airways by a former executive of Avis Rent-A-Car, why couldn't a pop tycoon start an airline?

It did not therefore take long for Branson and Fields to shake hands on an agreement that gave Virgin a 45 per cent stake in the new airline, with Fields himself retaining another 45 per cent through his holding company Fields Investments, and the rest divided between the company's employees. The day-to-day management of the business was left in Fields's hands.

One important question was left open.

'British Atlantic? The name doesn't really grab me,' said Branson. Fields replied that it was the best name he could think of, but that if Branson could come up with something better he would be happy to consider it.

A few days later, an excited Branson called back with the news that he had just had a brainwave.

'How about Virgin Airways?' he asked.

Fields was no fool. He realized immediately that whatever their shareholding agreement said, it would be difficult to maintain the independence of the airline from the rest of the Virgin Group in the eyes of the outside world if it shared the same name. But Branson was not to be put off. In the end, they 'compromised' on Virgin Atlantic Airways. It was only later that they discovered that Branson's original suggestion would have inadvertently made use of the name of a small Caribbean airline based in the British Virgin Islands. It was only by later paying off the aggrieved Caribbean carrier with tickets across the Atlantic that Branson was able to prevent the other Virgin airline from taking legal action against it.

Once he knew that Branson was prepared to invest, Fields reported the good news to Gardner and Tait. Neither was enthusiastic. Gardner saw Fields's approach to such an unconventional figure as proof of his lack of understanding of the airline industry. Tait, who had been living in the United States for some time, had never heard of Branson; but he knew that Virgin Atlantic was a crazy name.

As the public hearing approached, Fields became worried that Branson's lawyers, Harbottle & Lewis, were proving slow to produce a draft contract. He wanted the affair settled; Branson's signature would be accompanied by a cash influx into the business that would help to restore his dwindling pot of savings. Each successive letter from Fields's own lawyers about the agreement seemed to include a demand for money more urgent than the last.

On 29 February the two men appeared at a press conference at Maxim's Restaurant to announce the launch of the new Virgin Atlantic Airways. It was Branson's name that appeared in the following day's newspapers, promising to undercut People Express, and declaring his conviction that at least 250,000 British citizens would fly to New York if only the ticket price were low enough. What the assembled journalists did not know, however, was that Branson was not a director of the company. Nor did he hold any of its shares; while his handshake with Fields a fortnight earlier had yet to be formalized, he in fact held no legal interest in the venture at all.

As the toughness of Virgin's demands was spelled out in detail, Fields's lawyers became suspicious. They were concerned when Branson demanded that Fields himself should give personal guarantees for the debts of the airline – thus risking being made bankrupt and losing everything he owned if it failed. (There was no suggestion that Branson should do the same.) They also warned Fields in writing that Virgin would 'be able to control an important function of the company,' and expressed 'very grave doubts about the wisdom of the press conference held today.'

Undaunted by these cautions, Fields went off to the Civil Aviation Authority on 1 March to argue his case. The public hearing started inauspiciously. The three-man CAA panel, familiar with his style from earlier appearances, was irritated to discover that Fields had decided to make an impassioned speech himself instead of allowing the lawyer employed by his company to present the case in more measured terms. 'A man who acts as his own advocate has a fool for a client,' recalled one of the panel members later. It was not only the panel who were unimpressed: after hearing a report on the first day of the hearing from Colin Howes, his lawyer from Harbottle & Lewis, Branson also decided to come and speak on the second day. His presence soothed the panellists: although none of them had ever heard of Branson before – and were at first bewildered to find this unfamiliar presence from the music business invading their world of dark suits – the Virgin chairman's answers were convincing, and refreshingly to the point.

The question at issue was straightforward. British Caledonian Airways, which had been forced to wait a dozen years to acquire its own first transatlantic route, was determined to prevent an upstart like the new Virgin Atlantic from winning one in as many months. Specifically, BCal pointed out that it already had permission to fly passengers between Gatwick and JFK from 1985 onwards, and complained that if Virgin Atlantic were allowed a head start in operating the Newark route, the profitability of its own forthcoming flights would be put at risk. Since BCal had shown no great enthusiasm for the competitive North Atlantic run in the 1970s when it had the chance, this argument did not impress the panel. The CAA therefore seized on a detail of Virgin Atlantic's proposal – that it would run a scheduled daily service in summer, but might fly less frequently in winter if there were not enough passengers – and decided that the new airline counted as a sort of honorary charter airline. Since BCal had said that it would not oppose a charter service, concluded the CAA's written response triumphantly, Virgin Atlantic's application should therefore be granted. There was one condition: the airline was given a month to satisfy the bureaucrats that it was 'financially fit' to fly.

Until Virgin had a shareholding in the airline, it would not be in a position to make any formal promises to the Authority about underwriting the new venture. Fields had hoped that the contracts would be wrapped up within a matter of hours or days of the

29 February press conference. But, as the end of March approached, the draft agreement did not appear. The night before the two men were due to visit Clifford Paice, the CAA official in charge of financial vetting, Harbottle & Lewis had still not produced the paperwork. It was only by having the papers rushed round for signature at 10 AM on the day of the meeting that the two men were able to answer the CAA's financial inquiries as formal partners. In accordance with the deal they had shaken hands on, the two partners would have 45 per cent of the equity each, with the airline's founding employees holding the balance. Each side would have the right to appoint two directors to the company's board, though Branson would not at first be one. Day-to-day control of the business would stay in the hands of Randolph Fields, who would receive the title of chairman. His employment contract gave him thirty working days' holiday each year, a car 'of suitable standard for his business and private use', but no salary. Instead, Fields was to be paid £25,000 out of the first £1m that the airline made in profits, and five per cent of whatever profits it made after that.

With the helpful publicity generated by the newspapers, it had been a relatively easy matter to argue in the public hearings that a new carrier between Gatwick and Newark would help bring low-cost transatlantic travel to the masses, and would give a British business a chance to compete on a route dominated by People Express of the United States. But the financial experts at the CAA proved harder to please. Refusing to accept Fields's most pessimistic scenario, they started from the assumption that the airline would lose money heavily for most of its first year of operation, and demanded that £3m be injected into the company, either as share capital or as a loan from another Virgin company, to cover that eventuality. Under protests from both Branson and Fields, it relented. The airline need not come up with cash, said Paice; instead, the Authority would be happy to accept Richard Branson's offer for Virgin to guarantee whatever losses the airline might sustain.

This was not surprising to Fields, for he knew how conservative a view the Authority was apt to take of airline financing. What shocked him was Branson's reaction to the CAA meeting when they met back on his houseboat that afternoon. Without preliminaries,

Branson told Fields that the contract they had signed that morning would have to be torn up.

'My bankers won't let me do it,' said Branson. 'Unless we control the company, we'll have to walk away from this deal.'

Fields was crushed. He had come so close to realizing his dream; it would be cruel indeed if the prize were to elude him at the last minute. Recovering his dignity, he told Branson that he refused to be squeezed, and immediately left the boat with his lawyer to return to his chambers at Gray's Inn.

'Don't worry,' said the lawyer on the way back. 'He'll call you within twenty minutes of our return.' When the two arrived, Branson had already left three messages. He was almost in tears when Fields returned his call.

'All right, Randolph,' he said. 'You win.' But he was concerned that his attempt to renegotiate their earlier agreement should not sour the relationship. 'It wasn't me,' he explained. 'It was the bankers. I didn't want to do this to you. I was forced into it.'

Fields slept more soundly that night than he had done for months. The next morning, however, Branson was back on the telephone, harking back to the issue that Fields thought had now at last been settled. Once again he was demanding a greater share of the equity, and pleading that his advisers would not allow him to continue to support the CAA application on the terms they had agreed.

'Dear Randolph,' he wrote in a letter on 26 March.

> Please put yourself in my position. We have now been asked to give both unlimited guarantees to the CAA and to commit ourselves to Boeing for $13m [for the 747 whose lease they were negotiating] at a risk to us of $3,241,000. Furthermore – tomorrow – we have to outlay a considerable nonreturnable deposit. Unless we go with Boeing tomorrow, I don't see this venture getting off the ground in time for the summer.
>
> I genuinely didn't want to reopen negotiations. But – with the massive extra risk that we are having to incur – it would be irresponsible for me not to . . . If you want us to work together and for us to give this venture the 100% support it needs, it has to be on terms we feel comparatively comfortable with. At the moment, we feel very uncomfortable.

Fields retorted that Branson's demands were quite unreasonable, since he had known at the outset the risks that would have to be taken on. Yet still the pressure did not let up. On 2 April, just before the final meeting with the CAA at which the capital requirements were to be formally settled, Branson wrote to him once again – this time a rambling letter composed in the early hours of the morning.

> Dear Randolph
> Since I am having difficulty sleeping, I need to put my thoughts down on paper since tomorrow morning will be make or break day for the airline. I desperately need you to understand before everything is lost ... Neither of us are [sic] holding a gun to the other's head. Either one of us could throw everything away tomorrow. And I believe that if either of us applied to the CAA later, the chance of success another time (after what will be seen as something of a fiasco) will be nil.

Two days later, Fields gave in. He signed away majority control of the airline to Virgin, in return for a £200,000 cash payment to cover the investment he had already put in. The employees who owned what might have been a controlling 10 per cent stake were faced with a *fait accompli*. They might not have succeeded in blocking the new deal even if they had wanted to; and had they tried, Branson's withdrawal from the CAA application would have reduced the value of their shares almost to nil in any case. Roy Gardner, who had served Laker for years without receiving a single share, allowed his two per cent stake in Virgin Atlantic to be bought out without a murmur of protest. 'I thought it over for about five minutes, and then decided to stay with the company,' he later recalled.

Fields signed because he knew that Branson had him in a stranglehold. Without the Virgin guarantee, the airline would have no chance of starting operations in 1984. If he wanted to run an airline, it must be on Virgin's terms. After all, what hold had Fields himself over Branson? He had come up with the idea in the first place, and brought it to the houseboat; but now that Branson was aware of the opportunity, it was no longer of any value. Fields had done a great deal of work estimating traffic flows and had a detailed business plan – but Virgin had enough accountants to produce business plans of its own. He had identified a second-hand aircraft, and had thoughtfully sent Branson a model on which the Air Canada red stripe down the fuselage was left intact but the Virgin name was painted on the tail; but there were plenty of other 747s that would serve the purpose just as well. He had a team of good people, salvaged from the Laker wreck; but talented employees could easily be lured away. His only asset was a licence application that was nearing regulatory approval – in the name of Ritter PLC, Fields's holding company.

What Fields did not know, though, was that Branson had already made a discreet approach to Clifford Paice at the CAA to find out what the Authority would think of an application that did not carry the name of Randolph Fields. Had the regulators been willing for Branson to proceed without his partner, Virgin might have been able to start an airline of which it owned 100 per cent, rather than just 75 per cent, and to run it exactly as it wished. But the message that came back to Branson was politely discouraging. Although he was as welcome to apply for permission to fly a route as anyone else – and would have a good chance of succeeding, given the assets that he was able to bring with him – he could expect no special treatment. The application would have to be officially published by the CAA; other airlines would have the right to object, as they had done to the Fields application, and there would have to be another public hearing, and another investigation into financial fitness. If Branson wanted to part company from Fields, he should give up hope of flying any passengers in 1984.

While there was still a chance that he might be allowed to ditch his business partner, Branson had an incentive to postpone the signature of the shareholders' agreement. Once he understood that he and Fields were in it together, however, there was no point in further delay. The contracts could be signed, and it was up to Branson to secure as much of Ritter PLC for himself as he could. By increasing his shareholding from 45 to 75 per cent in less than a fortnight, he had certainly made a good start.

For his part, Fields was no more than dimly aware of these calculations. He believed himself still to be secure. He knew that Branson now had a controlling stake in the business, but his minority shareholding still gave him significant protection under British company law; and his position as chairman of the airline, with executive control of its daily management, seemed unassailable. Virgin Atlantic's board, he had agreed with Branson, would be made up of four directors, two nominated by Fields himself and the other two by Virgin. Only if it had reason to be concerned about the firm's management or its finances would Virgin have the right under the agreement to appoint a fifth director.

SEVEN

To Market, To Market

''ALLO,' SAID ROD VICKERY.

The man in the suit looked up from his desk, and threw a critical glance at Vickery's long hair. His eye took in the earring and moved down over the open-necked casual shirt, the jeans, and the highly polished cowboy boots.

'Hello,' he replied tentatively, 'I'm Don Cruickshank, the new MD. And you are?'

Vickery explained quickly that he was in charge of the company's car fleet, and dealt with its insurance and its property holdings. He had heard that this was Don's first day, he said, and since their offices were next door to each other, thought he should come and introduce himself.

They made an odd pair, wandering around the cramped Virgin offices in Ladbroke Grove. Vickery was the cockney wide-boy, affectionately known inside the company as Virgin's Arthur Daley, the man who used to tease the public schoolboys close to Richard Branson by pretending that he had graduated from Oxford University instead of Twickenham Art School. Cruickshank, his new neighbour, was fastidious, cerebral, and quietly spoken – and had 'management consultant' written all over him. Yet it was Cruickshank, not Vickery, who was the odd man out. Why, wondered the people Vickery introduced him to, had Richard brought in this man to run the Virgin Group?

Though only a handful knew it at the time, the reason was straightforward. Ten years after the foundation of the record label, nearly fifteen after the first discount LPs had been sold by mail-order, Branson had decided to take Virgin public. Knowing that the group would need some tidying up before it could be sold to investors on the stock market, he had resolved to bring in a manager from outside who could groom the company for its coming listing and who could reassure the City that someone who sympathized with its interests was inside.

Given the sensitivity of the appointment, and the special qualities that would be required of someone who could fit tolerably into the Virgin corporate culture while doing this job, Branson had been careful not just to accept the first recommendation of an outside firm of headhunters. In appointing Cruickshank, as with so many other people, the Virgin chairman relied on personal connections. David Puttnam, the film producer who made *Chariots of Fire*, had told Branson that he was talented and reliable. Robert Devereux, Branson's brother-in-law, had a healthy respect for his negotiating abilities, having dealt with him at Goldcrest Pictures during one of Virgin's sorties into the British film industry. Simon Draper had known nothing about him, but had met Cruickshank over lunch and come away with the conclusion that he was 'serious'.

A glance at Cruickshank's CV would have satisfied him of that. Qualified as a chartered accountant after graduating from the University of Aberdeen, Cruickshank had taken an MBA from Manchester Business School, and spent five years working for McKinsey & Co, the American management consulting firm, giving advice to a wide variety of industrial and consumer goods businesses and public sector organizations. He had served as commercial director of Times Newspapers and general manager of the *Sunday Times*. After Rupert Murdoch bought the Times group, Cruickshank had moved to the Pearson group, where he was a managing director of the firm's information and entertainment division, which included the *Financial Times*, the Goldcrest film company, and the publishing houses of Longman, Penguin and Westminster Press.

Only Ken Berry had not been consulted on Cruickshank's appointment. Since Berry was the administrator and the presiding financier of the company's music business (which was both the largest and the most profitable part of the Virgin Group), and since a new chief executive might well wish to become involved in the running of the record company, this was an astonishing omission. Berry would afterwards say charitably that Branson 'forgot to mention it' to him, introducing the two only after he had decided to install Cruickshank as the new group managing director over his head. But, although Berry was given a face-saving chance to meet Cruickshank before the appointment became formal, he was mortified. Berry was rather used to having the freedom to operate the business as he saw fit. 'Richard was never very demanding,' he recalled. 'He'd just say, "How's it going?", I'd say "Good," and that was it.' Cruickshank's arrival was an unmistakable threat to this friendly equilibrium.

Without making a scene, however, Berry fought off the threat. He agreed icily to the meeting that Cruickshank telephoned to propose. When the new group MD came over to his office to see how the record company was run, he left Cruickshank in no doubt that he neither needed nor would tolerate any interference in the way he ran the record business. Perhaps to Berry's surprise, his new boss decided not to impose his authority. Cruickshank beat a tactical retreat, leaving Berry and Draper alone at the helm of the record business, and resolving to concentrate at first on the job of knocking into shape the rest of the Virgin businesses. And Branson was happy to observe, after a rocky start, his management team settling down to an agreed division of responsibilities without requiring him to arbitrate.

It did not take Cruickshank long to realize the wisdom of his retreat from the record company – for running even the rest of the Virgin Group, he soon saw, would be a job to tax the most energetic manager. The group he was brought in to run in May 1984 was growing fast towards an annual turnover of £100m, but generating as a whole remarkably little profit. The record side was minting money, receiving handsome cheques twice a year from CBS in the United States in return for the rights to Culture Club and other top-selling Virgin artists. But the rest of the group was a rag-bag of different businesses, many of which lost money. What was more shocking to Cruickshank was that the group appeared to have no management structure, no believable information system, a set of professional advisers that it had long outgrown, and – most astonishing of all – a highly conservative bank, in Coutts, that was paranoid about lending to Virgin. As a result, the firm was struggling to expand with working capital that was wildly inadequate, and an overdraft facility that was minuscule by the standards of other businesses of comparable size. And to make matters worse, Branson was just about to launch an airline.

At first sight, it may have seemed that these features of the Virgin Group were intimately linked with Richard Branson's energetic style of management. Cruickshank believed, however, that they were not. In a number of discussions with his new boss, he argued that Branson should continue to dream up new ideas, to look at a bewildering variety of possible new ventures, and to start more of them every couple of years than most entrepreneurs would do in a lifetime. Branson should not try to change his own nature, he warned, by turning into an administrator and a financier. Instead, Cruickshank suggested, Branson should devote his energies to acting as catalyst; he should carry on motivating others and enthusing them with his conviction that every new business would succeed. All he needed was a corps of people to tidy up behind him, and to help him decide clearly what he was trying to achieve. This was the structure that Cruickshank intended to put in place.

Within weeks of his arrival, the Virgin Group began to change. Terry Baughan, the financial controller who had held the purse-strings for three years, soon departed; to replace him, Trevor Abbott was brought in, with the more senior title of group finance director. Abbott already had a background in the entertainment business, having for ten years served as finance director of MAM, the entertainment agency and conglomerate that Gordon Mills and Bill Smith had built on the artistic and commercial success of Englebert Humperdinck and Tom Jones. As soon as he met Abbott, Branson discovered that the two men shared the distinction of having left school at sixteen – though in Abbott's case, it was because his father could not afford the fees. Disqualified from becoming a barrister by his ignorance of Latin, Abbott had chosen accountancy as the next best thing, and spent five years as an articled clerk to John Wakeham, who later became Margaret Thatcher's chief whip and later became leader of the House of Lords. Abbott had become frustrated during his years at MAM with what he considered the company's growing conservatism, and its reluctance to take decisions.

The new arrivals made few concessions to the atmosphere of the company they had joined – and perhaps as a result, both of them were referred to derisively as 'suits' by the less conventional creative people inside the Group. Cruickshank became used to picking his way past piles of boxes of records every time he wanted to talk to Simon Draper, but continued to favour the sober tailoring that had helped him to the top of the *Sunday Times* and the *Financial Times*. Abbott traded in the Mercedes 450SEL that he had brought with him from MAM in favour of a more modest BMW, but the only move he would make towards casual clothing was to lower his tie to half-mast. The gold chain he had worn on his right wrist since the age of twenty-one remained untouched.

Undeterred by the initial hostility with which they were greeted, Cruickshank and Abbott set about reorganizing the Virgin Group into three divisions, Music, Retail and Vision, with the group's property interests tucked in at the end as discreetly as possible. The rest were to be got rid of: either by being closed down (as with Virgin's forays into film production, which Cruickshank deemed a disaster, and the Top Nosh sandwich delivery service), or by being sold off (as with one or two of the group's restaurant interests), or – in the case of the airline and the interests in hotels and nightclubs – by being demerged into a separate company owned mostly by Branson, in which Draper had a ten per cent shareholding. With that done, the next step had to be to make sure that each division had a financial controller with enough experience and authority not just for the size that the business was in 1984, but the size it expected to be in the years to come. On this they came into conflict with Branson: he took some persuading that the salaries such qualified people could command were a worthwhile investment for the company.

There was also a job to be done in disentangling some of the private interests of Richard Branson and his inner circle from the assets of the company. One issue that came up was the question of company houses. While Branson, Draper and Berry had for many years drawn only modest salaries from the company, the company had since the 1970s paid for the London houses that they lived in. Draper, however, was the exception; he had bought himself a flat in 1976. He was therefore far from happy when he received a call from the firm's accountants in 1982, asking to make an appointment to come and value the flat, on the assumption it belonged to the company just like those of his fellow directors. The revaluation was standard Virgin procedure: the more highly it could price its assets, the more it could borrow from its bankers. It required some effort for Draper to convince the accountants that there was at least one Virgin director who owned his own home.

One by one, the other Virgin directors began to buy the homes they were living in. In July 1986, Branson himself bought four different freehold houses from the Group for £985,000, and Cruickshank paid £172,000 for the London flat that had been bought by Virgin for him and his wife to live in. In October, Robert Devereux exercised an option to buy the flat which Virgin had bought for him at the end of 1984 at its original price of £61,000 – by then a considerable discount to its real value.

Another issue was benefits in kind. There was nothing wrong with the record company's tradition of organizing holidays – at first an annual weekend in the country, but later fully fledged weeks skiing at Zermatt, or elsewhere in Switzerland or France – for all its employees. But Virgin needed to sort out whether these were private or business occasions, and whether those who were invited should be taxed on the benefit they enjoyed by attending. Similar problems arose with Necker, Branson's private island in the Caribbean, which he bought back from the group in July 1986 for £1, also agreeing to take over £6m of debt owed to Virgin by the company set up to own it.

It was partly in order to lay to rest any doubts about these matters that Don Cruickshank and Trevor Abbott were keen for Virgin to leave behind the lawyers and accountants with which it had done business for years, and instead take its business to Freshfields and to Peat, Marwick, Mitchell (now KPMG Peat Marwick). The change marked the end of an era for Branson, who had become friendly with many of the group's long-standing advisers, and knew that Virgin had come to account for a significant proportion of their business. Harbottle & Lewis, the music-industry lawyers, survived the shake-out: they continued to provide legal services to Branson personally and to the airline.

Cruickshank had no trouble in persuading Branson to part company with Coutts & Co, the group's bankers. Branson had kept his personal account with Coutts since leaving school, just as his father and his grandfather had before him; and when he started in business it had seemed only natural to entrust to them the fledgling finances of *Student* and the mail-order business. The company and its bankers had at times seemed odd partners; while the doormen at the portals of its august banking hall in the Strand wore morning coats and striped trousers, the hippy staff who brought the takings of the early Virgin record shops used to arrive bedraggled and sometimes barefoot. In 1980, the bank had exacerbated a downturn in the company's fortunes by clamping down on its overdraft. When it did the same thing in 1984, however, the situation was different. Virgin was embarrassed by the temporary need to find £600,000 to cover the cost of an engine damaged during the test flight of its first aircraft, the *Maiden Voyager*; but it was by then the bank's second biggest customer after the Queen, and one of the country's top ten private companies. When Chris Rashbrook, a Coutts manager, came round to Branson's house after the inaugural Virgin Atlantic flight in June 1984 to tell him that the bank would not allow Virgin's overdraft to rise a penny beyond £3m – and would bounce any cheques that the company wrote past that limit – Branson was incandescent with rage. He ordered the manager out of his house immediately, and decided to find new bankers. It was not until several further crises had passed, and Virgin cheques to the value of almost £500,000 had been bounced by Coutts, that the matter was resolved. In November 1985, Virgin established facilities with six different banks and an increase in its overdraft to £30m.

But Cruickshank was not satisfied with putting these management changes in place. Before joining the company, he had wanted assurances from Branson that their agreed mutual goal was to take Virgin public – to have its shares listed on the London stock market. Despite his impatience with conventional financial analysis, Branson quickly grasped that since the banks set the interest rate on its overdraft while Virgin itself could decide how much to pay out in dividends, issuing shares to investors was a far cheaper way of raising the funds necessary to expand the business than borrowing from the bank. Once Virgin's shares were quoted on the Stock Exchange, other benefits would also flow. The greater prestige of being a quoted company, whose share price was reported daily in the papers, would allow Virgin to do bigger business deals. The group might also be able to borrow money at fixed long-term rates of interest by issuing its own bonds, and pay much less for this borrowing than the banks would charge. And once Virgin's shares were quoted, Branson would be able to secure his own financial future. By selling just a fraction of his shareholding, he could realize millions of pounds that would ensure lifetime security not only for himself but also for his parents and the rest of his family.

There was, of course, a downside. Once the company's shares were quoted on the stock market, Branson would have to exchange the relative freedom of a private limited company, in which his controlling shareholding meant that he could do almost anything he wanted, for the far more constrained world of a Public Limited Company. Virgin would have to publish a great deal more information than it ever had before, and would be obliged to obey more detailed rules. Not only would the business of keeping Virgin shares listed at the stock exchange be expensive; the very management style of the company would be at risk. To date, Branson had run the Virgin group with a view to maximizing its value in the long term. If he were to become answerable to shareholders, he would have to run Virgin so as to achieve the greatest value to shareholders over a period of months rather than decades.

Don Cruickshank and the advisers he brought in from the merchant bankers Morgan Grenfell had no difficulty in persuading Simon Draper of their point of view. The obligations that listing would impose on the group, they argued, would prevent Richard from squandering the profits of the record business on ill-judged projects in other industries. The new management and financial controls would give Draper himself more timely financial information about the record labels he was trying to run. And the listing itself would bring an influx of new capital that would allow him to embark on many of the expansion projects that he had been hitherto unable to put into effect.

There might be a personal advantage too, they pointed out. It would not only be Branson who would benefit from the public quotation of the shares. Draper, too, would find that with flotation would come not just immediate financial gain, but the first real opportunity to decide how long he wanted to continue in the business. As this point sank in, Draper began to think again. 'What

I wanted,' he said afterwards, 'was to have some real value in my shares, and have some independence from Richard.' It was a pleasant shock for him to realize that 'real value', in his case, was likely to mean £25m – and that a public offering of shares would allow him to place his shares in the hands of an offshore trust, and thus legally avoid the bulk of the tax that he would otherwise have to pay on his profits. Ken Berry, who had a far smaller shareholding than Draper did, found this argument less convincing. In fact, he was the only participant who could afterwards claim to have consistently opposed the idea from beginning to end. As the days and weeks wore on, however, Berry was forced to concede that he could not win the argument. 'Richard owned the company,' explained Draper later. 'He had a controlling interest. You could only go so far in running counter to him.' Once Branson had satisfied himself that a public listing was what the group should aim for, that listing then became the objective to which they all worked during the succeeding eighteen months.

The investment banker destined to take Virgin to market was named Roger Seelig. A bachelor of 41, Seelig was director of the corporate finance department at Morgan Grenfell, arguably the City's most successful investment bank at the time. With a salary of almost £250,000 a year, an immaculate haircut, a daring taste in striped shirts, and a penchant for talking excitedly into a mobile phone in cars, in restaurants, and in the foyer of the Royal Opera House, Seelig was almost a parody of the 1980s yuppie. But his flamboyance could not disguise a huge appetite for work – which impressed even Ken Berry, whose first reaction to investment bankers was inevitably one of distaste – and an unrivalled grasp of detail in the transactions in which he became involved. He had joined Morgans in 1971 after graduating from the London School of Economics and the London Business School, and had become its corporate finance director in 1979. Seelig also had a killer instinct for business that elicited fury from his competitors. After a meeting which he had attended as an adviser to Habitat Mothercare, which was supporting the Burton Group in a bid to take over Debenhams, Seelig tried to displace S. G. Warburg as the advisers to Burtons by having a quiet chat with Sir Ralph Halpern as the other participants in the meeting were walking out of the building to their cars. By 1985, Virgin was only one of many companies in which Seelig was involved. 'We were making presentations all the time,' he recalled afterwards. 'One had a pretty interesting client list.'

Seelig swiftly identified the issues that would have to be addressed before Virgin could be brought to market. One was what to do with Virgin Atlantic and the clubs in which Branson had invested. In late 1984, when the idea of a flotation first began to be contemplated, the airline was in administrative chaos and was losing money. Although its fortunes improved consistently thereafter, Seelig pointed out to Branson that investors on the stock market would not be willing to pay more than a nominal price for Virgin's airline interests, because they saw the market as so risky and the chances of ultimate success as so slim. To make matters worse, the airline's liabilities were secured by guarantees from other group companies. Investors might therefore actually mark down the price they were willing to pay for the rest of the businesses for fear that a collapse of the airline might bring the entire group to its knees.

There was also the question of Heaven, the gay nightclub that Branson had bought for the group for £500,000 in 1981. In public, directors of Virgin would later voice the fear that City investors might have been prejudiced against a business that appealed so openly to homosexual clients. Had that been the case, the investors would have been foolish: as the biggest gay club in Europe, Heaven turned in spectacular profits of £500,000 a year. It was an excellent investment; whatever the conservative businessmen thought of homosexuality, nothing could change that. The real problem was more subtle. Heaven was a source of friction between Virgin and the police; it would have been embarrassing to disclose this problem in the offer documents published before the company went to market, but unethical to hide it.

On 7 April 1986, two of the Virgin staff managing the club had been asked to a meeting at West End Central police station in London's Savile Row. It had come to police attention, they were told, that 'sexual acts were being carried out inside the club by patrons'. The police asked to be given two membership cards so that a pair of plain-clothes officers could come in at any time to patrol the premises discreetly to restrain the wilder excesses. Virgin was also asked to make sure that its own staff were keeping an eye on what was happening; to station staff in the toilets, in an attempt to discourage their use for sexual encounters; to print notices on the club's entrance tickets warning patrons that they would not be allowed to have sex with each other inside; and to install brighter lighting in the deliberately gloomy 'back room' that might serve as a venue for anonymous homosexual orgies. If the company was not willing to agree to these terms, the police insinuated, Virgin might find its club closed down by the Vice Squad. Two days later, Cruick-shank was wheeled in, and managed to help sort out the dispute. But he issued a blunt warning to Branson of the consequences that would follow if the goings-on at the club were to be exposed in public in the lead-up to flotation.

Seelig therefore advised Branson that he should separate his interests in the airline and the clubs from the rest of the Virgin Group, and exclude them from the flotation. (Ken Berry found it ironic that the newspapers would later praise Branson for his cleverness in having dreamed up the idea of the 'demerger'; in fact, his cleverness consisted in doing what he was asked to do to make the flotation viable.) Seelig's plan was as follows: Richard should set up a new holding company, to be called Voyager, which would buy the airline and the clubs from the Virgin Group. Although the airline and the other Voyager businesses would still be allowed to use the Virgin name without paying a fee for doing so, they would be forbidden to use the name to expand into other businesses without the agreement of the group, and they were not allowed to go into competition with the public Virgin. It was therefore clearly understood on all sides that the name Virgin was no longer Richard Branson's personal property. Now it was one of the assets that was to be bundled up and sold to the public.

The job of disentangling the airline financially from the rest of the group proved a little more difficult than Seelig had expected. The guarantees from the Virgin Group bolstered almost every major transaction in which the airline had become involved – its agreement with the CAA, the lease of its aircraft, the insurance bond needed by Virgin Holidays, and even the deal with United Airlines to service its aircraft on the ground. If Virgin's support

were to be formally removed from the airline, these business partners would require some other security against their risk. Fortunately, Branson himself was sufficiently convinced that the Voyager
businesses were worth investing in to agree to pledge some of his
own 94m Virgin shares as that security.

Before the sale, Morgan Grenfell therefore asked Deloitte Has-
kins & Sells, a firm of accountants, to go in and value the Voyager
businesses that Branson would be buying. The figure they came up
with was just over £5.1m. Since Heaven and the Roof Gardens club
had been bought five years earlier for knock-down prices totalling
£900,000, Deloittes probably valued the airline at under £4m. By
reference to the profits that the airline had made – or rather the
lack of them, since it lost almost £800,000 in the eighteen-month
period that ended on 31 July 1986 – that price may have seemed
appropriate. (It accorded neatly with the £1m that Branson had by
then paid in order to buy out Randolph Fields's 25 per cent stake.)
But the airline's fortunes had been improving steadily for a year by
the time the valuation was made in the summer of 1986. At the
end of the financial year in which Richard Branson bought it from
the other Virgin shareholders, Virgin Atlantic earned him a profit
of over £3m. A year later, it turned in profits after tax of more than
£12m. Branson therefore made in two years almost a four-fold
return on his investment. Not merely that: the details of the
demerger allowed Voyager legally to remain entirely separate from
the Virgin Group while still being legitimately funded on the security of Branson and Draper's holdings in the Virgin businesses.

Before these changes could be carried out, however, Virgin
urgently needed working capital. It fell to Cruickshank, as the MD
of the group, to lay down the law to those who were running the
various Virgin businesses. On 1 April 1985 the managing director
of one company in the group received a stern letter from him –
without the slightest hint that he might be joking – that 'cheques
issued and commitments made should, as a matter of highest priority, be kept at a minimum', and ordering him to provide a daily
list of all cheques over £5,000. Prior approval, the letter continued,
would be required for all spending over £20,000. Four days later,
Cruickshank reported to Branson that everyone was 'on hold' as to
payment of creditors.

It was in the present crisis that Seelig's skill came into its own. He suggested that rather than going public directly, Virgin should wait another year, but raise some immediate capital by privately placing some shares with a handful of institutional investors. The trouble was that issuing ordinary shares in Virgin would, from the point of view of Branson, Draper and its other owners, have two ill effects. First, it would dilute their control of the business, for the institutions together might be able to use their powers under company law to block decisions or to demand seats on the board. Second, an issue of ordinary shares might be selling Virgin for less than it was worth. The price at which privately placed shares are sold is usually decided by looking backwards at the profits that the company issuing them has made over the past few years. By contrast, shares listed on the stock exchange for the first time are usually priced on the basis of prospective earnings, the profits that the company expects to make in future. In Virgin's case, the difference could be worth millions: the firm's profits had been a modest £1.5m in 1982, but were due to come in at almost £15m in 1985. Since investors were also willing to pay more for publicly quoted shares because they can sell more easily than privately-placed shares, a normal private placement might bring in only one-fifth of what Virgin could expect to make when it went public.

Seelig therefore dreamed up a new kind of private placement that had never been tried in Britain before. The shares were preference shares, which carried no voting rights and therefore left the management of the business firmly in charge. They were also to be convertible, so that when the company went public the investors could turn them into ordinary shares. But to capture the full value for Virgin, the price at which the preference shares would be converted was not specified in 1985. Instead, it was agreed that the conversion would be at a certain fixed discount to the eventual price at which Virgin went public – and if for some reason the company decided not to seek a stock exchange listing, then the investors would receive their money back, plus a rate of interest for the money they had lent.

Morgan Grenfell and the banks that underwrote the listing were to be well paid for Seelig's ingenuity. On the full stock exchange listing, which was intended to raise a total of £32m in new capital for Virgin – £22.2m for Branson, £5m for Draper and £740,000 for Berry – they received commissions of £1.2m. Virgin agreed to pay a separate fee for Morgan Grenfell's services, and also to pick up the tab for the stamp duty, the accountants, the printing and postage bill and the advertising. The private placing itself cost £812,000.

But not even the private placing and the new overdraft facilities were sufficient to satisfy the voracious cash appetites of the growing Virgin Group. In February 1986, Cruickshank was once again forced to apply the brakes. In a secret memo to Branson, Abbott, Draper and Berry, he warned that the group was set to take itself into default of its borrowing rules by November 1986, when the listing was planned. He urged the Virgin directors not to make any commitments on the assumption that the group would go public in 1986.

'Let's just remind ourselves,' he wrote, 'of last year's crisis in the period leading up to the private placing. We should be in no doubt that Peat Marwick delayed signing our accounts because we had no contracted bank facilities to meet known cash needs in November 1985 ... We must not place ourselves in the position that the listing has to take place otherwise we go bust.'

EIGHT

'Too Liberal a Use of the Lawyers'

PENNI PIKE, RICHARD BRANSON'S personal assistant, had always believed that she and her employer worked harder than almost anybody they knew. So she was surprised to hear a reporter from the *Observer* warning her, just after the press conference on 29 February 1984, that by comparison with the coming task of running an airline, Richard would find that his adult life to date had been leisurely. The prediction turned out to be right. It took only four months to turn Randolph Fields's paper airline into a real one, but the dozen or so key people who were involved found themselves working harder than they had ever worked before or would ever work again. Nicholas Alexander, who had been drafted in from Virgin Games to apply his marketing skills to the new airline's customer handling, would leave his new riverside home at 6 AM and return after 10 PM day after day. After work, he was too drained to eat or talk, and could do little more than stand at the end of his garden, watching the grey Thames flow by in the dark.

The first task was to find an aircraft, since the owners of the Air Canada jet that Randolph Fields had originally intended to use were demanding too steep a price. Fields discovered that Boeing had a second-hand 747–200 sitting idle in the Arizona desert, which had been returned after flying only a modest mileage for the national airline of Argentina. The red stripe along the fuselage of the Air Canada jet had caught Branson's fancy, so he and Fields decided that the Argentine plane would be repainted similarly, with the Virgin logo on its tail.

More important, however, was to discuss the terms on which Virgin Atlantic would fly it. Both Branson and Fields made a stipulation: they certainly did not want to own the aircraft outright, but nor were they willing to commit Virgin Atlantic to heavy penalties if losses forced them to withdraw from the airline business and send the jumbo jet back to Boeing. The package that was eventually put together – by Freshfields, a leading firm of London solicitors, since Harbottle & Lewis did not feel that their expertise in the record industry qualified them to negotiate aircraft leases – was not a straightforward one. The 747 would be bought from Boeing by Barclays Bank, which was able to claim tax allowances for the aircraft's depreciation. Barclays would then lease it to a subsidiary of the Chemical Bank of New York, which in turn would lease it on to the airline. By comparison with the $100m cost of the same aircraft new, the $27.8m price-tag that Fields secured was very attractive, especially since Boeing promised to buy it back for $25m after a year (or two or three) if Virgin wanted. This limited the 'downside risk'; but Branson also insisted on being allowed to benefit from the upside. If the aircraft's value had risen by the time Virgin wanted to return it, the two sides agreed, Boeing would have to pay the market price for it.

Branson and his band knew little about how airlines present themselves to consumers – and what they knew they did not like. It was therefore necessary to start from scratch, sitting around a table and putting together a list of the myriad jobs that would need to be done. Only one feature of the new Virgin Atlantic service was certain. After a long talk with Sir Freddie Laker over lunch on the houseboat, Branson came to the conclusion that providing a good service to business class passengers would be essential to the airline's profitability. So Virgin put together a package that gave the business traveller not only a more comfortable seat and more space than on competing airlines, but also use of a free limousine service to and from the airports at both ends, and a free economy ticket for each business class ticket sold. Poking gentle fun at British social prejudices, the service was to be called Upper Class.

Deciding how to appeal to the mass-market traveller was more contentious. One thing was certain: with fares of £129 each way, the passengers would have to be jammed in as tightly as on other airlines, and there would be room for few frills. The old hands from the airline industry wanted this basic service to be called economy class, just like everyone else's. Nick Alexander, who had taken advantage of a slack period in the second year of the new

Virgin Games company to bring his entire team over to help with the airline launch, disagreed. Why not show a sense of humour, he thought, and call it Riff-Raff? Those who had come from Laker and British Airways were horrified by the suggestion: making people smile was not the way to encourage them to take Virgin Atlantic seriously. After a long dispute, Richard Branson was called in to arbitrate. He changed his mind three times; eight days before the airline was due to fly its first passengers, the matter had still not been settled. In desperation, Alexander ordered baggage tags and publicity materials to be printed – only to receive a call from the printers to say that his order had been countermanded. In the end, it was economy class, not riff-raff, that the budget travellers flew; and the airline's printing company, far from taking offence at Branson's inability to make up his mind, sent the story to its other clients in a newsletter, as proof of how quickly it could respond to changing demands.

With Roy Gardner's technical background, and the people he brought with him from Laker, Virgin Atlantic was on firmer ground when dealing with engineering matters. Since it would not be economical for the airline to set up its own maintenance team for a single aircraft, the job of keeping Virgin's 747 in good working order was subcontracted to British Caledonian. That left flying crew and cabin attendants still to be hired. Pilots were not hard to find: the fall of Laker had left many out of work, and British Airways, expecting soon to be privatized, had already shed a number of highly experienced staff who were surplus to requirements. By putting the word about discreetly, Virgin was able to pluck them from retirement and build a team of expert flyers who had flown more hours on average than almost any other commercial airline.

With cabin crew, the approach was to be the reverse. It was decided that the plane would be staffed by a mixture of people, half who had never worked aboard an airliner before and half who had. To keep a single plane in the air while allowing rest periods and back-ups, the company would need either six or seven separate crews – about 100 people. Jane Harrison was given the job of finding them. She placed a small advertisement in the *Evening Standard*, and soon found herself sitting on packing-cases in an otherwise empty office, interviewing a stream of applicants.

One thing was made clear to all the aspiring cabin crew at the outset: they would not join Virgin Atlantic in order to get rich. The salary on offer was a basic £4,500 a year – far below what other airlines were offering. When they were on the other side of the Atlantic, the crew would stay in modest Howard Johnsons or Quality Inns, not in Hilton Hotels. So low was the pay, in fact, that Freda Angus, one of the first cabin attendants hired, found herself actually earning less than her earlier salary in the notoriously underpaid occupation of schoolteacher. But to many of the young men and women who joined, this did not much matter. Flying was fun; flying a new young airline associated with a record label was certain to be more fun still.

This expectation was not disappointed. Time did not allow Virgin Atlantic the luxury of months of training that other airlines would put their staff through before allowing them to welcome their first passenger on board. In any case, the new airline did not have the fat instruction manuals that other airlines had built up, and nor did it want to drum into the staff a long list of rules and regulations. For their basic safety training, the new crews were packed off to the established training centre of British Airways. The rest was done in a single week at a small hotel near Gatwick airport. The precise wording of the in-flight announcements was left to the crew themselves. They were also given a preview of the uniforms that had been designed for them by Arabella Pollen, a leading young British designer, and asked whether they wanted to wear hats. (The answer was a resolute 'No'.) With that complete, the crews had time on their hands – so they were dragooned off to central London, at Randolph Fields's suggestion, to lend a hand in the reservations department. Long-serving crew members still remember the bonds forged as they answered the telephones together.

John Brown, who had been brought in from Virgin's publishing company, was given the job of putting together an in-flight magazine that could be tucked into seat pockets in the cabin. Airline magazines are usually bland, and for a good reason: they cannot afford to offend anyone, young or old, who boards the plane. From the airline's point of view, their primary purpose is to help sell duty-free goods and to give passengers information about the route and the film for which they would otherwise have to ask the cabin crew. Brown's first thought was that the title should be a pastiche of the British Airways magazine, *High Life*, which offered a drab middlebrow diet of features on British country traditions and interviews with ageing film stars. Others thought that nobody would see the joke if the Virgin magazine was called *Low Life*.

'Is this magazine eventually going to make money?' asked Branson at one meeting. When he was assured that it would, his response was immediate. 'Let's call it *Event*, then. I always swore that *Event* would make money.' He was not joking: it took half an hour to talk him out of the idea. In the end, someone suggested calling the magazine *Hot Air*; the company settled for that.

The name was more apt than any of them realized. By appearing at the initial press conference in old-fashioned leather headgear and flying goggles, Branson had offered newspaper picture editors and television news producers an irresistible photo opportunity – with the result that what might have been one-column news articles on the forthcoming service to New York grew into far more prominent features. As the launch date approached, the coverage became so intense that it was clear the airline would not need to spend a penny to advertise its launch.

There was a brass band to welcome the 440 guests, and waiters from Maxim's in white tie and tails were on hand to pour the drinks. But as the guests became more relaxed and the music grew louder – Madonna's new hit song, *Like a Virgin*, blasted from the loudspeakers – the staff gave up and let everyone help themselves from the bottles. Starlets, cameramen, cricket players, former Miss Worlds, assorted musicians and other minor celebrities danced unsteadily in the aisles. Uri Geller bent a spoon or two to demonstrate his famed supernatural powers. An all-female group called the Mint Juleps sang a capella with such feeling that Branson promised them an immediate contract on the record label without troubling to consult Simon Draper. A magician dressed up as a pilot pretended to be airsick, catching silver balls out of his mouth. Flashguns blazed as Branson strolled around, chatting to his guests. One of the staff, pausing to catch her breath, found herself cornered by a distinguished gentleman in his sixties who turned out to be

Richard's father, Ted. 'When I die, I hope heaven is like this,' he confided later to nobody in particular. 'Thirty-five thousand feet up, endless champagne, and surrounded by pretty women.'

The sixty or seventy cases of champagne consumed aboard the *Maiden Voyager* during the eight hours in the air – not far short of two bottles per passenger – were the best investment that Virgin Atlantic ever made. The dozen or so paying passengers on their way to New York on 22 June 1984 may have been bemused by the bacchanalian atmosphere; but back in London, the following Sunday's newspapers carried prominent articles about the new airline and its transatlantic service. Unmistakably, the articles were written with a tipsy goodwill towards the fledgling airline that was worth more than any paid publicity. There was no doubt about it; flying was fun.

But the launch had been more ulcerous than any of the journalists aboard imagined. They knew that the contract for the airliner had been completed only eight days before the first flight – and the aircraft itself was ready painted in Virgin colours only because R. Q. Wilson, the Boeing negotiator, had ordered the work at Boeing's factory in Seattle to begin while he and Fields were still haggling over the terms. What they did not know was that when the airliner had been delivered to Gatwick on 18 June, Roy Gardner had rejected two of its four Pratt and Whitney engines, complaining that their technical performance was below specification, and demanded that Boeing engineers spend the next eight hours on a swift double engine change. The change was complete only two hours before the aircraft was due to face the proving flight necessary to win an operations certificate from the Civil Aviation Authority. But no sooner had the jet taken off on a short trip to Holland and back, with both Branson and Fields aboard, than Gardner noticed a huge flame shooting out of the back of its number one engine. The oblivious pilot flew the aircraft to Maastricht and back before it could be checked by the British Caledonian engineers.

When they reported back to Gardner at 8 PM, they had bad news: one of the blades on the compressor, which forces air into the combustor driving the turbine at the core of the engine, had failed – and had flung out metal splinters that meant the entire compressor had to be replaced. If the aircraft was to win the CAA's blessing, there would had to be a swift change of plan. One of the rejected engines, which had already been shipped from Gatwick to Heathrow in preparation for return to Seattle, was recalled and fitted to the jet. The aircraft was allowed a second chance at its proving flight, and the story was kept out of the papers.

The publicity flight did not end without incident, either. David Tait, running the New York end of the operation, had made arrangements for the passengers to clear customs and immigration at the aircraft door and proceed straight to a reception inside the terminal building, rather than queuing in the arrivals hall to have their passports stamped. After returning to London to see the party off, he had dashed back to New York aboard a British Airways Concorde so that he could be ready to meet them. But when the 747 landed and the passengers emerged, Tait discovered that with all the excitement of preparing for the inaugural flight, Branson had forgotten to bring his passport. It was only because the head of immigration at Newark airport was at the head of the reception committee that Branson was allowed to welcome his guests inside US jurisdiction. Once inside, Branson had to be saved from another humiliating faux pas: he mistook the town's black mayor, who had come as guest of honour at the party to present Branson with the keys of the city, for one of the caterers.

Meanwhile, the real caterers discovered that the porcelain dinner plates from the incoming flight, which they were supposed to wash and replace on the plane for return to the company in London that had rented them out, had unwittingly been discarded by the cabin crew, and, following the rules that govern material thrown away by passengers on international flights, sent off for incineration. While the plates were being retrieved, the customs officers were tipped off by an anonymous telephone call that one of the pop stars aboard the *Maiden Voyager* was carrying drugs. It required all Tait's diplomatic skills to dissuade them from sending sniffer dogs after the aircraft and its passengers before allowing either to leave the airport.

A week later, after the cabin crew had been treated to lunch in Manhattan and the celebrities sent safely back to London, Branson flew across the Atlantic. He could not resist feeling a certain pro-prietorial satisfaction to be flying in a Virgin jet, painted in Virgin

livery, and staffed and run by enthusiastic young people wearing
Virgin uniforms. He noted, too, with satisfaction the comforts of
the Upper Class lounge in the 'bubble' on the upper deck of the
747. There was just one problem. Branson was entirely alone: he
had the upper deck to himself, as if he had invited friends to a party
and none had turned up. The trip was a chilling warning: unless the
new airline could swiftly begin to attract business class passengers, it
would be doomed to fail.

In the negotiations with the CAA, one aspect of Branson's
behaviour had puzzled Randolph Fields more than anything else.
Branson had proved unwilling to put £3m into the new airline,
either as shares or in the form of loans from other Virgin companies. Instead, he offered an unlimited guarantee of its debts,
backed by the resources of the Virgin group. At first sight, this
seemed extraordinary. He was already beginning to talk about listing Virgin's shares on the stock market, and had infuriated his
investment banking advisers at County NatWest by speculating as
to whether the business would be worth £100m, £200m or even
more. He had done all he could to place a limit on the potential
losses from Virgin Atlantic. But all the same, why should he wish
to risk everything he had built up so far? Why should he wish to
bet the entire Virgin group on the new airline?

One familiar reason was that finding a ready £3m was less easy
than Branson liked to admit to the outside world. Virgin was short
of cash. It had always been, and always would be; Branson had
always disliked the idea of leaving money idle in the bank when it
could be used to sign a new artist, establish a new label or start an
entirely new business.

But Branson had evidently realized something else, perhaps as
soon as he looked at Fields's original business plan. In most new
businesses, there are significant up-front costs that have to be paid
before income begins to come in. With the airline, however, the
situation was different. Few of Virgin Atlantic's bills had to be paid
far in advance. Some goods could not be purchased on credit; since
most of the airline industry expected the new venture to fail, suppliers of fuel and maintenance services were less easy on terms
than they were with existing customers. But for the most part, the

airline's inputs could be paid for either on delivery or afterwards. Its income from ticket sales, however, was a different matter: to make reservations, economy class customers had to pay when they booked – often weeks or even months in advance.

This meant that far from becoming a drain on the group's resources, the airline would in fact bring in a flow of cash that could be used elsewhere. How much? According to what Branson told the press a week before the inaugural flight, Virgin Atlantic had sold 25,000 tickets in advance. At a one-way fare of £129 – the £99 fare announced before the airline started up was for a brief introductory period only – that meant the company had already paid over £3m into the bank. Virgin Atlantic might make money or lose money; but it had cost Richard Branson nothing to start it up.

It was with this in mind that Branson paid close attention to the way that reservations would be handled. To save money, he suggested to Fields that Air Florida, one of the fastest-growing airlines that had been created by deregulation in the United States, should provide a computerized reservations service for Virgin. Virgin set up a small reservations office at Woodstock Street, in the heart of the West End of London; on the other side of the Atlantic, American passengers would either have to telephone London to make bookings by credit card, or go to Ticketron, a business that specialized in selling to New Yorkers tickets to concerts and Broadway shows.

Less than a month before the inaugural flight, this strategy suddenly became untenable. Air Florida had flown a jet into the Potomac river at Washington DC, and a collapse in customer confidence was threatening it with bankruptcy. Without warning, the company's central reservations computer went down – and took with it the records of thousands of Virgin customers. The advance publicity had already overwhelmed the reservations office in any case. There were not enough staff to take telephone calls, and not enough computers even for such staff as they had. Fields thought the best response was for the staff to take as many calls as they could, leaving hundreds of angry customers unable to get through to the perpetually busy Virgin Atlantic reservations lines. Branson saw things differently: after his experience with calling People Express, he had become convinced that the airline must answer its telephones promptly, no matter what the cost. He took to calling the reservations number several times a day, and lambasting Fields when he was unable to get through. Under his pressure, the staff made impromptu arrangements to try to take passengers' names and telephone numbers and the dates on which they wanted to fly, in order to call them back later. But this merely compounded the confusion. Maureen Connaughton, whom Fields had enlisted because of her computing expertise to head the reservations department, complained that Branson tried to stop her from taking a course to learn about computerized reservations; meanwhile, another member of the staff went directly to Branson to complain that Fields was mismanaging the office.

In New York, David Tait had meanwhile become convinced that selling tickets through Ticketron alone would never work. In Ticketron's favour was the extremely low commission rates it was willing to charge Virgin – only $5 a ticket, barely a quarter of the commission demanded by travel agencies. But the danger was that the American agencies, irritated to be undercut, would consequently refuse to handle Virgin tickets at all. Tait therefore made arrangements to sign up with a computerized reservations service in the United States. When he heard what had happened, Fields was furious. He tracked Tait down to an airport payphone, and ordered him to cancel the agreement that had been made.

'I can't do that,' replied Tait.

'I'm the company chairman, and I'm telling you that you must,' insisted Fields.

'I can't do that,' said Tait, 'because I don't work here any more.' Having thus tendered his resignation, Tait went to break the news to his wife, who had arrived from Europe to live in the United States, that he no longer had a job.

With only three weeks to go before the first flight, Branson was horrified to hear from Fields that the airline had lost its head of American operations. He telephoned Tait, and persuaded him to fly back to London for a meeting on the houseboat. At that meeting, there was another clash with Fields; but this was a battle that Tait won. Fields backed down over Ticketron, and agreed to relinquish responsibility for the London reservations department.

For all his charms, there was no doubt that Randolph Fields was a hard man to deal with. In a stiff memo to Branson after the houseboat meeting, Tait complained that his 'inability to argue without getting angry makes his management style (for want of a better expression) quite impossible to work with. Outside of an outright yes-man, I seriously doubt if any experienced airline executive will ever be able to work with Mr Fields.'

Fields conceded that he was sometimes difficult to deal with – though his manner had clearly not put off either the Boeing negotiator or the representative of Chemical Bank, both of whom were still his personal friends a decade later. But he insisted that the root problems with reservations was that even before the inaugural flight, Virgin Atlantic was wildly more popular than they had dreamed possible. Perpetually busy lines would have driven away many potential customers, he conceded; but Branson's short-term remedies resulted in an administrative nightmare for which he was later made the scapegoat.

Whatever the rights and wrongs of the controversy over reservations, Fields found little by little that members of his staff were talking directly to Richard Branson instead of to him. Branson was perpetually on the telephone, reassuring, encouraging, cajoling, praising. Although Fields still liked him, such trust as there had been in their dealings began to disappear. In early May, Fields's solicitor gently chided him for refusing to discuss with Branson face to face the straightforward question of whether Virgin Atlantic should be incorporated in the United States as well as in Britain, and instead handing the negotiations over to the lawyers. 'My only concern,' wrote Fields's adviser, 'is that too liberal a use of the lawyers might destroy the business relationship between Richard Branson and yourself.'

The warning proved prescient. Soon after the inaugural flight, Fields received an agenda for a forthcoming board meeting at which his own future as chairman of Virgin Atlantic was top of the agenda. A week later, on 11 July, he set out his grievances to Branson in a long letter.

> Dear Richard
> The essence of the problem is that Virgin Atlantic has begun, but cannot continue to be, operated as a wholly owned subsidiary

of the Virgin Group. This is not the structure which you and I set up and which is reflected in the Shareholders' Agreement and my employment contract. For example, the financial organization of Virgin Atlantic is reporting directly back into the Virgin Group and proving unwilling to provide me and the other directors with the information which we both need and are entitled to. Money is being removed on a daily basis from Virgin Atlantic's bank account without permission of the directors, and on at least one occasion Terry Baughan has made a contract on Virgin Atlantic's behalf without any authority from the Board. Complimentary tickets on the airline are being issued to Virgin group staff and customers without any prior arrangement with Virgin Atlantic. In my view, the airline simply cannot operate efficiently and profitably without a clear management structure and organization. That structure must start with me, since I am engaged as chairman in day-to-day charge of the business. Currently I am being frustrated in my duties by Virgin Group employees who countermand my instructions and fail to liaise properly.

Two days later, Branson returned a brief and not entirely convincing written response. 'I cannot agree that Virgin Atlantic is being operated as a wholly owned subsidiary of the Virgin Group,' he insisted. 'Please let me know what information you say are not being provided with . . . From what you say about money removed from the company's bank account, I think you misunderstand the way that account operates. The bank were not prepared to allow the Company [i.e. the airline] to run an overdraft, and therefore the Group is to some extent acting as banker for the Company. There are detailed records of the daily transfers.' The point that Branson did not answer, however, was this: once the advance ticket sales had started to come in, why did the airline need an overdraft? By skimming the balances of its account every night and transferring them into a bank account held by the group, Branson was wisely reducing the overdraft costs of his businesses. But he could not claim that this was being done in the interests of the airline.

On 17 July, Fields received a formal letter from Simon Draper addressed to himself and the other directors of the airline, informing him that the group had decided to exercise its right to appoint a fifth director to the airline's board. 'We have appointed Richard Charles Nicholas Branson as a director of Virgin Atlantic

Airways Limited,' the letter read. 'We are doing so because we are not reasonably satisfied with either the management or the financial position of Virgin Atlantic Airways.' The letter was drafted so as to make sure that the appointment was within the terms of the original shareholding deal; but Fields saw it as a declaration of war.

His first riposte – to write back to Draper demanding an explanation – was parried by Terry Baughan, with a smooth letter promising that the matter would be taken up at the next board meeting. But Fields was not satisfied with such a brush-off. Three days later he held a long meeting with his lawyers, and on 23 July he wrote to Branson through his lawyers threatening to apply to a judge in chambers for an injunction unless he received a promise that nothing would be done to interfere with the agreement governing the terms of his service as chairman. Having had no response, he carried out his threat – and won the injunction that he sought. Barely a week into August, however, he felt it necessary to go back to the judge, complaining that the Virgin Group was still trying to get rid of him. In a handwritten judgment, Mr Justice Otton said that he was 'left with a bad taste in my mouth arising out of the conduct of the Defendants [the Virgin Group, Branson *et al*], in particular the second Defendant [Branson himself].' He conceded that Virgin's aim was to protect the investment that it had already made in the airline, but he concluded that Fields had 'justifiably been given the suspicion that there is a movement to oust him and to terminate his service contract within a matter of weeks of its inception.'

By this time, Fields knew the partnership was over. On his lawyers' advice, he had begun to keep a daily diary of meetings and decisions. They had told him that he should 'be seen to act impeccably with a view to maintaining the bargaining position we have achieved.' Branson, by contrast, was willing to act less impeccably. Fields found that the locks had been changed on the doors of the Virgin Atlantic offices to prevent him from getting in. When later in the summer the airline took up his suggestion that it should feed passengers from continental Europe into its London–New York route by operating flights between London and the Dutch town of Maastricht, Fields was excluded from the inaugural flight. On one occasion, he was even subjected to the humiliation of being denied boarding at Newark airport on a Virgin flight back to London, even though he was the company's chairman at the time.

They settled in September. Fields resigned as chairman, and Virgin agreed to pay him compensation for his loss of office, most of which was gobbled up by the legal fees that he had incurred in winning them. It was not until May 1985 that Fields was persuaded to sell his stake in Virgin Atlantic back to Branson for £1m, and to resign as a director. He received his pay-off half in cash, and half in loan notes that were paid off in full by 1986.

Ten years later, the two still disagreed vigorously on where the fault should lie for the failure of their business partnership. 'I believe we dealt very fairly with Randolph, and put up with quite a lot over those three or four months,' said Branson. 'He's an extremely good litigious lawyer; litigation is his speciality.' Asked whether he felt ashamed of having approached the CAA with a view to cutting Fields out of the deal in the first place by making a separate licence applications, Branson offered no detailed defence of his actions. 'He [Fields] was negotiating extremely hard, and we needed to negotiate hard back. If you're negotiating, you've got to find out where your strengths and weaknesses are.'

Fields acknowledged that Branson was a better manager and a better negotiator than he, and conceded that 'by nature, I am a confrontational person'. He believed ever afterwards that he had fallen in love with Branson on the day they first met, while Branson had fallen in love only with the idea that Fields had brought him. The comments of Mr Justice Otton, Fields thought, vindicated his view that Branson had tried first to take his idea, then to hold him responsible for the airline's difficulties in its first few months of life, and finally to ease him out before the airline began to make money. 'It was not a matter of personalities; it was a conflict of vital interests.'

Who came out of the litigation better was a different matter. Had he held on to his stake in Virgin Atlantic, Fields might today be looking forward to selling it for anything between twenty and sixty times as much as he received in 1985 and 1986. (But it is far from clear whether Virgin Atlantic would still be around were Randolph Fields still its chairman. His subsequent attempt to serve Scotland and the north of England with a 747 service across the

Atlantic, went into receivership in 1987.) Fields complained that the fight with Branson had brought him to the verge of a nervous breakdown and nearly ruined his legal practice. For his part, Branson said that Fields had been so troublesome that he 'would have paid almost anything to get rid of him'.

Arguably, it was Fields who had the last laugh. As part of the 1985 settlement, Virgin Atlantic formalized the traditional perk of free flights when space is available given to retired senior executives in the airline industry. Fields received the right to unlimited free Upper Class tickets for life not only for himself, but also for his accountant, his mother, his wife, any children he might have, and two guests. The two sides agreed in a side-letter that Fields would avoid travelling on the busy days of Friday and Sunday, and in return the airline would allow his guests to travel without him on their return journeys.

Fields also kept up a lively correspondence with the editor of *Hot Air*, writing in to complain whenever the magazine gave an account of the creation of the airline that he considered failed to give due credit to his part in it. 'I get annoyed with the Trotsky treatment, being written out of history,' he said later. When Virgin Atlantic established a frequent flyer programme, he began to collect miles which he redeemed to buy tickets allowing him to commute by Dan Air between his office in London and his home in Jersey. The airline sent him several fulsome computerized letters, thanking him for being one of its very best customers, before Roy Gardner, the airline's joint managing director, realized from an analysis of frequent-flyer points what was going on, and put a stop to it.

Today, Randolph Fields still travels three or four times a month on Virgin flights. Most of the staff know him. He has a reputation for stretching out full-length in the lounge section of the Upper Class cabin as soon as the seat-belt sign has been turned off, and going to sleep. 'He makes himself very much at home,' says one of the cabin crew.

NINE

The Little Boys and Their Boats

DRIVING WAS NOT Richard Branson's strong point. Rod Vickery, the long-standing employee who was now in charge of Virgin's fleet of company cars, learned this to his cost one day while sitting in the passenger seat of Branson's car as the Virgin chairman drove across London and out towards the Manor in Oxfordshire. Branson kept up a sporadic conversation as they drove, his mind flitting along with his speech in a hundred directions at once. But he paid little attention to the road. Passengers, parked cars, buildings, bollards in the middle of the road – all seemed to appear to Branson without warning, and to require an urgent and stomach-churning lurch on the steering or the brakes. As he got out, Vickery swore to himself that he would never again sit in a car while Branson was at the wheel. To make sure that he did not have to do so, Vickery would afterwards make a point of offering to drive whenever he and Branson were due to go on a trip together. If that failed, the last resort was to grab Branson's keys and climb into the driver's seat.

Yet despite his lack of skill, Branson was unable to resist the thrill of driving. At Virgin's annual days out to the Goodwood motor-racing track, Branson would challenge all comers to races (sometimes giving himself a head start by rushing over to a car and driving off in a puff of smoking rubber before his competitor realized what had happened). On one occasion, he drove his car off the track and behind a barrier so that the others would think he had crashed – only to roar back on to the track at top speed, weaving dangerously between the other drivers.

Such antics were not confined to the race-track. Anyone else who had been stopped by the police for speeding on the M40 so many times would undoubtedly have lost his licence. But Branson's accent

– public school, with the braying edges smoothed off – was some help. So too was his ability to think of creative excuses on the spur of the moment. One set of magistrates, clearly unaware that Branson could easily have afforded a chauffeur, allowed him to stay on the road in case he might need to drive Joan to hospital in a hurry for the birth of their first child. On another occasion, he and John Varnom were stopped by the police while barrelling down the motorway at more than 90mph. By the time the officer had flagged down the car and taken out his notebook, Varnom was writhing in apparent agony in the passenger seat, his stomach racked by what looked like painful cramps. When Branson explained urgently that he was trying to get his stricken friend to hospital, the kind-hearted officer offered to escort him, with his blue lights flashing, all the way. To the great credit of his acting abilities, Varnom managed to continue the performance in the hospital casualty department, and the officer was somehow got rid of before the medical staff pronounced themselves unable to find anything wrong with the patient. The two went through precisely the same routine when they were stopped again for the same offence at almost the same place on the way back to London – but Varnom began to have second thoughts as the escort led them back to the hospital. Luckily, it was a different policeman, and they managed brazenly to ignore the quizzical looks Varnom was given at the hospital.

When all else failed, there was always a last resort: the driving licence of Kevin Ayers. Ayers, who became an increasingly frequent visitor to the houseboat *Duende* as Branson's marriage to Kristen Tomassi withered, had left his licence there once by accident. In the United States, where driving licences bear photographs, there would have been no temptation. But when the licence later reappeared in Branson's car, it was all too easy to show it to a recalcitrant police officer. After all, Ayers was in France or somewhere even further afield; and when the summonses arrived from the local magistrates' court, they would be sent back by the new occupants of his home, marked across the envelope with the words 'Return to sender – not known at this address'.

To some of the Virgin staff, Branson's competitive and exhibitionist streak seemed a little puerile. One senior member of the record company recalled that Branson's inclination to take his clothes off had become so familiar that a groan went up when during a trip to Switzerland he offered to bet everyone £10 that he would dare to ski all the way downhill stark naked, except for his ski-sticks. Nobody took him up on the bet, but Branson stripped off all the same and did the streak for nothing. The combination of a burning desire to win with only a limited dose of skill was common to many of his leisure activities, including tennis and chess as well as driving.

But this aspect of his character was to prove to be of incalculable value to the airline. Branson had already demonstrated by astute handling of the press during Virgin Atlantic's launch that he could generate as many column inches in national newspapers for free as his rivals were able to pay for. The trick was not just to be open and communicative with journalists who telephoned, but also to keep coming up with something new. When Virgin Atlantic had a new route to open, a new cheap fare, a new application or complaint to the Civil Aviation Authority, the need for novelty was easy to meet. But at the end of 1984 Branson discovered a way of combining excitement for himself with free promotion for the airline on a scale he had never before imagined possible.

The idea was brought to him by Simon Draper. A more serious fan of road cars and Formula One racing than Branson himself, Draper was frequently to be seen at Grand Prix meetings and became friendly with some of the promoters of the sport. It was on his way back from the Portuguese Grand Prix that Draper heard that a company which had long been associated with motor-racing teams was planning to break the speed record for crossing the Atlantic by sea. Would Virgin, he was asked, be interested in sponsoring the attempt?

Here, surely, was an ideal Richard Branson project. An exciting, and relatively brief, trip aboard a high-powered boat. A taste of danger – how could there not be, when the craft would have to navigate its way through a gauntlet of North Atlantic icebergs with land more than a thousand miles away? – but not too much. And a perfect opportunity for Branson to draw Virgin Atlantic to the attention of transatlantic travellers. For if the attempt was successful, this would be the first time that the record had been broken since 1952.

It was the arrival of the jet aircraft that accounted for the long period since the last attempt on the record. Ocean liners had survived the competition from aircraft until 1958, when Boeing's new 707 aircraft, with its lower costs and closely packed seating, brought air travel within reach of the average tourist budget. In that year, the number of travellers crossing the Atlantic by air overtook for the first time the number who went by sea. By the 1980s, travel on ocean liners had become a niche market, a curiosity for blue-rinse ladies of generous means and plenty of leisure.

Steamships had provided a service across the Atlantic for more than a century, stretching back to 1838. Then, the voyage had taken more than a fortnight; but the incentive of lucrative contracts to carry mail across the ocean prompted shipbuilders and shipping lines to compete in whittling back the journey time. It became the custom for the fastest ship across the Atlantic to fly a blue pennant, or riband, in celebration of its achievement. By the turn of the century, the holding of the Blue Riband had become a matter of national pride. In 1893, it was held by the British Cunard line; the riband then went in succession to three German ships; to Cunard's *Lusitania*, an ill-fated vessel whose sinking in May 1915 was one of the major atrocities of the First World War; then back to Germany in 1929; to an Italian ship that Mussolini named *Rex* in 1933; to the French *Normandie*; to the British *Queen Mary*; and then finally, as American commercial and industrial dominance after the Second World War became evident, to the *United States*. Transatlantic speed had become a surrogate for military strength and industrial prowess.

Yet the competition for the Blue Riband was also a matter of pride to the engineers who designed faster ships and more efficient engine turbines, and of adventure to those who piloted them across the dangerous and inhospitable waters of the North Atlantic. To celebrate the competition, the eccentric proprietor of an English shipping company, Harold Hales, commissioned a trophy in 1935 to be passed on to each successive holder of the riband. Like Richard Branson, Hales had left school without going to university and had begun a business career. He had served as an apprentice to an earthenware manufacturer; he had been one of the pioneering manufacturers of the motor-car; he had won three medals at the

Gallipoli landings in 1915, and had travelled after the war all over Asia before retiring to write his autobiography, *The Card*, in an imposing house in Golders Green which he named, using his own family name reversed, Selahdale.

If the baroque monstrosity that he called the Hales trophy was anything to go by, he also had more money than taste. Four feet high, its centrepiece was a 600-ounce globe of gilded silver in which the Atlantic crossing was traced in red on blue enamel. Above, a pair of gilded angels in loincloths fought over a small model of a cruise-liner. Around the equator were models of fifteenth-century galleons, with enamelled panels showing four ships that had taken the record. Two more gilded figures, one holding a pitchfork and the other a long scroll, completed the composition. The trophy, whose mixture of styles nodded in all directions from Greek Revival to Art Nouveau, was the masterpiece of a suburban jeweller in Stoke-on-Trent. Its dubious aesthetics might have had something to do with the decision by Cunard's directors in 1938, when the setting of a new record by the *Queen Mary* entitled them to claim it, to refuse the trophy. The *United States* was less snobbish. The trophy crossed the Atlantic in 1952 after the American ship demonstrated that it could outsteam the *Queen Mary*, and it had stayed in a merchant marine museum in the USA ever since. This offered unmistakable public relations potential to any new attempt on the record. Winning back the Hales 'for Britain' could be cast as a patriotic gesture.

At first sight, however, this patriotic gesture looked expensive. The company that was to build the boat was a private shipbuilder called Cougar Marine, which specialized in the construction of catamarans, or ships with twin parallel hulls. Cougar wanted to demonstrate to the world that its craft, derived from the kattumaram that Tamil tribesmen in Sri Lanka and southern India build by lashing together two hollowed-out logs, were suitable not just for small river boating but also for full-scale ocean shipping. Breaking the record would make Cougar's name, and prove beyond dispute that its boats were sturdy enough to withstand all the Atlantic could throw at them. But the craft would cost £350,000 to build, and all the other costs of managing and publicizing the operation would bring the bill past the half-million mark. Cougar was a subsidiary of Toleman Holding, the company that delivered almost one in three of the new cars on sale in Britain. But even Toleman, which had until recently had its own motor-racing team, could not meet the bill on its own. If Branson would pay, he was told by Chris Witty, a senior Toleman employee working on the project, he could choose the name of the boat – and he could also travel aboard it, and experience for himself the record-breaking Atlantic crossing.

Richard Branson knew even less about boats than he did about driving. After an accident in Mexico many years earlier, in which he and his first wife Kristen had narrowly escaped death when a small craft in the sea off the island of Cozumel had sunk in a storm, he had even sworn never to set foot aboard a boat again. But the temptation was overwhelming. The captain of the boat would be Ted Toleman, whose family owned the group, but safety would be assured by the presence of Chay Blyth, the celebrated round-the-world yachtsman. The public relations side was assured by the fact that 'Tomorrow's World', a popular science magazine programme on BBC Television, had agreed to devote a special programme to the attempt, and to send a reporter to join the crew. With luck, much of the cost to Virgin could be defrayed by finding subsidiary sponsors, who would provide goods and services and pay for their name to be printed on the boat alongside that of Virgin. Above all, it would be fun.

On 7 February 1985, the Virgin publicity machine swung into action. Four hundred journalists were invited to a press launch, which took place on Virgin Atlantic's solitary Boeing 747 during the gap between its arrival in London and its next departure carrying scheduled passengers to New York. As the aircraft described a gentle circle above the Bishop Rock lighthouse near the Scilly Isles, which marked the finishing-line of the eastbound trip, Branson and his colleagues told the story of the Blue Riband and the trophy, and outlined their plans for the attempt. The Virgin Atlantic Challenger would be the opposite of the great ocean liners of the past in almost every respect. It would be less than seventy feet long; it would need to be refuelled three times, since the 10,000 gallons of diesel that its two huge engines demanded to cross the Atlantic would be too heavy to carry; and it would be uncomfortable. To help get the story in the papers, Branson dressed up in a Long John Silver outfit, and posed for the photographers with a parrot on his shoulder. The presence of Chay Blyth was also a great help, since it was known that Simon Le Bon of the pop group Duran Duran had hoped that Blyth would join him in a round-the-world yacht race. The following morning's newspapers consequently reported that Branson had 'captured' the yachtsman for their attempt, as if the competition had already begun.

In fact it was Toleman who had captured Chay Blyth, who had agreed to join the project even before Branson was approached. He had negotiated his fee at a meeting in a hamburger bar with Steve Ridgeway, Toleman's project manager; but the partnership had almost come to naught when Blyth was invited to meet Toleman himself. The sight of the scores of trophies for powerboat and motor racing that crammed the office of the businessman sorely tempted Blyth to burst out laughing. As an ex-paratrooper who had rowed across the Atlantic with a partner and had circumnavigated the world solo, Blyth had an understandable disdain for those who wore their achievements too evidently on their sleeves. It was only with difficulty that he managed to restrain himself.

He was wise in doing so. Ted Toleman was a talented and likeable man, but he took himself very seriously. Where Branson was discreet in the way he treated his money, Toleman was happy for everyone to know that he was rich. With his bouffant hairstyle, his expensive cars, and the gold medallion that nestled amidst the hair that curled gently on his chest, he also had something of the air of an East London wide-boy. It was clear from the outset that there would be tension between these two very different millionaires; but it only gradually became evident how hurt Toleman was by Branson's effortless ability to steal the limelight. Chay Blyth noticed that whenever a photograph was taken of the crew, Branson would do something – raise his arms, wear a funny hat, put himself in an unusual pose – to attract attention to himself. The Virgin chairman was in any case already far better known than his car-transporting rival. When a television producer asked Branson to appear on a chat-show to talk about the attempt on the Atlantic record, one of the project managers asked whether he would like Ted Toleman to come too. 'Ted who?' the producer asked.

Yet it was hard to see that Branson had done anything deliberately to undermine Toleman's authority. When the 'Tomorrow's World' cameras were running, he would sit meekly along with everyone else while Toleman strutted backwards and forwards in front of a large map of the ocean, using a long pointer to give a military-style briefing about the weather. Consequently, Toleman was in a quandary; he knew that Branson was somehow hijacking the publicity benefits of the exercise, but was not sure what to do about it. A few weeks before the *Challenger* was ready, the puzzled participants had their answer. Toleman appeared at a meeting with a shirt prominently emblazoned with the word SKIPPER.

The night before Princess Michael of Kent was due to launch the craft, there was a furious row over the question of the sponsors' names. The contract between Toleman Holding and Virgin had laid down that since Virgin had paid for the boat, the placing and size of advertising logos on the craft would be subject to negotiation. Yet when Hugh Band, the marketing manager of Virgin Atlantic, arrived for a quayside inspection at Hamble, Hampshire, in the early evening before the morning launch, he found a vast Cougar logo stretching twelve feet across the top of the craft just in front of its windscreen. Chris Moss, Toleman's right-hand man on the project, conceded immediately that the logo had been painted on without Virgin's prior agreement. But he asked whether it might not be possible to have the problem sorted out after the launch. No, Virgin Atlantic were insistent. It must be removed immediately. At 2 AM, the boat's painters were still at work in the cool May air, despatching the advertisement for Toleman's company to oblivion.

Later that morning, Branson upstaged even Princess Michael. She had prepared a speech in which she intended to draw a contrast between the achievement of the Anglo-French Concorde, which was the fastest aircraft across the Atlantic, and the *Virgin Atlantic Challenger*. Yet she was only half-way through the sentence when Branson, sitting near her on the podium, made a face at the mention of the Concorde, and theatrically got up as if to leave, offended by the puff for British Airways. The poor princess, her *bon mot* ruined, was forced to interrupt her speech. 'No, come back, Richard!' she pleaded lamely. 'You're ruining the line that I worked out this morning.'

There was to be one final hitch before the preparations were complete. The curator of the US Merchant Marine Museum, which was holding the Hales trophy, announced that it would refuse to release it, whether or not the forthcoming attempt on the record was successful. The trophy was intended for commercial ocean liners, not speedboats, he maintained; Branson and his friends were quite welcome to cross the Atlantic in a twin-hulled aluminium craft, but they must invent their own speedboat trophy if they wished to do so. In his defence, the curator pointed out that with 35 vessels and over 2,000 passengers already lost, Hales had ordered that the trophy be withheld from any ship that endangered the safety of its crew or passengers in the course of breaking the record.

Not only was there doubt about whether the attempt would succeed; there was now also doubt about whether the dastardly Americans would hand over the prize if it did. But, if anything, this merely added to the zest of the exercise. The challenge would go ahead.

Two months after its launch by the princess on the eastern side of the Atlantic, the *Challenger* tied up at the midtown Manhattan dock. Its crew were ready to start as soon as the meteorologists could predict four days of clear weather. Unfortunately, that prediction was obstinately slow in coming: conditions in the North Atlantic sea lanes were worse than in any July for the past 60 years. As the weathermen continued to deliver reports of heavy seas, thick fog, and late-melting icebergs, the nine-man crew was doomed to wait. Not Richard Branson, though: he had a business to run, a heavily pregnant girlfriend to keep an eye on, and an airline on which he could fly to and fro across the Atlantic without charge. To the amusement of the rest of the crew, Ted Toleman left New York soon afterwards, deciding that he also was too busy to sit around waiting for the right weather.

Early in the morning of 10 August, the meteorologists gave their blessing and the crew was hastily reassembled in Manhattan. Two days later the *Virgin Atlantic Challenger* cruised out of harbour, and headed for the Ambrose Light Vessel at Nantucket, the starting-point from which the 2,949 nautical mile Atlantic crossing was measured. It was sixteen minutes before noon, Greenwich Mean

Time, as the ship passed Nantucket. To beat the record set by the *United States*, and thus to regain the riband, the ship would have to arrive less than three days, ten hours and forty minutes later. Its average speed over that period would have to be higher than 35.59 knots. For Branson there was a special urgency about the trip; Joan's labour was now imminent. Even if the record-breaking attempt were successful, he would still have only an outside chance of fulfilling his promise to be present at the birth of his second child.

That was the first ambition to be abandoned. Joan gave birth to a boy during the first day of the journey, and Branson was given the news over the radio by his mother. But it soon became clear that the celebration that followed was premature. Some seventeen hours into the voyage, the skies darkened and *Challenger* ran into a storm. For almost twenty hours the crew were thrown backwards and forwards, up and down, with nauseating and exhausting regularity. It was only with the greatest difficulty that Peter Macann, the reporter from 'Tomorrow's World', was able to operate his hand-held video camera. Outside the ship, visibility was low; radio communication was cut off. Despite this, the craft continued to press forward at 40 knots.

No sooner had the storm abated than the crew realized that the boat was running out of fuel. It had only just managed to make its first refuelling rendezvous, off the Newfoundland coast; now it seemed certain to fall short of its second – so far short, in fact, that it would not reach the refuelling vessel even if it began to steam swiftly towards the *Challenger*. Thankfully, a reconnaissance aircraft of the Royal Air Force, circling the ship in broad sweeps 30,000 feet above, was able to come to the rescue. It identified a French cargo ship that was willing to help. Within a matter of hours, the 65-foot craft was alongside, and barrels of diesel were being winched overboard from which the *Challenger*'s tanks could be refilled. Despite an accident in which one of the barrels dropped by mistake into the side of the craft, narrowly missing two members of the crew, the refuelling was completed, and the boat was once again on its way. The tanks were refilled for the third and final time on the fourth day, after long hours of miserable discomfort for the crew in the choppy North Atlantic waters. With only another 255 miles to go to the Scilly Isles, the Riband seemed at last within reach.

It was not to be. Less than two hours short of the Bishop Rock lighthouse that marked the finishing line, after the *Challenger* had successfully covered 2,850 nautical miles, the boat hit a piece of floating debris on its starboard side. Nobby Clarke, the engineer, was sent with Steve Ridgeway, who had overseen the building of the craft, to crawl along the still-moving craft to inspect the damage. He glanced back at Chay Blyth, who had been awoken from a sleep, and gave a thumbs-down signal. The boat had been badly holed; water was already sloshing around inside the hull. After crawling out to have a look himself, Blyth took Branson and Toleman aside. There was a slight chance that the hole could be patched, he said, but no more than that. Given the risks, it would be better to concentrate on making sure that everyone aboard got safely off the boat. They agreed; the crew were told to put on their survival suits, and the *Challenger* was throttled back to a standstill.

Blyth, who had once spent nineteen hours in cold water after capsizing a boat off Cape Cod, already had plenty of experience of abandoning ship. He ordered everyone to keep calm and not to hurry as the lifeboats were filled and boarded. With one small hitch – Dag Pike, the navigator, threw the first life-raft over the starboard side of the ship's prow, with the result that the gash in the side of the boat tore it as soon as it inflated – the crew began to board the lifeboats in an orderly fashion. 'Hey, Skipper,' shouted Blyth to Ted Toleman. 'Come back here. You're supposed to go off last!'

Blyth earned his fee several times over in the six minutes it took before the crew were safely in the two lifeboats. With admirable sang-froid, he picked up only one item from the ship to take as a souvenir: a pair of high-technology night glasses worth about £45,000. As the rest of the crew watched the *Challenger* sink, Blyth talked with the crew of an RAF Nimrod aircraft overhead about rescue. There were three choices, he was told by the Nimrod's radio operator: a banana boat, a boat bound for Lagos, or a Sea King helicopter. The trouble was that the first two were heading west towards the Caribbean, but they might just have been out of the range of the helicopter. The round-the-world yachtsman was not panicked by the knowledge that he and his comrades were bobbing about in rough cold seas far out of sight of land. 'You can bugger off if you think I'm going on a banana boat,' he told the Nimrod. 'I'm waiting for the helicopter.'

Wiser heads prevailed on him to accept the first offer. Two hours later, the nine crew members were duly lifted aboard a container ship owned by Geest, one of the world's largest banana traders. On board were a dozen or two privileged passengers, dressed in black tie and waiting to sit down to dinner. An elderly woman passenger in evening dress gave Branson a warm and unexpected hug, and handed him the previous day's London newspaper. Inside was a picture of his as yet unnamed son.

TEN

Hales and the Lionheart

A MONTH AFTER the sinking of the *Challenger*, one British newspaper estimated that the abortive record attempt had brought Virgin Atlantic £5m of free advertising. Yet there was a difference
between press coverage and sales. At home, the crossing produced
an immediate sharp increase in bookings on Virgin's New York
route. In America, journalists were not merely more cynical of
celebrity businessmen, but also more parochial; as a result, potential
US customers for the airline read less about the attempt in their
daily newspapers, and saw less of the drama on television. But the
effect that the affair had on Richard Branson's own public image
was beyond dispute. The airline's launch had established him in
the public mind as a plucky fighter for the interests of consumers.
Challenger turned him into a daredevil, and a good sport who
behaved well when he lost. His reappearance in the weekend newspapers, holding his new-born son above his head to demonstrate
how much more important this was to him than a mere race, was
almost a parody of the stiff upper lip expected of the British sports-
man. So, too, was his insistence that he would try again next year
with exactly the same team.

Over the following weeks, there were a number of loose ends to
pick up. Against Chay Blyth's advice, Branson had given permission
immediately after the rescue for a salvage vessel to try to retrieve
the holed catamaran. Luckily, however, it was too late, and the
Challenger disappeared beneath the waves. Instead of being forced
to pay a salvage fee and being left with a damaged and unsaleable
boat full of near-worthless waterlogged instruments, Virgin was
therefore able to claim in full on its insurance policy. Part of the
money it received could be used to replace equipment that had
been lent to the project by 54 different sponsors.

The company also managed to head off the threat of bad publicity surrounding the rescue. A handful of cynics, quick to observe that the Royal Navy and the rescue services had incurred substantial costs in fishing Branson and his party from the Atlantic, asked whether it was right that the company should reap the publicity benefits of the voyage without picking up the invoice for saving the lives of the crew. The navy, which had participated vicariously in the glory by virtue of the current and former servicemen who were aboard, presented a bill to the Department of Transport for its services but said in public that providing support for *Challenger* had been an invaluable training exercise. Those in charge of the rescue helicopters maintained stoutly that they had merely been doing their job. In the end, Branson and Toleman put an end to the controversy by offering to give £10,000 to the Royal National Lifeboat Institution as a gesture of their gratitude.

It was harder for Branson to deal with another complaint. The original idea for the trip had come from James Beard, a talented ship designer who had been one of the founders of Cougar Marine until his death from leukaemia in 1982. Princess Michael's agreement to launch the boat had been secured with an undertaking that the crossing would be used to raise £1m in charity sponsorship for a new children's leukaemia extension at a Surrey hospital. Unfortunately, this purpose had become lost in the excitement of the project, and the total raised for the hospital was less than ten per cent of the intended amount. When Branson neglected to mention it during an appearance on Terry Wogan's television chat show, the sister of the deceased designer, the Countess of Normanton, was unable to restrain herself. She aired her frustration to a gossip columnist from the *Daily Mail*, and the newspaper duly carried a highly unflattering article about Branson. It accused him of squeezing 'every last ounce of personal publicity' from the attempt, and contrasted Branson's failure to mention the hospital's fund-raising drive when 'in the full glare of world attention' with his talk of 'his own enterprises which he boasts are worth in the region of £150m'. Although Branson was given a chance to comment, he was unable to change the tone of the piece. 'There were a variety of reasons for [the crossing],' he was quoted as saying. 'The charity was just one of them ... I didn't want to play it up because then cynical people accuse you of using charity to get publicity.' It did not help that Branson was already on record as having admitted the commercial imperative behind the trip. Speaking to a reporter from *The Times* before the crossing took place and trying to appeal to a business audience, he had put the point plainly: 'As far as Virgin is concerned, this is a way of promoting the airline. It is not an indulgence.'

The first to discover how hard-headed Branson was behind his very public love of adventure was Ted Toleman. As discussions of the second attempt on the Blue Riband began, Toleman's first inclination was to take it for granted that his own firm would be arranging the project, and simply to present Virgin with a package for approval. Branson was fully aware of the great commercial benefits that would flow from a crossing that broke the record. But he was also aware that the exercise could take place without the co-operation of either Toleman Holding or Cougar Marine. As the two sides got down to negotiating the price of a new boat, Toleman found that the price Branson was willing to pay was more than £100,000 short of Cougar's demand. The Virgin chairman was also asking searching questions about the second-hand value of the craft, and coming to the view that a vessel with a single hull would be easier to resell than the catamarans in which Cougar specialized. It soon became clear that the only terms on which Virgin would agree to continue the partnership were highly unattractive. Ted Toleman would of course be welcome to participate in the second attempt; that much had been promised. But the boat would be built not by Cougar but by another company, so Toleman would derive no profit from building the craft. Furthermore, he would actually have to pay for his passage like any other sponsor.

The obvious response was for Toleman just to go ahead with a second attempt using a Cougar boat, and to challenge Branson to a race. But Chay Blyth, whose fame as a round-the-world yachtsman brought in significant publicity, was already in the Virgin camp. He had been charmed by Branson the first time around; the two had started to negotiate a fee for Blyth's participation in a second Virgin Atlantic challenge; and Blyth had also suggested a bigger project in which Virgin would join in a business with him, using modern versions of the clippers that had plied the Atlantic before the arrival of maritime steam power.

Even Toleman's own employees had fallen under the Branson spell. He discovered this one afternoon late in 1985, when he strolled into Chris Witty's office for a chat. Witty, one of the key members of the team that had put the project together, had bad news for him. He was leaving, he explained, to go and work for the Virgin group as its general manager of publicity and promotions. Toleman looked at him in disbelief. There was a long silence.

'Well, in that case,' said Toleman, 'you might as well go now', and he stormed out of the room. The bemused Witty knew that relations between the two men were hardly cordial, but he was surprised at Toleman's outburst. It was only in a conversation with the company's finance director that he later discovered that Chris Moss, who had been Toleman's closest adviser and assistant, had already announced his intention to leave for a job as second-in-command to the marketing chief at Virgin Atlantic. The brain drain from Toleman Holding to Virgin was only complete with the later departure of Steve Ridgeway, Toleman's project manager for the first challenge, also to the airline.

There can be little doubt that Richard Branson would have been equally furious to have good staff poached by a former business partner. But Branson later defended his actions in luring away three key staff from Toleman by pointing out that no compulsion had been necessary to make them leave; they had chosen to join Virgin of their own accord. In Japan, such a transfer could easily be prevented by a telephone call to the chairman of the employee's destination company; but agreements between employers not to poach staff from each other were contrary to workers' interests, Branson believed. It was a case of every man for himself – and companies that could not keep their workers·happy must expect to see them change jobs.

With the distasteful business of severing relations with Toleman behind him, Branson could now get on with the job of preparing the second attempt on the record. Despite his enthusiasm for acquiring the team that had worked on the first challenge, he did not lose his habitual negotiating skill. Witty and Moss were hired for salaries that were slightly higher than they had received from

Toleman, but lower than they had demanded. With Chay Blyth, matters were more complicated. The two men talked long and hard over the terms on which the yachtsman would participate. Blyth favoured a fixed fee; Branson wanted to pay an amount that depended on all sorts of things, including how many days Blyth spent on the project, whether it was successful or not in winning the Riband, and so on.

Agreeing the sum involved was difficult enough. 'It was peanuts [to Branson],' Blyth later recalled, 'but Richard can't leave a deal straightforward; it's got to be complicated. He thrives on bartering [*sic*]. Finally, we were driving to Bracknell Weather Station and I said as I got in the car, "Right, Richard, if we haven't agreed a fee by Bracknell, I'm not going on the boat." All the way he was haggling, till we get to Bracknell and I open the door and he looks at me and says, "All right, I agree." '

It required a lengthy second session, this time at Branson's house in Oxford Gardens, to pin down the details of the formula. In the end, the two men shook on it, and walked together down the stairs towards the front door. When Branson put his arm around Blyth's shoulder, the yachtsman suddenly stopped and looked at him, knowing that there was something wrong with the formula they had just agreed. Branson, who knew exactly why he was pausing, burst out laughing. It was only then that Blyth suddenly realized that one of the clauses in the agreement would favour Branson more than he had expected. Yet far from being offended, Blyth saw Branson's ruthless negotiating technique as an endearing characteristic. The story later became a standing joke; Blyth used to say that he had only ever been ripped off by three people in his life. Two were Cornish farmers, notorious for their shrewdness; the third was Richard Branson.

Meanwhile, preparations for the financing of the project and the building of a new boat were well in hand. Chris Witty picked up sponsorships from Vodafone, a mobile telephony company, and from the makers of the game Trivial Pursuit. *Virgin Atlantic Challenger II*, as the new boat would be called, was already being designed and constructed at Brooke Marine, a formerly state-owned shipyard at Lowestoft. Since the sponsors who had provided equipment for the first attempt on the Riband had been paid in full for what they had lent – after expecting only to receive their second-hand equipment back again, possibly damaged – they were only too keen to donate their latest technology for *Challenger II*. The only participants who were less enthusiastic about the second trip were the company's insurers at Lloyd's of London. They had received a premium of £80,000 for the first vessel, and had paid out £1m when it was lost. To insure the new craft for almost the same sum, they asked for £150,000. Branson was outraged. He resolved not to buy insurance at all, though in the end the others involved in the project paid the premium discreetly without mentioning it to him.

There was a sticky moment during the winter of 1985 at the Lowestoft shipyard, when Brooke's workers, who had been irritated by a number of changes to their working practices demanded by the yard's management since privatization, seemed set to go out on strike. A shipyard strike might have spelled disaster for the attempt; if the weather window of summer 1986 were missed, the entire exercise would have to be postponed until the following year, by which time the public might have lost interest and other challengers come into the race. Once again, however, the famous Richard Branson charm conquered everything in its path. When he heard what was up, the Virgin chairman flew down to Lowestoft by helicopter for a look around. He slapped people on the back, asked them how things were going, and told them what a great job the shipyard was doing on the boat. The excitement of the arrival and departure of the celebrity, and the realization that his success in the summer depended on the shipyard, helped the threat of a dispute to evaporate.

Once again, this time in late June rather than late July, a boat bearing the Virgin insignia sped out of New York harbour bound for Newfoundland. Once again it refuelled, courtesy of Esso, from a vessel that put out into the Atlantic from an oil-rig. Despite heavy fog, *Challenger II* made good time for its first twenty-four hours. It was only on the second refuelling stop, on the second full day of the journey, that things began to go wrong. For some reason, water was mixing with the diesel fuel as it came across from the refuelling vessel to the powerboat. It took seven hours of work, in which the ship's engineer and the relevant refuelling specialist worked together under enormous pressure, before the craft was ready to set to sea again. Even then, it was only able to proceed on its path courtesy of the two men below decks, who constantly changed and rechanged the fuel filters to keep the sputtering engine alive.

There was barely more time for leisure in the cabin above. Chay Blyth had broken his toe when it had been crushed under a chair, and was lying back in some discomfort, knowing that it would be some time before he could see a doctor. Richard Branson, the captain of the craft, had a radio in front of him that was linked to the operations headquarters in one of the company's record shops in England by a frequency different from that of the boat's main radio. On dry land, Virgin staff were going through a directory of the country's regional and local newspapers, calling the papers' editors one by one and offering to patch Richard Branson through to them for a live interview from the *Challenger*. While Branson answered questions from one newspaper, the next would be receiving background information from the land staff, or waiting on hold to be put through. The Virgin chairman kept this up for hours, answering the same questions and making the same jokes time and again. Finally, he turned to Blyth.

'This is getting boring,' he told the yachtsman. 'We've got to tell them something else.'

Blyth's reply was characteristically quick-witted. 'We've just missed a whale,' he said.

'Where, where?' asked Branson, leaning forward towards the windows. 'I didn't see it.' It was only when he looked back that he realized that Blyth had not seen a whale either, but knew what made good newspaper copy.

'Oh yeah,' Branson said, 'I've got it.' And he regaled the next half-dozen interviewers with a vivid account of the great sea creatures that had swum so perilously close to *Challenger II*.

In the end, they did break the record; and once again, they owed a debt to the military. Extra fuel filters were flown out from London by the RAF, and parachuted into the boat's path. The Irish navy provided not just the third refuelling stop, but also platefuls of steaming stew for the gallant captain and his crew. The weather was miserable for several hours after that, with a reminder of the stomach-churning swell that had been almost a permanent feature of the last attempt. But as the Bishop Rock lighthouse drew closer, the sea appeared miraculously to calm. A flotilla of small boats and a handful of helicopters came out from the coast to meet the conquering heroes. *Challenger II* crossed the line two hours and nine minutes faster than the *United States* had in 1952, and thus became the new holder of the Blue Riband.

After the generous coverage of the 1985 attempt, Branson and his team had high expectations of the publicity they would derive from the 1986 success. But even those expectations were surpassed. As luck would have it, *Challenger II*'s arrival slotted neatly into the half-time of the live televised final of the World Cup in Mexico. A newsflash was superimposed over the football; and there was enough time for the pictures of the arriving crew to be sent to London for broadcast as the top item of the evening news bulletins of both BBC and ITN. The delays and the problems with the fuel filters had served only to make the story more exciting; had the crossing proceeded according to plan, the powerboat would prob-ably have crossed the ocean ten or more hours faster than the previous record-holder. Without the suspense, more commentators might have come to reflect that with the benefit of thirty-four years of developments in engine and hull design to draw on, it would have been astonishing if *Challenger II* had not been able to break the record.

There was a minor delay as the craft came in to dock, because another vessel had to be moved from its berth. After some minutes of waiting around, Branson noticed that the assembled newspaper photographers, only twenty yards away from the prow of the craft, were getting restive. It was clear that if they had to wait around much longer, they would be in danger of missing their deadlines and would leave without bothering to photograph the boat's historic arrival and the welcome by Princess Michael of Kent. He turned to one of the crew, and murmured: 'Get the guys to throw me in.' Twenty seconds later, Branson was in the water, and already swimming the few yards to the quayside. The newsmen had their pictures, and the publicity benefits to Virgin were secure.

As expected, the US Merchant Marine Museum refused to hand

over the Hales trophy. But the terms of its refusal – the museum's curator dismissed *Challenger II* as a ' little toy boat', pointing out that it was even smaller than the lifeboats of the ocean liners for which the Hales had been intended – merely added to the wave of public acclaim in Britain. A few days later, the craft was given special permission to break the speed limit on the River Thames; Tower Bridge was raised especially in her honour. As the powerboat planed at sixty knots under the bridge and along the still water towards the Houses of Parliament, children of all ages waved Union Jacks from the banks. A fire tug blew a jet of water high in the air as a salute. Two figures could be seen at the tiller: Richard Branson and Margaret Thatcher, the prime minister.

Branson had clearly struck a chord in public sensibility. Three years after the new militarism of the Falklands War, at a time when the economy was booming and confidence was apparently restored in the new Britain, here was a national hero, an adventurer, a patriot whose inspired amateurism epitomized everything that it meant to be British. The Tory tabloids paid him due tribute. BLUE RIBAND BRANSON: HE'S DONE IT!, said the *Mail*. The *Express* went further still; it published a long and adulatory profile of the Virgin chairman under the title RICHARD THE LIONHEART, accompanied by an interview with his mother.

A cartoon in the *Express* raised a more important issue: the continued refusal of the US Merchant Marine Museum to hand over the Hales trophy. A man and a woman, both wearing sweatshirts emblazoned with the words BRAVO BRANSON looked in through the windows of an old-fashioned carpenter's workshop, where a half-completed wooden hull stood at one side. Sitting on a stool, carving a piece of wood with a penknife, was a grizzled, bearded seafarer with a cantankerous expression on his face and a large patch on the left knee of his trousers. The caption underneath expressed the paper's irritation at the American museum's insistence that a modern powerboat could not be eligible for the trophy: 'He holds that none of them have beaten the *Cutty Sark* yet, under sail.'

In the event, the museum's recalcitrance did Branson no harm. It allowed him to be cast as the underdog even after having broken the record, and ensured a continued drip of newspaper articles about the dispute. Branson himself considered establishing his own prize for future challengers; but there was no shortage of alternatives. First, the jeweller that had been responsible for the original Hales came forward with the suggestion that it might make a facsimile of it; since it was not made clear who would provide gold and silver to the value of £75,000 that would be necessary, little more was heard of that. Later in the summer, however, the *Daily Express* came to the rescue. True to its support for Branson, the paper commissioned its own trophy and presented it to him.

The *Express* profile had described Branson as 'the tycoon who can't help making money even when he's making waves in the Atlantic'. Others too, perhaps enchanted by what the paper described as 'that easy charm which makes everyone from Premier to form prefect warm to him', had taken up the theme that the profitability of the *Challenger* projects had just happened as if by accident.

That was not how it seemed behind the scenes. When the project team suggested that the boat might be taken on a tour around the south coast of England to celebrate its victory, Branson was at first unenthusiastic. He had a business to run, after all, into which he had plunged himself soon after the crossing. And why should he wish to pay for a tour? Chris Witty had a better idea: with luck, he said, Esso would offer to cover the fuel costs.

Thanks to the subsidy from the oil company, the *Challenger II* therefore embarked on a tour starting at Bristol and ending at Lowestoft. At each of the more important stops, there would be a special promotion inside a Virgin store. The public would be allowed to walk all over the boat, and a lucky few would be taken for a short ride on her. If the local mayor or some other dignitary was willing to come to the Virgin store or to hold a civic reception, Branson would make himself available. Everywhere he went, local newspapers and television cameras followed. At Plymouth, a queue of people stretching fifty yards outside the Virgin shop waited in the driving rain. Bemused, Witty went up to a man at the end of the line and asked him why he was waiting. 'Oh,' said the man. 'It's not every day that you get a chance to go aboard history.' Such activities spread the benefits from the project across the entire group, from the airline to the retailing division.

That left only one question unanswered: what should happen to the boat? Virgin briefly considered offering it to Greenpeace so that it could be used for high-speed harassment of whaling vessels and other ecological vandals. An altogether better solution would be to sell *Challenger II*. But Greenpeace was manifestly unable to pay for the craft, and it would be unreasonable to expect it to do so. The vessel was displayed at a boat show in Britain; it elicited huge public interest, but no offers. This was perhaps not surprising, since the sort of well-heeled enthusiasts who might wish to spend £1m on a powerboat would be more likely to spend their time in the warmer climate of the Mediterranean. So Dag Pike, the maritime journalist and navigator who had participated in both crossings, was given the job of taking the boat down from England to the south of France, dropping in at Minorca on the way so that Eve Branson, Richard's mother, could show the boat to some of her friends. The outward passage was traumatic: so bad were the storms between the straits of Gibraltar and Majorca that Pike very nearly lost the craft altogether. He swore after the *Challenger II* limped into Mahon harbour that the journey had been far more frightening than the Atlantic crossing. One point was beyond doubt: had disaster struck during the Mediterranean run, Pike and his crew could not have been assured the swift rescue that the publicity of the record attempt had guaranteed during the two Atlantic crossings.

The shipping brokers charged with the sale had asked Branson to fly down to St Tropez to help attract buyers to view the boat after a nearby yachting festival and regatta. *Challenger II* raced out of Majorca harbour against *Fortuna*, a boat belonging to King Juan Carlos of Spain, and won; it then beat another boat in St Tropez. Yet the most enthusiastic buyer who materialized did not come through the brokers. He was a wealthy Arab who had heard that the boat was for sale from Megan, Chris Witty's girlfriend and later wife, with whom he got chatting in a bar. When it became clear that he was seriously interested in acquiring the craft, the team took him on a jaunt from St Tropez across to Monte Carlo. Given that the trip took an hour by sea, while it would have required two hours or more by road, the buyer was impressed. On his arrival, Richard Branson took him out to lunch at the Hôtel de Paris to discuss terms, leaving the rest of the team to eat at a restaurant on the Monte Carlo waterfront. Before the lunch,

Branson asked Chris Witty how much he should ask for the craft: £1.5m, or £1m? Witty warned that he would never get the higher figure – he would be doing well to receive £1m. Two hours later, the two met again; the buyer had agreed to pay Branson his £1m. But he wanted some work done on the powerboat before he would accept delivery; he had therefore agreed with Branson that he would pay a deposit of £100,000, and come up with the rest after the work was completed.

Unfortunately, that was not the end of the transaction. For all his connections with the Saudi and Jordanian royal families, the buyer drove a hard bargain. On inspecting the work that he had required on the *Challenger II*, he declared that it had not been done properly to his specification and refused to pay. Unwilling to frighten away their purchaser, Witty and Branson were at first emollient. Gradually, however, they realized that some pressure would be necessary in order to persuade their buyer to complete the purchase that he had agreed. Branson remained polite whenever they spoke; it was left to Witty to play the hard cop, to issue the threats of legal action unless payment was made, and to point out to the shipping brokers that their own commission would depend on successful recovery of the debt. More than a year later, with the £900,000 balance still unpaid, Branson and Witty were beginning to suspect that they would never see it. But their buyer was as unpredictable as ever: as quickly as he had made difficulties, he delivered a banker's draft for the balance, and came around to Branson's home to offer a present in apology for his slowness. The gift was a brand new Range Rover, which Branson at first resolved to sell but was prevailed on by Joan to keep so that the children could drive it around the grounds of their Oxfordshire house. The Branson family kept the car until 1994, when it was destroyed beyond repair in the late-night accident on the motorway. The timing of the buyer's change of heart proved to be perfect. A matter of weeks later, an American vessel broke the Atlantic speed record that *Challenger II* had established. Without the cachet of the Blue Riband, the powerboat's value dropped overnight from £1m to £250,000. But by then it no longer belonged to Richard Branson.

It was not only the boat whose value proved transitory. None of those who followed Branson in attempting to break the Atlantic sea speed record ever received more than a fraction of the publicity that he had achieved – not even James Sherwood, the flamboyant Kentucky founder of the Sea Containers travel group, who won the Riband with a catamaran high-speed ferry that was large enough to displace a Boeing 747. By taking the record with a sea-going craft expressly intended to carry fare-paying passengers and freight – and by threatening legal action if he were not given the Hales – Sherwood managed to force the myrmidons of the Merchant Marine Museum at last to hand over the trophy. But by then, the British public was bored with Atlantic racing. The trophy undoubtedly helped to win custom for Sherwood's high-speed Sea Cat service across the English Channel. But it never made him a celebrity like Branson.

Hippie, musician and producer of *Tubular Bells*, Tom Newman was put in charge of the recording studios at Shipton Manor. When he resigned abruptly after a dispute with Richard Branson, no attempt was made to persuade him to come back. Branson later commented that the shares Newman forfeited might have later made him a millionaire.

Below Mike Oldfield, composer and performer of the album that put the new Virgin record label on the map. The deal he signed with Branson on the Manor's kitchen table gave him royalties of five per cent on the sales of *Tubular Bells*; the contract was later renegotiated.

Nik Powell, Branson's boyhood friend and first business partner. The payment he received on leaving Virgin in 1981 is believed to have included £1 million in cash, a cinema and some other company assets. When Virgin went public in 1987, the shares he had sold back to Branson rose in value to about £96m.

Below Shipton Manor, Oxfordshire, which Branson bought for £30,000 with the help of a loan from his aunt and a mortgage from Coutts Bank. The Manor is still used as a recording studio by Virgin Music, now owned by Thorn-EMI; its vast dining table has been moved to Virgin Atlantic's Upper Class lounge at Heathrow Airport.

Johnny Rotten survived his time as a member of the Sex Pistols and subsequently changed his stage name to John Lydon. The Pistols put an end to a fallow patch at the Virgin record label, and helped to re-establish its artistic credentials in the age of punk.

Below Malcolm McLaren signed the Pistols to Virgin after the band's shocking behaviour prompted other record companies to terminate their contract.

Below Boy George, discovered performing in a gay club by a Virgin talent scout, was the brilliant new star who provided the cash flow that sustained the Group through the turbulent launch of Virgin Atlantic Airways. Here he is pictured with soulmate Marilyn.

Some of Richard Branson's employees found his practical jokes endearing; others found them tiresome. He challenged friends on a skiing trip to bet him £10 that he would not dare to strip and then ski down the piste naked; when there were no takers, he performed the streak anyway.

At company parties, Branson would be among the first to throw the bread rolls or to let off the fire extinguishers.

One of his party pieces was to upturn attractive women. Here his victim is Ivana Trump, then wife of New York property millionaire Donald Trump, at an airline awards dinner.

Steve Lewis joined Virgin at the age of sixteen, and spent over twenty years working for the Music Group before it was sold in 1992. He now occupies a post at the top of the rival Chrysalis Music Group.

Below Don Cruickshank, former management consultant and newspaper executive, joined Virgin as managing director to help take the company public. He stayed about five years with the group, leaving after Branson withdrew from the stock-market.

Right Trevor Abbott, Virgin's present group managing director, left school like Branson at sixteen. Trained as an accountant, he joined Virgin as group finance director. He is Branson's most senior adviser, and usually assumes the thankless job of firing unwanted senior executives.

Left Tony Elliot, publisher. When his *Time Out* magazine was hit by a strike, Branson offered to go into partnership with him. Elliot turned down the idea; Branson then decided to set up *Event* as a rival magazine, which later folded after incurring heavy losses.

Right Randolph Fields brought Branson (*right in picture*) the idea of starting an airline. Before the launch of Virgin Atlantic, Branson won majority control by renegotiating their original equal partnership. Fields later resigned as the airline's chairman, and sold Branson his shares. He still has the right to fly free in Upper Class, which he does 'two or three times a month'.

Ted Toleman, an Essex millionaire (*left in picture*), got more than he bargained for when Branson joined his attempt to break the Atlantic sea speed record. Branson's talent for publicity – aided by his penchant for dressing up, in this case as Long John Silver – brought commercial benefits to Virgin while Toleman and his firm remained largely unrecognized. When a second attempt was organized, award-winning yachtsman Chay Blyth (*right in picture*), parted company with Toleman and joined Branson's crew.

The two attempts on the sea record turned Branson into a celebrity. *Challenger II* brought useful publicity for his airline (*above*) and was then sold for £1m. Prime Minister Margaret Thatcher honoured him by joining his lap of honour up the River Thames (*below*).

From the rock market to the stockmarket: Branson's public-relations skills, and his apparently extensive wardrobe, were put to use once again when Virgin's shares were quoted on the stockmarket in 1986.

Right Roger Seelig, the investment banker at Morgan Grenfell who advised Branson on the flotation, feared that Virgin would receive a flood of applications from individual investors but fail to win support from the big institutions. He was right.

ELEVEN

Enlightened Capitalism

BY THE SUMMER OF 1986, the size of the Virgin Group and the fame of its chairman had reached such a point that a call from a cabinet minister was no longer a source of excitement. Lobbying ministers – about airline regulation, or about the copyright protection for recorded music in Japan – was an essential part of Richard Branson's job. Distant though he felt from the world of Whitehall, he was by now quite used to receiving invitations to lunches or receptions in government departments. But this call was different. It was someone from the office of Kenneth Baker, the environment secretary; and the request was that Branson should come to the department to talk to Baker about taking charge of an exciting new project.

Baker's offer was straightforward. The government, he said, wanted two jobs done. It wanted to find some useful work experience for up to 5,000 unemployed youngsters; and it wanted to bring together the different voluntary organizations that were trying to improve the urban and rural environment of Britain. If the two aims were put together, Baker said, the government would be willing to put £30m into a new umbrella organization dedicated to achieving them. And Richard Branson, a businessman with proven skills of leadership and with undeniable credibility among young people, seemed just the man to run it.

Flattered, Branson could not hide his enthusiasm. But after asking a few questions, he said that although he was keen on the idea, he would like to think about it. Over the next few days, he spent several hours consulting his colleagues at Virgin – Simon Draper, Ken Berry, Don Cruickshank and Trevor Abbott.

His Virgin colleagues pointed out to him the risks of taking on the job. Until now, they reminded him, Virgin had been a non-political company. Although Branson's entrepreneurial methods, and the speed of his rise in the 1980s, may have seemed to many outsiders as quintessentially Thatcherite, he had taken care never to give money to any political party and never to show any interest in the honours that Margaret Thatcher was dishing out with increasing speed to her favourite industrialists. Whatever Branson said in public, the new job would destroy this independence for ever. He would be identified as a Conservative sympathizer.

The Virgin chairman therefore took the unprecedented step of consulting the opposition. If Branson asked the advice of Labour and the Liberals before accepting the post, it would be hard for them to rubbish it afterwards; and he would maximize his chances of being able to do a good job unhindered by politically motivated criticism. And there was undoubtedly a job to be done; with 3.4m people unemployed, and with youth unemployment a particularly acute problem despite the healthy growth of the economy, it seemed absurd to pay people to stay at home on the dole instead of doing something healthy and useful that would make British towns and open spaces more attractive.

Before Branson had formally made up his mind, however, the environment department had already leaked the news that he would accept the job to the newspapers. An enterprising reporter from the *Sun* tracked Branson down to the Scilly Isles, where he was visiting local people who had helped him in his first attempt to cross the Atlantic by boat, and flew down in a chartered helicopter. Asking Branson to pose unwittingly for the *Sun* photographer with the broom that he had brought with him specially, the reporter returned to London in time to write a characteristically chirpy story about Branson's acceptance of the new job.

Worse was to come. The prime minister returned a few days later from a trip to Israel, and threw the tabloid press into a storm by complaining about the rubbish she had noticed lying at the sides of the roads on her way back from the airport. If the Israelis could keep their streets clean, she asked, why couldn't Britons? Mrs Thatcher had a point. The amount of rubbish on the streets of cities does not depend only on the efficiency with which it is removed; it also depends on the tendency of the locals to drop it in the first place. If a public campaign could make people aware how much less appealing litter made their cities, then there was at least a chance of achieving a change of attitude so that people would simply drop less litter in future.

Yet the matter was more complex than that, and the prime minister's comments created a political storm. Labour's environment spokesman observed wryly that only Mrs Thatcher could have had the gall to talk about Britain's dirty streets while putting downward pressure on the budgets of local councils. 'They are as much her responsibility as they are of the individuals who drop litter,' he said. The *Financial Times* went further, pointing out that her conclusions from the Israel trip had been based on a misapprehension. Its local correspondent discovered that local people in Ramat Gan, a district near Tel Aviv she had visited, were furious at the cost of the special clean-up campaign that had preceded her arrival, and at the flowers that had been trampled by her entourage and the security staff accompanying them. 'Moreover,' added the article, 'the litter left by the crowd guaranteed more overtime for the road-sweepers.'

It was Branson's bad luck to become embroiled in this dispute. Perhaps because of the *Sun* photograph, the rest of the tabloid press reported his new job as if were solely a matter of clearing up litter. He was dubbed the 'Tidy-up tycoon' and the 'Minister for Rubbish'; even the *Sun* itself, in the course of an otherwise sympathetic editorial, offered to bestow on him the title of 'Sir Litter'. Believing that his proven touch with the press would come to the rescue this time as it had before, Branson fired off a number of letters to newspaper editors in an attempt to correct the misapprehension. But it was too late. The story of a pop tycoon as a sort of national dustman-in-chief was simply too good to allow the facts to get in the way. Newspaper coverage of the project thereafter, and even discussion of it in Parliament, seemed shackled to the assumption that Branson was only in it for the rubbish.

The Virgin chairman also discovered that he had become a surrogate target for those who wished to attack Mrs Thatcher. A week after the project was announced, one newspaper reported gleefully that Branson had been prosecuted for speeding down the M40 at ninety miles an hour. The *Daily Express* suggested that Branson had an ulterior motive for becoming involved in the litter project, insinuating that the post might be the beginnings of a political career, and saying that the project 'could bond the Virgin million-aire to Mrs Thatcher's team for good'. The *Daily Mirror* dug up the old story that amyl nitrate was being sold at Heaven, and recycled it under the title SLEAZY DISCO SECRET OF MR CLEAN. 'Atlantic hero Richard Branson arrived home yesterday to be confronted with the sleazy side of his empire,' began its self-styled 'exclusive'. 'A sex drug that is causing increasing concern to doctors is being sold in his gay disco in London . . . The *Mirror* warned Branson four years ago that Alkyl Nitrate [*sic*] was being peddled to the dancers there. Branson . . . promised to investigate. But the *Mirror* can reveal that the drug was STILL on sale when our investigators called.'

The *Daily Star* was even more unashamedly vicious. It said that Branson was 'an odd bird for Mrs Thatcher to have befriended'.

> At 19, he was prosecuted for distributing leaflets telling teen-agers how to cope with VD and contraceptives.
>
> A few years later, he was found guilty of defrauding the Customs and Excise. He just escaped going to jail, but was fined £50,000 instead.
>
> Much of his fortune – £320m passed through his hands last year – comes from his chain of multi-sexual [*sic*] nightclubs.
>
> And he once refused to advertise in two leading music papers – because THEY refused to carry advertisements which recommended making pot-smoking legal.
>
> To crown it all, he hasn't yet married Joan Templeman, mother of his two children, although he's lived with her for 10 years.
>
> Come to think of it, perhaps Mr Branson is the ideal man to pick up our rubbish. At least he won't be shocked by anything he finds.

With a sinking heart, the Virgin chairman set to work on some projects which he hoped might set the record straight. Three useful schemes were proposed: a Forest of London project, whose aim was to encourage the planting of as many trees in the capital as possible; a Green Line across the country, turning waste land into city farms or local parks; and a Blue Line, drawn by opening up disused waterways for boating or for pleasure walking.

There was a minor public row over the name of the new organization. The environment department wanted to call it NEWS –
National Environmental Work Scheme. Branson, complaining that
this sounded too much like bureaucratic self-parody, suggested
something more catchy. The civil servants responded by vetoing
the inclusion of the word 'Virgin' in the name; in the end a compromise was reached by calling it UK 2000.

The press launch, held in Halifax soon after the initial storm of
press coverage, was more of a success. Two people in particular
were impressed by Branson's style: Kenneth Baker, the environment secretary who had bounced him into accepting the job in the
first place; and David Young, a businessman who had attracted Mrs
Thatcher's attention after being brought in as head of the Man-
power Services Commission, and was then given a peerage and a
seat in the cabinet as her employment secretary. 'Both Ken and I
thought we knew a bit about how to handle publicity and how to
sell things,' Lord Young recalled. But Branson's techniques made
him realize he was dealing with a master. It had been arranged that
the two ministers would speak first, followed by Branson. There
was a pregnant pause before Branson came on; the lights and sound
only appeared when he appeared. Relaxed and informal as ever,
Branson stole the show – and the two ministers, outdone at what
they had believed to be their own speciality, joked about it for
months afterwards.

Not even Branson's drive, however, could do much to increase
the glacial speed with which British civil servants and voluntary
organizations move. By November, only 34 of the intended 5,000
work places on the programme had been filled; and despite Branson's strenuous efforts to demonstrate what the project was really
about, the litter label stuck. On one occasion, Branson foiled an
attempt by the *Today* newspaper to set up a photograph of him
holding a broom – and was rewarded with an article the following
morning accusing him of giving 'a road-sweeper the brush-off'.
'He refused to shake hands [with a Greenwich dustman who
approached him while he was launching a new Virgin business
venture],' wrote the paper, 'and even threw away the dustman's
broom.'

By the following year, Branson had lost patience. Frustrated by the difficulty of getting things done inside government, hurt by what he saw as relentlessly critical coverage of his attempt at public service, Branson began to reconsider his earlier intention to stay in the job for more than a year. But the papers were no more sympathetic to his departure than they had been to his arrival. As soon as it became formal, the *News of the World* reported that 'Maggie' had given him the 'order of the boot': 'Mrs Thatcher RUBBISHED his efforts to lead her Clean-up Britain campaign and FROZE him out as head of the UK 2000 group. The move follows her complaints that the group has not done enough to keep Britain's streets litter free.'

The irony was that even before Kenneth Baker had made Branson the UK 2000 offer that he could not refuse, the Virgin chairman was already working on a charitable scheme that was not only more important but also more innovative.

Branson had been talking to Norman Fowler, the health secretary, about the problem of AIDS, which had suddenly become a public health issue in 1985 and 1986. Asked why the government was not doing more to promote the use of condoms, which were known to reduce drastically the risks of spreading the human immunodeficiency virus (HIV), Fowler's response was blunt. It was not the responsibility of government to promote the use of condoms, he said; it was up to the private companies that manufactured them.

As the gravity of the AIDS crisis became apparent, even Conservative ministers came later to recognize that a laissez-faire government might have good reasons for spending taxpayers' money to promote the use of condoms. But Fowler had made an interesting point: one of the main reasons that condoms were barely advertised in Britain was that London International Group, previously known as the London Rubber Company, dominated the market. Accounting for more than nine out of every ten condoms sold in the country, the firm simply had little incentive to spend money on advertising. What LIG needed, if condoms were to receive some private-sector publicity, was a little competition.

Branson went away from the encounter with Fowler with nothing more than a few words scribbled on the back of his hand. But the more he thought about it, the more he came to think that there might be an opportunity here for an entrepreneur to perform a great public service. London International had grown fat on its years of monopoly, and was charging very high prices. A new entrant into the condom market could undercut LIG, force it to advertise to defend its market share and thus to raise public awareness of the importance of avoiding unprotected sex, and could make condoms available to the public at a much lower price than before. With luck, the new entrant would be able to do all these things, and still have profits left over at the end of the year which could be given to an AIDS or other public health charity.

The Virgin chairman knew instinctively how well he was suited to the job. Launching a major new consumer brand would be an exciting business challenge. Pitching it at young people who had hitherto ignored the finger-wagging of doctors and government ministers was just the sort of task he was suited for. And the idea of enjoying himself in a project that would do good to society and raise money for charity made the entire package irresistible.

In April 1986, Branson therefore asked a headhunter to find him a chief executive for his new not-for-profit condom company. The man he identified as his target was John Jackson, a specialist in pharmaceutical and consumer goods. Trained as an accountant, Jackson had switched into general management and risen to the top of the pharmaceutical division of Bristol-Myers. He had then become chief executive of Cheseborough-Ponds, a diversified company that manufactured everything from a moisturizer called Pond's Cream to tennis rackets. Now that the firm had been taken over by Unilever, Jackson was looking for a job. The two men discovered over lunch on the houseboat that Branson's project was the job for him.

Since Richard Branson had never before made the mistake of thinking small, there was no reason to think he might do so now. Jackson told him that he was delighted to be associated with a project that would do some good for society – but not prepared to live like a pauper in order to do so. 'I'm not the type of person to go into the voluntary sector,' said Jackson afterwards. 'I like running companies to make a profit.' Accordingly, Branson agreed to match

Jackson's former salary at Cheseborough-Ponds of £100,000 a year. There was one proviso, however; Branson insisted that only £60,000 of that sum should be paid as salary. The remaining £40,000 would be a bonus, dependent on Jackson's ability to establish a new brand of condoms and operate it profitably within eighteen months. But with the bonus taken into account, Branson was paying Jackson more for participating in this charitable venture than he was paying even Don Cruickshank, the managing director of the Virgin Group at the time.

That decision proved to be one of the best he ever made. Jackson set to work with enthusiasm, drawing up a feasibility study of what it might cost to establish a new brand, and doing some discreet research into what it would cost to buy condoms from one of LIG's global competitors. His first approach was immediately successful. Ansell, a subsidiary of Pacific Dunlop, the largest manufacturer of condoms in the United States, was ready and willing to provide the nascent charity with as many condoms as it could hope to sell – and to do so at a price so low that the charity would be able to undercut LIG's Durex brand by more than 60 per cent. Jackson and Branson would be buying packets of three condoms for about 9p, and selling them on at over 15p to retailers, who would then price them for the general public at 30p.

Now that he knew the venture made sense in principle, Jackson was ready to go ahead in earnest. He and Branson got together for a brainstorming session to decide what the new condoms should be called. After rejecting scores of other possibilities, including 'Passion', they finally adopted a suggestion made by Joan Templeman. The new brand would be called 'Mates'. Early market research warned against this choice, for too many people appeared to associate the name with gays and homosexuality. But Mates was the name that Branson and Jackson liked most, so Mates it was to be.

Branson's colleagues at Virgin were none too enthusiastic about the idea of moving into the condom business. In particular, they did not want the company name to be associated with the venture. So the Virgin Healthcare Foundation that Branson had intended to set up was called instead simply The Healthcare Foundation; and the Mates logo, although upside-down it looked suspiciously like the capital letter V in the Virgin logo, was ostensibly quite separate and distinct from that of the company owned by the foundation's chairman.

Jackson's next task was to establish a distribution channel for the new product. He contacted Boots, the country's largest seller of condoms, to ask whether the retail chemist chain would be willing to stock the condoms and sell them on without taking profits. The answer was a polite but unshakeable no; but the good news was that Boots, and most of the country's other big retailers of condoms, were more than happy to stock a rival brand to Durex. Better still, Jackson also set up an attractive deal to sell the condoms through vending machines. A vending company agreed to invest its own money in establishing a network of 18,000 vending machine in pubs and petrol stations across the country – far outflanking the Durex distribution system of only 2,000 machines.

A handful of agencies were discreetly invited to pitch for the Mates advertising account. The runner-up came up with the best slogan – 'If it's not on, it's not on' – but it was Still, Price, an agency that had worked for Branson before, that won the account. Its approach was to be whimsical and serious by turns. One television commercial it produced dealt with the embarrassment of a young man trying to buy condoms in a chemist, but unable to say the dread word; another focused on the fear felt by young people after a night of unprotected sex. The Mates ads were thus ready to go out, each one ending in the punchline 'You make love; Mates make sense.'

Branson had invited two key people to join him on the board of his new foundation. One was Anita Roddick, founder of the Body Shop empire; the other was Michael Grade, then controller of BBC but later to take over at the helm of Channel Four. As the advertisements neared completion, the foundation was therefore able to approach the BBC with an unusual request: since the wider use of condoms was an issue of such importance in terms of public health, and since the Healthcare Foundation was trying to encourage their wider use, would the Corporation consider running a series of Mates advertisements that had been doctored to remove any mention of the brand? The answer, perhaps surprisingly, was yes; and so it was agreed that a number of advertisements would go out on a number of different days, at the peak time just before the beginning of the main nine o'clock news on BBC1.

Branson and Jackson never discovered who it was that leaked the story of the Healthcare Foundation and its planned new product launch to the press. But in the summer of 1987, a story appeared on the front page of *Campaign* magazine – strongly suggesting that the guilty party had been one of the advertising agencies that pitched for the account but failed to win it – revealing with some accuracy what Branson's plan was. The first effect of the story's publication was to knock 10p off the share price of London International Group: investors correctly suspected that competition in the condom market would reduce its profits. But the leak was also an inconvenience for Richard Branson. The Virgin chairman, who was in America waiting to try to cross the Atlantic by balloon, was forced to come home to give a hurriedly arranged press conference.

With LIG now forewarned of the onslaught that was coming, it became imperative to capitalize on the publicity and launch the brand as soon as possible. The first Mates condoms were therefore sold in early November; and their impact was immediate. Significantly cheaper than Durex, the new brand immediately took more than a quarter of the condom market. It also prompted Durex to cut its prices, and to reverse its long-standing policy against realistic advertising spending. Later in that autumn, the Independent Broadcasting Authority approved the first condom product advertisements to be shown on British television. Branson did not achieve his declared aim of selling 70 million condoms in the first year; but with average annual sales for the entire market of only 140 million, that had perhaps been too optimistic to begin with. Nor did he succeed in provoking a sharp increase in the total size of the market, and thus encouraging many people who had never used condoms before to take them up. But Branson could congratulate himself, and John Jackson too, on a number of highly impressive achievements. Between them, they had launched a major new consumer brand and established it as profitable within a year. They had forced down the retail price of condoms, making it cheaper for young people to have safe sex. And they had made £1m in profit in the first year, which could be passed to the Healthcare Foundation for forwarding to worthy causes.

There was still far to go in promoting open discussion of the link between unprotected sex, HIV and AIDS. Right-wing Conservatives would jump up in Parliament from time to time, complaining that the promotion of condoms seemed to be an invitation to promiscuity; abstinence, they suggested, would be a better message to bring to young people. These attitudes were not confined only to Parliament. When the Health Education Authority commissioned a series of safe sex advertisements aimed at businessmen travelling abroad, it encountered surprising resistance to placing them in airline magazines. British Airways refused to run the campaign in its in-flight magazines, after taking fright at the line: 'When you've had a few and you're miles from home, it's not your brain that does the thinking.' Perhaps more surprisingly, so did the publishers of Virgin Atlantic's in-flight magazine. It required Richard Branson's personal interference to persuade the *Hot Air* editors that they should swallow their scruples about a family readership for the sake of the wider benefits of slowing the spread of AIDS.

It was never Branson's intention, however, that either he or his foundation should remain the owner of a condom company indefinitely. Maintaining the position of Mates in the market, Jackson had warned him, would require continued marketing spending and constant attention. So Mates was sold. Ansell, the company that had manufactured the condoms, gave £1m to the Foundation as an advance on future royalties. Thereafter, it was agreed, Ansell would pay the Foundation a royalty of 2 per cent of its annual sales.

By 1994, Mates were still to be found in British chemists. The brand no longer belonged to Ansell; that firm in turn had sold it on to Johnson & Johnson, the international toiletries conglomerate. But proof of the longevity of the brand could be seen in the fact that it had diversified out of condoms. Also available, through vending machines, were Mates toothbrushes and Mates toothpaste. Even when he was not making money for himself, it seemed, Richard Branson was a successful entrepreneur.

TWELVE

'I've Got to Believe You're Serious about It'

As 1986 PROGRESSED, Virgin's flamboyant investment banker, Roger Seelig, observed with growing admiration Branson's brilliant orchestration of positive coverage for the Virgin group in the press. Virgin hired the advertising agency Still, Price to prepare press and television commercials for the flotation, with the punchline 'From the rock market to the stock market'. Branson himself began to talk in public about the possible flotation. But Seelig's admiration soon turned to dismay when he realized that the Virgin chairman was in danger of doing too well for the company's own good. Many of the teenagers who had bought its records in the 1970s, and had now grown up into thirtysomethings with children, liked the idea of making a quick couple of hundred quid by 'stagging' Virgin – subscribing for its shares before the stock market listing, and then selling the shares on at a quick profit a few days later. *Challenger II* and the airline had also generated extra publicity for Branson, and by 1986 the nightmare of the overbooked summer flights of 1984 had begun to fade.

As a result, there was already a market out there for Virgin paper; the more Branson did to raise interest, the more inflamed the demand would be when it came to listing. Yet Virgin should not be trying to achieve the same public awareness as British Telecom had in November 1984, Seelig urged. BT was Britain's biggest company; Virgin, by contrast, was trying to sell off shares only to the value of £60m – and it was intending to give employees and artists priority over the first ten per cent of that. Too much hype among the public at large would simply give Lloyds Bank, which the company brokers Rowe & Pitman had hired to handle the registrations, a mountain of excess application forms to deal with.

What mattered more was winning the support of the pension

funds and other institutions which invest the billions of pounds of savings of working people across the country. Institutional share-holders are cheaper to deal with, since the administrative costs of sending out annual reports and dividend cheques to a single £1m shareholder are only a fraction of the cost of doing the same to 1,000 shareholders who each own £1,000 of shares in a company. And since enthusiasm from the amateurs was likely to die away after the initial hoopla, the institutions would also be important in providing a pool of ready buyers for Virgin's shares after the listing.

It was in the autumn of 1986, then, that Branson and his col-leagues had a foretaste of running a public company. They had to take time out from their day-to-day work, and instead troop around the City by taxi, having cups of tea with fund managers and lunches with brokers. The object of the exercise was to convince these specialists, who in turn would convince other institutional investors, that Virgin had progressed far from its ragged beginnings as a mail-order record discounter. Their audiences, serenaded with extracts from *Tubular Bells*, had first to be disabused of one mis-understanding. Virgin did not, as its bank managers at Coutts had for years persisted in believing, make most of its money from the record shops. Retail was not the core of the group; as Virgin would later admit in the formal offer documents, the shops had 'not to date achieved an adequate return'. It was in fact Virgin Music – the record labels, the publishing arm, the studios – that was the group's 'cash cow'. In the eighteen months to 31 July 1986, that division brought in operating profits of £22m. Retailing, despite eating up capital at an enormous rate, lost money; Vision was grow-ing nicely, but had so far achieved operating profits of just over £1m – 5 per cent of turnover, compared with the fat 16 per cent that the music side was bringing in.

Unfortunately, the brokers and fund managers knew too little about Virgin's businesses to appreciate the finer details. At one meeting, Simon Draper listed the company's hit bands in an attempt to convey its strengths. One by one, the names came out: Culture Club, China Crisis, Japan, Orchestral Manoeuvres in the Dark, UB40. All were greeted with stony silence, observed a reporter from the *Washington Post* who was present, until Draper finally lost his cool. 'You may not have heard of any of these bands,' he blurted

at the besuited gentlemen, 'but I can assure you they sell millions
and millions of records all over the world.'

The other question that was always asked concerned the role of
Richard Branson himself. Having created the public perception that
the record business was Branson's personal creation, it was hard
for the Virgin directors to admit in public that it was nowadays
run from day to day entirely by Simon Draper and Ken Berry. But
that was precisely what they needed to do if they were to convince
investors that the Virgin Group would still survive if Branson fell
under a bus.

Roger Seelig himself was more aware of this than anyone. A few
weeks before the 'roadshows', as the investors' presentations were
known, had begun, he had turned up for breakfast at Branson's
house in Oxford Gardens one morning, and asked as they sat down
to their cornflakes and coffee whether Richard had had a good
weekend. Branson strolled over to the television, and switched on
a video recording of himself, diving out of an aircraft with a parachute on his back. Instead of pulling the string to open the
parachute, however, he by mistake pulled the ripcord that released
the entire parachute harness – and went promptly into free-fall,
spinning furiously without a parachute on his back, 10,000 feet
above the ground. Although the film showed the two military
instructors who had accompanied Branson out of the aircraft skydiv-
ing down to catch him, this documentary proof that the Virgin
chairman had come close to death was too much even for Seelig.
He advised urgently that Branson should in future be as discreet
as possible about his dangerous hobbies, or expect the company's
share price to take the consequences.

Another precaution he suggested was that Virgin should invite
on to its board some non-executive directors. As the stock market
had begun to rise, and chief executives of public companies had
become greedier, institutional shareholders were beginning to wake
up to the reality that free-wheeling managing directors and chairmen could not always be relied on to act in the company's, rather
than their own, interests. Most often, the issue came up when corporate executives were deciding how much to pay themselves: a
large number took advantage of the fashion for performance-related
pay to set up share option programmes whose rules gave them huge

pay-offs. The rising number of takeovers had raised a second issue: with their luxurious offices, chauffeur-driven cars and private jets, company executives often became highly reluctant to relinquish their posts. When another company, believing that it could manage the business better, tried to buy out the shareholders, there was a great temptation for the incumbent managers to protect their own livelihoods by fighting off the bid, even if resisting it was not in the interests of the shareholders. The most extreme conflict of interest arose when the incumbent managers would use inside knowledge to trump an outside bid with their own buy-out offer – without answering the question why, if they knew how to run the company in a way that would bring greater value to shareholders, they were not already doing so. For all these reasons and more, the fashionable City view in 1986 was that public companies needed non-executive directors, who could make sure that the executives who were running the business full-time kept the shareholders' interests at heart.

At Virgin, there was little danger that the directors would do otherwise. Simon Draper and Richard Branson, the two most important directors, stood to gain far more from long-term improvements in the value of Virgin's shares than from anything they might earn on a monthly basis. Branson drew £60,000 a year in salary; because he would still control a majority of the company after flotation, a one per cent improvement in the Virgin share price would be worth ten times that sum to him. The disparity was less for Draper, but the principle was the same. Under the circumstances, there seemed little reason to bring in any outsiders to the Virgin board. But Branson and Draper both conceded that the style in which they had become accustomed to operating might discourage big institutional shareholders from entrusting their capital to Virgin. The answer was to find two people who would reassure the City, but whom the Virgin founders would be able to work with.

It was proof of Virgin's attractiveness that the first person suggested was willing to serve on the board without even demanding a fee. Sir Phil Harris, who had built up the Queensway discount carpet chain, had proven expertise in retailing, the area of the Virgin business that was doing least well. Given the dramatic rise in value of his company's shares on the stock market, it was also fair to assume that institutional shareholders would warm to his presence. The other non-executive director was Cob Stenham, former finance director of the multinational consumer-goods conglomerate Unilever and current chairman of the European operations of Bankers Trust, a New York investment bank. He was known as an imaginative financier, but a stickler for corporate correctness. On first impressions, Simon Draper found it hard to distinguish Stenham – Etonian, Cambridge graduate, chartered accountant, barrister – from any other of the bankers or brokers in the establishment that he had recently had to deal with. Later, however, he came to like him, and discovered that they shared an interest in modern art: among Stenham's string of posts were the chairmanships of the Institute of Contemporary Arts and the Royal College of Art. Branson agreed to pay Stenham for his services; the figure of between £10,000 and £15,000 recorded in Virgin's first public accounts a year later reflected the fact that Stenham had given extra financial advice and put in extra time on top of the formal board meetings.

The listing documents were issued on 7 November 1986, but Seelig could not hold back Branson's instinct for public relations. The company had run television advertisements showing a City type in pinstripe and bowler dancing around his office to the slogan, 'After the Big Bang, how about a little pop?'; its chairman, unable to resist another outfit to dress up in, had appeared at the press conference to announce the details of Virgin's plans in the same garb, rented from Moss Bros.

Those who wanted to buy shares were given until Thursday 13 November to apply. Early that morning, Branson went down to the Lloyds Bank offices at Bishopsgate in the City of London with his mother to see the last applications for Virgin shares handed in before the 10 AM deadline. A queue of people stretched around the corner, and many of them wanted Richard Branson's autograph; the television and press cameras were out in force. The assembled journalists and photographers could not resist pointing out that Branson had by some oversight succeeded in putting on a left shoe from one pair and a right shoe from another. His explanation was disarmingly upbeat: he was tired, because he'd been awoken at five o'clock that morning with the news that a record by the Human

League, a Virgin act, had just reached number one in the United States singles charts.

Roger Seelig's fears were confirmed at a meeting held the following morning to look over the applications that had been received. Over 100,000 private investors had wanted to buy shares in Virgin – but the institutions, spurning the careful briefings of Branson and Draper, had turned up their noses at the issue. This presented the brokers at Rowe & Pitman with a dilemma. In order to take advantage of the rising market, no fixed price had been put on Virgin's shares. Instead, the offer documents had invited investors to bid, or 'tender', whatever they thought Virgin shares were worth, with a minimum price of 120p a share. Once the applications were in, the brokers would then be able to pick the highest possible price at which the offer would still be fully subscribed to Virgin's satisfaction – and then, for the sake of fairness, to allot shares at that price to everyone who had bid the same or more.

The enthusiasm of the small investors was such that Virgin shares could have been pegged at well over 160p each – and Branson's inclination was to do just that. But Seelig and the advisers from Rowe & Pitman warned that such a course might be disastrous. Were Virgin to price itself so high, the after-market as the shares were traded on the floor of the stock exchange over the coming few days would be a disappointment. Few institutions had been willing to come in on the tender offer; fewer still would want to buy Virgin shares at what they deemed inflated prices in tiny parcels from private individuals. With no buyers, the share price would plummet. And although it would not be Branson or Draper who lost, tens of thousands of small investors would find themselves not merely making no profits but actually out of pocket. This was not exactly the kind of public relations that Virgin wanted.

They ended that meeting by deciding to set the price at a less ambitious 140p. As it turned out, however, even that was too optimistic. The shares opened firm, then dropped 4p, then rose again. It was a foretaste of what was to turn out a thoroughly unsatisfactory relationship with the stock market, and a disappointing period for the business as a whole.

Yet fortune was to prove kinder to Richard Branson than to Roger Seelig. A few weeks after Virgin's flotation was wrapped up, inspectors from the Department of Trade and Industry began an investigation into the Guinness bid to take over Distillers, which Seelig had orchestrated at the beginning of 1986. Seelig himself was forced to resign from Morgan Grenfell, and was arrested in October 1987 and charged with securities fraud and two counts of false accounting. Unable to bear the seven-figure costs of defence lawyers, Seelig was forced to defend himself under increasing stress. The case against him was abandoned in 1992 after the judge concluded that he was no longer fit to conduct his own defence.

Before he agreed to join the Virgin Group in 1984, Don Cruickshank had made a point of having a talk with Richard Branson about the company's future. Privately owned companies, he knew, are different beasts from those whose shares are quoted on stock exchanges. Lines of command are often less precisely defined in private firms, and styles of management more idiosyncratic. If he was to join as group managing director, Cruickshank needed reassurance that Branson understood what running a public company would be like. He had to believe that Branson was serious.

As he came to know his employer better, it began to dawn on Cruickshank that certain aspects of Branson's character would make it difficult for him to survive tough times as a public company. For all his qualities, Branson hated deep down to be held accountable to anybody. He had insisted on going his own way from his early teens onwards, to the chagrin of many of those who came into contact with him. His parents, his schoolmasters, his first wife Kristen, his business partner Nik Powell, his colleagues: all had suffered the consequences of trying to restrain or control Richard Branson. It was only later that consideration for Joan Templeman and his children was to prompt Branson to abandon the perilous hobby of hot-air ballooning.

For the first few months after Virgin went public, all seemed to go well. Cruickshank felt that he had been successful in persuading Branson to jettison some of the less successful businesses in order to concentrate on what he was good at. For instance, he had forced Branson to insert a statement into the tender documents to the effect that after winding down the projects in which it was currently involved, Virgin had no further ambitions in the film-making business.

Cruickshank had also succeeded in making the Virgin Group board more systematic both in the regularity with which it met and the matters it discussed when it did so. Aware that the non-executive directors had other business interests, he also convinced the troika of Branson, Berry and Draper that they should try to cut the length of the meetings back to half a day.

Another of his achievements was to make sure that the group had a respectable share option scheme. While Virgin was still a private company, even its senior managers had accepted below average salaries in return for the excitement of working with Richard Branson and the confidence that they would one day be rewarded handsomely for their loyalty. Once the firm had gone public and grown far past the point where every employee had regular personal contact with its chairman, new arrangements had to be put in place. The route chosen was the conventional one at the time: a number of different schemes, some of which gave bonuses to employees based on the profits earned in the businesses they worked for, and others (mostly confined to more senior staff) which gave them the option to buy Virgin shares below market prices at specified times in the future. Trevor Abbott, who had put in a similar scheme in his previous job, arranged the details. Apart from Draper and Branson, who already held huge quantities of Virgin stock, options on nearly 1.8m shares were given to Trevor Abbott, Robert Devereux and Cruickshank himself. Given that their salaries ranged from £57,500 to £75,000 a year, these options gave the Virgin directors a strong financial incentive to make the company grow and become more profitable. The incentive was even more necessary for other Virgin employees; as the accounts for the company's first public year were later to show, only one Virgin employee apart from the directors earned an annual salary above £30,000.

But it was not long before Cruickshank found that he and Branson differed on a number of important questions to do with the running of the company. One early debate was over dividends. With his public-company background, Cruickshank saw it as a matter of routine that a generous proportion of the firm's profits should be remitted back to the shareholders every year in the form of dividends. Branson did not agree. 'How is it possible', he used to ask, 'that the shareholders can put this money to better use than I can?' It was a legitimate argument, of course: having entrusted him with their money in the expectation that he would produce a better return on it than they could alone, why should the shareholders then demand that he should return part of it every year in the form of dividends? But this view failed to take into account the wish of some investors to take their profits from the growth of Virgin year by year rather than in a single lump when they sold, which would incur capital gains tax in the process. But there was also an expectation on the London and New York stock markets that equity investments produced a dividend return. Branson would have been more at home with Japanese investors, who until the early 1990s were willing to tolerate far lower dividends (and indeed far lower levels of profitability in general) from their shares. In London he stuck out like a sore thumb.

Cruickshank also found Branson's attitude to tax puzzling. If there was one thing the Virgin chairman was pathological and obsessive about, it was his dislike of paying more than he had to to the Exchequer. During the 1970s and early 1980s he had bought a number of highly complicated tax schemes designed by Godfrey Bradman, which resulted in a flood of transactions that reduced or postponed the tax that the Virgin companies had to pay. Cruickshank saw no evidence that Branson was in danger of crossing the fine line between legal tax avoidance – finding ways, quite legally, of minimizing tax bills – and the illegal evasion of tax by lying to the Inland Revenue. With top-ranking firms acting as Virgin's solicitors and auditors, there was no question of that. But even after the company had gone public, Branson was still inordinately keen to find ways of putting off his tax bills. On one occasion, he dreamed up the idea of investing in a seismic survey ship in the North Sea, and Cruickshank was obliged to sit down with him in the houseboat for several hours with piles of computer printouts in order to prove that the costs of entering into the deal, and the risks that it might bring to Virgin, were too high to justify the modest cash-flow advantages of postponing a small tax payment. In any case, the company was growing so fast that even tax avoidance schemes that seemed rational at the time were dwarfed by the size of the company's normal transactions later on.

The Virgin chairman was equally uncomfortable with the idea of holding regular meetings with the brokers and analysts, and explaining to them how the business was going. One reason for this was a purely practical one. There were only two other record companies quoted on the London stock market, Thorn-EMI and Chrysalis. Of the two, the former was a stodgily managed business that had delivered unspectacular results for years, whose record labels were far from the most important parts of its business; the latter, a firm that had disappointed investors' expectations. With a market of this size, it was simply not economic for stockbrokers to set up a team of analysts to study the record business in depth; there would not be enough share turnover to bring in the commissions that would cover the cost of the research. As a result, the industry in which Virgin found itself was probably the least understood sector of the market – and the questions that analysts asked were banal in the extreme. Particularly irritating was the analysts' apparent inability to understand the notion that a third of the music business's turnover came not from new releases but from 'back catalogue'. The company was less dependent than they realized on Simon Draper's ability to pick the next hit, and its results were less likely to suffer if Boy George were to drop dead from a drug overdose.

Branson having lost patience with the City, the taxi run eastwards from the familiar Virgin territory of Notting Hill Gate was delegated to Cruickshank and Abbott. Occasional appearances were made by Simon Draper (who hated it even more than Branson himself did) and by Ken Berry. Berry – the restrained, sensible, unflappable, ever-polite Berry – never let on that he was not enjoying himself. Analysts and brokers appreciated his laconic, factual answers, and the glimmers of dry humour that he would occasionally reveal. Such goodwill as Virgin enjoyed among institutional investors was partly due to him, even though he continued inside the company to be the director who was most unshakeably convinced that the company's decision to go public had been mistaken.

As the anniversary of its listing approached, Virgin's auditors were doing the final accounting checks on the company's most successful year ever. Turnover was up 27 per cent to nearly £300m; profits after tax had more than doubled to £18m, with the sale of the airline and clubs to Branson's private Voyager group contributing a net extraordinary item of £4.6m. Overcoming Branson's misgivings, Virgin also distributed a total of 2.65p a share in dividends in respect of its first public year. Yet before these achievements could be reported to the shareholders in October 1987, the London stock market suddenly crashed, taking more than £60m off the company's market value in three days. Instead of breaking through the £2 barrier, Virgin's shares fell back to 83p. It was not until the spring that they would begin to recover.

Worse was to come. One of the uses to which the company intended to put the new capital it had raised in 1986 was to start a new record label in the United States from scratch. This was not the first time that Virgin had made a direct foray into the American market. Branson had sent Ken Berry, then his valued personal assistant, to New York to set Virgin up as an independent in the United States. He had established an office in a house in Greenwich Village that had previously been occupied by Mick Jagger and by Chris Blackwell, founder of Island Records, but, despite his efforts, the attempt had failed ignominiously. Virgin had then reverted to the safer but ultimately far less profitable approach of licensing its British artists to American labels in return for a royalty percentage. With such a clear demonstration of the risks of trying to go it alone in the United States, most public companies in Britain faced with such a second chance would have used their financial muscle simply to buy into an existing record company.

When the influx of cash from the listing brought that chance, Branson still preferred to start small, and build his own label entirely from the ground up. He had earmarked $30m for the cost of hiring staff and finding offices, signing up artists and distributing their records before the new label turned into profit. This strategy produced one startling early success: a record by the group Cutting Crew, which was the label's first singles release in the US market, rose to the top of the American charts in May 1987. Virgin Records America Inc was also able to boast four other Top Twenty singles, and one gold album in its first year.

Yet as 1987 turned into 1988, Branson was forced to admit that more money would have to be poured in, and that consequently the new US operation would not break even until its third year of operation. In the first year, it had proven a drag on the growth of the profits of Virgin Music as a whole. Although the division's 1987 profits of £20.3m were a whisker higher than those of the year before, they would have been several millions higher still without the heavy investments in the American market. This strategy of building up from the bottom would improve Virgin's value in years to come; but the company had to concede that its immediate effect would merely be to reduce the dividends. This trend became more pronounced by the time Virgin announced a less attractive set of half-year results in May 1988: profits were weighed down by a £3m interest charge, reflecting the money the company had borrowed in order to build up its labels in the United States and Japan. Ken Berry was once again sent scuttling eastwards to have a discreet word with a handful of big City institutions, to explain that the short-term hit to Virgin's profit and loss account that would result from this policy would bring long-term benefits.

Looking back, some Virgin executives would later complain that the company's difficulties in the stock market were the fault of the analysts. In fact, the evidence is exactly the opposite: although their questions may have been ill-informed at first and hostile later, the firm convinced the analysts of its case. Of the 45 or so brokers' circulars on Virgin issued during the company's first eighteen months on the stock market, the overwhelming majority advised investors to buy the company's shares, and only one rated Virgin a 'sell'. Even after interim results below expectations, all six of the circulars published described Virgin as a long-term buy, or a long-term hold – meaning that clients who already owned shares should retain them, even if the company was not a promising enough short-term investment to be worthy of the attention of those who did not.

Unfortunately, the analysts could compel neither the traders in their own firms nor the fund managers to whom their circulars were sent to take their optimistic advice. Within a day of the publication of the half-year results in May, a rush to sell had wiped out eight per cent of the firm's value. By that point, investors who bought shares when Virgin went public had done 60 per cent worse than they would have simply by buying into the FT index and riding upwards with the market as a whole.

To a great extent, this behaviour by big investors could be blamed on their notorious short-termism. Given the choice between a Virgin Group that was making little money now but hoped that its present investments would bring in fat profits later, and a firm whose management was squeezing its business for every last penny of profit and dishing the proceeds up as dividends in the present half-year, the institutions had no hesitation. Like Saint Augustine in his prayer to God, they wanted to be 'good, but not yet'.

But there were other reasons for investors to shun Virgin's shares. Even occasional readers of the newspapers could see that the promise not to spend more than three days a month on the affairs of the Voyager Group was not being kept. Branson was clearly devoting the bulk of his energies to the airline. Only those who knew the group well were aware that this was less of a reason to worry than it seemed, since the most profitable parts of the group were its record and music publishing interests, run by Simon Draper and Steve Lewis respectively. There was also the question of Branson's high-profile adventures. Had the Virgin chairman been risking his neck in boats and balloons for the greater benefit of his shareholders, well and good; but the companies that were primary beneficiaries of the publicity were once again the private businesses of the Voyager Group. To the Virgin Group itself, therefore, there was little upside from the ventures' success; but if Branson killed himself, the public businesses would be deprived of their chief source of inspiration.

Branson and his lieutenants clearly found the City's conservatism stultifying – so much so that eight years later, long after Virgin's time as a public company was over, Simon Draper rejected an invitation to speak to a group of stock market analysts about the record business with the words: 'It's the last thing on God's earth that I'd want to do.' They might have been forgiven for their sensitivity, since Branson's increasingly high public profile was beginning to make his private life the object of interest in the popular press.

In August 1987, just after the end of Virgin's first public financial year, *Mayfair* Magazine dug up some nude pictures of Joan Templeman, Branson's girlfriend, for which she had posed more than a decade earlier, and splashed them across its cover with the words VIRGIN BRIDE SHOWS OFF ALL HER ASSETS. Before they could be published, however, the pictures were leaked to the *News of the World.* The paper instantly ran a sanctimonious 'exclusive' on them, claiming that she had agreed to spend a week-long photo session in Crete in return for £150 of 'easy money' while she was married to Ronnie Leahy, 'who she dumped in the 1970s'. The article, entitled BRANSON GIRL IN NUDE SNAPS SHOCK, explained that the pictures left 'nothing to the imagination', and suggested that they were 'bound to embarrass mega-rich Virgin boss Branson'.

They did not. While other tycoons might have attempted to buy back the pictures in order to prevent their publication, Branson was delighted that the world should know how beautiful the mother of his children was. When one senior employee at Virgin Atlantic teased him about the pictures, saying that he and his colleagues had all had to take cold showers after seeing the *Mayfair* pictures, Branson was able to reply that he had asked the magazine for copies – and was now the proud owner of a huge colour enlargement of the naked Joan, which he proposed to hang over his bed.

Two months later, Branson's own behaviour was to become the focus of attention. During a weekend away for Virgin staff at a hotel in Cornwall, he entertained the party by dancing a strip-tease on a restaurant table in fishnet stockings and lacy suspenders. This time it was the *Sun*, also owned by Rupert Murdoch's News International, that found out; the story ran under the headline SHOCK-ING STOCKINGS CAPER BY POP TYCOON. A few days later, the paper even managed to get hold of a photograph of the incident, in which Branson was immediately identifiable by the brightly pat-terned sweater that he wore incongruously above the waist. The article was clearly friendly; it described Branson's 'down-to-earth' antics as 'Virgin on the ridiculous', and quoted a member of the company's staff as saying that 'some of the blue-rinse grannies staying there complained, but it was all in good fun'. 'Even with all his millions,' the paper observed, 'he likes to show he's still one of the lads . . . despite his taste in undies!' The sole note of criticism came at the end of the story, when the paper claimed that the weekend, including drinks, four-course meals and sports facilities, had cost 'a staggering £¼m'. Draper later insisted that the real figure was nearer half that sum.

If any of this did Branson's standing on the stock exchange real harm, it was probably that last detail. Contrary to the view from inside Virgin, City people were more tolerant of private eccentricities than they perhaps seemed. This had already been demonstrated earlier in the year, when Sir Ralph Halpern, the flamboyant 48-year-old chairman of the Burton retailing group, was reported as having had a brief but sexually athletic affair with a topless model of 19. After the sniggers had subsided, the model's lurid account of the story might actually have been positive for the Burton's chairman, since it proved that the onset of middle age had left him full of energy and with an undiminished appetite for work. The company's share price fell sharply during the week that the story broke, but that probably had more to do with the fact that Halpern and his fellow-directors were trying to win approval at the company's annual general meeting for an exceptionally generous and controversial performance-related pay scheme.

If tales of Branson's private life with Joan had any ill effect on investors' views of Virgin, it was probably only in one respect: the coverage gave rise to the view that Branson was not a serious businessman. Rich, famous, gregarious, uninhibited, he gave the impression that his life was a succession of adventures and mildly debauched parties. How could it be otherwise, if the man worked on a boat and never wore a suit?

Had they only known the reality behind the tabloid stories, the pension funds and investment trusts might have taken a different view of Virgin's shares altogether. The boat and balloon stunts? A brilliant way of achieving millions of pounds of press coverage that the Voyager businesses could never have afforded to buy. The parties and weekends away? To achieve the same team spirit among the employees that made up most of the guest lists, Branson would have had to pay substantially higher salaries. The cross-dressing, the pin-up girlfriend? The best possible way, surely, for a record company to establish a corporate image with which fashionable young musicians of powerful libido would identify.

THIRTEEN

Hot Air

IT WAS PERHAPS inevitable that the Virgin chairman should be asked, almost as soon as he returned home from the successful assault on the Blue Riband, what he planned to do next. His answers were as amiable and mumbling as ever. But in fact, discreet preparations were already under way for a stunt that was far more ambitious than either of the two Atlantic sea crossings. Richard Branson was going to fly across the ocean by hot-air balloon.

The idea had been brought to him by Hugh Band, the marketing manager of the airline. Early in 1986, Band and a colleague had visited the offices of Thunder & Colt, a company which manufactured hot-air balloons from an industrial estate at Oswestry in Shropshire, in order to discuss a huge balloon that would be used to publicize Virgin Atlantic. Underneath the designs for the new Virgin Atlantic balloon – which had giant bulges that would be painted to look as though a jet aircraft had crashed into it – Band noticed a different set of blueprints.

'What's that?' he asked Per Lindstrand, the founder and chief executive of Thunder & Colt.

'Oh, that's just my pet project,' said Lindstrand. 'It's a design for a balloon that will make the first hot-air crossing of the Atlantic.'

Knowing how much the first *Challenger* had already stimulated demand for tickets on the airline, Band realized immediately that a more innovative and technically demanding balloon venture might be an interesting project for Virgin to take on. He asked Lindstrand a few quick questions on the subject, and promised to talk to Richard Branson about it. They then returned to the discussion of the aircraft-shaped publicity balloon. His business done, Band later drove back to London.

Hearing nothing further that week or the week after, Lindstrand assumed that Virgin had no further interest in the matter. The development of his prototype, he believed, would continue to be a private hobby. But Lindstrand was mistaken. A month later, on a rainy grey morning, his telephone rang. It was Hugh Band, calling from Virgin, to invite him to lunch with Richard Branson.

'When?' asked Lindstrand.

'Today, at one,' came the reply.

'But I'm in Shropshire, near the Welsh border,' he said. 'It's 11 AM, and it takes three or four hours to drive down to London from here.'

'Oh.'

Lindstrand then added that he did have a small private plane, which he could fly to an airfield near the capital. If he hurried, he might just be able to arrive by 1.30.

By the second cup of coffee, they had agreed in principle that Lindstrand would build, and he and Branson would fly, the world's largest ever hot-air balloon across the Atlantic.

'Don't you want any references?' asked Lindstrand.

'I have just one question,' replied Branson. 'Do you have any children?'

Lindstrand replied that he had two.

'Well, that's all right, then. That shows I will be safe, because you aren't likely to want to kill yourself.'

As Branson was later to discover, Per Lindstrand was more than just a balloon manufacturer. By background he was a pilot of both military and civilian jets, who had been trained in Sweden's air force. He was a good theoretician, too; by adding long experience to aeronautical engineering qualifications, he had become one of the world's leading authorities on balloon design. But Lindstrand was no armchair balloonist. By piloting two highly advanced balloons, he had helped to win world records for the highest ever parachute jump and the highest ever hang-glider flight. He was also thoroughly trained in survival techniques. For there was always the risk that either or both of them might have to jump out of the balloon in the skies above the mid-Atlantic and parachute to the cold seas below.

As they basked in the weak London sunshine on the deck of the *Duende*, Lindstrand outlined his plan to Branson. He started off by reminding the Virgin chairman of the crucial difference between a hot-air balloon and one that is filled with a gas that is lighter than air, like helium or hydrogen. Lighter-than-air balloons, Lindstrand explained, require very little fuel. Once the ropes that tether them to the ground are cut, they will float up into the sky and stay there without further effort, unless the balloon's skin is punctured. Hot-air balloons are altogether more difficult. They have to carry enough fuel not just to get them from one place to another, but also to supply the lift necessary to keep them above the ground. That is why, by 1986, the Atlantic had been crossed many times by airships filled with helium or hydrogen – but never by one filled with hot air alone. Nobody had managed to design a combination of balloon and fuel efficient enough to provide the lift and go the distance. If the two men could pilot a hot-air balloon all the way from America to Britain, they would not merely break the world distance record for hot-air ballooning. They would travel three times further than any hot-air balloonist had before.

Lindstrand's design incorporated not one but three major advances in ballooning technology. First, he hit on the idea of saving fuel by riding piggy-back on the 'jet stream' of powerful air currents far above the ocean. So far, no balloonist had dared to try such a thing, for fear that the violence of the currents would tear the balloon's envelope to pieces, leaving its pilots to fall to a lonely death beneath the clouds. But Lindstrand, with his experience of high-altitude ballooning behind him, believed that the conventional wisdom just might be wrong.

His second innovation was a consequence of the decision to try to fly in the jet stream. Since the balloon would be nearly 30,000 feet above the ground, it was out of the question for it to carry just a wicker basket. At such an altitude, the air temperature is far below freezing, and the pressure too low for a human to breathe unaided. For its pilots to survive, the balloon's capsule – known to the professionals as a gondola – would have to be pressurized and heated, like the cabin of a jet aircraft.

But it was Lindstrand's third innovation that was most interesting. Part of the reason why traditional hot-air balloons were so thirsty of fuel was that they had little insulation to prevent the huge volumes of air inside them from cooling down. Lindstrand wanted to go one step further than mere insulation. He wanted the material from which the balloon was made to act as a combination of greenhouse and Thermos flask. In the daytime it would trap the energy from the rays of the sun (which is much brighter above the clouds than below), and use it to warm up the air inside; at night, it would insulate the contents and prevent them from cooling down. By this combination, the balloon would be able to stay aloft for much longer and on less fuel than a standard design.

Richard Branson was undoubtedly impressed by Lindstrand's presentation. But that did not prevent him from negotiating hard over the terms on which they would do business – so much so that it took many meetings over the next three months before a formal contract between the two sides was agreed and signed. Branson was insistent on three points. First, he would not on any account pay Lindstrand a pilot's fee. Second, he demanded that Thunder & Colt should provide the balloon to Virgin at cost price. And third, he wanted detailed assurances from Lindstrand on how the publicity surrounding the trip should be handled. Lindstrand would be forbidden to talk to the press for the duration of the project and the preparations running up to it without prior written permission from Virgin; he would be forbidden to write a book about his experiences; and he must make sure in public to refer to Richard Branson at all times as the captain of the craft.

Though these demands may have sounded ludicrous, Branson's staff and advisers had persuasive arguments for them. On the pilot's fee, he pointed out that the Atlantic crossing was clearly something that Lindstrand wanted to do anyway, so there was no reason why he should be paid for it. On the question of the manufacturing fee, Branson knew that even though Thunder & Colt would win little recognition among the general public for having made the balloon, its involvement in the project would be well known in the ballooning world. Customers would beat a path to its doors when they read about the crossing, and Thunder & Colt would undoubtedly profit from extra business. There was no reason, therefore, why Virgin should do any more than cover the manufacturing costs of the balloon. As for the publicity, Lindstrand should know that achieving increased bookings for the airline was the primary reason for Virgin to become involved. Unless the group had compete discretion over the handling of public relations, the benefits could not be assured. In particular, it was important for Branson himself to be seen not as a mere passenger, but as the leading light of the adventure. After all, Richard Branson was not just a millionaire record boss. He was a *daredevil* millionaire record boss.

For an independent-minded man like Lindstrand, this was a galling list of stipulations. It appeared to pay too much attention to the commercial imperatives of the sponsor, and not enough to the experience, the skills and the courage that would be needed to make the project a success. But there was at least one respect in which Branson had read Lindstrand absolutely correctly. The Swede's enthusiasm to build his balloon and cross the Atlantic in it burned visibly in his eyes. He was therefore willing to accept terms that a less dedicated balloonist might well have refused.

Lindstrand's acceptance of the Virgin terms, and his growing liking for Branson as they began to work together on the project, was tempered by a distaste for what he saw as the contrast between Branson's private style and his expansive public persona. When there was business to be done, Branson loved to haggle; he had a street trader's aptitude for negotiation, knowing exactly when to talk and when to stay silent, when to press his counterpart on a point and when simply to walk away. In public, however, Branson disdained small economies, and loved to dispense the patronage that was at the disposal of someone who owned an airline.

Thunder & Colt had a standing arrangement that would allow its employees to fly free on Virgin Atlantic when they needed to cross the Atlantic on business, in return for providing free balloons or associated services up to the same value as the air tickets used. Virgin was always fastidiously insistent that Thunder & Colt employees travelling under this 'contra' deal must be treated as standby passengers – and thus denied the automatic rights such as seat reservations, limousine pick-up and use of the Virgin airport lounge that passengers paying full business class fares would receive. Yet Lindstrand had been told about an incident that took place while Branson was checking in at Gatwick which contrasted sharply with this attitude. An elderly couple at the desk were arguing with the Virgin ground staff over a flight delay, asking to be switched to another airline's flight to New York rather than to be forced to wait for the next available Virgin flight. Faced with a flat refusal, the couple explained tearfully that they were flying across the Atlantic for the funeral of their son. Unless they were switched, they would be unable to see his face before the coffin lid was closed. Couldn't something be done, they begged. That was the point at which Branson stepped in, to the astonishment and delight of the other passengers watching the incident. 'Put them on Concorde,' he said.

Virgin had two good reasons to keep secret the preparations for the balloon crossing. One was that work on the balloon started well before the second attempt to break the Atlantic sea record; releasing any details of what Lindstrand and Branson were up to would have made no commercial sense. The excitement over the proposed balloon crossing, which was technically more interesting and photographically more spectacular than any surface crossing could be, would have cannibalized the press coverage of *Challenger II*.

The other reason was that Virgin was in the process of going public. Roger Seelig had decided to make a virtue out of Richard Branson's adventurous nature, since he could not disguise it, but he knew that there was a limit to what institutional investors would take. It required little technical knowledge to realize that for all the perils of rough seas, travelling in a powerboat across the surface of the ocean was a great deal less dangerous than flying across the ocean in a tin can suspended beneath a ball of fire almost 30,000 feet above the water. Until Virgin was quite ready to tell the world about the balloon that Thunder & Colt were building, the project was to be kept absolutely secret.

It was by mistake that the news was let out in December 1986. Chris Witty, project director for the second powerboat expedition, got chatting to a journalist from the *Daily Express* during a flight across the Atlantic on which the two were sitting together. When the journalist asked him a question about 'hot air', Witty forgot for a moment that *Hot Air* was the name of the airline's in-flight magazine. Instead, he assumed that the journalist already knew about the balloon project. Unaware that his comments would later appear in print, he explained that Branson was very keen on the idea, but that his staff at Virgin were still trying to persuade him not to do it. 'It could be very dangerous,' Witty said – adding that since Branson headed the Virgin Group, his safety had become a matter not just of his own personal concern, but also of the vital interests of the business he had founded. A day or two later, Witty read with growing horror an article in the *Express* gossip column entitled WHAT A GAS! NOW IT'S BRANSON THE VIRGIN BAL-LOONIST. The article described the crossing as 'a madcap scheme' and 'a dangerous new stunt', and pointed out that by comparison with the boat crossing, it would be 'far more risky and would cost many thousands in rescue back-up services'. Branson's 'anxious staff', however, were 'trying to talk him out of it by dreaming up less dangerous challenges'.

When the article appeared, Branson was already far from London, beginning an early Christmas holiday on his private Caribbean island. There might therefore have been some hope that the article would either not be noticed, or would have been forgotten by the time he returned. But Witty was not to be so lucky. Alerted to the story's publication, Branson lost no time in telephoning Witty from his holiday retreat. Accustomed since his arrival at Virgin to a boss who was quicker to praise than to condemn, Witty was astonished to hear a stream of vitriol down the telephone, with Branson 'effing and blinding' at him for having allowed the news of the balloon crossing not only to get out prematurely, but also to cast such an unfavourable light on the Virgin chairman himself. It was some weeks after his return from Necker before relations between Branson and Witty cooled.

Luckily, the aspiring balloonist had a great deal to occupy himself with. As a good swimmer who had already been fished out of the Atlantic once, he did not need to undergo any special training for a possible sea rescue. But there were many other skills to pick up before Richard Branson could serve as a competent partner to Per Lindstrand. One was radio operation – a course which he passed more because of the instructor's goodwill than because of the level of skill that he had attained. A senior Virgin employee involved in the project, conscious that the survival of the two men might well depend on Branson's ability to operate the radio, was understandably horrified to be told by the instructor that a student bearing a less illustrious name might not have been awarded the certificate.

Another was parachuting: since the two might have to abandon ship at 28,000 feet, Branson would need to have at least a rudimentary knowledge of the techniques of free-fall and parachuting. It was on his first jump that disaster very nearly struck – producing the video recording that gave Roger Seelig such disquiet over his breakfast. Even with the hours of work that he put in, however, it would have been unfair to expect Branson to reach the same level of expertise as Lindstrand. With his military training, his experience as an aircraft and balloon pilot, and his knowledge of survival techniques, Lindstrand could board and fly a balloon with a deep sense of calm that was the consequence of not having to think before he acted. But there was a limit to what Branson, who had never been up in a serious balloon six months before the take-off date, could do. The Swedish airman later heard one of the project team joke that the crew of the *Virgin Atlantic Flyer*, as the balloon was to be called, would be made up of three members: Lindstrand himself, Branson and a dog. Lindstrand's job was to fly the balloon; Branson's was to feed the dog; and the dog's job was to bite Richard Branson if he touched any of the controls inside the cabin. In the event, Lindstrand was to estimate after the flight that Branson had spent little more than ten minutes in full control of the *Atlantic Flyer* – and to wonder whether the purpose of the 'gagging clause' of his contract was to prevent the general public from learning just how little Branson had to do with the job of actually flying the balloon.

Although he may never have been cut out to be a professional balloonist, the Branson name and the business skills that came with it were of indisputable value to the project. After finding around half a million pounds from Virgin's own coffers for the construction and delivery of the balloon, and putting in more than the same amount again to pay the bill for the ground staff and the publicity that would be needed, Branson worked hard to find sponsors to offset Virgin's risk. Once again, his eye for a good picture story came to the rescue: TVS, a regional British television company, agreed to commission a documentary film about the project, whose working title was *Two Men in a Balloon*. In return for unrestricted access to Branson and Lindstrand – and the right to use all the footage from a small video camera that Branson himself would operate inside the cabin – the company would pay a fee of £100,000, and also make a satellite feed of live television pictures from the launch site available free of charge for the BBC and ITN to show on their evening news bulletins. This would ensure that the pictures so essential for publicizing Virgin Atlantic would be available to news editors in London even if they did not consider it worthwhile to send their own camera crew and equipment truck to the launch site in the United States. It was thanks to this agreement that Richard Branson was later to make an unprecedented two appearances in a single week on the 'Wogan' chat-show.

Branson also managed to cut through red tape that might otherwise have put a stop to the project. On one occasion, for instance, Lindstrand telephoned him with the news that an essential altitude-chamber test on the prototype could not be carried out because the aerospace company that owned the tunnel had booked it out to other customers every day for the next two years. 'Give me the name and phone number of the chairman of the company,' said Branson – and two hours later, he called back with the news that not only was the chamber now immediately available, but also that, as a gesture of goodwill to the project, the normal charge of £2,000 an hour would be waived.

The welcome that awaited the two balloonists when they arrived at Sugarloaf, Maine, was characteristic of the warmth of rural New England. The area, chosen for its proximity to the coast and for the shelter from winds necessary to inflate the world's largest ever balloon, is a popular ski resort in the winter. In the summer it is beautiful but sleepy. The local radio station broadcast almost non-stop *Atlantic Flyer* bulletins, while local restaurants offered 'ballooning specials' to the visitors and to the hordes of television, radio and newspaper journalists who had descended on Sugarloaf to report the launch.

With the experience of the *Challenger* crossings behind him, Branson was not surprised to discover that the good weather promised by Bob Rice, the team's meteorologist, had disappeared by the time he arrived at Sugarloaf. As day after day passed, the team amused themselves by spending their free time white-water rafting down nearby rivers. But there was much for Branson and Lindstrand to do. Not all the equipment for the balloon capsule and its launch had arrived; spare parts and components continued to dribble in, and to be checked and fitted under Lindstrand's supervision, for several days. For the Virgin chairman, the balloon itself was enough to concentrate on. He realized that, with little more than a weekend's orientation at Thunder & Colt's headquarters in Oswestry under his belt, he had come dangerously unprepared. The extra few days offered by the adverse weather could be usefully spent familiarizing himself with the switches and dials in the circular aluminium gondola in which he would be spending three or more sleepless days and nights.

But there were distractions. One was the management of the Virgin businesses back in London. While Lindstrand did his best to drill his fellow traveller in all the things he would need to know, Branson's attention was all too often drawn by pressing questions at the airline, the record business or the communications division. With faxes and telephones easily available, courtesy of the cheap and efficient American telephone network, it was all too tempting to spend several hours a day talking to colleagues, business partners, lawyers and accountants.

The other distraction was the vast press corps that had assembled to witness the take-off. This was excellent news for Branson and Lindstrand; it ensured that their attempt on the ballooning record would be fully reported to Virgin's advantage. The height of interest in their expedition was to a great extent the consequence of the friendly, easy-going approach that the company took in its dealings with the press. From Branson himself downwards, everyone at Virgin seemed to be aware of how important it was to feed the journalists with interesting, punchy quotations for their stories. They also understood the importance of dreaming up a fresh 'angle' on the story every day that would enable the journalists on the spot to convince their editors that something genuinely new that required reporting had happened since the day before. Providing good 'photo opportunities' mattered, too: given the greater attraction to editors of stories that can be easily and dramatically illustrated, Virgin's ability to generate exciting pictures helped win it coverage that might otherwise have been missed.

But in part, the attraction of the story to journalists was the risk: even with Lindstrand's experience and skills, the proposed crossing was a hazardous enterprise that might well cost Branson his life. Such an outcome would be regrettable, certainly; but it would also be a powerful and sensational story, comparable in its scale and visual force to the destruction of the space shuttle *Challenger* earlier in the decade. Any television company or newspaper that resisted the temptation to send a reporter to cover the beginning of the crossing had to prepare for the possibility that the two men might be killed in a sudden and spectacular fireball only a few hundred feet above the forests of Maine. No serious news organization would wish to lose such a story to its rivals. Branson may have been dimly aware that this was the reason for the presence of so many journalists, but he only realized it fully on dropping in to a mobile editing suite being used by the staff of Independent Television News for a chat with one of the station's staff. Inside the vehicle a film was running on a video monitor: an early version of his own obituary.

The other members of the project team were initially astonished at the amused calmness with which the Virgin chairman told this story, as if it were nothing more than an elaborate joke at his own expense. But they realized gradually that this was Branson's way of dealing with stress, with fear, and with the pressure from Joan to stop doing things that would endanger his own life and his family's happiness. Proof of the underlying gravity of the issue came the day before the balloon was scheduled to lift off, when a pair of lawyers paid a discreet call on Branson at his hotel. The man who always seemed to behave as if he believed himself immortal had decided to make his will.

Branson and Lindstrand retired early in the afternoon of the day before they were due to fly the Atlantic. Though both men usually slept soundly, they realized that it was imperative for both of them to get some rest. With a flight ahead of them that could well keep them awake for two nights in succession, they would need to be as alert as they possibly could be at the beginning of the expedition; yet the adrenalin might keep them going anyway. The solution to the problem was found courtesy of America's National Aeronautics and Space Administration. The organization responsible for launching dozens of astronauts into space was familiar with the problem of insomnia the night before take-off, and had specially formulated sleeping pills for the purpose. A couple of swallows, a sip of water, and Branson and Lindstrand slept deeply and calmly for eight or nine hours.

At three o'clock the following morning, the two men were awoken and driven by car into the wide open space among the trees where the balloon had been inflated. It was an impressive sight; taller than Nelson's column, the *Virgin Atlantic Flyer* was a vast balloon whose top half was almost spherical, its heat-retaining coating black and glistening in the arc lights installed for its inflation. Beneath the envelope and above the gondola, powerful burners threw jets of blue and yellow flame upwards to heat the air that would carry Branson and Lindstrand across the Atlantic. Ropes tethered the craft tightly to the ground; there was barely a quiver of wind in the sky.

Dawn was already breaking by the time the two climbed into their seats inside the aluminium capsule. When Branson got up to wave a final goodbye through the transparent observation dome at the top of the capsule, however, he had a shock. The gentle bump that he had assumed was something to do with the removing of the guy ropes holding the *Flyer* to the ground had in fact been more serious. A line had tangled around one of the craft's six pairs of fuel tanks, and had ripped them forcibly off their mounts. The tanks had tumbled to the ground, luckily without hurting any of the ground crew still close to the balloon. But the loss of the tanks had reduced the balloon's weight by several hundred pounds; and as a result, it had risen majestically off the ground with several large sandbags still attached to it by ropes. As Branson peered from the observation dome, he saw that the ground was already more than a hundred feet below, and the *Flyer* was climbing with almost imperceptible acceleration towards the sky. After checking in with air traffic control, Lindstrand jettisoned the sandbags at 12,000 feet by climbing out of the capsule and cutting the ropes with his Swiss Army knife. It was now too late to bring the balloon down in order to reattach the fallen tanks; yet without them, the two men no longer had enough fuel to be confident of reaching land on the far side of the Atlantic.

FOURTEEN

Flying Across Two Oceans

RICHARD BRANSON and Per Lindstrand considered their options. The capsule in which they were sitting was by now high in the sky above Sugarloaf, Maine, and the *Virgin Atlantic Flyer* was performing exactly as predicted in all respects except one: it had left one of its six pairs of fuel tanks on the ground. Should they play safe by aborting the crossing and trying to land the balloon in the United States? Or should they take a chance and continue? The argument against the first option was that there was no way to navigate the *Flyer* back to the point from which it had taken off; but if it landed anywhere else, there was every chance that the envelope would be torn and the attempt on the record would have to be abandoned for the year. The argument against the second option was that the fuel they were to carry had been carefully calculated to get them across the Atlantic with just the right safety margin. Any more, and the balloon would be heavier than it need be; any less, and they would face an unacceptably high risk of being forced to ditch in the ocean before reaching Europe. The loss of two tanks had dangerously reduced the balloon's effective range.

They decided to continue. And with the luck of the brave, the two balloonists soon found that conditions were improving sharply. The *Flyer* climbed smoothly upwards, and its capsule pressurized correctly as planned. It continued to rise until it reached 27,000 feet, the centre of the jet-stream that would carry them across the ocean. After six hours, they had covered 500 miles; after ten, they had broken the world distance record for a hot-air balloon flight. But Branson and Lindstrand had no opportunity to quit while they were ahead. They were by now almost a third of the way out into the Atlantic, and simple prudence dictated that they should continue the flight until they were over land at the other side.

Only a couple of mishaps interrupted the smoothness of the crossing. At one stage, the balloon jerked fiercely upwards as if it had collided with something; it was only a minute or two later, as a message came through on the radio from a passing Concorde, that the two realized that they had merely been shaken by the sonic boom caused by the airliner's supersonic flight miles above their heads. Later, a Virgin Atlantic 747, carrying Eve Branson and most of the project team across to Britain from the United States, described an elegant figure-of-eight around the balloon, its passengers oohing and aahing through the windows at the sight of the airline's chairman floating serenely in his balloon nearby.

When the *Flyer* was only a few hundred miles short of the Irish coast, however, a more serious problem came up. The heat-retention system that Lindstrand had designed into the envelope was working spectacularly well; the warmth of the daytime sun was keeping the air inside the envelope so warm that far less fuel was needed to provide lift than they had imagined. But an apparently trivial detail of the system proved its weakest point. To prevent the balloon from rising further than it should during the middle of the day, the envelope was equipped with a small vent at the top, from which hot air could be released. The winding mechanism to this vent, however, seemed to have failed – with the result that the *Atlantic Flyer* began to climb swiftly. If the balloon rose too high, lack of oxygen in the outside air would douse the engine that kept its cabin pressurized and provided electricity for its radio; and the two would have to perform a record-breaking parachute jump, from an altitude at which the air was too thin and too cold to breathe.

Richard Branson had good reason to wish, as he fastened the parachute harness around his waist and prepared to bail out of the balloon, that he had taken his parachuting lessons more seriously. But by some happy chance, his skills were not to be tested on this occasion. As Lindstrand continued to work the winding mechanism that controlled the vent in the balloon, he suddenly felt a tug of movement as the vent reopened. The *Atlantic Flyer* started its descent back towards its cruising altitude of 27,000 feet. Just after lunch on the Friday, after less than thirty hours of flight, the craft passed over Donegal, on Ireland's west coast. The objective of crossing the Atlantic was now achieved in all but name. The job that remained was to bring the balloon safely down to earth.

That proved harder than either of the men aboard expected. So efficient had been the heat-retaining envelope designed by Lindstrand that three of the *Flyer*'s fuel tanks were still unused. It would not be prudent to risk a bumpy landing with the potentially explosive tanks still aboard, so the obvious solution was to drop them – and to do so from beneath the clouds, so that it would be possible to confirm beforehand that the tanks would not hit anything. But manoeuvring the vast balloon gently downwards to below the cloud line and then back up again proved more tricky than Lindstrand had expected. As they approached the hamlet of Limavady, in the Ulster countryside, the *Atlantic Flyer* was suddenly pushed downwards without warning by a draught of cold air, and crashed with a sickening jar into a field. The tanks had fallen off without requiring any action at all, and the radio aerials underneath the capsule were broken; Branson and Lindstrand were now effectively isolated from the outside world. Meanwhile, the sudden reduction in its weight pulled the balloon sharply and uncontrollably upwards.

Lindstrand decided that the unpredictability of the *Flyer*'s movements gave them only one option for landing. They should try to bring the balloon down on water, as close as possible to the shore. Once they had touched down again, Lindstrand would push the two buttons that fired the explosive bolts releasing the capsule from the envelope, and the two men would wait inside the capsule, floating on the surface of the sea while the vast envelope billowed gently away towards the heavens.

Subsequent investigation suggested that it was because of a short-circuit in one of the batteries that the bolts failed to fire. But as soon as Lindstrand felt a second sickening impact as the capsule hit the water, and felt it pull up again still attached to the envelope above, he knew that the bolts had failed – and that therefore the two men must eject immediately. The risk was too great that the capsule might detach from the balloon a few hundred or a few thousand feet above the sea, at an altitude far too high from which to jump safely but not high enough from which to parachute. He yelled at Branson to jump, pulled himself out of the *Flyer* through the observation dome, and dived into the cold waters of the Irish Sea. He was counting on his partner to follow immediately, for while Lindstrand had been strapped to his seat, engrossed at the controls of the balloon, it was only Branson who had had time to don a safety suit, and to attach to his belt the life-raft and other survival equipment that the two would need when they hit the water.

But Branson did not jump. Perhaps it was because the balloon jerked upwards as soon as Lindstrand jumped out of the capsule, making it impossible for Branson to get his footing until it was too late and the sea was already a hundred feet below. Perhaps it was because Branson himself, facing the uncomfortable prospect of a long swim back to shore in a very cold sea, hesitated for just a few seconds too long. Whatever the reason, however, Richard Branson stayed aboard the *Virgin Atlantic Flyer* – and as Lindstrand wildly waved and shouted at him from below, he floated away beneath a balloon with neither electricity nor fuel, whose capsule was liable to be torn from its envelope at any moment.

The textbook response to the situation, which Branson's trainers had sought to instil in him during his training, was to wait until the balloon had attained an altitude from which it would be safe to parachute, and then bail out. Accordingly, the Virgin chairman put on his parachute harness, checked his life vest and life-raft, and took a deep breath. 'I had done all this exercise blindfold time and again before leaving Sugarloaf, and I should by now have been one hundred per cent comfortable with it,' he said later. 'I knew this was the most important decision I would make in my life. I also knew the chances were that these were the last few minutes of my life. I also knew that the fuel was just about to run out.' Following the strictures of his training, Branson opened up the remaining burners in order to help the *Atlantic Flyer* upwards, and stepped out of the opening at the top of the capsule in preparation for the jump.

But he could not do it. It was a lonely feeling, looking down at the clouds and wondering what hazards he would meet below if he parachuted out. So instead of jumping, Branson strapped himself back into his seat and scribbled a note to Joan and his children telling them he loved them. He then sat at the controls for another five or ten minutes locked in thought. At the end of that period, his mind was made up. 'It dawned on me that rather than taking the risk of parachuting, that if I was to use the balloon as the parachute, and hurl myself off just before it hit the water, that would be the best chance of survival.'

Once again, his extraordinary luck held true. Despite the perilous instability of the bolts that were still holding the capsule to the balloon's envelope, the two main components of the *Flyer* held together for the next twenty minutes or so that he remained inside the capsule. Meanwhile, the balloon floated downwards and westwards through the clouds; and before night fell and reduced visibility destroyed his chances of being found in the water, Branson once again saw the crests of the waves as the balloon floated gently back to earth. Better still, he saw something else: a Royal Navy ship, complete with a military helicopter. He was about to land right in the middle of a naval exercise. Branson waved his spare pair of red underpants at the helicopter pilot, and felt his heart leap as the pilot waved back.

It was only a matter of seconds after Branson bailed out of the balloon above the water before the helicopter was able to winch him out to safety; and only a minute or two more before he was in a hot bath on board ship, a glass of reviving navy grog in his hand.

'Where's Per?' he asked.

'Where's who?' Branson's naval rescuers had recognized Branson on sight. But they had not been following the story of his attempt on the record so closely that they knew he had a travelling companion. So it was not until almost an hour after Per Lindstrand ditched into the water that the expedition to rescue him began in earnest.

More than two miles off the north-eastern tip of Ireland, with the day turning into evening, the water temperature was about 12 degrees centigrade. Without the protection of a survival suit, Per Lindstrand knew, a human being should expect to survive in the sea only about forty-five minutes. Yet the Swedish air force had one of the world's best methods of training for sea survival, since its pilots knew that they might be required to eject into the icy waters of the Baltic. Lindstrand was therefore aware of precisely what he needed to do. Rather than succumb to the natural inclination to curl up into a ball for warmth, he knew that he must swim vigorously. Even if the currents were too strong for him to reach the shore – the tide was going out, so he had little chance of doing so – the resulting boost to his blood circulation might keep him alive for the few minutes that mattered. He also knew what to avoid at all costs: if he allowed his head to be fully submerged, the drop in temperature of the blood circulating around the brain would produce a feeling of euphoria which would be followed in turn by relaxation and then a peaceful, sleepy death by drowning.

Only a few minutes after he hit the water, Lindstrand saw something that raised his spirits tremendously. A lifeboat of the Royal National Lifeboat Institution came speeding across the waves straight towards him. He waved wildly, and shouted at the top of his voice in order to let the boat's pilot know exactly where he was. But the boat merely surged straight ahead and past him, and Lindstrand could just see two figures at its helm looking intently in front of them as the huge balloon carrying Richard Branson glided off into what would soon become a sunset. Half an hour later, a rescue helicopter clattered overhead. But once again, nobody spotted the pilot of the *Atlantic Flyer*. Within a minute, this second possible rescue had moved on without noticing the bedraggled and now weakening figure in the water below.

It was a tribute to the professionalism of the navy helicopter rescue crew that when the machine came to search the area where Branson had said the balloon had first hit the water, it took less than half an hour to locate Lindstrand. But it proved impossible to pull him to safety with the winch. Branson had mistakenly sat in the harness as he was rescued, instead of hooking his arms around it and allowing himself to be pulled upwards by the shoulders. As a result, the cables had become twisted as the winch was pulled back on to its drum, and it could not be disentangled enough to be paid out to Lindstrand in the water. Since the waves were too choppy to allow the helicopter to hover only a few inches above the surface, the helicopter pilot had no alternative but to retreat. It took more time before a dinghy could be found to motor out to Lindstrand and bring him back to land. The Swedish balloonist, his face blue and his teeth chattering uncontrollably, was pulled bodily aboard the dinghy. It was not the fault of those aboard the dinghy that they did not realize the gravity of Lindstrand's condition; the airman was unable to say a single word except 'Branson'. But he was given nothing more than a woman's sweater to wear, and his hypothermia worsened as gusts of cold air tore into his body as the dinghy sped back to the shore at 35 mph. The perilously ill Lindstrand was immediately put aboard a helicopter to be flown to the nearest hospital, at Kilmarnock in Scotland.

A crowd was waiting for the returning hero when Richard Branson and Per Lindstrand dismounted from the helicopter at Kilmarnock. What seemed like 2,000 people had vaulted over the hospital fences and rushed towards the machine before its rotor blades slowed to a stop, desperate to catch a glimpse. Branson, dressed fetchingly in a Royal Navy jumpsuit covered with impressive zips and pockets, stepped out first. Behind him, obscured by the brightness of the Virgin chairman's smile, was Lindstrand. He was still alive, but wore nothing but a grey blanket and some underwear. On catching sight of the crowd of well-wishers, Lindstrand wrapped the blanket around his head and closed his eyes. When he opened them again, the crowd had disappeared. Richard Branson was galloping towards the entrance of the hospital; the spectators, like children following a latter-day Pied Piper, were trotting obediently behind him.

They had a celebration dinner in a nearby hotel that night. The head waiter was asked to leave the telephone off the hook, in order to give the two balloonists some respite from the flood of calls from newspapers across the world. Lindstrand's wife was present, and so were the rescue crews; Penni Pike, Branson's secretary, served as a proxy for Joan Templeman, for whom the prospect of this perilous journey had been too traumatic to contemplate. A wedding was being celebrated in the hotel on the same evening; so it was only natural that the visiting celebrity should make a funny speech. As the evening progressed and successively more raucous toasts were drunk, an exhausted Per Lindstrand looked on in bemusement as Richard Branson once again became the life and soul of someone else's party.

*　　*　　*

Merely having survived the crossing was excuse enough for celebration. But the coverage of the crossing in the American press during the succeeding week guaranteed that the flight would also prove a commercial success for Branson in his most important overseas market. The story of the *Atlantic Flyer* not only made it to the front page of the *New York Times*, but also appeared as a full-page article in *Newsweek*. Once again, the story won blanket coverage in the British media; and it was not hard to see why. Virgin had thought carefully at a very early stage about how to make the story attractive to print and broadcast journalists, and once again had made arrangements for Richard Branson to give interviews over the radio during the flight itself.

Only one cloud appeared in the otherwise blue sky of public adulation. Late in the day on which the two men had been rescued, a journalist from the *Observer* telephoned the centre in the Post Office Tower from which operations were being managed with an odd question. Was it the case, he asked Chris Witty, that the reason the explosive bolts had failed to fire, and the two men had thus been forced to ditch in the sea rather than landing safely on dry land, was because Richard Branson had depleted the balloon's electrical supply by spending too much time giving interviews over the radio? The exact details of that conversation remain the subject of controversy. But the indisputable result was that the next issue of the *Observer* contained a prominent story under the headline BRANSON'S OWN HOT AIR TO BLAME. 'Pop millionaire Richard Branson's thirst for publicity may have contributed to the near-disaster in which his transatlantic balloon crossing finally ended,' the story began. It quoted Witty, Virgin's manager of special projects, as saying: 'There were long interviews using the radio and we knew power was low. You can't stop Richard talking to the media.'

Soon after the story's publication, the hapless Witty was once again carpeted by his irate employer. He was warned formally by letter that it was only his otherwise exemplary performance in the job that had saved him from the consequences of this public relations setback. Had it been another member of the Virgin staff, the story might well have led to an immediate dismissal. It was not simply that the Virgin chairman was personally irritated that he had been made to look foolish by an allegation which both he and Lindstrand later could prove had no foundation at all in fact. More importantly, Richard Branson was becoming increasingly aware that his reputation was a bankable asset for his businesses. Nothing must be allowed to reduce its value.

Given the lengths to which the Virgin chairman had gone in order to make sure that the balloon trip paid its way, Per Lindstrand did not expect to receive a sympathetic hearing for his next proposal. Within a matter of months after the Atlantic landing, he had put together a more ambitious plan to fly the far longer distance across the Pacific. There was just one difficulty; the obvious route for such a flight would be from south-eastern Japan to California – and although Virgin Atlantic already flew between London and California, it was only just beginning to establish a route between London and Tokyo. Until there was a Japanese business big enough to promote, Lindstrand feared, Richard Branson would not be interested in ballooning across the Pacific.

To his surprise, the Swedish balloonist realized that Branson had been bitten by the ballooning bug. Despite the lesser commercial attractions of the venture, despite his brush with death when the Atlantic crossing went wrong, despite even the fact that the Pacific crossing would be significantly more dangerous, since a balloon would be out of helicopter range for far longer, and there would be fewer ships close enough to effect a sea rescue – despite all these concerns, Branson was immediately gripped by the idea of spectacularly breaking the record that the two men had just set. The fact that eight lives had already been lost in attempts to conquer the Pacific by balloon did not deter him in the least.

Yet he did not allow enthusiasm to overcome his commercial instincts. Once again, the negotiation of the agreement between Virgin and Lindstrand's firm took many meetings. Once again, Virgin went to enormous lengths to secure the sponsorship from other companies that would reduce the cost of the project. This time, however, the prize was potentially greater still. With the help of Dentsu, Japan's largest advertising agency, Virgin secured a lucrative deal with Otsuka, a Japanese pharmaceutical company that had a thriving soft-drinks business. As a result, it became clear at the planning stage that the six massive fuel tanks needed to send the new balloon across the Pacific would be in the shape of drink cans. They would carry the words Pocari Sweat – for this, unlikely as it sounded, is the name of one of the leading soft drink brands in the Japanese market. As part of the deal with Otsuka, Branson and Lindstrand agreed to be photographed drinking Pocari Sweat; because neither of them found Otsuka's product palatable, however, they were forced to empty the cans and fill them up with something else.

It was in October 1989 that the capsule for the *Virgin Pacific Flyer* was completed. Together with the balloon's envelope, neatly folded so that it would fit inside a standard 20-foot freight container, it was shipped off to Miyakonojo, the small town on the Japanese island of Kyushu from which Lindstrand had decided to attempt the crossing. Small-town Japan gave the two men a generous welcome. Miyakonojo's town council provided hundreds of tiny Union Jacks (but no Swedish flags, since Lindstrand had long since assumed British nationality) for the local schoolchildren to wave. Songs of welcome were sung. In an attempt to match this warmth, Virgin flew a British military band over to Japan to participate in the celebrations. The company also paid £87,000 for the services of the Shinto priests who arrived to bless the balloon before its intended departure; though Lindstrand observed to his chagrin that the scale of the spending necessary did not prevent Richard Branson from disputing an item costing £150 on his invoice as the two men travelled together in a taxi.

Since the experience of the Atlantic crossing had taught Branson not to expect the take-off to proceed on schedule, he was not surprised when the first two attempts to launch the balloon had to be called off because of bad weather. In any case, he and the rest of the team had plenty to entertain them in the bars and restaurants of the town – and the locals, unaccustomed to visits from Westerners even towards the end of the twentieth century, were intensely curious to meet them. Four thousand cars, and more than ten thousand people, turned up in the middle of the night to see the inflation of the balloon when the weathermen finally gave their blessing. It was a spectacular sight: a huge darkened sphere, glistening with frost and with the light of ten thousand flashguns.

Yet the sight struck fear into Lindstrand's heart. Because it had been only a last-minute decision to abort a take-off the previous evening, the launch helpers had decided to leave the envelope out on the ground overnight – and the frost, unprecedented in the semi-tropical climate of that part of southern Japan, had caused the different layers of the *Pacific Flyer*'s energy-saving envelope to separate. Lindstrand watched in silent horror as silver foil peeled off in ever larger strips as the balloon grew larger. When he realized that the lining was coming off inside the balloon, he concluded that the launch would have to be aborted.

A lump in his throat, Richard Branson assumed the responsibility of making the speech that would so sorely disappoint the spectators and the team members. He explained why it would not be possible to fly the Pacific; he admitted that since the manufacture of a new balloon would take many months, the crossing would have to be postponed for a year; and he apologized and thanked everyone in equal measure.

The sponsors were not pleased. Nor were the two companies that had been responsible for the manufacture of the envelope fabric, for they detected in the reports of Branson's speech an implication that it had been their own defective workmanship that was the reason for the cancellation of the attempt. They consequently refused to participate in a second try, one of them even resisting the ultimate pressure of a lunch for its company chairman with Richard Branson himself. Per Lindstrand was therefore forced to find two new suppliers, and to start rebuilding the envelope from scratch. During the succeeding months, negotiations with Branson once again took a turn for the worse – and the suspicion began to grow in his mind that the narrowness of his escape from death on the Atlantic run had belatedly rattled the Virgin chairman. Was Richard Branson now looking for an excuse to avoid flying the Pacific?

Even if he was, Branson was given no opportunity. When Virgin's staff in Tokyo proved unable to issue a new date for the next attempt on the Pacific record, the mayor of Miyakonojo took it on himself to fly to London and to remind Branson face to face that he had promised to return and try again. The implication was clear: if he failed to keep that promise, Branson should no longer expect his businesses to have a good name in Japan. But in the event, the warning was unnecessary. Richard Branson was ready and willing to come back for a second try, and he was prepared to set a provisional date in December 1990 on which he would do so.

Once again, it was weeks before the weathermen could predict a clear pair of days for the flight; once again Branson, Lindstrand and their team whiled away almost a month in Miyakonojo. With a business to run, the Virgin chairman spent many hours every day on the telephone, and took every opportunity to slip away to America or Europe for a few days to keep an eye on things. As Christmas approached, it became clear that the reduced rescue cover over the Pacific during the public holidays made it essential for the launch to be postponed until the New Year; so Branson took his family off for a holiday in the sun.

Soon after their return, the two balloonists were able to wish good luck to a rival. Fumio Niwa, a Japanese balloonist, was hoping to accomplish the far easier task of crossing the Pacific in a helium balloon – but to do so alone, rather than with a companion. But Niwa's attempt turned out to be an alarming reminder of the perils that had befallen Branson and Lindstrand. After calling off his first attempt (and in the process making himself unpopular with the Japanese rescue services), Niwa eventually lifted off at 4 AM on 11 January 1991. Less than 200 miles away from land, however, the Japanese balloonist ran into difficulties and was forced to ditch. With the help of the ground crew who were intending to track the *Pacific Flyer*, it took no more than a few hours for the authorities to discover the position of Niwa's life-raft, and to dispatch a flying boat to pick him up. Unfortunately, the waves were just a little too high for the flying boat to land; so its pilot dropped a marker buoy and radioed for a helicopter to winch up the shivering but still healthy balloonist. The helicopter, however, did not come. A bureaucratic problem arose over where the helicopter should be dispatched from and whether one was available; and by the time the machine was found and sent, it was dark. The marker buoy could not be found; nor could Niwa. When the helicopter returned at first light, he was found floating peacefully in his life-raft very close to his original ditch position. He was dead.

After this, the launch of the *Pacific Flyer* was certain to be a graver affair than the previous attempt. To Lindstrand's surprise, it was a textbook take-off: the vast balloon glided serenely into the air, the cabin compression system worked perfectly, and the two men soon found themselves sailing along in the middle of the jetstream at breathtaking speed. But getting out of Japanese airspace turned out to be more difficult than expected. The Japanese air traffic controllers, who were in radio contact with the balloon just as if it were a commercial airliner, told Lindstrand that he should change course in order to pass through one of the official 'reporting points' used by airliners entering and leaving the country's airspace. Lindstrand tried to explain over the radio that since he was piloting a balloon, he was unable to steer it sufficiently precisely to obey this instruction. Unable to understand his response, the Japanese ground controller became angrier and angrier, telling him finally that he would be forbidden to leave Japanese airspace unless he passed through one of the reporting points. In the end, Lindstrand did the only sensible thing; he read the name of one of the reporting points off his map, and said that he was changing course to pass through it. Unable to confirm whether or not the balloonist had done so, the controller was mollified. But the incident served only to increase Lindstrand's resolve to get into United States airspace, and into the hands of American rescue teams, as soon as possible.

Knowing the effect that sudden changes in weight could have on the behaviour of the balloon, the two men took particular care as they prepared to jettison their first empty fuel tank. As soon as the switch was thrown, and the explosive detonator had severed the tank from its housing, the balloon wrenched upwards with a horrifying jolt, and swung over to one side at a sharp angle. White-faced, Branson and Lindstrand knew that something had once again gone wrong with the system of holding the fuel supplies to the capsule. As well as dropping a single empty fuel tank, they had jettisoned two further full tanks – leaving themselves with little more than half the fuel they needed to get to America. Branson continued to talk quickly into the video camera installed inside the capsule; but the camera could not fail to pick up the anxiety in the exchanges between the two men after they discovered the disaster.

LINDSTRAND There's always a chance. We'll go swimming otherwise.
BRANSON Bloody electricians! [. . .] Instead of 70–80 hours' duration, we have about 35 left. So we have a few headaches

ahead. It may seem ridiculous me carrying on filming at the moment, but there's not much else we can do and in some ways it's quite therapeutic. I hope we get as close to the Californian coast as possible. [. . .] We want to know, if we're not going to make Canada or landfall, where the most stable seas are. [Speaking into the radio] As a rough idea, how rough is it near Canada, over? [. . .] America is not important if we can find out about [the seas] . . .

LINDSTRAND We want to get to America. The chances are we have a much higher chance of finding a boat near America. The coast guards have helicopters that can go 500 miles.

BRANSON Well, I think almost definitely we're going to have to do a sea landing.

LINDSTRAND I'm not so sure.

In the event, it was Lindstrand who was right. A fire broke out briefly when blobs of frozen fuel caught light and dripped incandescently on to the transparent observation dome above the capsule, only to be doused by lack of oxygen by a speedily executed climb towards thinner air. Radio contact was lost between the balloon and its US control station for more than seven hours, leading the project controllers on the ground to declare 'Operation Spanner' (the code word previously agreed to keep secret the bad news that things were going wrong), and prompting Branson's press chief Will Whitehorn to prepare for the task of telling the world's media that his employer was dead and executing his final wishes. Frantic airline staff had to be restrained from sending the nearest Virgin Atlantic 747 out over the Pacific to look for their lost chairman. Then the balloonists' voices crackled reassuringly back across the ether as unexpectedly as they had disappeared.

Despite these upsets, the balloon rode the jet stream safely towards America at such a good speed that it would clearly make land even without the two lost fuel tanks. The landing was to be no simple matter. Instead of touching down gently in California or Oregon, which was the route they had hoped to take, Lindstrand and Branson found themselves swept uncontrollably northwards past Canada and towards Alaska. Their eventual landing-point was to be in the middle of a frozen lake deep in the frozen wastes near Yellowknife.

The capsule hit the ground at speed – Lindstrand later described the feeling as similar to being aboard a 'rocket-powered sledge' – and for once, the explosive bolts fired perfectly. The *Flyer*'s envelope lifted gracefully off, floated upwards for a few seconds, began to empty itself of air, and glided majestically off to the trees a few hundred yards away.

Outside, it was almost thirty degrees centigrade below zero. Lindstrand gave silent thanks that he had been persuaded, against his better judgement, to pack the insulation overalls that would keep them from freezing to death in the snow and ice. After an attempt to get out and explore – of which the two men hastily thought better when they were hit by the freezing blast of wind – Lindstrand and Branson settled down inside the capsule to wait to be rescued. Five hours later, having seen no living creature but an otter in the meantime, they heard the clatter of a helicopter's rotor blades. The rescue team, making use of two chartered executive jets and such rescue helicopters as they could lay their hands on, and braving appalling Alaskan winter conditions, had found them. It was not a moment too soon: Branson already had a touch of frostbite on one foot, and Lindstrand on a finger. But now they were safe. Gathering up the video tapes that would be used to make a television documentary about the crossing, and leaving the balloon itself to be dismembered and turned into superior tenting material by a band of local native Americans, Richard Branson prepared to go home.

It was not Branson's fault that the Pacific crossing was such a disappointment in publicity terms. Everything had been carefully prepared. The standard arrangements had been made for radio interviews during the flight. Journalists had been flown to Japan and to America to make sure that papers unable to afford the air tickets could still cover the story. Film footage had been made available. And Virgin's staff had fought for the company's interests as vociferously as ever. At one stage, before the balloon had lifted off from Miyakonojo, a dispute had taken place inside the capsule itself between the rival representatives of Virgin and its Japanese co-sponsors over the question of which company would have the right to place its advertising stickers in the locations that would be most prominently visible in the television programmes made from the video footage shot by Richard Branson.

There was just one difficulty: the Gulf War had broken out soon after the balloon took off. This made the project more exciting, and more worrying for its participants, for it raised the risk that Branson and Lindstrand might either be denied landing rights in United States airspace because of the level of alert on which the military was placed, or worse still might actually be mistaken for an enemy aircraft and shot down. But in news terms, the beginning of the campaign to eject Saddam Hussein's troops from Kuwait dwarfed the breaking of a mere record, no matter how heroically the Pacific had been flown. For once, it was hard to interest the world's press in the doings of Richard Branson.

Once he was rescued, Branson immediately threw himself into the urgent task of preparing his airline for the slump in traffic that would inevitably result from the outbreak of hostilities. On receiving the news of the Gulf War on the radio during the flight, Lindstrand had observed that worries about the future of his business made Branson immediately more pensive and silent. He had good reason to be so.

For Lindstrand himself, however, the trip was a triumph. Just as Branson had suspected during their negotiations, the successful flight helped to establish his firm as the biggest supplier of civilian balloons in the Japanese market. And Lindstrand had the extra satisfaction of knowing that his technical expertise as a designer and builder of balloons was unsurpassed. The scientist and inventor in him took great pride from knowing that the balloon in which he and Branson had flown the Pacific was 216 per cent more fuel efficient than the Atlantic balloon he had built less than three years earlier.

Branson's satisfaction was of a different kind. His ballooning days were now over: for after receiving a talking-to from his father, he resolved that for the sake of his wife – Joan, who he had finally married the year before – and their children he would never again undertake such perilous exploits. But the knowledge he and his employees acquired from their dealings with Per Lindstrand and the sponsoring companies allowed them to build up a new business. The Virgin Group was itself now in the ballooning business. A subsidiary company called the Virgin Airship & Balloon Company was having increasing success in persuading big British companies that putting their name on the sides of balloons and other dirigibles was a good way to promote their products.

FIFTEEN

Recovery in Woodstock Street

As Randolph Fields withdrew first from daily management of Virgin Atlantic, then from the company's chairmanship, and finally from its board of directors and its register of shareholders, Richard Branson began to acquire the power to run the airline as he wanted.

Fields had been a useful scapegoat. The minutes of early Virgin Atlantic board meetings – which were themselves a source of dispute, because Fields brought his lawyer with him and complained that the record of discussions was slanted in favour of Branson's point of view – show that while Fields was still nominally in charge, Branson and his people sought to attribute many of the airline's difficulties to his misjudgements earlier on. His departure meant that the Virgin team had no further distractions or excuses. The job of sorting those difficulties out was theirs alone.

The conflict over the reservations office in Woodstock Street had left behind it such chaos in 1984 that nobody knew exactly how many passengers had been booked on Virgin's flights or whether they had paid. This was particularly the case for flights returning from New York to London: David Tait would afterwards joke that people who turned up at the Newark check-in, said their name was Smith and demanded two tickets would instantly be flown across the Atlantic gratis. Carrying the occasional freeloader was no disaster. More serious, however, was the fact that the company's reservations records sometimes showed flights as fully booked that were not. On several occasions during the peak period of high summer, while Branson was distracted by his legal battle with Fields and therefore spending much of his time with solicitors, the aircraft had to leave London with almost 300 empty seats. Branson knew that full flights in the summer were essential if the airline were to survive the leaner winter months – and that it would run up huge losses unless it met its capacity targets. He therefore authorized the reservations staff to adopt a desperate remedy: deliberately to accept reservations from significantly more passengers than the airline could carry.

The results were infuriating to Virgin's customers, and damaging to the company's public image. With remarkable swiftness, the previously friendly press began to turn sour. On 30 July the *Daily Mail* reported that there had been 'angry scenes at Gatwick airport as Britain's newest cut-price airline flew into a storm'. At first Branson hoped that the difficulties could be blamed on the seasonal rush to leave the country. 'The trouble is,' he explained with humility, 'we lacked experience. We simply failed to appreciate what happens when universities and colleges break up and students flock to get away.' Many travellers were willing to accept limited over-booking as the commercial reality of the industry. They became less sympathetic when it became clear that Virgin had no idea how many tickets it had sold for each flight.

On 4 August readers of the *Daily Telegraph* discovered that Branson had been forced to cross the Atlantic on Concorde in order to avoid bumping one of his own passengers. On the 25th, *The Times* reported an incident at Newark the previous evening during which the police had to be called in order to protect Virgin ground staff from furious travellers, 'yelling and chanting and pushing to get past the desk' with 'several babies and old people and one woman getting married in London today'.

Branson's response was commendably frank, but hardly diplomatic. 'To break even,' he was quoted as saying, 'we must regularly fill 405 seats on every plane. If we only book 405, with the rate of no-shows in the United States, we only get about 310 passengers who take the flight.' Asked whether he was beginning to wish that he had never become involved, he was adamant: 'I do not regret starting the airline. It is challenging, and there are teething troubles. But I believe that we can make it work.' With so much on his mind, it was no wonder that Branson promised to subscribe £1,000 to an appeal by Radio Oxford for monitoring equipment for premature babies at the John Radcliffe Hospital, but then forgot to send in his cheque. (Another tycoon, Robert Maxwell, had done the same thing: but Maxwell's secretary had the presence of mind to say that the cheque was in the post.)

Given what had come before the airline's launch, it is hard to see how Branson could have avoided that first disastrous summer. An established airline with a corps of experts in customer handling, telephony and computing would have been hard put to install a new system during the busiest period of the year, and train its staff how to use it, without bringing daily business to a halt. For the novices at Virgin, the task was evidently an impossibility. So it was not until later that Branson was able to turn his attention to the development from scratch of a new system for recording customers' reservations and keeping track of who had paid for tickets and who had not.

As autumn approached, the congestion decreased, and Branson began to look for ways to woo business travellers. He conceived the idea of a new 'Space Class', in which customers would be guaranteed an empty seat beside them in return for a higher fare. But in the meantime, the airline began to face real competitive pressure in the economy cabin. After wishing Virgin luck before its launch, and tolerating its low fares and daring publicity tactics during its first months, British Airways at last made its first counter-attack. It asked for official permission to drop its lowest fare to within £1 of Virgin's prices.

Branson was outraged, but not surprised. His lunchtime chats with Laker had alerted him to the risk that at the first sign of the new airline's success, established carriers would move in to undercut its fares. At first sight, it might seem impossible for them to do so: with modest salaries, a cheaply leased second-hand aircraft and minimal overheads, Virgin's costs were undoubtedly lower. But the larger airlines had the luxury of flying scores or even hundreds of routes, while Virgin had only one. They could afford to lose money on the London–New York run for a while, since profits from elsewhere would be able to subsidize it; and if a price war on the route prevented Virgin from generating enough profits to expand (or better still, forced it to withdraw from the industry altogether), the money would be well spent.

In most jurisdictions, including Britain, the United States and the European Union, such a strategy – known as 'predatory pricing'

– is illegal. It is unfair, in the sense that it allows companies with higher costs to drive out of business another company with lower costs, when straightforward economics suggests that the opposite ought to happen; and it acts against the interests of consumers, since most predators intend to raise prices again, to a level higher than they were to begin with, as soon as the low-cost competitors have been seen off. Yet despite the web of government regulation in the airline industry – in which airlines have to receive permission either to raise or to cut fares on international routes, and such little competition as exists is regulated by international treaties – there is in practice not much protection against these tactics. Proving that prices are below cost, let alone that two or more companies have got together with the intention of driving a competitor from the market, is both difficult and time-consuming. Laker's wide-ranging claims against the big airlines had come to court so slowly that they were still pending two years after the failure of his airline – by which time Virgin had battles of its own to fight.

On Laker's advice, Branson had tried to pre-empt any attack from the established airlines by winning an assurance from the British government that it would move swiftly to protect him from predatory pricing. Unfortunately, an approach before the inaugural flight to Nicholas Ridley, the government transport secretary at the time, was politely rebuffed: Ridley said he could not promise in advance to prevent a price war from breaking out.

As Laker had warned, the request from British Airways to cut fares was followed promptly by similar requests by TWA and Pan American. Branson realized that he could not complain in public against lower air fares. The argument that prices were being cut in order to drive him out of business and then raise them to a higher level than before was too subtle for the public to understand. In any case, Branson knew that he would look like a bad loser if he made any demand for higher fares. Instead, he chose a different tack. Rather than be seen to oppose lower prices, he decided, Virgin Atlantic should call for BA and other airlines to make the same cuts on their fares to other destinations as they wanted to make on the New York route. This ingenious strategy allowed him to present himself as a consumers' champion (despite having denied before the airline's launch that he was on a crusade for lower fares), while preventing the other carriers from cut-throat pricing. Unfortunately, the demand was ignored by the authorities.

In the event, it was the interests of the British Exchequer that helped to relieve the pressure on Virgin Atlantic over its first winter. The reason was that Margaret Thatcher's government was determined to take British Airways out of the public sector. The firm had been bought by a Conservative government in 1939, and merged with Imperial Airways under the chairmanship of John Reith, previously of the BBC. It had been renamed British Overseas Airways Corporation, but then given back its old name in 1974 when it was merged with British European Airways.

Public ownership had done British Airways no more good than it did scores of other flag-carriers across the world. The airline was not only inefficient – its disgruntled passengers used to refer to it as 'Bloody Awful' – but even with government protection from competitive forces, it still lost money. The prime minister was determined to be rid of it. Laker's decision to sue British Airways in the US courts, along with a host of other international carriers, had cast a cloud over the proposed privatization, since his $1bn lawsuit, if still pending, would have to be disclosed to potential investors. Branson's threat to follow suit – and his announcement that he had consulted Laker's aggressive American anti-trust lawyer – made matters worse. Investors could view one pending lawsuit against an airline coming to market as forgivable; two looked like carelessness.

Before approving the proposed low fares, the British government therefore tried to protect its stake in BA by asking the United States government to exempt the British flag-carrier from any legal consequences that might arise from the price war. The response was, not surprisingly, an unequivocal 'No'; the executive branch of the federal government could give no such undertakings on behalf of the US judiciary. The British government therefore announced on 25 October that it would not approve the new fares. But this blatant attempt at diplomatic blackmail brought unpopularity down on the government's head – for the airlines, expecting approval to be a formality as usual, had already sold cheap tickets to 130,000 people who would now have to pay a supplement at the airport before boarding their flights. By the end of the month, Ridley was forced to back down. Muttering lamely that he wanted to 'leave the passengers out of this', he agreed to allow tickets to be honoured if they had been sold before the government refused permission for the new fares.

Although prices did fall later in the winter, the uncertainty over that crucial few weeks had been enough to keep Virgin afloat. On 9 October, before the government stepped in, Branson had threatened to fold the company altogether unless it was protected from the predators, and sworn to start his own anti-trust suit if the low fares were approved. By November he had decided not to go to court after all, and he made no move to liquidate Virgin Atlantic.

The next few months were not without incident, however. The following spring, Virgin Atlantic narrowly survived an attempt by Chemical Bank to repossess the *Maiden Voyager* – not because of worries about Virgin's solvency but because of an internal dispute over whether the deal put together by its leasing arm in London had technically infringed US banking law. Once again, however, Branson's instinctive reliance on highly paid advice and quick legal action saved the day. He sent his lawyers to the High Court to seek an immediate injunction against Chemical, and threatened to sue for $10m if the bank repossessed the aircraft. Chemical reconsidered; while it hesitated, Virgin had enough time to arrange a new leasing deal with Security Pacific that would keep the aircraft that was registered as G-VIRG in the air.

Luck was the final ingredient necessary for the airline to survive. Although Branson had done everything he could to minimize the start-up costs of the operation, and to reduce the risks if it failed, there was one element he could not control: the exchange rate. Like other aircraft leases, Virgin's 747 lease was priced in dollars, while the majority of the airline's income came from British residents who paid for their Atlantic crossing in pounds sterling. When the deal on the *Maiden Voyager* had been struck in spring 1984, the pound was worth $1.45. By Christmas, the dollar had strengthened so much that it appeared to be heading for parity with the pound. If Virgin had been forced to return the plane that winter, it would therefore have had to find about one-third more pounds in order to realize the same amount in dollars after currency conversion.

But the familiar Branson sorcery held once again: by July, when the foreign exchange contract expired, the dollar had fallen back and a potential £6m loss had evaporated. When the airline turned in a loss for the financial year to 31 January 1985 of only £1.5m, Branson and his advisers felt they deserved modest congratulations.

During the course of 1984, Nick Alexander found himself constantly being second-guessed in his job as marketing director by Richard Branson. In most ways, Branson's approach was impressive. He was fully open to new ideas, and gave as much credit to the opinions of the office cleaner as to those of the managing director. He was also quite willing to attempt what appeared to be the impossible. Early one morning, he telephoned Alexander and asked him to place an advertisement for the airline in that afternoon's *Evening Standard*.

'That's impossible, Richard,' replied Alexander. 'We're far too late for the paper's copy deadlines.'

Branson insisted that Alexander should do his best all the same. The sceptical marketing man then spent the entire morning on the telephone – to the newspaper, to Virgin's advertising agency, to the production people who would turn the copywriter's idea into camera-ready artwork. By dint of superhuman efforts on all sides, an advertisement did just make the last edition of the newspaper. Branson thanked him gracefully for his work; but there was an unmistakable triumph in his voice as he did so. Branson wanted people around him who, when asked to do something, would do their best to succeed, rather than expend effort arguing over whether it could be done or not. The establishment of the airline in less than four months was testimony to that.

But this admirable quality had a drawback, too: it tempted Branson to interfere in the decisions being taken by his line managers. When a business was stable and running successfully, he was as able to stand back as any good delegator. In the face of uncertainty and failure, however, he disrupted the chain of responsibility, and undermined the ability of his managers to get the job done. Incidents like these wore down his relationship with Alexander to the point that he was pleased to leave the job of running the airline's marketing to someone else, and return to the greater independence of his old job at the games company – even though he knew that in doing so he would remove himself from the magic circle of Branson's close confidants.

Yet in one crucial respect, Nick Alexander left his mark on Virgin Atlantic's strategy. Late in 1984, Branson and his colleagues had stepped back from the airline's daily concerns, and asked themselves during a weekend meeting at Branson's house in Oxfordshire what sort of airline they were trying to build. Branson's answer was unequivocal: to attract the backpacking, record-buying public, Virgin Atlantic must charge low prices. Alexander argued strongly to the contrary. The airline should certainly offer its customers the best value, he believed; but that did not necessarily mean the lowest prices too. Passengers were already coming aboard the Virgin Atlantic jet expecting a Skytrain-style service, and finding themselves pleasantly surprised. Branson should be trying to capitalize on this advantage, he urged. The Virgin chairman was not convinced – and for the moment, the airline's strategy remained unchanged, and its prices remained lower than those of its competitors.

By early summer 1985, the New York route had stabilized to the point where Branson was ready to start thinking about acquiring a second aircraft and opening up a second destination. The company decided on Miami, which was a less popular route with business travellers, but had the advantage that Florida's year-round warmth made it more seasonally stable than other tourist destinations. Setting up Virgin Atlantic's second route proved to be more time-consuming, however, than setting up its first. It took a year for Virgin to win the necessary permissions from the British and American authorities, and to put in place the local management needed to maintain the service on the far side of the Atlantic. Subsequent launches took longer still: when Virgin Atlantic made an application to fly between London and Tokyo in July 1987, Branson had no idea that the route would not be launched until May 1989. But the delay did not matter much. With the Miami and Los Angeles routes open, the airline almost doubled in size: the accounting period that ended in July 1986 saw turnover shoot up to the annual equivalent of £34m and after-tax losses fall to £775,000. By summer 1987, the airline's turnover was pushing £60m, and it turned in an after-tax profit of £3.2m – enough to cover not only the cost of buying out

Randolph Fields, but also all the losses the airline had sustained from its start.

Much of the credit for this was due to David Tait's nurturing of the US operation. The job of marketing the airline was much harder on the far side of the Atlantic than at home, since Branson was much less well known there. Tait knew the difficulties he faced, for he had been the local manager who established Laker's Miami routes. As in many businesses, the highest hurdles were at the start. Tait found it very hard to hire anyone before the airline's inaugural flight, since the company was entering a market that had just claimed two victims (Laker and Air Florida), had no aircraft, and had no licence. Its first New York operational centre was a spare room at the top of the record company's offices in Greenwich Village – and with nowhere else to live, Tait slept in an even smaller room across the corridor. Although the planning consents did not allow the airline to operate from the building, it had to take reservations calls there for its first few months all the same. Only when the insistent pounding of rock music from the record executives' offices next door became too much, and the number of calls was large enough to justify the rental of a proper office, did the airline move to premises of its own.

The Virgin Group had always had plenty of talented individuals who could come up with a constant stream of new ideas; as it had matured, it had also acquired a smaller corps of professional managers to keep an eye on details. Tait had both of these skills. He ran a tight ship in New York. He was able, thanks to his growing friendship with Richard Branson, to fight his corner in corporate battle when necessary. Yet his approach to marketing the airline in the United States was highly inventive and successful. With the help of an innovative New York advertising agency, Virgin Atlantic in the United States ran a powerful advertising campaign that managed to appeal simultaneously to the sense of tradition that American travellers often associate with Britain, and a younger picture more in keeping with Virgin's image. Its first slogan was 'Eat, drink and fly with an English Virgin'; the airline also made highly successful use of Tracey Ullman.

During one later brainstorming meeting, Tait and the agency sighed over the fact that their best idea – to use Phil Collins's new hit song, 'In the Air Tonight', as background music for a television commercial – would be far beyond their budget. It was quite by chance that Branson called him a few days later, and asked whether he would like to use Collins or his colleagues from the band Genesis in the airline's US advertising campaign. Tait laughed; since their fee alone would swallow up his entire year's budget of £2m, he assumed that this was one of his boss's less funny practical jokes. It was not: as part of the negotiations over Collins's latest contract with the record label, Branson had suggested a television commercial. In the event, the advertisements went out on the networks without music, but with the band talking to each other. They brought in floods of calls to the airline's reservations counter.

The independence with which Tait was allowed to run Virgin Atlantic's American operations was partly the result of his authoritative knowledge of airline marketing in the United States. But it was also due in no small part to his personal relationship with Branson. The two men seemed to be on the same wavelength. Both felt they knew how to have a good time; and Virgin employees visiting from London, seeing the two men get drunk together, would later muse on the fact that despite the thousands of miles that separated them – and the numerous occasions on which Tait had turned down senior positions at the airline in England – the head of Virgin Atlantic's US business seemed to know their boss better than they did. So strong was the relationship, in fact, that it survived even after Tait committed a major indiscretion. Interviewed for a feature published in the British edition of *Esquire* magazine in May 1993, Tait told the following story about Branson:

> He's a little bit shy, particularly with strangers. Virgin was opening the Miami route, and Richard and I were driving along in Florida and he wanted to buy some condoms. So he disappeared inside this pharmacist [*sic*] and came out a few minutes later, visibly flustered. He slammed the car door and said, 'Bloody idiot! You could have told me. In this country, they don't know what a Durex is.' But that wasn't the worst part. He couldn't remember they were all called condoms.

On the inaugural flight to Miami in April 1986, a reporter asked David Tait what Virgin would do if a competitor began to undercut its Miami fares.

'Eastern Airlines already have,' he replied sharply. 'Why don't you ask about our quality of service?'

Tait was right. In the space of less than two years, Virgin Atlantic had begun to establish itself as one of the best carriers across the Atlantic. Its economy class was good, with better food than average, and a longer pitch between the rows of seats than other carriers; if its staff were less deferential than those of British Airways, they were certainly more friendly. But it was in catering to the business customer that Virgin excelled. The waiters provided by Maxim's for the inaugural flight had been dropped soon after, for their wing collars and tailcoats proved impractical during the long hours in the air. The Upper Class seat, however, was an instant hit: it was almost as broad and as far from the seat in front as other carriers' First Class. Rather than showing a succession of movies on the screen in the cabin, the airline provided miniature portable video recorders for its Upper Class passengers, with a menu of 100 or so films to choose from and watch when they chose throughout the flight.

The airline also offered its Upper Class passengers a free chauffeur-driven car service between their homes and Gatwick airport, which was helpful in persuading business travellers who had never considered flying out of any airport but Heathrow. Later, after one passenger asked to be driven up to the Highlands of Scotland – at a cost to the airline of over £300 – the service was limited to within a 50-mile radius of the airport. The 'amenity kits' given away on Virgin flights were better than the standard package of cosmetics, eyeshades and toothbrushes: until economies later forced Branson to cut back in this area, Upper Class passengers received a growing choice of high-quality toys, including Cross ballpoint pens, powerful miniature torches, and aromatherapy kits. It was no wonder that the empty seats that Branson had surveyed with such disappointment a week after launch were soon occupied. Within a year of launch, the Upper Class section of the aircraft on the New York route had filled not only the 'bubble' upstairs, but also the front of the aircraft's main cabin downstairs. Later on, the entire front half of the 747 was to be taken up with Upper Class passengers.

By the time Virgin Atlantic had been flying for four years, there was no longer any doubt that it had become a success. Partly this was due to Branson's exquisite sense of timing, for the industrial countries of Europe, North America and Japan were in the middle of the longest economic boom since the war just as the airline had reached full speed. Interest rates were low, the stock market crash of October 1987 had been shrugged off, and British and American citizens were crossing the Atlantic as if it were their last chance to do so. Virgin Atlantic was also putting its assets to highly intensive use: it had exactly two aircraft, and in the words of one of its senior executives at the time, it was 'flying the arse off them'. The *Maiden Voyager* continued to ply the North Atlantic, with its Upper Class section full of highly profitable business travellers on their way from London to New York. The Miami route was operated six times a week by the other 747, which packed in more that 500 economy passengers at a time. Since the jet also flew to Orlando, carrying British tourists to and from holidays at Disney World, the engineers had only one day in fourteen in which to maintain it. In the heat of summer, when the temperature was high and the pressure low, it was sometimes necessary to reduce some of the aircraft's lucrative load in order to ensure that the pilots could take off safely from the short Gatwick runway.

This highly efficient use of aircraft did have a drawback, however. With only two 747s, Virgin was unusually susceptible to technical problems: if one flight had to be delayed for six hours for repairs, it could take three or four days for the timetable to be restored to normal. If something serious came up during a busy period such as Easter week, it would be impossible to find another airline willing to take Virgin passengers, and the airline's flights could run late for as long as a week. The airline's marketing staff spent much of their time reminding journalists and the public that not even large airlines like British Airways had spare aircraft sitting at every airport in the world that they served. But they could not wriggle out of the fact that on outbound flights from London, Virgin's punctuality record was doomed to be worse than that of its competitors. Luckily, no proper statistics were kept for the first years of Virgin Atlantic's operations.

Yet these problems were symptoms of a wider success. The airline was filling as many seats as it could ever hope to, and flying its planes for the maximum possible number of hours each fortnight. British Caledonian was providing a good and economical maintenance service. The wages of cabin crews were still low (despite early signs of greed among the airline's pilots), and the routes on which they were flying were the longest that a single crew could be asked to serve. Ground costs at Gatwick were significantly lower than those of competitors at Heathrow. And a campaign by Branson's senior managers to persuade him to abandon the airline's Dublin and Maastricht routes had finally succeeded after Branson overheard a passenger aboard one of the decrepit 1950s turboprop aircraft with which Virgin was serving those destinations joke that with planes like this in service in Europe, it was no wonder he could afford to offer low fares across the Atlantic. As a result, the airline's turnover rose more than £15m to £75m in the financial year to July 1988. With gross margins touching 35 per cent, profits after tax were a promising £12m.

The temptation was strong to stand still. Branson's senior advisers had repeatedly been obliged to restrain him from what they considered ill-judged diversifications. Now, they believed, their point was proved. Four years after launch, two years after paying Randolph Fields the second half of his £1m, the airline was minting money. If only Branson could be persuaded to resist the hubris that had brought down Freddie Laker, the Virgin Atlantic managers believed, their joint future would be secure.

But Branson was like a gambler who was unable to pick up his winning chips and leave the casino. He would not be content with a small but profitable airline, occupying a comfortable niche that larger competitors were willing to ignore. Within a year, he had thrown Virgin Atlantic once more into turmoil. In an aggressive programme of opening up new routes to Tokyo and Los Angeles, he doubled the size of the fleet by buying two more 747s – this time far more expensive aircraft, since the engines fitted to the Boeings that Virgin already owned were not powerful enough to take off from Gatwick and fly non-stop to Japan or to the West Coast of the United States. The airline had also decided to start doing its own maintenance. Even though it had no hangar – Virgin jets had to fly to Stansted or Dublin for any work that could not be done in the open air on the tarmac – this was expensive, for Branson had to invest in a stock of valuable spares.

More daringly still, Branson now had his eye on a greater prize.

So far, few incoming Virgin passengers flew on from London after crossing the Atlantic to other European destinations, so the 'interlining' commissions that Virgin Atlantic received from the airlines on to which they transferred did not account for a significant proportion of its profits. In future, Branson expected this to be different. If Upper Class was to attract business passengers to its full potential, the airline would have to fly out of Heathrow Airport. This, however, would result in a sharp increase in costs, for instead of maintaining staff at a single hub, Virgin would have to pay separate bills for Gatwick and Heathrow.

Branson's programme of expansion had exactly the desired effect: by July 1990, Virgin Atlantic's turnover had more than doubled to £180m, and its associated holiday company and cargo handler had grown more impressively still. But it was nowhere near so profitable. The airline's after-tax profits had fallen from 16 per cent of turnover to just over 3 per cent. And the full weight of recession and the collapse in air travel resulting from the tension in the Persian Gulf was yet to come.

SIXTEEN

A Man of Property

WHEN THE VERNON YARD OFFICES became too small for the Virgin Records business, Richard Branson learned an expensive lesson. A huge old Victorian mansion had been found on the Harrow Road, a couple of miles north of the traditional Virgin territory in Notting Hill Gate. The house was set back from the road behind a wall, with a huge dilapidated front garden that could easily be turned into a car park. On the left side of the mansion was a drab but serviceable bungalow; on the right hand side was an equally drab building that had once been used by the Department for Health and Social Security as a local office for giving out unemployment benefits and income support. Virgin had a choice: to buy the entire site for £600,000, or to acquire only the main block for a lower sum. Rod Vickery, who looked after the company's property interests at the time, advised Richard Branson and Simon Draper to buy the lot. Branson, still smarting from the company's earlier financial difficulties, saw no reason to spend a penny more than he had to. The issue remained controversial for several weeks, as Vickery and other Virgin staff tried unsuccessfully to persuade their employer that buying just part of the site would be a false economy. A few years later, their predictions came true. The record company had grown as they expected it would, and Virgin was obliged to buy the rest of the site in order to make space for its new employees. The difficulty was that another company had now acquired what Virgin needed to buy; and secure in the knowledge that it would cost Virgin still more to find another site and move elsewhere, the firm was able quite legally to hold Branson to ransom. In the end, Virgin paid £1.2m for the space that it could have bought a few years earlier for only £600,000.

Branson was therefore in a receptive mood when Laurie Dunn,

the managing director of Virgin Australia, sent him a message to say that an old friend wanted to talk to him about the possibility of starting a property company. When the standard invitation to the houseboat was taken up, Branson discovered that the friend turned out to be old in more senses than one. His name was Arthur Viccary, and he was almost 60 years old. Not only was he old enough to be Richard Branson's father; he was also probably the oldest employee the group had ever taken on.

Yet as Viccary unfolded his proposal, Richard Branson realized that this would probably be an advantage. Viccary had started out in the construction business in 1948, after serving for four years in the Royal Artillery. He had worked as a surveyor; he had taken part in the 1950s property boom in which an inexperienced industry found itself required to build at great speed everything from synagogues to blocks of flats; and moving to a small property company in Surrey, he had built it up gradually over almost twenty years and then sold his shareholding to a larger construction company. Viccary could claim to have done everything in the business, and to have seen it through both boom and bust.

The deal was wrapped up in fifteen minutes. Arthur Viccary would set up a new property company, to be called Vanson Developments (the name borrowed the initial letter of his own name and combined it with the rest of Branson's). He was to build up a small team of specialists who would devote half their time to handling the property work that needed to be done inside the Virgin Group – looking for new sites for Virgin Megastores, and negotiating the rents on them – and the rest to setting up and running a small property development company. The firm would have 10,000 shares of a pound each, and Viccary himself would buy a quarter of them. He would become the firm's managing director, and he would receive a salary of £25,000 a year. Branson would provide all the funds necessary for the property investments that Viccary decided to make. Although Viccary did not know where the ultimate source of the funds was, he knew that it was channelled through a company called Virgin Management, and he knew that the interest rate at which the money was being borrowed was a point and a half above base rate.

None of this was put in writing until Viccary's contract of

employment and the company's memorandum and articles of association were formalized. But Viccary went away, set up a small office in Surrey, a county on the southern borders of London's suburbs, and acquired a Mercedes-Benz 280 to serve as his company car. He had always driven Mercedes, and he saw no reason to change his habits now.

The first deal that Viccary brought in was close to home. It was in Redhill, Surrey; and his plan was to buy a plot of land and build between thirty and forty houses on it. In the event, after consultations with Branson, Viccary never went through with the deal. But a few months later, they entered into a similar project in Surbiton. As luck would have it, a buyer approached the company after it had acquired the land and before it had started building; and Viccary was able to sell at a modest profit without having done anything other than hold the property for three months.

Other deals on a similar scale followed. A site in Wandsworth, just south of the River Thames in central London, yielded nine flats and a small profit. A farm in Dorking was reborn as an attractive retirement home of 39 sheltered dwellings for old people. That development was less profitable than it had first promised to be, for the government imposed value added tax on building work half-way through. But Vanson Developments still scraped clear with a profit of £100,000 or more.

It was only in 1986, as the increase in property values was accelerating, that the company hit the jackpot. Viccary decided to acquire an old house in Carlton House Terrace, in a peaceful enclave between Piccadilly and St James's Park. The house, which had previously served as Crockford's Club, was acquired for £950,000. Viccary's plan was to renovate it and sell it on as offices, but once again a buyer materialized before any work needed to be done. The Crown Commissioners, guardians of the government's properties, wanted the building for the use of civil servants; and it was willing to pay Vanson £300,000 more than it had paid only six weeks earlier for the property. There was a bonus in the transaction for Viccary, too, which he discovered while strolling around the empty house, admiring the elegant chandeliers and paintings that had been left in the grandiose reception rooms by its previous owner.

'They'll be clearing all these out,' said Viccary.

'Oh, no,' replied the agent. 'You've bought the lot.' Viccary therefore found that Vanson Developments was the proud possessor of a collection worth almost £40,000, which included a handsome portrait of a lady by the eighteenth-century artist Sir Thomas Lawrence. The collection was not quite Richard Branson's taste; luckily, the agent who had found the house for Viccary was willing to forego part of his fee, in exchange for chandeliers and pictures.

The company's most successful deal to date was also in central London. Viccary found an office building at the bottom of St Martin's Lane, in the middle of the city's theatre district, which a Finnish bank had bought and intended to turn into its London headquarters. The building was known as Cavell House, because it overlooked the statue of Nurse Edith Cavell, who had been shot by German troops during the First World War for helping British soldiers to escape back to their homeland. Vanson invested just under £3m in an option to buy the freehold of the building after its refurbishment. When the work was done, Viccary was able to exercise the option for another £14m – and to sell on the building to the National Westminster Bank at a profit of more than £3m. It had cost the company less than £200,000 to borrow the money needed to buy the option only six months earlier.

By 1987, Vanson Developments was doing so well that Viccary's salary, which included a profit-share element, was rising fast. In keeping with his policy of retaining firm equity control in other Virgin businesses, Richard Branson accepted Viccary's offer to sell part of his 25 per cent shareholding in the business. A deal was struck under which Virgin would take Viccary out of the lucrative profit-sharing scheme, and would acquire three-fifths of his shareholding in Vanson. In return, Viccary would receive £700,000 in Virgin shares.

Then came an unpleasant shock. When the matter was under negotiation, the Virgin shares which Viccary had accepted in payment for his options and his holding in the property company looked as if they might well rise in value past £2 each. But in a few short weeks came the 1987 stock market crash; and Viccary found that the coin in which he had been bought out was suddenly worth only half what he had expected. Richard Branson was not to be blamed, of course; he had had no more inkling of the equity collapse than anybody else. But Viccary must have wondered for an uncomfortable year whether he had undersold himself badly.

In the event, the property developer was to discover that he had not. Vanson carried on growing the following year, and a new partner whom Viccary had brought in to help him began to look aggressively for bigger sites to develop. Tony Bland, as the new director was called, came up with a highly promising deal in Crawley, the town near to Gatwick airport in which Virgin Atlantic had its administrative head office. The idea was that Vanson would buy a large empty site in the town centre for £28m in partnership with another company, and then turn it into an office development built around a huge new distribution centre for J. Sainsbury, Britain's largest supermarket chain. The bid for the site was successful, but then things began to turn sour. Vanson's partner pulled out, leaving the firm with the unpleasant choice of either proceeding with all the risk on its own balance sheet, or jettisoning the £3m which it had paid as a non-returnable deposit. Bland was in charge of the deal, and Viccary was on holiday at the time.

After a little heart-searching, Richard Branson and Trevor Abbott decided provisionally that the purchase should go ahead. But they checked with Viccary first. On the very day that he returned from his holiday, Trevor Abbott telephoned him to ask his advice.

'We have £3m non-returnable on the table,' he said. 'You're the managing director. We're not going to take the final decision until you say what you think.'

Viccary gave his blessing, but began to regret his decision within a matter of weeks. First Sainsbury's decided not to proceed with its distribution centre; then the local council announced that it had changed its mind about the planning permissions which it had informally indicated that it would be willing to give to the developers. As a result, Vanson found itself the proud owner of a vast empty site, on which it was no longer able to build the offices that it had hoped for. Under the planning regulations, however, the company had the right to appeal against the council's decision directly to the Secretary of State for the Environment. That cost another half-million pounds – and, more significantly, it resulted in a long delay. While the site was lying empty and the planning dispute was in the hands of the lawyers, the British commercial property market had begun to turn. By the time the appeal was settled in 1989, it became clear that Crawley town centre was not so valuable as Tony Bland had thought it to be in 1988. Vanson tried to unload it at a loss, but could not find any buyers.

Viccary felt sick at heart. The development had contravened what he believed to be the cardinal rule of property businesses: never to take on a single project so large that it could sink the rest of the company. He had never been an enthusiast for the idea himself, but he had given the final authority to proceed when challenged either to approve or veto at short notice. And his own exit route from the business – the Virgin shares he had received in return for his Vanson Developments holding and the cancellation of his attractive profit-sharing arrangements – was in 1989 still worth only half its value on the day the agreement with Branson and Virgin had been signed.

Viccary's personal problem was later to be solved by Branson's dramatic decision to buy Virgin back from the stock market. When the company was taken into private ownership once again, Viccary was able to unload his shares at 140p each, the price at which they had been first floated. But Vanson itself was left with a large portfolio of unsaleable properties, of which Crawley was only the largest and most unsaleable. In the end, the Group was obliged to write off £12m in its accounts to cover the losses made by Vanson Developments.

Far from disclaiming responsibility for the crash of Vanson Developments, Trevor Abbott would speak of it afterwards as his greatest failure. He had proposed to the board at the end of 1988, as part of the process of taking the company private, that the property company should be sold outright. Surveyors were appointed to value the company's assets, and set to work putting together a detailed package of information showing the planning consents that the company had obtained, the size in square feet of every site and every building that it owned, its rents receivable, and photographs of every building. This package took three months to assemble; but by mid-1989, after three months of trying unsuccessfully to find a buyer, Abbott realized that Virgin would now never be able to sell it until the property market revived. 'The principal reason that we didn't sell,' he admitted later, with commendable frankness, 'was because I refused to sell this company at a loss.' Prey to the usual inability of an investor to accept his losses and walk away from them, Abbott had told the surveyors that he would not consider selling any of the assets at prices below their book value in the Vanson accounts. 'What makes me sick – what makes me throw up in the bin – is that my decision to get out couldn't have been more right.'

But there was one further humiliation which Virgin would have to undergo before it could draw a discreet veil over the Vanson fiasco. This concerned the future of Tony Bland, the director who had proposed the Crawley project. Before joining Vanson in 1988, Bland had run his own property company, and had been a partner in Hillier Parker, a prominent firm of estate agents. He had come to Vanson because he was under the impression that Virgin had both the commitment and the financial muscle to turn it into a major development company that would be able to engage in ambitious projects taking years to complete. A couple of discussions with Don Cruickshank, who served as Branson's chief executive when the group was still public, had confirmed this impression.

What Bland found once he set to work with Arthur Viccary, however, was quite different. 'Our philosophies were different,' he recalled. 'Arthur was not so much an investor as a dealer.' As he looked more closely into the transactions that Vanson had been involved in, Bland came to the conclusion that the company's strategy – exemplified by the Crockford's and Cavell House deals – was to move in quickly to buy up cheap land or buildings; and then to sell them on, often equally quickly, with the minimum of development work. This was not what he thought property was about. 'I had a background in which I advised major institutions on their property investments. Even though I was involved in development, most of my experience was with long-term investors.'

The Crawley project was therefore Bland's opportunity to make his mark on Vanson. It was a huge investment – so huge, in fact, that Bland warned Branson, Abbott and the other directors of the Virgin Group, that they should think of it as what he called a 'flagship-type operation'. They should go forward with the transaction only if they were willing to put the full weight of the group's influence and resources behind it. 'It's not something one could possibly recommend as a development for Vanson as a development company,' he told them. 'It's something Virgin will have to make a decision on.'

Bland lived to regret those words, for his attempt to turn Virgin and Vanson with a single transaction into a property company of the first order failed disastrously. As things began to get worse, Abbott and Viccary made it clear that they held Bland responsible for Vanson's over-expansion. Relations between Bland and Viccary deteriorated, and the younger man soon found that Viccary was holding private meetings with Trevor Abbott behind his back. He therefore prepared to take pre-emptive action of his own. Bland began to make sure that the minutes of Vanson board meetings recorded who had argued for and against every decision that was made, and he took care to inform Abbott formally that he thought Vanson as a whole was being mismanaged. 'Everything I did was minuted and agreed by the whole board,' he insisted.

Bland stayed on as a director of Vanson in a state of undeclared war with Arthur Viccary until May 1992, when Abbott abruptly called him into his office and told him he was sacked. Then Abbott, usually known for his ability to deal ruthlessly with difficult situations, made an uncharacteristic move. He wrote Bland a letter about the circumstances of his dismissal, which conceded that the group still had contractual obligations to him. Soon after his dismissal, Bland complained to the company that he had been unable to find another job. He had done his best, Bland said; but market conditions were terrible, and he could not be held responsible for the problems that had arisen. He would have been happy to stay on and continue with the long-term job of sorting them out; instead, he had been unceremoniously dumped by Virgin. He therefore wished to claim all the salary he was due until the expiry of his contract, and some expenses.

For once, emotion overcame reason in the Virgin response. Instead of looking carefully over the sympathetic letter that Abbott had written, and making an honest assessment of whether this had compromised Virgin's right to sack him by appearing to concede that Bland had not been at fault, the company and its lawyers at

Harbottle & Lewis decided to fight Bland all the way. The result was that notes had to be placed in the Vanson accounts recording the removal of a director under the provisions of the Companies Act; a formal legal reply to Bland's claim had to be sent; Bland's attempt at a conciliation directly with Richard Branson had to be ignored; and some months later, Virgin was forced to defend itself in the High Court. After turning down an offer of settlement worth £100,000, Bland won – and walked away from Virgin in 1993 with about £250,000 in his pocket.

Two years were to pass after Bland's departure from Vanson Developments until the British commercial property market was ready to recover. In the meantime, Virgin had been forced to write off the bulk of the money that had been invested in the business; so it was an unexpected bonus when a tenant was at last found for a large building at Crawley that had been erected and then sold to the Prudential insurance company. The tenant was Unilever, the Anglo-Dutch consumer goods conglomerate, and it was paying a rent of nearly £2m to occupy the building. Vanson benefited from the deal only because the presence of a tenant relieved the company of the obligation to pay the rates and insurance on the building while it remained empty, so the immediate effect on its profit and loss account was limited. But the occupation of one big building would clearly make it easier to build and later rent out other office buildings on the site. In time, Vanson Developments might produce a decent rate of return, and might even pay back the millions that had been so disappointingly invested in it.

But there was a lesson for both Virgin and its chairman in the fiasco. Virgin had first entered the property business through an unusual route – by noticing that the values of its own buildings were rising so quickly. Yet within a very short period of time, and on the basis of a handful of successful small deals, the group had committed millions of pounds to a project that was too ambitious. To make matters worse, its top management had been bewitched by the broader hysteria in the property market that helped to drive prices to an all-time high in the middle of 1988. This was not the first time, and nor was it to be the last, that Richard Branson would lose money by abandoning his normal principles in favour of an attempt to make apparently easy and swift returns from speculation. The moral of Vanson Developments was that Branson should stick to building businesses that delivered goods or services that consumers really wanted.

SEVENTEEN

Branson Succumbs to Takeover Fever

UNTIL VIRGIN WENT PUBLIC, Richard Branson had always been seen as an unconventional kind of entrepreneur. It was not merely his choice of dress and his straight talking that set him apart from the corporate pirates who were rising to the top of British business in the 1980s. It was also his sense of scale: his preference for small offices over big, for building companies from scratch rather than buying them, for recruiting novices and promoting them when they had learned the ropes rather than hiring in big-name managers from outside on high salaries. Yet Branson was not immune to the broader fashions sweeping across British business. Proof of that came in 1987, when he prepared to throw all his old habits and principles to the wind – by making a vast, leveraged bid for another company.

Branson had long nursed a secret ambition to take over the giant of the British music business, Thorn-EMI. The company had its roots in Thorn Electrical Industries, a firm started in 1931 when Sir Jules Thorn opened a shop in Twickenham that specialized in hiring out electrical lights and appliances imported from America to the suburban English middle class. Even before it added music to its portfolio, merging with EMI in 1979, Thorn was already a sprawling conglomerate. By the late 1980s it controlled the Elstree film studios and a chain of EMI cinemas, and it made a bizarre range of products including semiconductors, light-bulbs, Kenwood food mixers and Ferguson television sets. It also owned the country's biggest television rental business, which had helped to make the video-cassette recorder a standard consumer product in Britain more quickly than in any other European country. Yet Thorn was also looking like a tired and sluggishly managed conglomerate, in which selling pop records came low on the list of priorities. Its head office had become bloated, and its middle managers bereft of any sense that they were entrepreneurs. Instead of fighting for business like the lean beast that Virgin was, Thorn-EMI was content to sit back and rely on the distribution power that its network of HMV shops gave it. In almost every area of the company's business apart from retail, Branson believed, his own methods could do better. Put together, he thought, the Virgin and EMI empires could become a world-beating music business.

There was just one difficulty. Thorn-EMI was almost ten times Virgin's size. Even to contemplate the takeover of a company so much bigger than his own was an act of bravado for Branson. The bravado was compounded by the fact that since music was no more than a part of the company's business, he would if he succeeded have to manage a number of divisions in industries of which neither he nor his senior directors had any experience whatever. Inexperience had never stopped Branson in the past, though; look at the success he had already made of the airline. Why, with the confidence that the stock market listing had given him, should it stop him now?

And why should the mere size of Thorn-EMI be an obstacle? Ten years earlier, Virgin would have been quite unable to contemplate such a takeover. For until the 1980s most companies had two ways to raise money for expansion: either to issue shares, as Virgin had just done, or to overdraw from the bank. It was only the largest and most conservatively run businesses, known as 'blue-chips', that had enough credibility with pension funds and other big investors to issue bonds. These bonds – certificates guaranteeing that the company in question would repay a fixed capital sum on a fixed date, and would make pre-agreed interest payments in the meantime – were traded in the markets like government bonds or like shares.

It was Michael Milken, of the US securities firm Drexel Burnham Lambert, who found a way to help lesser companies raise huge capital sums. Money lent to them would be less safe; but this would not necessarily make their bonds less attractive for investors, since they would offer a higher interest rate to compensate for the risk. By both helping companies to issue bonds in the first place and acting as an intermediary between buyers and sellers of the same bonds afterwards, Milken created – almost single-handedly – a new market. Because they were beneath the attention of traditional bond investors, the new bonds became known disparagingly as 'junk'. Maybe, but it was by issuing junk bonds that companies in the US were able to raise huge sums of money with which to take over other companies.

In principle, the method was straightforward. Having decided on a target, the buyer would work out how much it would need to finance a buyout from the shareholders. The next step would be to work out how much the target company might be worth when managed more aggressively – with a cut in contributions to its pension fund, with redundancies among the pen-pushers at head office, and with the selling off of valuable buildings and some (or perhaps even all) of the company's different businesses to other buyers. Once the figures were in place, the buyer could then form a small company, and arrange to issue a junk bond that would raise the huge sum needed for the buyout. The paperwork could then be circulated to institutions, who would buy the bond in the expectation that with the buyer's tougher management style, the raised cash flow from the target firm would be high enough to meet the schedule of interest payments on the bond and then pay back the capital in due course.

Branson was bored by finance, by accountancy and by formal techniques of management. When he had been in partnership with Nik Powell, he had poked gentle fun at the jargon that Powell had picked up from his reading of American business magazines. In the run-up to taking Virgin public, he had astonished the specialists at Morgan Grenfell by claiming not to know that 'earnings per share' simply meant the company's profits divided by the number of shares it had in circulation. But by 1987, Virgin's listing had forced Branson to pay more attention to what was going on in the stock market – and he was therefore presented with a model that would show how a small company like Virgin could take over a larger one like Thorn-EMI.

The model was Martin Sorrell's WPP. Sorrell, a graduate of Cambridge and the Harvard Business School, first made his name as the financial controller of Saatchi and Saatchi, masterminding the series of takeovers that turned a small London advertising agency into a global services conglomerate. In 1985, he left the agency to take over Wire and Plastic Products, a company that manufactured supermarket trolleys. With the same techniques as he had followed for the Saatchi brothers, Sorrell used WPP as a vehicle to buy, on borrowed money, a succession of increasingly big companies in the marketing business. In 1987, Sorrell won control of J. Walter Thompson, the Madison Avenue advertising group, for £351m. In a matter of months, the advertising industry's horrified reaction turned to admiration as Sorrell raised the company's margins from 4 per cent to 10 per cent, and unearthed $100m buried in the value of the office building that the company's Japanese subsidiary occupied in Tokyo. WPP's shares, worth 35p in 1985, were by 1987 up to 700p. If Sorrell could do all this with JWT without claiming any specialist knowledge of advertising itself, what could Branson not do with EMI?

Following Virgin's placing of preference shares in 1985, his first line of attack had been to consider a bid for EMI's screen entertainment division. Since this was flatly contrary to the principle that Branson had already agreed with Don Cruickshank of getting out of the film business, it was not surprising that it came to nothing. A year after Virgin's flotation, in late 1987, the idea reappeared in a different form. This time the plan was that Virgin should go into partnership with Mountleigh, a property company that had prospered during the bull market under the leadership of Tony Clegg. Virgin and Mountleigh agreed secretly that the two companies would mount a joint hostile bid for Thorn-EMI. When the quarry had been captured, it would then be dismembered: Branson would take the music business for Virgin, and Clegg would take the television rentals business for Mountleigh. Dealing with the lighting business that made up the rest of Thorn-EMI's interests would be the responsibility of Mountleigh, but the plan was that Clegg would sell it on swiftly for a profit soon after the takeover was complete.

Trevor Abbott, then Virgin's finance director, spent many hours working on the bid in meetings with Mountleigh and with investment bankers and advisers. That early preparation was to a great extent simple guesswork, since British company law allows public companies to keep more information about their interests and their

performance secret than United States law would allow. To avoid
the risk that their plan would be exposed before the bid was
fully ready, and that an alerted Thorn-EMI would be better
able to defend itself, the two partners took a further precaution.
Rather than mounting the bid on their own account, Virgin and
Mountleigh spent £100 on buying a shell company called Early-
gallop Ltd, changed its name to SMQ Ltd, and each agreed to put
in £3m. They then put together an agreement with the Bank of
Nova Scotia, one of the banks to which Virgin was most friendly,
that the bank would lend money to SMQ Ltd to pay for the early
purchases of shares. In a rising market, the shares of a company as
solid as Thorn-EMI would be highly unlikely to fall more than 10
per cent, so the £6m put up by Virgin and Mountleigh would allow
the bank to underwrite purchases of up to £60m with little risk to
itself. That would allow the two companies to build up a reasonable
stake in secret before being required under company law to declare
their hands as substantial minority shareholders in Thorn-EMI. It
would also allow Don Cruickshank, when telephoned by newspaper
journalists who had picked up rumours that Virgin might be preparing a bid for Thorn-EMI, to say without formally lying that Virgin
was not currently a holder of the company's shares. Unknown to
Cruickshank, however, Richard Branson was not content just to
build up a stake in Thorn-EMI through SMQ. With his usual
impulsiveness, he had gone ahead and arranged to buy a big block
of shares directly. That way, he hoped, Virgin's profits would be
all the greater when the bid was announced.

Then disaster struck. The stock market crash of October 1987
took 20 per cent off the share prices of all three of the players –
Virgin, Mountleigh and Thorn-EMI. Clegg realized quickly that
he would no longer be in a position to participate in the bid, and
withdrew. That left Branson with a dilemma: Thorn-EMI was now
a great deal cheaper than before, but Virgin's own borrowing power
was still further diminished. The company was facing not just the
loss of the £3m with which it had guaranteed the Bank of Nova
Scotia's loans to SMQ, but also a heavy loss on the shares it had
acquired on its own account.

To make matters worse, there was a separate problem with those
early purchases: Branson had not troubled to seek the authority of

the board before acquiring the shares, and there was some doubt as to whether it was proper for him to have used company money in such a venture. At the insistence of Cruickshank and Cob Stenham, one of the company's two non-executive directors, the Virgin board had agreed that each director on his own would have the right to commit the company to expenditure of £2.5m. Transactions up to £5m required the consent of a committee of three members of the board; above that, the full board had to give its approval. Given the fact that Virgin had amended its Articles of Association so that board meetings could be held on the telephone, Branson could hardly claim that the urgency of the matter gave him no choice but to act on his own. Had the Thorn-EMI shares held their value, the matter could easily have been cleared up with a retrospective approval. Now that they were worth a great deal less, the problem was more acute. In the end, Branson resolved it by agreeing to bear a loss of £700,000 on the shares himself.

A larger issue still remained, however. Could Virgin afford to swallow up the much larger Thorn all on its own? Cob Stenham's corporate finance specialists at Bankers Trust were asked to prepare for Virgin a secret dossier, exploring the possibility of a hostile bid for the whole of Thorn-EMI. Dated 22 October 1987, the document avoided any mention of the two companies involved. Virgin it referred to merely as 'V'; Thorn-EMI was codenamed Rose, and the takeover under contemplation was Project Rose.

'We assume', wrote the specialists at Bankers Trust, 'that there are two, not necessarily coincidental, aims in the proposed exercise, namely (1) to purchase Rose's music business for a price which is reasonable in the short term and will look cheap once V has applied its superior management skills; and (2) to make a profit on the resale of businesses not wanted.'

The paper went on to consider in turn three possibilities: a hostile break-up bid for the whole of Thorn-EMI, which would require a staggering £2.6bn in finance; a purchase of the EMI music business on its own for £400m, without the HMV shops; and a friendly joint venture with the company. The first idea had to be dismissed out of hand. 'It is clear', concluded the Bankers Trust specialists after several pages of figures, 'that without a partner for V to take any of the unwanted divisions, the uncertainties are too great and the breakup figures do not make a sufficient return to the equity holders [of Virgin] to justify their making the investment.'

In considering whether the second idea would work, the paper started from the assumption that 'the effect of V's superior management skills will raise profits from Rose's music division from the £26.4m for the year to March 1987 . . . to £30m in June 1988 and to £51m by June 1989.' Even with this dramatic improvement in financial performance, however, the deal would be hard to justify. There were different ways of finding the £400m, some involving more fixed-rate bank debt, others involving the issue of more new shares in Virgin with which the Thorn-EMI shares could be exchanged. But each had difficulties. All of them would result in 'an unattractively sharp drop [in Virgin's earnings per share] in the immediate future'. The analysts at Bankers Trust had two recommendations: Virgin should either offer much less for the EMI businesses – perhaps £330m, rather than £400m – or lower its sights, and try to go into partnership with EMI. The ideal solution, they concluded, would be to set up a joint-venture in which each side could concentrate on what it was good at: Virgin would run the combined record-label and publishing businesses, while EMI would run the combined record shops. Each would take a 75 per cent stake in the business it was running, with an option to go up to 100 per cent. If exercised, the options would thus leave Thorn-EMI with all the shops and Virgin with all the records. This, said Bankers Trust, would achieve a number of objectives simultaneously. It would reduce the initial outlay for Virgin; it would increase, rather than reduce, Virgin's overall financial performance, since the transaction would rid the company of its worst performing business; and by throwing a sop to EMI's pride, it might just win the agreement of Thorn-EMI's management.

Unfortunately, it did not. Branson had already made contact with Sir Graham Wilkins, Thorn-EMI's chairman; the two men had spoken over the telephone several times, and Wilkins had consulted Sir Colin Southgate, his chief executive, on the matter. Invited for a chat aboard the *Duende*, the chairman ate his lunch stolidly but politely, and told Branson doggedly that his company was not for sale – neither in whole nor in part. Wilkins had received prior intelligence from his company secretary's department that somebody was building up a stake in his shares. Snippets in the papers indicated that it might be Branson (though the papers were convinced that the deal was to be done with Alan Sugar's Amstrad, rather than with Mountleigh); and Wilkins knew that being only a tenth of the size of its prey was not necessarily a problem for Virgin. 'If you've got access to money,' Wilkins mused afterwards, 'it doesn't matter what your size is.' Although his company was in play, the 62-year-old industrialist saw no reason to concede to Branson's pressure. Far from taking Branson's offer seriously, he made a counter-offer: Thorn-EMI would make an offer for Virgin. On hearing that Branson did not want to sell, he finished his coffee and departed.

Branson knew when to cut his losses. Soon after it became clear that Virgin could neither afford to buy Thorn-EMI against its will nor gain its consent to a joint venture, he began to wind down the shareholding that had been acquired through SMQ. Thanks to the goodwill of the Bank of Nova Scotia, there was no need to do this in too much of a hurry. From time to time during the first half of 1988, rumours would sweep the market that Virgin was still considering a bid; rather than quashing them fully, the company was able to take advantage of the rising price of Thorn shares to mitigate its losses. By mid-May, the conglomerate's share price had recovered the setback of the October crash and more. Virgin's share price, however, had not. The disappointed Branson could not fail to notice that his aim to build a single British world-class record company was as far away as ever.

But the failure of the bid was also a lucky escape. As Ken Berry was later to observe, Virgin had no experience of running a conglomerate of the size of Thorn-EMI, and it was highly doubtful whether its management would then have been up to the job. EMI had many thousands more employees than Virgin, and while the smaller company specialized in signing artists and working hard on marketing and promoting them, the larger one had big investments in manufacturing and distribution.

Even had it succeeded in getting a grip on the problems of the troubled giant, ruthless tactics would have been required. There would have been no question of applying to EMI the mildly chaotic, small-is-beautiful principles that had governed Virgin's scattered offices. On the contrary: as the new owners of the business, Virgin would have been forced to make substantial cuts in order to repay the loans it had taken on to finance the purchase. The obvious strategy would have been to merge the staff that were duplicated across the two previously competing businesses – and since salaries were lower at Virgin, the firings would have had to take place mostly among EMI staff. In the past, Virgin had on occasion been forced to make a few people redundant; but the numbers had rarely risen above twenty, and the redundancies had taken place at times of recession when the company could reasonably claim that they were the only alternative to outright closure of Virgin businesses. There was no question that Trevor Abbott and Don Cruickshank had the toughness necessary to do this unpopular job. But the steps necessary to knock a Virgin-owned EMI into line would have given Branson quite a different reputation. Had he been unable to keep up the debt repayments, the resulting crisis might well have brought the rest of the Virgin group down along with the EMI acquisition. Had he succeeded in doing so, Branson would have emerged from the 1980s with a slash-and-burn reputation little different from that of any other bull-market entrepreneur.

By the time the last Thorn-EMI shares had been unloaded, Branson had already moved on to other concerns. The failure of Virgin's share price to recover properly from the October 1987 crash was becoming a source of irritation. Going public had brought an influx of money into the group, which was fast being spent on expansion of the record label in the United States, on the building of an expensive new Virgin Megastore in Paris, and on acquisitions and growth in the businesses for which Robert Devereux was responsible. But the listing had brought with it substantial costs, too, in the changes it dictated to the way in which Virgin was managed.

From day to day, it was true, not a great deal had changed. Simon Draper and Ken Berry still had the freedom to sign which artists they pleased to the record company; Richard Branson, for his part, was still able to pursue his extracurricular activities, whether ballooning, serving as the figurehead for the UK 2000 project, or drumming up publicity for the airline. It was more at the quarterly board meetings that the shoe pinched. The days in which the three had lounged in armchairs at Branson's house in the country, chatting informally over a free weekend, had long gone. Now the Virgin board meetings were set months ahead. There was a formal agenda, with board papers attached which they were required to study in advance. A secretary was present to take detailed minutes. And the three were required to justify their actions to the new directors who had been brought in.

Don Cruickshank, who was finding that he was by now devoting the greater part of his time to sifting through the new business ideas that outsiders were sending to Virgin in every post, and finding and interviewing candidates for managerial jobs, was determined to make his mark. Likewise the two non-executive directors: although Ken Berry remembered the board meetings when Virgin was public as undemanding affairs, Simon Draper would often lose patience when Sir Phil Harris, wishing to contribute something of his retailing expertise, turned the discussion around to his encyclopaedic knowledge of every High Street in Britain. Cob Stenham was perhaps the most rigorous financial analyst at those meetings, and would subject budgets, management accounts and new business ideas to colder scrutiny than anyone else.

In many ways, this new formality was an advantage. It meant that the Virgin Group was being run more as a single entity than as a federation of businesses that had little more than Richard Branson's equity stake in common. Draper and Berry found that they were being informed of new ventures – particularly in the communications empire being built by Robert Devereux – far earlier than before, and that more informed discussions were taking place about what Virgin should spend its money on. But the meetings were dull, there was no getting away from that; and they seemed to symbolize the unwelcome demands that institutional investors placed on the company.

Relations between Cruickshank and Branson were also becoming strained. Cruickshank saw his job as trying to bring to Virgin the standards of corporate governance that were later to be formalized by a committee under Sir Adrian Cadbury. Branson found it hard not to view this as obstruction. Too often, Cruickshank seemed to wish to scale back his good ideas, to slow down his expansion, to bureaucratize his relations with Virgin staff. Worst of all, he had taken to sending Branson finger-wagging memos. One of Cruick-shank's memos cast a distinctly unsympathetic eye over one of Branson's pet projects, the opening of a Virgin Megastore in Paris. It argued that the megastore was unlikely to deliver an acceptable return on the commitment of between £7m and £9m that it entailed. Cruickshank advised Branson to write off the idea, at a cost of up to £2.6m including what had already been spent. He could not resist the final sting: 'There is a real lesson here,' he wrote to his chairman, 'for the way we organize our retail activities around the world and exercise financial control'. Branson was always keen to learn from mistakes, keen to take advice from specialists; but he was not used to receiving his lessons from employees in such a peremptory way.

The clash of cultures came to a head at the February 1988 board meeting. Sensing the change of mood among the company's founders, Trevor Abbott had brought with him an extraordinary proposal, which was later to become known as Project Experience. He started off by giving a list of the advantages that Virgin had gained from the listing of its shares. It could use its own equity to buy other businesses. The listing had given the founders a way of taking money out. Virgin's new status as a PLC allowed it to borrow more easily and at lower interest rates. It was able to attract better management. It was being run in a more disciplined way. Potential deals had become easier to attract. And so on.

But there were also disadvantages in being public, Abbott argued. Keeping its shareholders informed and complying with the stricter obligations of a public company was expensive, he said. Since Branson and Draper did not want to lose control of the company, Virgin was able to issue new paper in theory, not in practice. Virgin shares were still not yet an institutional stock: although most of the shares sold in 1986 had now been sold to professional investors – apart from the Branson-Draper-Berry holdings – only 4 per cent of the equity was in the hands of individual investors. Virgin was getting on well with its bankers, but pension funds and investment trusts had not yet been convinced of the stability of the company's business. Yet the pressure to produce short-term profits was still there.

There was another consideration that Abbott did not mention. The fall in the company's share price since October 1987 had proved an embarrassment all around. It mattered little to Branson, Draper and Berry, though the lower value of their personal holdings made Virgin equity less valuable as collateral on which they could raise loans. For others, however, the consequences were worse. Plenty of employees had bought shares. So had a number of Virgin artists – including Phil Collins, Bryan Ferry and Mike Oldfield – for whom a loss of £150,000 was hardly more than a few months' royalties, but who nevertheless had no hesitation in conveying to Richard Branson their irritation. Peter Emerson, Branson's neighbour in Oxfordshire, had put in £30,000. Sir Phil Harris had put in £250,000. Trevor Abbott himself had done the same, and the fact that he had recently moved into a large new house had given rise to rumours inside the company that the losses on his Virgin shares were causing him financial difficulties. Although the collapse of Virgin's share price had 'not been a happy moment' to him, he would later maintain that the profits he had already made on the rest of the portfolio with which he played the stock market on his own account bailed him out.

Abbott's conclusion was stark: Virgin should go private. He asked the board for permission to look into the feasibility of buying back from the company's shareholders the £90m of new shares that had been issued as a result of the private placing and the listing.

Although it had evidently been cleared beforehand with Branson, the suggestion provoked uproar. Don Cruickshank went down the list of pros and cons, taking issue point by point with Abbott's analysis. With the backing of Robert Devereux, he argued forcefully that being a public company was not a fair-weather exercise: the disciplines it involved could be painful during difficult times, but Virgin should not shirk its responsibilities. Simon Draper agreed. He believed it would harm Virgin's reputation to change course so swiftly and with so little apparent reason. Ken Berry, the most vehement opponent of listing in the first place, kept his own counsel. What else could he have said, but 'I told you so'?

Despite Cruickshank's hostile response, the eventual outcome of the meeting was that Abbott won the approval he had asked for. Barely fifteen months since the listing, he was now free to go away and work on Project Experience – sorting out the financial, managerial and regulatory issues that would be involved in taking

Virgin's shares off the stock exchange list. That meeting also marked a subtle change in the politics at the top of the company. The non-executive directors became aware that their job as guardians of the interests of Virgin shareholders would now become far more taxing, since those interests now clearly diverged from those of Richard Branson, Simon Draper and Ken Berry. Don Cruickshank realized that his days at the company were numbered. He had joined Virgin in order to run it as a public company; once it returned to the private ownership of Richard Branson and his inner court, there could be no further place for him inside it. But it was for Trevor Abbott that the meeting was most significant. He had been brought in soon after Don Cruickshank, and subordinate to him. On his arrival, he had been not merely a 'suit', as the creatives liked to call those who had financial expertise, but a second-ranking suit at that. Increasingly, however, Abbott had discovered an affinity with Branson. Whereas Cruickshank appeared somehow to be in the way of Branson's ambitions, Abbott was someone who helped them become reality. If and when Virgin was bought out of the stock market, his position was certain to change. With the non-execs off the board, with Cruickshank out, with Simon Draper and Ken Berry and Robert Devereux once more devoting their energies to the businesses they ran themselves and spending little time worrying about the group as a whole – with all these changes, the man who took Virgin private would become Richard Branson's right-hand man.

Nobody knew how the leak had taken place. But on 7 July 1988, Richard Branson started to receive calls from journalists asking whether it was true that he was considering taking Virgin private. By the end of the day, he had been forced to make a formal statement confirming that he and some of the other Virgin directors were working on a plan to buy the company back from its stock market shareholders. The statement – put out on plain rather than on Virgin paper, to reflect the fact that Branson was acting on his own behalf rather than as chairman of the group – summarized the issue in three crisp sentences. 'Virgin's strategy of investment for long-term growth, with its effect on short-term profitability, has had an adverse effect on the share price . . . As a result, the benefits of a listing which Mr Branson anticipated at the time of the flotation 18 months ago [*sic*] are not being realized. In view of this he is exploring the possibility of a management buyout.'

The statement had two immediate effects. Since Branson made it clear that he was intending to buy out the company's small shareholders at the issue price of 140p a share, which was 40 per cent higher than the current market price at the time of the leak, the quoted price of Virgin shares immediately began to rise. They would continue to rise over the succeeding months as the buyout became a reality. The other effect of Branson's statement was to set off a stormy debate in the City and in the newspapers on the question of why the London stock market seemed so inhospitable to entrepreneurs. The influential Lex column of the *Financial Times*, for instance, conceded that the uncharitable view of the buyout was that 'Mr Branson, finding his charm wasted on the hard faces of the City, is taking his bat home in a huff.' But it went on to observe that Virgin had issued no new paper since the flotation, and to point out that there should be no reason for investors to be less tolerant of a company that grew organically than of one that grew by acquisition. It concluded by pointing out an irony: some of the same institutions that had spurned Virgin shares in the market would probably be willing to lend the money that Branson would use to take the company private. If Virgin set a trend, then a rival method of financing growing businesses would be established, and the stock market itself would be the loser.

Trevor Abbott had moved fast in the three months before the buyout proposal became public. The board had been split into two, with a committee set up under Don Cruickshank and Cob Stenham to look after the interests of the shareholders, and Abbott, Branson, Draper, Devereux and Berry working together to buy the company back. The board proposed that Stenham receive a fee of £40,000 for the extra work that would be required. Raising the finance proved a little more time-consuming than the *Financial Times* had expected. Despite the fact that the buyout team was taking corporate finance advice from its broking subsidiary Samuel Montagu, Midland Bank did not lend. In the event, it was a consortium of international banks led by Citibank that provided the £182.5m loan. The transaction price valued the company at £248m, and made it the largest company ever bought back from the stock market. That figure – and the apparent size of the loan – was perhaps misleading. Since 63 per cent of the shares had never left the hands of Branson and his team, they could be used as security against the £90m needed to buy out the outside shareholders.

The management buyout was to be carried out by a newly formed company called Glowtrack Ltd in which Branson and his colleagues had taken shares in proportion to their Virgin holdings; it would succeed only if three-quarters of the outside shareholders agreed to sell. To avoid the problem of a recalcitrant minority standing out, Samuel Montagu had advised Abbott to put to the vote not a straightforward offer to purchase, but a 'scheme of arrangement', whose passage would allow the offer to be implemented automatically for all the Virgin shares.

The contrast between Virgin's highly trumpeted entrance to the stock market and its more discreet withdrawal could hardly have been more startling. The shareholders' meeting took place on 21 November, a rainy Monday, at the wood-panelled Stationers' Hall in a back street behind St Paul's Cathedral. Forty shareholders turned up, many of them small investors who remained loyal to Branson and wanted to retain their stake in the company. Suitably sombre, Branson explained repeatedly that he had been forced into the buy-back by the collapse of the company's share price after the October 1987 crash. The two resolutions needed to effect the buy-back were passed by overwhelming margins – 24m votes to 1,140 for the first, and 27m to 365,000 for the second. And in a matter of barely an hour, Virgin was set back on its old private course.

For Cruickshank, who had at one stage suggested as a half-way house that a private placing of airline shares might serve as a substitute for Virgin's full listing on the stock exchange, this conclusion was accompanied by a further straining of relations with Branson. He knew that Branson would take direct control more forcefully than before, and that without restrictions on the amount of time he could spend on Virgin Atlantic, his interests would inevitably become focused on the airline. The strategy on which Cruickshank had worked so hard – that the Virgin Group should specialize in audio and visual businesses – was being abandoned without ceremony. He departed swiftly, on good terms with Branson and his former colleagues, but with an inevitable sense of melancholy.

Branson, by contrast, had a new spring in his step. He was quite sincere in thanking the shareholders at Stationers' Hall for their support, and saying that he had no regrets about their relationship over the previous two years. Nor had he reason to. The process of going public and back again had undoubtedly been accompanied by upheaval inside the management of the group; but this would have happened anyway. And even after the transaction costs involved, the fees payable to lawyers, brokers, underwriters and advisers, Virgin had not done badly out of its period in public. It had benefited in effect from an unsecured interest-free loan of £90m for more than two years, during a period of great expansion. By January 1989, when the transaction was complete, Virgin was more than twice as big a business as it had been in 1985 when the private placing had first been contemplated.

EIGHTEEN

Loos, Booze and Upper Class

As it grew older, Virgin Atlantic continued to dream up new ideas for its Upper Class service. Manicurists and masseuses were made available on some of its routes, though they had to be withdrawn from the Tokyo run launched in May 1989 after embarrassment was caused by a number of Japanese male passengers who misunderstood the nature of the service they were being offered. Board games, always a favourite Branson pastime, were offered in the lounge area of Upper Class. There was a Snoozzone for passengers who wanted just to sleep, with fluffy pillows and quilts provided, and the disturbance from lights and PA loudspeakers kept to a minimum after take-off. Passengers for whom time rather than comfort was the deciding factor could choose to be taken from central London to the airport not in the back of a limousine, but as a pillion passenger on a motorcycle.

Many of these ideas came from Branson himself – or to be more precise, from people he met. The airline's top management began to talk affectionately of what they called the Virgin Sample of One, referring to their employer's habit of having a long chat with someone, often a person with no knowledge of or expertise in airlines, and coming away with a page of notes in his day book and a determination to put some new idea into practice immediately.

The raft of unconventional ideas was more than just an expression of Branson's personal preferences. It was also a deliberate attempt to appeal to a younger, less stuffy kind of business traveller – particularly women. The most striking demonstration of this approach to the outside world was a memorable television advertising campaign which unashamedly sent up the sort of advertisements that Cathay Pacific and Singapore Airlines had made popular. Instead of a businessman settling into the comfortable seat, there was a businesswoman; instead of a deferential hostess in soft focus to bring the drinks, the camera showed an attractive young male steward. And, as if to add the final touch to the role-reversal, the female executive gave his shapely rear a leer as he moved away. Virgin had succeeded in having the best of both worlds. Many of its print advertisements concluded with the sentence: 'And we haven't even mentioned our stewardesses' – which managed to convey just the right impression of political correctness, while at the same time hinting to male customers for whom a pretty face was important that there would be no shortage in that department.

Some of Branson's ideas were perhaps before their time. While Virgin was negotiating with Airbus in 1993 over a new fleet of aircraft, Branson raised the idea of configuring the A340s he wanted without windows – an idea that had so far been confined to cargo freighters. In principle, the suggestion made good sense. American Airlines had saved itself millions of dollars by leaving the shiny bottom half of its aircraft fuselages unpainted, thus economizing simultaneously on paint and on the weight that the aircraft had to carry. Why should Virgin not go one better? The installation of windows required extra weight in the aircraft's hull, Branson argued, so removing them and installing video screens on the inside of the cabin would reduce the weight of the A340s, and thus the amount of fuel required to fly them. Wiser heads warned Branson that passengers' preferences might be irrational, but they were no less strong for that. His colleagues reminded him of the situation with aircraft seats: although it had been demonstrated conclusively that seats facing backwards were safer than those facing forward, no commercial airline had dared to install them.

The Virgin business class lounge that opened at Heathrow in 1993 was a more typical Branson project. The Clubhouse, as it was called, had all the fax machines, the bar and the showers that were becoming standard in airport lounges. But it also boasted an old-fashioned library, with a wooden model of a galleon made by French prisoners of war, and a three-tonne table brought from the old recording studio at the Manor, so vast that it had to be lowered through the roof. (Staff at the Manor were astonished when the removal men came to take away the table. They knew that the Manor and its contents had been sold, along with the rest of the business, to Thorn-EMI the previous year; so the table no longer belonged to Branson. Ken Berry, who was by then in charge of Virgin Music Group under its new owners, was hastily contacted, and agreed to telephone his former employer to raise the issue. In the event, the table was taken away to Heathrow all the same; but Branson agreed to pay for it.) There were three rooms of electronics – one each of Sega video games, of Linn hi-fi equipment, and of Philips interactive computer technology. A toy train trundled its way around a track. Fresh croissants and coffee were on offer at all hours; for passengers who had time to kill, specialists were on hand to offer facials, manicures, pedicures and haircuts. It was character-istic of Branson that although the brochures boasted that the cost of the lounge had been £1m, by no means all of the bill had been paid by Virgin. The airline had persuaded the makers of the cos-metics used in the beauty salon and the various electronics goods to make their products available for nothing – in return for the right to take passengers' names and telephone numbers so that they could send salesmen around to their homes after their return from abroad.

Branson was always ready to reconsider ideas that did not work. When a television documentary was made in 1994 about the service aboard his airline, an undercover BBC reporter observed that the toy train in the lounge was not working properly. Asked what the train was there for in the first place, the barman on duty, unaware that he was being filmed by a concealed camcorder, muttered that he thought it was 'a waste of time'. Two weeks later the reporter played Branson the videotape of the incident. With creditable good humour, the Virgin chairman promised to reconsider the toy train.

No sooner was the Clubhouse complete than the airline started planning an even larger lounge near the airport perimeter, where business travellers could leave their cars and take a dip in a swim-ming pool before boarding their flights. It was no surprise that by 1994, Virgin Atlantic had won awards for Best Transatlantic Airline and Best Business Class six years in succession.

With most of the businesses he owned, Richard Branson had made a point of allowing the managers in charge to take the decisions. This principle was applied most clearly to the record label, where the team of Simon Draper and Ken Berry were evidently admirably equipped to run Virgin Music Group without interference. Robert Devereux, too, enjoyed broad independence in the running of Virgin Communications. Yet even after the airline had turned into profit, Branson continued to interest himself in its daily affairs.

One reason for this was that he had simply been bitten by the airline bug. Many of those who have worked in airline management insist that the business is more exciting than anything else they have done, even if they cannot quite explain why. International air travel is a service industry in which customer satisfaction matters more than almost anything else, where (given the infrequency with which most passengers fly) the company has only one chance to get it right. It is also a twenty-four-hour business: an airline that flies passengers from Britain to both coasts of the United States and to Japan will always have an office open, or an aircraft flying, somewhere in the world.

Branson therefore found himself paying constant attention to small details. He would make a point of calling the Virgin Atlantic reservations lines, just as he had in the days of Randolph Fields, to make sure that telephone customers were being treated properly; and he later took great personal satisfaction from the fact that the firm was given an award for the best customer telephone service in Europe. On boarding a Virgin flight, he would first visit the cockpit, spend the next two hours with the cabin crew, then devote two hours to discussions with the in-flight supervisor, and pass the rest of the time strolling up and down the aisles talking to the passengers.

Copies of the visitors' book aboard each aircraft, in which Upper Class passengers were invited to write their comments, were forwarded to him so that he could write back if necessary. Every month, he would pick up the telephone and call fifty or so passengers to apologize for a mistake or comment on an idea. Branson found it no less of a chore to make these calls than anyone would, but he believed the self-imposed obligation was useful in keeping customer satisfaction at the front of his mind. This habit often led to hilarious results, though: many of the people he called were convinced that he was not the chairman of the Virgin group at all, but a practical joker playing a trick on them.

Station managers across the world had standing instructions to call him if an aircraft was delayed for more than two hours; if a delay was particularly severe, he would telephone the departure lounge and ask the staff to pass on his apologies to the passengers. This too was occasionally apt to backfire, however; at least some customers refused to believe that Branson himself had made the calls, and dismissed the messages as inept and insincere.

Branson also knew that until his airline could match the massive advertising budgets of giants like British Airways, he would have to generate free publicity for it. Aboard the inaugural flight to Miami, he appeared dressed up as Peter Pan; by the time the aircraft had landed, he had changed into the garb of an old-fashioned city businessman, complete with striped trousers, black jacket and furled umbrella. When the Civil Aviation Authority first allowed Virgin to operate flights from Heathrow, Branson decided to turn to his own advantage the fact that Lord King, BA's chairman, had described him as a 'pirate'. With a black tricorn hat on his head and a patch over his left eye, he posed in front of the model Concorde that stands at the entrance to Heathrow. The BA insignia on the aircraft behind him had been redecorated in Virgin livery, and a sign informed passers-by that the grass verge on which it stood was now Virgin Territory. Branson even managed to deflate a worldwide promotion in which BA flew tens of thousands of passengers free on 23 April 1991. Advertisements for Virgin reminded business travellers that they might not be able to make paying reservations on BA flights on that day, but they would always be welcome aboard Virgin Atlantic.

Although these antics translated directly into higher ticket sales, they worried the City. Virgin Atlantic formed no part of the public company that Branson had sold to the stock market. Nobody inside the group had taken remotely seriously Branson's legal undertaking at the time the Group had gone public 'to devote substantially the whole of his working time' to the development and management of the record business and retail, and only 'to spend on average some three days a month' on the airline and the other businesses that he owned privately under the Voyager umbrella. But investors could not fail to notice that Branson seemed perpetually to be on television and in the papers talking about his airline. Sooner or later, the institutions would begin to ask why he was not spending more time on the Group.

A year after the Group had gone public, Branson decided to recruit a managing director for the private interests of the Voyager Group whose presence could reassure the City that the airline's demands on his own time were being kept within limits. Head-hunters found for him a man who knew all about marketing travel businesses: David Benson, a top manager at the Sea Containers group who had run the recently revived Orient Express train service between London and Venice.

Benson arrived at Virgin Atlantic in November 1987 with two titles: managing director of the Voyager Group and commercial director of the airline itself. He immersed himself in airline affairs with gusto. Soon after his arrival, he put the entire company from directors downwards through a Dale Carnegie course, teaching the staff how to remember names, how to motivate themselves if they were feeling low, and how to make the most profitable use of their time. He started to collect the airline's first punctuality statistics, and drummed into the ground staff the understanding that business class travellers would begin to get twitchy if the aircraft sat at the gate even five minutes longer than it should. He established an On Board Products Group, whose job was to sift through the ideas that came through Branson and others, and put into effect only the most important so that the airline could continue to improve its service without jeopardizing the stability that its operations had already achieved.

The new Voyager Group managing director also became the first top manager of the airline to serve as a member of the cabin crew. He decided to fly a round trip on the busy Miami route, and chose to work at the back of the plane, where smokers and drinkers congregate. He was given basic safety training, though it was taken for granted that he had already flown across the Atlantic often enough to have a good idea of how to serve drinks. The crew knew who he was, but not the passengers. Since he was twenty years older than all his colleagues, they must have assumed that he was a senior steward who had been downgraded for some reason.

The two flights were a salutary experience, from which Benson learned two important lessons. One was to appreciate just how hard the cabin crews aboard a packed airliner have to work. The job was a cross between barman and a lavatory attendant – 'loos and booze', he later described it, recalling with particular distaste the Sisyphean task of keeping the outdated toilets presentable for eight hours at a stretch. The other lesson was that the control of stock on board needed badly to be done by computer. At the beginning and end of the flight – the times when the cabin crew ought to be as visible as possible to the passengers, welcoming them and helping them settle in their seats and get together their belongings – he discovered that they were instead spending their time counting whisky miniatures. He was flabbergasted to see how many hours of each flight had to be spent filling in forms. It was only much later that the stock sheets could be replaced with barcodes and portable computers.

In most companies, a chief executive with Benson's qualifications and experience would have spent much of his time keeping track of the Voyager Group's finances, and making strategic decisions about its future. He soon discovered, however, that Trevor Abbott wanted to keep the Voyager purse-strings in his own hands; and that Branson, behind the public façade of 'three days a month', was beginning to take more interest in the future of his airline than in the other businesses. Benson's master's degree from the Sloan School of Management at the Massachusetts Institute of Technology would clearly have to be applied to the more junior job of helping to run the airline from day to day. He accepted this effective demotion without a murmur – but the quality of his skills soon became evident from the growing sense of purpose and *esprit de corps* inside the airline's management.

It was not only the junior staff at the Virgin Atlantic head office who were impressed by David Benson. When Branson and Abbott started to look around for minority investors willing to inject new capital into the business, Benson reminded them that when he was working for Sea Containers he had held talks with the Seibu-Saison Group of Japan. In the event, he reported, those talks had come to nothing; but it might be worth making an approach. Benson was right. The introduction made, Trevor Abbott was left to negotiate the eventual deal, signed in May 1989, that gave Seibu-Saison a 10 per cent share in the airline, plus an option to acquire a further 10 per cent. The Japanese firm paid £6m for its shareholding, and lent the company a further £30m at a preferential interest rate. A large chunk of this sum was immediately set to work paying for the new maintenance department that the airline had established.

But Benson was not around long enough to see the completion of the deal that he had brokered. A month after the Virgin Group had been taken private, an odd incident occurred at the airline. Benson and his colleagues were told that Michael Batt, a star marketing man from British Airways, had been headhunted to take over as the airline's new commercial director. Batt arrived on a rainy morning in November 1989 and, after receiving a long briefing from Benson, spent his first day in meetings. Benson explained at the end of the day that he was about to leave on a short business trip, but suggested that they should talk later in the week. When he telephoned Batt to see how he was getting on, he was told by one of the secretaries that Batt had 'gone househunting'. In fact, Batt had decided not to take the job at Virgin Atlantic. Having worked for the company for a grand total of two days, he left and went back to his old employers at British Airways.

Only a handful of people at Virgin Atlantic know what led to this bizarre chain of events. On Batt's first day, it was clear from his sketchy knowledge of commercial matters that he was an odd choice for the job of commercial director; on the other hand, he was equally clearly a marketing expert with a good overview of the business as a whole. Batt had in fact been offered the job of Joint Managing Director of the airline, in a move to put in an Abbott loyalist at the top of the airline.

Michael Batt had clearly not been warned what to expect. The reception he received from Roy Gardner, the airline's current managing director, was so chilly that he could only conclude that he had been placed in an impossible position. Since he was not based at the airline's head offices in Crawley, Trevor Abbott had been unable to help him over the stormy introduction. Richard Branson was in Japan, preparing to fly over the Pacific in a hot-air balloon. So Batt walked out, and decided never to return – not even to collect the two days' pay he was owed. 'The moral of the story,' he said afterwards, 'is never to accept any title with the word "joint" in it.'

With the Virgin Group now no longer listed on the stock market, Branson was free once again to devote to the airline such time as he wished. David Benson therefore withdrew from daily involvement in the affairs of Virgin Atlantic, and concentrated instead on doing those parts of the Voyager Group managing director's job that had not already been annexed by Trevor Abbott. Yet the responsibilities he was left with were clearly unmatched to his talents and experience. When, one day in April 1990, Abbott walked into his office and closed the door, Benson knew that he was about to be either promoted or sacked.

It was the latter. Abbott told him bluntly that there was no longer a job for him to do, and ordered him to clear his desk. Benson's contract specified that he should be given six months' notice; Abbott offered eight months' salary instead. Benson saw no point in appealing to Richard Branson directly. He knew that Branson hated firing people, preferring others to do it for him; and he felt sure that Abbott must have consulted Holland Park before making his move. A personal appeal might shame Branson into reinstating him, as similar appeals by others in the past had done. But Benson's pride prevented him from putting himself into the position of a supplicant. He took the money and went back to Sea Containers, where his experience at the airline soon won him a more senior job than he had left. He allowed his Virgin Atlantic share options to lapse, but spent two years arguing with Abbott over a bonus that he claimed he was due. In the end, unable to wring from Abbott the full value of his bonus in cash, Benson settled for a bonus paid in Virgin Atlantic air tickets.

Benson's departure left unresolved the airline's lack of direction at the top. On the departure of Randolph Fields, Roy Gardner had been promoted from running the technical side of the airline – he held the air operator's certificate, without which no airline is allowed to carry scheduled passengers – to the job of managing director. The move made sense at the time, for a bad safety reputation would have done the airline more harm than almost anything else. When Virgin Atlantic was launched, Branson had joked that with only one aircraft, the company would have either the world's best safety record, or the world's worst. His decision to give the title of managing director to the man who was in charge of safety was testimony to how seriously he took the issue.

Gardner's conservative approach to maintenance had also helped to keep costs to a minimum. When serviced to the exacting standards he demanded, the ex-Argentine 747 that was Virgin Atlantic's first aircraft turned out to be a highly reliable machine, losing only a few days of operation in its first three years of life. It had been Gardner who refused to accept delivery of two of the *Maiden Voyager*'s four original engines, successfully demanding that Boeing replace them without charge; and it was to be Gardner again who extracted compensation of £1.5m from Airbus Industrie after the European aircraft manufacturer failed to honour its promises on the delivery of the new A340s that Virgin acquired in 1994.

But Roy Gardner was not a marketing man, and nor was he a personnel manager. Some of those working for him observed that behind his bluster, he was a gentle man who shrank from taking ruthless decisions. Others, noticing how often he would telephone his wife from work and discuss office matters with her, took to teasing the couple gently by introducing them at parties as 'the managing director of Virgin Atlantic and her husband'. Although the airline had a good finance director in Nigel Primrose and a good marketing manager in Chris Moss, it still needed someone at the top to impose some management disciplines and to remind the airline's staff how important it was to please its customers. Consistency was not yet the airline's strong point, despite David Benson's good work. The service aboard a Virgin jet could be highly sensitive and attentive on a good day, but spectacularly offhand on a bad one.

Achieving that consistency was not a job for Richard Branson himself. He was, as he acknowledged, much more interested in starting new businesses than in running established ones; and since he had, according to one of his senior managers, 'the powers of concentration of a gnat', it was hard for him to focus on the myriad small details that combined make the difference between a tolerably good and an outstanding airline. Yet there were precious few world-class service companies in Britain. It was only in the United States, with its Disneys, IBMs and McDonalds, that there was a big pool of talented managers who knew how to run businesses in service industries. So there was no way in which to find an outsider who could instil into the airline the discipline that Branson realized it needed but he could not provide alone.

What Britain did have, however, was a retail sector that was more efficient than that of any other European country, driven forward by a handful of powerful and innovative companies like J. Sainsbury, Tesco, Asda and Marks & Spencer. In September 1989, just before the Virgin Group withdrew from the stock market, Abbott had brought into the management of the European megastores one of the crack retailers in the country: Syd Pennington of Marks & Spencer. The solution to the problem at the airline, Branson realized, was staring him in the face.

Pennington came from a working-class family in Glasgow, and his father was a joiner. He left school, like Branson, without going to university. He had joined the civil service and resigned at 21, as soon as he realized that he would have to wait seven years for his next promotion. He had then moved to Marks & Spencer, and spent the next seventeen years in different stores across the country's national chain of mainly city-centre outlets, ending up as manager of the company's store at Enfield, a northern suburb of London. Soon after Pennington arrived there, M&S started an experiment; as well as selling basic food ingredients, it began to stock chilled cooked meals suitable for reheating at home. The trouble was that the products were scattered around the store: chicken Kiev in the cabinet with the raw chickens, fish pie along with the plaice fillets, and so on. Pennington wondered whether they might sell better if the different products were brought together in a single refrigerator. The results of moving them were astounding: sales rose fourfold, and within a month the company had established a prepared foods department to exploit the new opportunity.

But Pennington was not content. As he saw sales of prepared dishes exploding, he began to ask why M&S insisted on confining its food departments to the basements or the back of stores, where customers had to walk past rail after rail of sweaters and blouses in order to buy a sandwich. Why not open some shops that sell only food, he asked. The company's management was shocked; to do so, after all, would put M&S in competition head on with

Sainsbury's and the other supermarkets. Once again, Pennington won a corporate battle. He persuaded the firm to open a new food store at Islington, just north of the City of London, on the site of an old Budgen supermarket that had been driven out of business by a Sainsbury superstore. When M&S opened its first all-food store on the same site, it took £350,000 in its opening week – and Pennington's reputation was made. He was swiftly taken out of line management and told to come up with a business plan for developing fifty more food-only stores. It was then that he was headhunted, and brought in to oversee the development of the Virgin megastores across Europe. One day in February 1990, Richard Branson called him, and asked him to take some time off his job and spend a few days putting his retailing expertise to work at Crawley looking at the airline's duty-free operation.

Pennington found that the business was a mess. Nobody had identified which goods should be sold on which routes, or at what margins. Perhaps because the cabin crews had been paying more attention to the passengers, the inventory control systems on board were inaccurate. Pennington pointed out to Branson how expensive it was for Virgin Atlantic to load unnecessary stock on to an aircraft: every can of Coca-Cola carried back and forth across the Atlantic for a month, he pointed out, cost the airline $6.32 in jet fuel. Such details may seem trivial, he conceded; but retailing, whether in a supermarket or in an aircraft 37,000 feet above the ground, is all about detail. He asked for permission to spend more time at the airline's offices in Crawley and at Gatwick, and found that there were similar problems in the food operation: it was less tightly and effectively controlled than it should have been. 'The good news,' he reported in conclusion to Branson over breakfast a few days later, 'is that you don't have a duty-free problem. The bad news is that you have a structural management problem.'

Abbott was aware of that; he had been trying for years to persuade Branson that Roy Gardner's engineering expertise did not qualify him to run an entire airline. When Branson asked Pennington what changes he would propose, the former retailer agreed to spend two or three days the following month looking at the airline in more detail, and to report back with an action plan of changes that should be put into effect. Three days later, Branson pre-empted him. On Pennington's return from a trip to Milan, where he was negotiating a site for a new Megastore, his secretary greeted him with the news: 'You've been made joint managing director of the airline.'

Three years after Pennington moved into the Crawley offices, the airline's duty-free sales had risen from £1.8m a year to £6m. He had raised the gross margins in the department to 50 per cent, and was preparing to open a new business selling casual clothes to Virgin passengers by mail. Plans were also in train to add a shopping channel to the multi-channel television systems that were installed in the back of the economy-class seats, and to offer a casino-in-the-sky for the benefit of travellers on the Hong Kong route who wished to gamble against themselves on the television screen in front of each seat, paying for their stakes with cash advances drawn electronically from their credit cards.

Pennington also introduced a third class to Virgin travel. Not first class – even though the airline felt that it could do a better job on the caviare-and-roast-beef brigade than most of its rivals. Instead, Virgin Atlantic began to offer a Mid Class. The uninspiring name was a compromise: David Tait, with his eye firmly on the US market, had wanted to call the new service A Touch of Class, while Chris Moss, the London-based marketing director, had preferred to take the joke on British snobbery a step further by establishing a Middle Class. But the creation of a new class of service was a recognition that two new markets had grown up who were currently falling between the cracks of the existing three-tier air ticket system. One was made up of the growing number of business travellers whose employers were unwilling to pay hundreds of pounds extra for fancy food, but who still demanded the flexibility of a full-fare economy ticket on which they could change the return date or routing at any time. The other was the new middle-aged rich: the group of people whose dead parents had bequeathed them a house which they did not need, and who therefore had more disposable income than they had ever possessed before. A study of the demographics convinced Pennington that these people would be willing to pay full economy fares – twice the price of the cheapest available discount fares, or more – for a wider and more comfortable seat, and for bags that emerged more quickly on the airport carousels upon arrival than those of the tourists at the back of the aircraft.

As 1990 turned into 1991, the skies above Virgin Atlantic began to darken. Recession in the European Community and United States began to bite, and airline traffic to suffer accordingly. On 1 August 1990 the forces of President Saddam Hussein of Iraq had invaded Kuwait, and by Christmas the world was convinced that the American-led multinational forces stationed in Saudi Arabia were poised to strike back against Saddam. Oil prices – and consequently the cost of jet fuel – began to rise. Big corporations all over the world, whether in Los Angeles, Osaka or Munich, began to tell their staff not to travel.

The year 1991 was the worst ever in the history of aviation. Collectively, the world's airlines lost a total of over $4bn (£2.5bn); Virgin Atlantic did less badly than many, but could not avoid losing money on its normal operations. Nigel Primrose, the company's finance director, did his best with the figures, and managed to come up with two improvements for the accounts. He took advantage of the provisions in the Companies Act that allow a business to change its accounting date once every five years, and moved the end of Virgin Atlantic's accounting period from 31 July to 31 October. This made good business sense, since it had always been an inconvenience for the airline to end its financial year in midsummer, when business was at its busiest. Now that the Virgin Group was no longer public, the bankers were not so insistent that the airline's year-end must match those of other businesses that Branson owned. But the change made financial sense too, since the fifteen-month accounts that the company now had to prepare would include two summers – 1990 and 1991 – but only one winter. This made the figures as a whole look greatly more attractive.

Primrose also discovered that he could liberate £6m by selling one of the fleet of aircraft – the second 747, which was being used on the Miami route – and leasing it back. Entering the profit made on this transaction in the accounts as an exceptional item, Virgin Atlantic was just able to scrape by with a profit of £734,000. With a tax credit thrown in of £873,000, Branson was thus able to show his bankers a retained profit for the financial period of £1.6m.

He was less fortunate the next year. With only a single summer in the figures, and with no more aircraft available for sale and lease-back, Virgin Atlantic plunged £21m into loss in the twelve months to 31 October 1992 – thus swallowing up the profits of the fat years from 1987 to 1990, and throwing the venture as a whole since its beginning in 1984 back into the red. Particularly depressing was the Tokyo route. The sharp recession that had now begun in Japan had produced a dramatic fall in traffic on this once lucrative route. With British Airways, Japan Airlines and All Nippon Airways fighting for customers between London and Narita, Virgin lost well over £3m on that route alone.

Although the two years of miserable results could be blamed in part on the inhospitable economic environment, there was a sense of desperation inside the top management of the airline during that financial year. Richard Branson had been given an opportunity to keep his airline small and to milk to the full the profits from its two routes; but he had not taken it. By opting instead for expansion, he had done the commercial equivalent of playing double or quits. Not only had the airline's growth gone into reverse; its turnover had shrunk by 10 per cent to £303m in 1992. Worse still, it seemed clear that in percentage terms at least the airline could never be so profitable again as it had been in 1988.

Branson continued to maintain a brave face in public. But for the first time since the airline's disastrous opening summer, he would have been forgiven for wondering whether he had in fact made a terrible mistake in entering this business in the first place.

NINETEEN

The Price of Privacy

THE DEAL THAT took Virgin private put an end to Richard Branson's ambitions to take over Thorn-EMI's music business. Yet paradoxically, the aborted takeover and the privatization were similar transactions. In both cases, Branson raised the necessary finance with debt rather than equity – by borrowing money at a fixed rate of interest, rather than by issuing new shares that gave outsiders control of the business. The privatization of Virgin, which entailed the borrowing of £182.5m, was only a tenth of the size of the Thorn-EMI deal that never happened; but in both cases the debt was so large that it could only be repaid if Branson could raise money both by selling off peripheral businesses, and by showing a sustained and dramatic improvement in profits in the core businesses. And in both cases, the result of the deal was to increase the risks and the rewards to Branson personally. If his ambitions were fulfilled, he would make a very large sum of money. If they were not, he would be sunk.

The terms of the loan that enabled Branson and his co-directors to buy back Virgin from the stock market were a mixture of favourable and strict. The interest rate demanded by Citibank and the other 21 banks in the consortium was only 1.5 percentage points above LIBOR – the rate at which banks in London routinely lend money to one another. That was proof not just of the high standing in which Branson was held by the lenders, but also of the professionalism with which Trevor Abbott had put together the buyout proposals during months of negotiation. To avoid conflicts of interest at Virgin's bankers and brokers, the buyout group were formally advised separately by a team from Samuel Montagu. Since the vast majority of work was done in-house, Samuel Montagu received only a modest commission, reflecting the few days of work that its staff put in.

Abbott's ability to do most of the buy-back work without the help of outsiders was all the more impressive given that an earlier plan to raise money by issuing preference shares in the now highly profitable Virgin Atlantic Airways had been abandoned. In the absence of new finance for the airline, Abbott had not only to rearrange the divisions of the Virgin group, but also to refinance Voyager's debts. Branson had used his Virgin shares as collateral for the money he had borrowed to finance Voyager. Shares in a private company were much less easy to sell than shares traded on the London stock exchange; so it was only understandable that Voyager's bankers should ask for new security arrangements as the group went private.

Although the interest rate looked favourable, the Abbott plan set high targets for the newly private Virgin group. Its covenants to the banks showed that the group was promising to turn in retained earnings totalling £7m by the end of the year to July 1989, £20m by the end of the 1990 financial year, £45m by the end of 1991, and £85m by the end of 1992. It also undertook to find £55m-worth of businesses to sell. Even by the standards of the cracking growth that Virgin had turned in over the previous three years, these targets would require impressive performance. An internal projection, which was not made public, showed what the plan would mean in practice. The retail and property businesses had turned in disappointing figures while Virgin was public; had the published accounts separated the two, it would have been impossible to hide the fact that the retail businesses were actually losing money. Yet the buyout arrangements made some optimistic assumptions about their performance over the coming five years. The two divisions were expected to contribute combined profits of £10.4m in 1989, £11.8m in 1990, £13.8m in 1991, £15.7m in 1992, and £18.3m in 1993.

For the first few months after the buy-back, Branson's plans proceeded on track. Don Cruickshank departed in January, and the two non-executive directors ceased to come to board meetings; only after their departure was Branson able to confess that he had never quite understood the point of people helping to make decisions about a company without actually working for it. Trevor Abbott won his prize for successfully negotiating the privatization: he took over as group managing director in early 1989, soon after the company's small shareholders had received their cheques. The disposals that Virgin had promised its bankers, however, were a little slower in coming in. Vanson Developments, the group's property company, had been put on the blocks early in 1988, but the market had peaked and begun to decline and it had still not yet found a taker. In August, Robert Devereux sold off the film and distribution businesses to Management Company Entertainment Group, a company from Los Angeles. The price of the deal was $83m, but only a proportion of that sum came in cash; the rest was paid in shares in MCEG, which were quoted on NASDAQ, the electronically traded second-tier stock market of the United States. Better news came from Virgin Records America Inc, which was at last turning into profit: by the 1990 financial year, its sales would rise to a healthy $100m.

In public, Branson now felt able to say how relieved he was to have relinquished Virgin's quoted status. But he could have been forgiven some gentle gloating, too. The airline, which the brokers and underwriters had assured him was too cyclical and risky to be worth selling, had now had three successive years of profits; the £5m that Branson had put at risk in the Voyager Group, when he split it off and bought it as a separate business, now looked like a spectacularly good investment. The success of the record labels in America, and to a lesser extent Japan, was still more satisfying: these, after all, were the investments that the City had not dared to make – the investments on account of which his share price had been marked down and the big institutions had snubbed him. Branson had been proved right with unexpected speed.

But the job of repaying the money that had been borrowed in order to take Virgin private was now beginning to look a little daunting. The economic background had swiftly become less hospitable. Economic growth slowed down sharply as the bull market came to an end, and the floating interest rates to which Virgin's £182.5m was linked began to rise. Branson could console himself with the thought that base rates at 15 per cent were crippling other British businesses, too. But the privatized Virgin, taking also its other debts into account, was particularly highly leveraged. Having expected trading profits to rise and to receive a further windfall from asset sales, Virgin now began to look a little overborrowed.

It was against this background that the group began to look for ways of raising capital to pay off the debt. Early in 1989, Ken Berry went to Tokyo to talk to a giant Japanese media group that had ambitions to move into the global record business. The company was called Fujisankei; it had sales of over $5bn a year, and interests in television stations and tabloid newspapers, but ambitions to expand its business abroad. The deal that Berry laid before a pair of senior Fujisankei executives at the Intercontinental Hotel in the Shinjuku district of western Tokyo was straightforward: a quarter of the Virgin Music Group (the record labels) for $150m (£96m). At first sight, the implied $600m value that this placed on the empire of Simon Draper and Ken Berry might have seemed astounding for a business that only two years earlier had made profits before interest of £20m. But Virgin was now one of a dwindling number of record companies that were both large and independent; and its value could not properly be assessed only by looking at its profit-and-loss account. Invisibly locked inside its balance sheet was a treasure-trove of copyrights, including the rights not only to a large number of hit singles and albums that were continuing to sell well year after year, but also to a great deal of music not yet even written by artists under contract to Virgin.

It had been agreed inside Virgin before Berry's departure that the proposal would be put before the Japanese company, with the clear message to take it or leave it. In the event, the deal took ten weeks' hard negotiations in London and New York. Fujisankei was helped by its long-standing adviser, the Industrial Bank of Japan; it also hired Skadden, Arps & Co, a leading firm of New York lawyers, to act on its behalf. With so many professionals on the Fujisankei side, there was very often a mismatch across the boardroom tables at which the contract negotiations took place. On one side would be a leather-jacketed Ken Berry and Trevor Abbott, accompanied by a brace of lawyers from Freshfields; facing them would be a dozen or even more Japanese and American faces.

It had taken two or three months for Fujisankei's record company, Pony Canyon, to persuade two other companies in the group,

Fuji TV and the radio station Nippon Broadcasting, to contribute half of the $150m it was being asked to pay. But Akira Ijiji, the head of Pony Canyon, did not see the deal as only financial. He wanted two other things from Virgin: a joint-venture deal allowing Pony Canyon to distribute Virgin recordings inside Japan and in Korea, Taiwan and Singapore; and he wanted some knowhow. The Japanese side proposed that they should be allowed to send ten employees to London to work inside Virgin and learn how the company – and the European music business – worked. Armed with this knowledge, Fujisankei hoped, it would be able to do business in continental Europe and the United States more easily in future. Ken Berry was willing to negotiate on the first idea, but not on the second. It was therefore agreed that Pony Canyon would be given the right to distribute Virgin recordings in Japan, which was currently held by JVC. Fujisankei was welcome to nominate a director and an auditor to attend the quarterly board meetings of Virgin Music Group; since the board was largely a ceremonial affair now that Virgin had gone private, the concession meant little. But only one Fujisankei employee would be allowed actually to see inside the Virgin operations.

Fujisankei conceded on these points, but the firm could be forgiven its caution. The price it was being asked to pay made the proposed deal not only Japan's largest investment in the European media business, but also the biggest ever equity acquisition in Britain by a Japanese company. When the negotiations got difficult, Abbott resorted to his nuclear option: he told the Fujisankei executives that he had received a written offer from Thorn-EMI of $90m for 10 per cent of the company, and threatened to walk out of the negotiations and take that offer unless Fujisankei saw reason. In the end the Japanese company conceded; but it won an all-important concession in increasing the proportion of the company it was getting for its $150m from 24.99 to 25.1 per cent. The significance of this was that the larger holding allowed Fujisankei if it chose to block any decisions of the Virgin Music Group board to change the capital structure of the business, for instance by issuing new shares or bonds, that might harm Fujisankei's interests. There was also an agreement that each side would give the other first refusal in the event that it ever sold its stake.

The proceeds from the Fujisankei deal removed much of the pressure on Virgin's management. But as the months of 1990 went by and the recession began to develop, it became clear that bringing in nearly £100m was not enough. Further sales would have to be made if Virgin was to service the debts it had taken on. Not only were the Megastores struggling against a general background of slowing retail sales and failing to deliver the promised profits; Vanson Developments was running into more serious trouble still. It had managed to sell off almost none of its portfolio, and the accelerating fall in property prices was making it seem less and less likely that the company ever would.

Under the circumstances, the deals that Branson and Abbott struck in the early summer of 1989 were startlingly advantageous. In May, Seibu-Saison, the Japanese travel and leisure group that had bought Inter-Continental Hotels in 1988, paid £6m for 10 per cent of Virgin Travel Group, the airline's new parent company, and made a £30m loan at a highly advantageous 7 per cent rate of interest, which it would have the option to convert into a further 10 per cent of the airline group's equity under an agreed formula in 1992. In June, a joint venture deal was signed with Marui, one of Japan's largest retailers, that gave Virgin a chance to try out the Megastore on the Japanese record-buying public without having to sink millions of pounds into high-priced Tokyo real estate. The exact terms of the deal were never disclosed, but Marui was reported to have paid $20m for half of the newly formed Virgin Megastores Japan. The company's first shop opened in the basement of a department store in Shinjuku, one of the capital's busiest shopping districts. Virgin put a few hundred thousand dollars into the company, but Marui made the vastly more valuable contribution of 10,000 square feet of prime selling space in the world's most expensive capital city.

By the end of 1990, however, Virgin seemed as far as ever from its target of reducing the debt to manageable levels – so once again, Ken Berry was sent on the road. This time his job was to look for a deal that would bring in much larger sums of money by ceding partial control of the record business to one of the five multinational companies. The key was in the fact that Virgin had always contracted out to others its manufacturing and distribution. Companies that already had pressing plants for vinyl records and CDs, and that had the sales staff on the ground to distribute records across the world's major markets, could cut their costs sharply if they were given the chance to distribute Virgin records as well. A deal that gave one of these firms a large minority stake in the business and a permanent right to manufacture or distribute for Virgin in the territory in which it was dominant would have been far more valuable than a traditional minority stake. Berry's tentative approaches revealed two conclusions. There was certainly demand out there: Warner was keen to distribute Virgin records in the United States, and Bertelsmann Music Group of Germany wanted to do so in the rest of the world. But neither firm was willing to offer a high enough price. In any case, it would have been hard to structure the huge interest-free loans that the two companies were willing to offer in such a way as to ease the wider difficulties of the Virgin Group as a whole.

It was therefore after all other possibilities had been exhausted that Branson had to face the inevitable: Virgin Music Group, the crown jewels of the empire, the business that had produced most of its profits over the past decade, the fruit of more than fifteen years' work by Simon Draper and Ken Berry, must now be put on the block. The decision was a gutwrenching one, even for Trevor Abbott who had only joined the company as it was preparing to go public. But by early 1991, what else was there to do? Robert Devereux had boasted of the huge increases in value of a number of Virgin Communications businesses; but the offers that had been received failed to live up to his predictions. With the exception of the retail operations in Europe, all the joint ventures that could be made already had been; all the minority stakes that could be sold had been. Virgin was in no immediate danger of becoming insolvent; but the airline, the retailing businesses and communications could not continue to expand at the rate that Richard Branson wanted if he kept the record company. It was a simple choice: keep the record business and shrink – or sell it and expand.

In March 1991, Branson asked Anthony Salz, his lawyer at Freshfields, to invite three groups of investment bankers to the house in Holland Park for meetings. He knew that he could rely on Salz's discretion not to say too much before the bankers arrived. What he was allowed to let out, however, was a piece of information that would send a shock wave through the world record business. Virgin Music Group was up for sale.

John Thornton, sitting in his managing director's office at the London office of Goldman Sachs, responded swiftly when Salz called.

'Are you approaching any other investment bankers?' he asked. 'And have you called any of them yet?'

On hearing that the answer was yes to the first and no to the second, Thornton immediately swung into action. He explained confidentially to the lawyer at the other end of the telephone that this was a small industry. It would be disastrous for the rumour-mill to get hold of the news that Branson wanted to sell, for there was a risk that he would then get a lower price for Virgin Music. The difficulty with talking to the three different bankers that Virgin had decided to approach on the transaction was that whichever Branson chose, two must inevitably be disappointed. It would be too much to expect them to keep the news secret for the months that it would take to find a buyer and pin down all the details. Thornton therefore suggested an alternative strategy. Why not hold the first meeting with him, have a general chat about it, and then approach the others if Branson felt it necessary to do so?

Salz was too quick to miss the advantage that this approach would give to Thornton. Without seeing the other bankers, Branson would be unable to judge whether Goldman Sachs was the best; he would also be negotiating blind on the bank's fee for handling the transaction. He knew this; and he knew that Thornton knew he knew it. But Thornton's argument sounded plausible. The possible loss that would come from a premature leak of the news that Virgin Music was for sale could outweigh tenfold the difference in fees or in expertise between one specialist and another.

Thornton's presentation at the Holland Park meeting was impressive. He began by reminding Branson of what a valuable commodity he had on his hands. Virgin Music was the last remaining record company of any size that had not yet been swallowed up by one of the international majors. It had a freewheeling, hip image, a market niche, that more established companies would find it impossible to replicate. It had a stunning list of artists, of which it had lost almost none. And finally, there was the Branson factor: the involvement of its celebrity chairman in the business conjured up certain associations that made it more attractive to record buyers, and hence to potential owners. But there was one point which was more important than everything else. Selling a record company, Thornton argued, was nothing like selling a manufacturing company. It was about romance; about creating a wonder. About making purchasers feel not merely that they wanted to, but that they *had* to own Virgin Music.

Then the conversation turned to specifics. Branson said that he would prefer to sell the record business to a British company rather than to a foreign one; Thornton agreed that this pointed to Thorn-EMI, and added that he already knew well Sir Colin Southgate, Thorn's chairman. There were obvious merits in taking the company to Thorn-EMI first, without offering it to any other takers. But that strategy would have disadvantages too; psychologically, the lack of competition would make it hard for Virgin to bid up the price that Thorn-EMI offered. Thornton and Branson therefore agreed on the following plan of action. They would take to Southgate a detailed and specific proposal, with the message that Virgin would be willing to deal with him and him alone. If Southgate was not willing to accept it, then the sale must be thrown open to other bidders.

Thornton was given instructions to go away and prepare some financial projections based on confidential management information from inside the music group, and call a meeting with Southgate. In the event, Southgate brought with him two colleagues to the meeting: Jim Fifield, the head of the EMI music division, and Philip Rowley, his financial guru. Denuded of its statistics, Thornton's case was a simple one. Virgin Music was still a fast-growing company whose profits were lagging behind its exploding turnover; any valuation based only on profits must therefore be doubtful. Historic profits alone would undervalue it; estimates of profits to come would be contentious, because the Virgin side were certain to be more optimistic than the Thorn side. Instead, Thornton proposed, the two sides should sit down and look at the annual cost savings and revenue increases that would result from putting

Thorn's music interests together with those of Virgin. That, rather than Virgin's profits as an independent, was the number on which the valuation ought to be based. And his hope was that by building up a picture from the same financial details, the two sides would be able to come to an arrangement within a month. 'What we want to know,' he told them, 'is whether we're in the same ballpark.'

They were not. Thornton's figures argued that the net present value to Thorn of the stream of future savings and earnings ought to be well over £500m; Southgate and his colleagues argued that Virgin's music publishing company was easier to price, since its value was mostly based on the book of copyrights that it held. They suggested, therefore, that this part of the business, along with the recording studios, should be taken out of the calculation and valued separately. According to their method, they said, the calculations came up with a range between £320m and £400m. Calmly and politely, Thornton told them to go to hell. 'You've missed a real opportunity here,' he said. 'We could have shut this down right away. If you think better of it, we're happy to talk. But now we'll shake hands as friends, and start talking to other purchasers.'

The next company on Thornton's list of potential purchasers was MCA, the Music Corporation of America. Founded in 1924 by Dr Julius Stein, a former vaudeville back-up man to Mae West, MCA had become by the late 1980s one of the most powerful forces in the entertainment industry of America, and thus the world. Its interests had diversified from booking dance-bands to representing actors and musicians as an agency to making and selling television shows and films. Known as 'the Octopus' because of the reach of its tentacles, MCA also had superlative political connections resulting from its long association with a B-movie actor called Ronald Reagan who was elected US president in 1980. MCA had already made clear its wish to expand in the record business by purchasing Geffen Records, a rising US independent label, for the astounding price of $710m. Virgin, which was still a minor player in North America but would be able to help MCA assure its place in the single European market, seemed to fit neatly into the company's strategy. There was just one difficulty: although MCA was still managed from day to day by Lew Wasserman, the cinema usher whom Dr Stein had appointed its vice-president in 1936, it now

had a new owner. MCA had been sold to Matsushita Electric Industrial, the world's biggest maker of consumer-electronics products,
a year earlier. On a transaction as big as the purchase of Virgin,
the shots would be called at Matsushita's head office outside Osaka,
not in Hollywood.

Unwilling to talk to Wasserman until he knew which way the
land lay, but equally unwilling to face the humiliation of an outright
rebuff from MCA's new owners, Thornton decided that his best
strategy was to find out discreetly whether MCA would be allowed
to buy Virgin Music if it wished to. Outside Japan, there was only
one man to call: Michael Ovitz, head of Creative Artists Agency, a
Hollywood fixer who had brokered the purchase of MCA and was
therefore considered to have the confidence of Akio Tanii, the
chairman of the Japanese electronics firm. Ovitz's answer was
encouraging: he understood that Matsushita wanted MCA to grow
into a world-class entertainment conglomerate; Virgin Music was
just the sort of thing Matsushita would want its new child to spend
$1bn on. With this blessing, Thornton swung into action. He
enlisted the help of John Eastman, a leading New York entertainment lawyer, and the two men went to see Felix Rohatyn, a director
of the investment bank Lazard Frères who advised MCA.

It was in a letter from Lazard Frères that Thornton received the
bad news. Based on the figures he had been given, Rohatyn told
Goldman Sachs that he did not believe Virgin Music was worth
more than $600m – which, with the pound at $1.70, came to significantly less than the £400m that Thorn had been willing to pay.
Like any good negotiator, Thornton poured scorn on the idea. The
offer was so absurdly low, he told Rohatyn, that he wouldn't even
dare to show the letter to Branson. But he had a better idea. Just
as he had with Thorn-EMI, the Goldman banker suggested that
the two sides should meet to discuss the $80m revenue enhance-
ments and cost savings that he believed would come to MCA from
acquiring Virgin.

It was illustrative of the hierarchy established by size and wealth
in the US media industry that this time Branson and his colleagues
had to go to the US in order to make MCA take seriously the idea
of purchasing Virgin Music. The negotiations culminated in a big
meeting at MCA's Californian headquarters, at which Branson and

Berry, with their new American lawyer and banker, were grilled by a panel of the MCA top brass. Lew Wasserman, the company's octogenarian president, was in a placatory mood; it was David Geffen, the 39-year-old president of MCA's Geffen Records subsidiary, who asked the difficult questions. Having built Geffen Records in a decade and sold it to MCA less than two years earlier for shares that he had recently cashed in, Geffen was ideally placed to assess a fast-growing independent record label. There was also some personal pride at stake; at the time he had sold to MCA, the price Geffen had been paid was the largest ever for a record label. If Branson wanted almost the same amount in pounds for Virgin Music, he would have to explain why it was a more valuable property than Geffen Records had been.

The Virgin pair and Thornton returned to London without an offer – but also, more importantly, without a firm refusal. MCA was evidently keen on the idea of the acquisition, but it would have to clear the suggestion with Osaka. If the transaction took anything like as long as Matsushita's $6bn takeover of MCA itself had taken, it would probably be months rather than weeks before a firm answer came back. Thornton, like any good salesman, refused to be downcast at this. From his point of view, the important thing was not to allow negotiations with MCA to progress to the point where Virgin received a definite no; once that message had crossed the Atlantic, Thorn-EMI would begin to press Branson to sell at their price rather than his. Luckily, that had not yet happened. 'We're still in the game; we've bought ourselves some time,' Thornton told Branson and Berry. Later in the summer he duly went back to work on Sir Colin Southgate and his colleagues at Thorn-EMI.

From a detailed point of view, the negotiations with Thorn-EMI were proceeding quite satisfactorily. After having at first rejected Branson's price outright, the British conglomerate was beginning to warm to the idea of owning Virgin Music. Not only were the columns of figures produced in spreadsheets by Thornton's staff at Goldman Sachs sinking in; more significantly, Ken Berry's understated authority had begun to impress Jim Fifield. Personal chemistry also helped. Sir Colin Southgate, born the son of a wholesale fruit merchant from the old Covent Garden market, had a humble background in common with Berry; as a maths enthusiast and computer programmer, he shared Berry's accounting knowledge; and by 1992, the pair had both acquired a taste for fine wine. The old antipathy between the T-shirts-and-jeans mentality of Virgin and the suits at EMI was beginning to disappear.

But the need to sell was now becoming urgent. Virgin had made the mistake of telling its bankers early in 1991 of its decision to sell the music group, and the bankers had duly marked their diaries for repayment of the group's still heavy debts some time in 1991. As summer came, and then autumn, the bankers became concerned, and asked to speak to Thornton directly about the progress of the transaction. Their temper was not improved by the appearance on 2 October of a large feature stretching across an entire page of the business section of the *Guardian* newspaper. WILL BRANSON'S BALLOON BURST?, asked the headline. In the text, one of the paper's senior business writers argued that 'behind the image of a man with a Midas touch running a loose-knit empire of diverse businesses is a picture of a highly indebted and not very profitable conglomerate, faced with huge financing requirements over the next few years.' Roger Cowe's description of Branson's 'grasshopper mind, which led him from one adventure to another in an apparently haphazard business progress' was irritating enough. But Cowe homed in ruthlessly on the airline and the music business, identifying them correctly as the pair of activities that brought in four-fifths of the group's profits, and asking searching questions about their future. More damning still, the paper published a table showing the group's cash flow and debt, purporting to demonstrate that only the records businesses produced enough money to fund the investment they needed – and that as a whole, the group had a funding requirement of £139m in its 1990 accounts. Trevor Abbott, quoted in the article, had sought to limit the damage by pointing out that the underlying picture was healthier than it appeared because of the new accounting policies that the group had followed since it left the stock market. 'The glory of being private,' he was quoted as saying, 'is that we can choose accounting policies to suit us and the taxman. We don't have to worry about what the City will think.' But the overwhelming conclusion – that Richard Branson needed to sell Virgin Music – was left unchallenged.

When he saw the published article, Branson was incensed. His first reaction was to telephone Peter Preston, the *Guardian*'s editor, to protest at the unfairly bad light in which he believed the article portrayed his company, and to complain that he had not himself been given the chance to discuss it with Roger Cowe. In fact, Branson was wrong; his press chief Will Whitehorn had been fobbing off Cowe for weeks, and the interview with Abbott had been arranged as a last-minute alternative to an unavailable Branson. But by a combination of charm, pleading and veiled threats to resort to other means if he were denied a satisfactory right of reply in print, Branson won from the *Guardian* an undertaking to publish an article by him the following week.

The article was the subject of detailed negotiation between Virgin and the newspaper; on being shown a first draft, Cowe protested to his editors that it contained errors of fact which Branson should not be allowed to get away with. In it, Branson gave a potted account of his approach to business and a litany of Virgin's achievements before, during and after its minuet with the stock market. 'From this comfortable position [i.e. as a private group],' he wrote, 'we have been able to take a very Japanese approach to doing business. Go for growth. Go for quality. Go for creating valuable assets. Do it – if necessary – at the expense of short-term profits.' He pointed out that the published 1990 accounts on which the article had been based were fifteen months out of date (though that was hardly the writer's fault, since Virgin could have supplied more recent figures had it chosen to do so). He picked up on some detailed points, complaining about a mistake in a chart accompanying the original article, and correcting the source of an £8m interest charge which the *Guardian* had wrongly put down to the airline instead of to Virgin Holdings. He also argued that 'our accounts do not reflect the value of our businesses because our businesses are not asset-based'. For instance, he wrote, the glittering list of copyrights that the music group owned – Phil Collins, Peter Gabriel, Janet Jackson, Paula Abdul, Belinda Carlisle, Bryan Ferry, and many others – were undoubtedly worth hundreds of millions of pounds; yet their value did not appear on Virgin's balance-sheets.

Yet there were only a few sentences in his reply about the core argument of Cowe's article, which was about cash flow rather than about assets, and which was addressing the question of whether

Virgin would be able to sustain its investment programme. The investment numbers had been distorted, Branson said, by the splitting of the single Virgin empire into separate businesses the previous year. This had produced a net funding requirement for Commmunications of £53m, a business that was generating cash of £1.7m when the demerger was excluded from the calculations. The 'real' investment figure for retail, he added, was £15m, not the £42m which resulted from the fact that one part of the group was buying assets from another. Overall, Branson insisted, the company's net assets of £334m outweighed its £242m net debt by a comfortable margin. It was his penultimate sentence, however, which gave the game away: 'Indeed,' he insisted, 'if we sold any one of our major businesses, we would wipe out our group debt totally and, if we chose to, could then leave all our companies with considerable cash.'

The damage limitation exercise was completed with a sentence at the foot of Branson's reply, inserted over the protests of the writer of the original article, in which the *Guardian* said it accepted 'that it in its analysis of the accounts it did not take sufficiently into consideration the intangible assets and copyrights of the Virgin Group of companies and some of the effects of the demerger and reconstruction'. This was far from an apology. But bearing in mind that Virgin had used in its defence more recent and detailed statistics than it had made available earlier, it was a more satisfactory outcome than Branson deserved.

TWENTY

Playing at Retailing

IN AUGUST 1987, Richard Branson received an unpleasant shock. The finance director of Virgin Retail, the group subsidiary that owned the record shops and Megastores, discovered a 'hole' in the company's accounts – a big accounting error that suddenly revealed the firm as having over £1m less to its credit in the bank than its managers had believed. To make matters worse, the company was already losing £1m a year, and there were no signs of improvement in its trading conditions.

The discovery that the record shops were doing so badly came at a sensitive time. Don Cruickshank had just produced another of his strategy papers on the future of Virgin, arguing strongly that the Group should be trying to focus on what it was good at and should look much more carefully at the rate of return it received on the money it invested in its different ventures. The retail business was unable to stand up to the rigour of such analysis. Over the years, the amount of capital tied up in it had risen gradually to £35m. Not only was there little evidence that the record shops would ever set that money properly to work; also, there was ample evidence that better returns could be made if the money were given to Simon Draper to invest in the record labels, or to Robert Devereux for the group's burgeoning publishing and video interests. In any case, Virgin's public reputation as a company willing to take risks on good ideas was such that not a week passed without the arrival of a letter from an aspiring entrepreneur, suggesting a venture in which Richard Branson might wish to invest. The board therefore took a swift but brutal decision: it would give the retailing businesses a stay of execution until Christmas 1987. If matters had not improved by that date, then the shops and megastores would be sold in the New Year for whatever price they might fetch.

Although the economy was growing rapidly and consumers were spending in the high streets, the Christmas 1987 season produced no better results for the group's retailing interests than the previous Christmas or the Christmas before that. Negotiations were accordingly opened with W. H. Smith, one of the leading stationery chains in the country. After seventeen years in retailing, Richard Branson was finally preparing to cut his losses and get out.

Virgin's entry into the retailing industry had been an even more hasty move than its decision to exit. The first shop had been opened in 1971, when Tom Jackson had led the country's 240,000-odd Post Office workers into an all-out strike against the Conservative government of Edward Heath. Until the strike began, Branson had been the owner of a fast-growing but rather chaotic mail-order record business, which banked cheques and postal orders from customers all over the world, and dispatched several weeks later the LPs and singles that they had asked for. The daily delivery of letters was life-blood to the business; and Branson had realized, as soon as he knew the strike was in earnest, that something must be done quickly if his fledgling business was to survive.

The first shop, which was no more than an upstairs room above an Oxford Street shoe shop, was immediately successful. Lack of time and money made it impossible to fit it out luxuriously; but the relaxed staff of the mail-order business proved congenial shop assistants. Customers would never be turned away from the Virgin shop because they looked young and a little bedraggled; on the contrary, they were welcome to sit inside the headphone cubicles and listen to records all day long, if they so wished. There was often a slight whiff of marijuana about the premises, too.

Nobody bothered too much about the dull details of retailing. Unless the austere Nik Powell was around, stock was checked when people felt like it. Staff were paid in cash from the till. Even the working hours were flexible. Those who felt like coming in late could do so; since those same latecomers would probably still be in the shop at 7 PM, chatting with the last customers, there seemed little reason to be strict about morning opening times. The store was a great success, and it was not long before another had opened in Notting Hill Gate, close to Virgin's ramshackle offices.

With the exception of Nik Powell, the casual approach to the stores went all the way to the top. Often finding himself temporarily short of cash, Richard Branson thought nothing of taking a few five-pound notes from the tills and leaving scrawled IOUs in their place. On one occasion – which Powell only discovered years later – Branson went into the Notting Hill shop after hours, and borrowed a rather larger sum. With his wife Kristen and Tom Newman, he went off to the Playboy Club to try out his new system for beating the bank at roulette. The three set to work playing the tables, and very nearly lost the entire sum. By dawn, however, they were back to where they had started. Like naughty schoolchildren, they crept back into the shop; exhausted and chastened, they replaced the money they had borrowed.

(In principle, Branson's system was infallible. By betting on red, starting with one chip and then doubling the stake every time black comes up, a gambler can be sure of winning – for the payback when the ball eventually drops on red will equal the total number of chips lost on black plus one. In practice, however, two difficulties make the system unworkable. First, it requires deep pockets. To survive a run of ten consecutive blacks and still have one chip left for the next bet, the gambler will need 1,024 chips; to survive a run of seventeen blacks, 131,072. Second, most casinos – including the Playboy Club – impose a limit on the largest stake that can be wagered at any one time. The system cannot work, however, unless the gambler has the right to keep doubling up indefinitely.)

Branson's brush with Her Majesty's Customs & Excise provided a paradoxical reason to keep the retail business expanding. The £53,000 penalty which he had agreed to pay in order to avoid being prosecuted for his purchase-tax fraud was cripplingly high – and only by expanding the business could Branson and Powell see a way of earning it. New record shops provided a glimmer of hope. Virgin could get sixty days' credit on the new records with which it stocked the shops; but customers would pay for the records in cash or with cheques that could be cleared in less than a week. As a result, every new record store – whose opening was timed carefully in order to open on the precise day of the month that would maximize the delay between selling the records to customers and

The second of Branson's balloon crossings, this time over the Pacific instead of the Atlantic, was sponsored by the Japanese makers of a soft drink called Pocari Sweat. Branson and Per Lindstrand, the Swedish balloonist he flew with, dutifully drank water out of Pocari Sweat cans for the camera.

Left Take-off from Japan.

Below The beginning of the Gulf War diminished the publicity value of the balloon's spectacular landing in the northern wastes of Canada.

Branson felt personally hurt that his community work attracted more criticism than his business ventures. The launch of his Mates condoms raised £1m for charity, but had little effect on condom use among young people.

Branson advertises the Barcelona megastore by waterskiing behind an airship, and simultaneously the airship itself.

The compact-disc factory in the basement of the Oxford Street megastore was opened by Branson with Mike Oldfield and members from Virgin's latest discovery T'Pau. Unfortunately, the CDs it produced were expensive and of poor quality.

Branson would often put into effect ideas suggested to him by friends or members of the public – a practice that his employees called the 'Virgin Sample of One'. Here he launches a service for carrying Upper Class passengers to the airport by motorbike instead of limousine.

So strong is the Virgin brand that Branson can use it even to launch products which have little to do with his business – such as computers.

Branson joked he thought that he and Joan Templeman, his long-standing girlfriend, should get married before their children did. The ceremony took place on Necker, his private island, and was attended by fifty close friends. Branson parachuted in to the ceremony carrying a box of Milk Tray chocolates.

Right John Thornton, the investment banker from Goldman Sachs who sold Virgin Music Group for £560m.

Sir Colin Southgate, Thorn-EMI's chairman, asked Branson to take on the honorary title of president after the sale.

Branson's High Court victory against British Airways brought a flood of positive coverage, and gave aircraft makers the confidence to offer him a new fleet. He distributed the £500,000 that he received personally to Virgin Atlantic's staff; the payments of £161 became known as the 'BA bonus'.

Lord King resigned as chairman of British Airways soon after the conclusion of the affair.

Powerful friends: Princess Diana, a guest of Branson's private island in the Caribbean, wrote him a friendly postcard after his libel victory against British Airways. She brought a flood of publicity to Virgin Atlantic by launching the first of its new fleet of Airbus A340 aircraft only days after she had announced that she would be withdrawing from public life. In keeping with the aircraft's name, *Lady in Red*, Branson persuaded her to remove the jacket from her green suit, and don instead the red livery of a Virgin Atlantic stewardess. He later tried to spray her with champagne; she ducked.

Virgin Atlantic took delivery of a fleet of Airbus A340s in 1994. Cheaper to run and maintain than its Boeing 747s, the new jets promised to help the airline back into profit after the miserable recession that followed the Gulf War.

Branson's bid to run the National Lottery and to give his profits to charity was a success with the general public – not least because he used Desert Orchid, the prizewinning racehorse, to deliver the application. The Office of Lotteries was less impressed; it turned him down, and awarded the franchise to Camelot instead.

The dejected Virgin chairman first threatened to seek a judicial review of the decision, but later relented and decided to concentrate on trying to run a lottery in South Africa.

The Range Rover in which the Virgin chairman and his family narrowly escaped death on the M40 motorway in June 1994, shortly before his 44th birthday. Realizing Branson's publicity value, Range Rover later supplied a fleet of 640 vehicles to carry Upper Class airline passengers to the airport – and ran advertisements in the press saying that it owed the deal to its 'hard cell'.

Left His mother always wanted him to be Prime Minister rather than a business man. Could her wish come true?

having to pay suppliers for them – brought a flow of new cash into the Virgin empire as it settled into its stride.

It required little retailing expertise to see that the sleepy business practices of traditional record shops provided a tremendous opportunity. From his visits to the United States, Richard Branson knew how differently things were managed across the Atlantic. To rival the tiny neighbourhood record shops, with their eclectic collections of records, many of which would sit in the racks for months before being bought, a new kind of record store was coming into being. It was big; it was well-lit, and records were arranged clearly in alphabetical order by artist; it covered most tastes in pop music comprehensively; and it turned over its stock much faster than the smaller record retailer. Instead of choosing a record sleeve from the rack and taking it up to a counter, where a shop assistant would demand payment and then provide the vinyl disc to go inside the sleeve, customers could simply pick shrink-wrapped records off the racks themselves, and take them up to a cash desk on their way out. This was the musical equivalent of a supermarket; and the equivalent of Sainsbury's was Tower Records, a company whose stores were spreading swiftly all over the United States.

The expansion of the record labels forced Branson to spend much of his time travelling in Europe and the United States, negotiating terms with licensees and companies from whom Virgin wanted to license new acts in its own territories, so the expansion of retailing was not on the top of his list of priorities. In 1975, however, a snippet of market intelligence gave added urgency to the long-term plan to set up a Tower-style operation in Britain. Our Price Records, another company that had sprung up to serve the needs of the new generation of music buyers, was negotiating a deal on a huge site in Oxford Street near Marble Arch that had formerly served as home to scores of different small shops. Unless Virgin got there first, Our Price seemed set to become Britain's first new-style record retailer – and to achieve this alarmingly close to Virgin's own record shop at the other end of the street.

Virgin therefore moved quickly. Swooping under Our Price's nose, it acquired the Oxford Street site and prepared to establish what would later become the first 'Virgin Megastore'. In keeping with Nik Powell's notions of good research, two different missions were sent to the United States to spy out some ideas that might usefully be borrowed. Powell himself went with John Varnom; a little later, Jon Webster and Pete Dolan crossed the Atlantic, strolling around record shops as if they were customers and only later approaching the store manager to ask a question or two. To British eyes, the managers were unexpectedly friendly; even after they heard that their interlocutors represented a small chain of record shops in Britain, they were still quite happy to talk about how they managed their own stores and what their English cousins could learn from it. Only one chain was less than co-operative: Tower itself. The Virgin advance guard was frogmarched out of the door of a Tower Records store as soon as it identified itself – but not before Webster had taken a couple of dozen pictures of the store interior so that he could come home with some ideas about how to fit out a megastore.

Much thought had been put into the question of what to do if the initial sales were below expectations. Nobody had considered what would happen if the new venture were actually *more* successful than Branson and Powell had expected. Yet that was to be the problem. The shop was mobbed by customers; so many, in fact, that the clusters of cash tills which Branson had insisted on placing in the middle of the sales floor, rather than by the doors as barriers to the customer's escape, had to be moved. It was the heavily discounted prices that brought customers from far and wide. Germans and Italians would routinely walk up to the information desk with a list of thirty or more albums they knew they could buy more cheaply than at home. So great was the megastore's buying power, and so deep the discounts that it was able to demand of the record labels that supplied it with stock, that occasionally even the owners of small record shops would walk in and buy a hundred copies of an album that was on sale at Virgin for less than their own wholesale buying price. Soon after the store opened, one Virgin employee discovered that the fear of Our Price that had been the primary motivation behind its creation had been misplaced. Our Price had not, after all, been planning to turn the entire space into a single vast record store; its intention had been to establish a normal record shop, and sublet the rest of the space. But Virgin's mistake was a blessing in disguise. The megastore was profitable, and it helped tremendously to raise the company's profile among fashionable young record buyers.

The same could not be said of the other record stores, unfortunately. By 1981, Virgin had 35 shops up and down the country, ranging from hole-in-the-wall to megastore, and with a bewildering number of gimmicky sidelines. Clothes had been sold in the record shops for a while, under the name Virgin Rags; that had been discreetly terminated when it became clear that the business was losing money because nobody in the company knew the first thing about clothes retailing. By 1984, when Don Cruickshank was in place, the retailing business was looking still more problematical. True, the turnover of Virgin Retail made it the country's third biggest record retailing chain. But it was not, with the exception of the flagship store at Marble Arch, making money. The prospectus published before Virgin's shares were listed on the stock market admitted shamefacedly that the retailing businesses had 'not to date achieved an adequate return'. They lost money again in 1986. Not even the high street expertise of Sir Phil Harris, the Queensway carpet king, could make a difference to the dismal financial performance of the business.

By the time the 1987 crisis occurred, every possible idea seemed already to have been tried. One of the most outlandish was Richard Branson's own suggestion that a machine for pressing compact discs should be installed in the megastore's basement, visible through glass walls to the customers browsing in the store. In principle, it was a magnificent idea. But the quality of the discs that the machine turned out was appalling; a huge number of them had to be thrown away. Ken Berry was furious at being forced to buy even the good CDs that it produced, for he knew it was cheaper to have discs pressed at a proper manufacturing plant. And an alarming number of the discs were somehow pilfered from the store anyway – perhaps because staff and customers alike saw it as the musical equivalent of a public drinking fountain, pumping out its shiny silver circles at zero cost.

Once it had decided at the beginning of 1988 to sell the chain of shops lock, stock and barrel, Virgin therefore set to work squeezing the best possible price out of W. H. Smith, which as owners of the

Our Price chain had expressed an interest. But the sale of the entire retail division was never to be achieved. For one thing, Smith's were interested only in the smaller shops, not the megastores; for another, Branson himself was unable to resist a pang of regret. At the time that the sale of the chain had been decided on, he was hard at work preparing to open a new Virgin megastore in Paris, on the Champs-Elysées. Simon Draper had delivered a withering put-down when Branson announced this venture. 'Frankly, Richard,' he said, 'if you can't make money with megastores in Oxford Street, how do you expect to in other parts of the world?' Stung by this rebuke, Branson decided to proceed with the sale of the smaller shops to W. H. Smith. But he resolved to keep the megastores and see whether they could be turned around.

Many an entrepreneur, recalling the depressing hours of management time that had been wasted in trying to make the smaller record shops turn a profit, would have been willing to get rid of them at almost any price. Not Branson. In breathtaking defiance of financial logic, he demanded £43m from W. H. Smith for the 67 stores and seven undeveloped sites that constituted the chain of smaller shops. What made this figure more astonishing still was the scale of the losses that the businesses were making. According to one Virgin employee at the time, the £89,000 profit which Branson claimed the stores had made in their last financial year might have been calculated before central overheads. 'The truth is that they were losing at least £2m a year,' said the employee, 'and if you took a straight approach instead of capitalizing everything down to the wastepaper bins, I'd say the true rate of loss was anywhere from £2m to £3m.'

It took a month for Branson to lower his sights from £43m to £23m; and several more months before Virgin and W. H. Smith were able to agree on the details of the deal. The negotiation was made more difficult for Virgin by a lawyer who represented Smith's with unexpected robustness, and for Smith's by Virgin's determination not to pay any tax on the greater proportion of the money it would receive from the sale. A complex transaction was arranged whereby the shops to be sold to Smith's were first sold to a new company created by the Virgin Group. That company paid for the shops by issuing £23m in loan stock, which was also subscribed to by the Virgin Group. The new company was then sold to W. H. Smith for a nominal sum, and the loan stock which Virgin held in it was sold at the same time for its face value of £23m. As a result, the taxable profit made by the Virgin Group on the sale fell from almost £23m to almost nothing. The Inland Revenue took several months to approve this arrangement, but more because of the deal's complexity than because of any dispute over the legality of the tax avoidance inherent in the transaction. Since the sale would give the newly expanded Our Price chain a total of 274 shops, and a 20 per cent share of the record retailing market, it had to be referred to the Office of Fair Trading. Approval was routine, but took time. So it was not until the end of July 1988 that the deal was done. Within a few days of the sale, the managing director who had failed to rescue the retailing company from its difficulties was also out.

Don Cruickshank, ever the orthodox managing director, had organized a traditional head-hunt in order to find a replacement. Four candidates appeared; then, when the news broke that Richard Branson was planning to take Virgin private again, they lost enthusiasm, finding the idea of working for an unlisted company less prestigious. Branson and Cruickshank were at a loss. Who should be the new managing director of Virgin Retail? There was clearly no experienced hand inside the company; equally, it had proven impossible to lure someone in from outside.

Cruickshank was a little suspicious to receive a memo from Simon Burke, a trained accountant who had served as Virgin Retail's new business manager until the sale, proposing himself for the job. Burke knew a great deal about corporate finance; he had spent a year working as a company doctor. But he had no retailing experience at all, not much experience of mainstream management – and he was willing to admit that he had put himself forward for the job with 'extraordinary rashness'. Simon Draper and Ken Berry, sensitive to the fact that the retail division had for years made a habit of frittering away profits they made at the record company, were suspicious. But when Abbott indicated his approval, Richard Branson invited Burke around for a talk, and decided immediately that he wanted him to take the helm of Virgin Retail. Grudgingly, the others agreed.

Burke took over on 10 August and began to move fast. His first priority was to streamline the company's operations. The ill-fated machine in the basement of the Oxford Street megastore pressed its last CD and was taken away. Virgin Retail concessions in Burtons, Hamleys and Debenhams stores were sold off. A sweetshop called Butterfly and a mail-order firm called Megamail were closed down. 'There were seven or eight of these things,' Burke said afterwards. 'They had nothing much in common except that they were all losing money.'

Burke's next task was to deal with the Virgin Retail management team. The company's employees were miserably demoralized; there had been rumours about redundancies following the sale which the company had been forced to deny and which then proved true. The staff were emotionally burned out, and seemed not ready to accept a dramatic change of pace. The new managing director therefore cheerfully provoked two waves of resignations, at the beginning of 1989 and then again in the spring. With the top ranks of the company cleared out, he was ready to start again. By the autumn, he had put together a revival strategy for the megastores businesses, so that Branson and his colleagues could agree on the marketing and financial strategies needed to make it work.

There are different accounts of the meeting at which the revival strategy was discussed – but the tone was set when Simon Draper and Ken Berry expressed bitter disappointment that despite the continuing profitability of the record company, Virgin had just been obliged to sell a stake in it to Fujisankei, the Japanese media group. 'It would never have happened if Richard hadn't squandered the money on other businesses,' one participant remembers Berry as having complained. Given the jibing between Branson and the two men who ran his most profitable business, it was perhaps not surprising that the meeting was less than conclusive. Simon Burke won approval for his plan; but he never received a firm commitment to provide the resources necessary to put it into effect.

From that point on, Virgin Retail's progress was one of steady recovery. The more closely he looked at the business, the more Burke discovered that turning it around would not simply be a matter of imposing a few financial controls. 'The place had been badly mismanaged for years,' he remembered. 'They didn't have in stock the items people would want. While they had reasonably large quantities of records that you couldn't get anywhere else, they wouldn't have the current number two album.'

The firm's buying systems were equally awry. Store managers operated a system which they called 'memory buying', which meant that a member of staff would stroll around the racks with a clipboard, looking at the list of the total catalogue of artists whose work was normally sold in the store, trying to remember what had been bought earlier and adding new orders to his list accordingly. Staff turnover was also a problem: so demoralized were the shop assistants in the various megastores that they lasted on average less than a year each. At first sight, the fact that the business was being run almost without rules might have seemed an attraction. But the company's employees did not seem to like being able to turn up as they wished from day to day and receiving their salaries in cash from the till. Nor, of course, did such a system make it easy for the store managers to make sure they had enough staff on any given day. Burke concluded that the staff wanted a greater sense of structure. 'They wanted an understanding of where they stood,' he said. 'Laissez-faire freedom doesn't appeal to people when they have it.'

As Burke was to learn over the coming years, retail businesses have to be run tightly. At 30 per cent, the gross margins of music and entertainment retailers are among the lowest in the business; once expenses have been taken into account, music retailers are lucky to bring in a five per cent net return on sales. The tightness of these figures helped to explain why the megastores had never made money. It was impossible to make a success of the business if 'you didn't know what your gross margins were, what your stock was or where it was'.

Burke also realized the urgency of reversing the reckless diversification by which the different store managers had attempted to boost their returns. In one megastore, the first sight greeting the customer on crossing the threshold was a washing-machine. This was because Comet, a white goods discounter, had been given a prominent concession at the front of the store. Nearby was a stand for Athena greetings cards. Records, it seemed, were relegated to the corners.

Burke cut costs, and won support from above to reduce the company's total headcount by two dozen. By the end of his first year at the helm, he had produced a trading profit. At a few hundred thousand pounds, it was not much; but it was better than the company had ever achieved before, and Burke and his new management team had worked hard to get it.

It was another year before they were ready to start opening new stores. Belfast, Burke's home town, turned out to be the first site of the new generation of megastores: not by his preference, but because that happened to be the first place where the agents the company had retained were able to come up with a suitable site at a reasonable cost. Cardiff followed in late 1990; then a refurbishment was carried out on the Edinburgh store. In 1993, six new megastores were opened, bringing the number of locations in the chain back up to 24. In a vastly more competitive market than a decade earlier, the pared-down Virgin Retail was the fourth biggest music retailer in the country. More important, it had acquired a reputation among suppliers and competitors as the sector's most innovative company.

The last area that required Burke's attention was technology. When he became managing director, the company was half-way through a computerization programme which was badly misconceived. 'We had to throw the system out,' he recalled. Within two more years, he had invested £3m in an entirely new electronic point-of-sale stock control system. By 1992, the new system was revolutionizing his business. Burke was able to sit in his office and read off a computer screen which titles had sold how many copies in which stores the previous day – and was busy planning further refinements which would produce a daily report showing which stores had sold more or less than average of each title, and which stores needed a given title to be restocked most urgently.

That left only one piece of unfinished business – what to do with the last remaining peripheral activity of Virgin Retail. When Burke took charge, he discovered that the company owned a pair of small shops selling video games, one of them in Bristol and the other at 100 Oxford Street. Richard Branson had acquired them in 1984, when an independent company called Game Centre had run into difficulties from overtrading during a year when demand for video games suddenly collapsed. Ironically, Burke himself – who was not working for Virgin at the time – had put together a plan with a couple of friends to buy some of the assets of Game Centre from the receiver; his plan had fallen through when Branson beat him to it. Burke felt flattered to discover that Branson had seen the same business opportunity as he had. He was to discover later that Virgin had bought the Oxford Street shop for a much simpler reason: it was surrounded on both sides by the Virgin megastore; once it had been bought, the megastore was able to gobble up its selling space.

But Simon Burke was an occasional player of video games himself, and fancied the idea of trying to make something of the games business. In 1990, he hired an associate to develop the idea and to open some more video-game stores. By the end of 1992, the number of shops in the new chain had reached 30, and Virgin found itself in possession of a highly profitable company that was the only serious video-game chain in British retailing. But Burke began to worry about the future. Just as they had done nine years earlier, video-game sales suddenly collapsed in February 1993; and Burke realized that his budget for the current year showed that more money was to be tied up in stocks of video-game hardware than in stocks of compact discs for the entire megastore chain. He halted the expansion immediately, and resolved in future to keep a tighter grip on the affairs of the business.

As if by magic, Burke received an approach later in 1993 from Rhino Group PLC, a company that had ambitions to build its own chain of video-game stores under the brand Future Zone. The two sides met in October, and Burke was made an offer of £6m for the 30 stores he had built up over the previous two years. He haggled for a quarter of an hour over the price, bidding the offer up to £9m for the stores and another £3.5m for the stock. A month later, the game centres were gone, and Virgin Retail was £12.5m richer.

Burke had only one source of regret in his time at Virgin Retail. While he had been working so hard sorting out the consequences of the fevered expansion of the megastores in Britain earlier in the 1980s, Virgin was busily opening new stores across continental Europe. The Paris megastore was an extraordinary success: despite Cruickshank's warnings, the millions of pounds spent on refitting

a vast floor-space on the Champs-Elysées proved a good investment. The store was spectacularly busy; on Sunday afternoons, 'le
tout Paris' appeared to be there, idly flipping through the racks of
new compact disc releases beneath the pilasters that adorned its
imposing interior. Within weeks of its opening, however, the store
became the source of a dramatic political controversy. Encouraged
by a rival retailer, the city government ordered the Paris megastore,
a project masterminded by Patrick Zelnik, head of Virgin France,
to obey the local ordinance that forbade Sunday trading. When
Virgin France ignored the instruction, it found itself in court and
threatened with a fine of 4m French francs (£400,000) for every
Sunday thereafter on which it continued to break the law. Under
the threat of such draconian penalties, the store was forced to disappoint the thousands of customers who had made Sunday its
second biggest trading day of the week. But Richard Branson flew
to France to make his point. He warned that jobs at the megastore
would be lost; and he threatened to curtail Virgin's ambitious
expansion plans throughout France unless the law were changed to
his satisfaction.

Simon Burke might have wished that Branson had lost the legal
battle. But France's regulations on Sunday trading were eventually
changed – and in honour of the company that had been responsible
for the reform, the new piece of legislation became known as the 'loi
Virgin'. Emboldened, Branson spent almost £10m on developing a
vast new megastore in Bordeaux. The success of the Champs-
Elysées proved impossible to replicate, however. Bordeaux lost
money; and Burke was forced to reflect wryly that he had to pay
the price for Branson's misplaced daring. For without sufficient
funds from the parent company, Virgin Retail had to look outside
for money if it was to continue to expand.

The moment of truth came in February 1992, when the financial
pressures on the Virgin group were as great as they had ever been
since the withdrawal from the stock market two years earlier. Virgin
made a deal with W. H. Smith, the company that had bought the
smaller record shops from him in 1988, that turned the megastores
into a joint venture and brought in a substantial injection of new
cash. The stationery chain agreed to lend £10m to the British retail

businesses, and paid £12.5m to acquire a half-share in them. This transaction provided Burke with a cash injection large enough to keep his recovery plan on track; but he could not resist a pang of regret that this business – which he fully believed would be big enough and profitable enough to be floated on the stock market in its own right a few years down the line – was no longer entirely in the possession of the Virgin Group.

But there was a tension in the partnership. Relations between Branson and the managers at W. H. Smith were perfectly cordial and Burke was left to continue to manage the megastores without interference. As the half-owner of the megastores, however, W. H. Smith found itself facing a conflict of interests. As they continued to expand out of London and into middle-sized British towns and cities, the megastores came increasingly to compete with Our Price – which had cost W. H. Smith a total of over £100m, including the investments made since it bought the chain from its two entre-preneurial founders. To make matters worse, the Virgin megastores were winning the battle hands down. Our Price had stores in towns like Swindon, Peterborough and Northampton that were earning nicely while they had a monopoly. But as soon as a larger competitor came in – particularly the aggressively managed and highly success-ful HMV chain – the Our Price store would find its turnover knocked down by a third or more and its profits turning with alarming speed into losses. There were two difficulties: the standard Our Price format was a store of around 1,500 square feet; while HMV stores, more likely to be 5,000 square feet, could offer a much wider range of records, videos and games. To make matters worse, the management of Our Price stores had become flabby and unfocused. Whereas in 1988 it had been the Virgin megastores that needed tightening up, by 1992 it was Our Price. Having turned in profits of £15m in 1988, the chain was now barely making money at all. Yet if Burke suggested the opening of a megastore in a town where Our Price was already suffering under an onslaught from HMV, the result was inevitably tension between his office in Lad-broke Grove and the W. H. Smith retailing headquarters in Swin-don. Something would have to give: Virgin and Smith's would either have to dissolve their partnership or cement it more firmly.

Trevor Abbott, Virgin's group managing director, therefore

opened negotiations with W. H. Smith. It was a highly delicate situation: the decision inside Smith's to buy Our Price had come directly from Sir Malcolm Field, the group's chief executive. Charming though he was, Field was intensely sensitive to any suggestion that Our Price was badly managed – for that would inevitably reflect on his own decision to buy the chain and the price he had paid for it. As a result, Virgin found that any criticism of Our Price, no matter how mild or inadvertent, produced a swift and angry reaction from W. H. Smith. By early spring 1994, Burke and Abbott had almost given up on the partnership, for Smith's seemed incapable of coming to a decision on the matter. The company had gone 'into blancmange mode', as one manager close to the negotiations put it. Suddenly, however, W. H. Smith had an attack of realism; and it decided to go ahead with a merger.

On 2 March 1994 the two firms announced that the 305 Our Price stores and 24 Virgin megastores would be combined into a single business. Virgin would own 25 per cent of the new company, and W. H. Smith the rest. The larger firm would have the right under some circumstances to buy Branson out later on. While the two firms waited for approval from the Office of Fair Trading – with expected 1994 sales of £350m, the combined business would be a sufficiently powerful force in the market to raise questions about a dominant position – a bland press release was published by W. H. Smith announcing the agreement. 'We are all very excited by this opportunity,' Simon Burke was quoted as saying. 'The combined business will be able to achieve far more than either of the constituents alone, and both the Our Price and Virgin brands will be vigorously promoted under a single management structure.' An executive committee would run the joint venture, including a representative each from Smith's and Virgin. But there would be no doubt as to the identity of the managing director of the new business. The managing director of Our Price was to be found a new job inside the senior management of W. H. Smith. The chief executive of the combined Our Price and Virgin megastore chain would be Simon Burke.

Whatever Burke's misgivings about the decision to hand over majority equity control of the megastores business to W. H. Smith, there were two points in its favour. First, the deal itself was very attractive. Virgin now owned a quarter of a very much larger chain that was indisputably the country's biggest music retailer. Yet Virgin continued to exercise in the person of Simon Burke day-to-day management control over the business. The value of its holding would be great; and proof of that would come either when W. H. Smith bought Virgin out of the business altogether, or when the joint business was floated on the stock market as an independent company. But there was a second, and equally important reason: the establishment of joint-venture businesses in partnership with other companies was now a highly successful pattern across Virgin's retailing interests all over the world.

The idea of a joint venture had first come when Virgin was looking for ways to get into the Japanese retailing market. Highly lucrative though it promised to be, Japan raised a problem: the price of entry. Under standard business arrangements, Japanese commercial landlords demand large up-front payments from their tenants before they are willing to let out a building. For a company like Virgin, the cost of opening, fitting out and stocking a megastore seven thousand miles from London would be prohibitive enough. It would rise from alarming to ridiculous if the company were also forced to pay millions of pounds in advance just to secure premises.

The solution that Branson found, and Trevor Abbott negotiated, was elegant in its simplicity. Virgin could capitalize on the strength of its brand, and the growing presence of its megastores across Europe and the United States, to persuade an existing Japanese retailer to come into a partnership. The chosen partner was Marui, an innovative retailer known for its appeal to young people. Under the agreement between the two firms, a Virgin megastore would be opened in the basement of one of Marui's department stores in the Shinjuku district of western Tokyo. The precise terms of the deal have never been made public. But informed sources inside Virgin suggested that by 1994, the company had made a total cash investment in the Japanese retail business of not more than a quarter of a million pounds. In return it had a half-share in a chain of megastores that promised to be fifteen strong by the end of 1995. The new store opened in 1994 in Ikebukuro, a railway terminus just north of central Tokyo, did more business on its first day of trading than any other megastore in the world. Virgin could plausibly claim to be the most successful foreign retailer in the Japanese market. The American chain Toys 'R' Us, which had overcome initial public hostility to build an out-of-town toy supermarket, might dispute that claim; but the US firm had probably invested a hundred times more money in order to achieve the same objective. Once again, Virgin had assured itself of an exit route: the five-year plan agreed with Marui in 1994 provided for the joint-venture company to work towards achieving a flotation on Japan's unlisted securities market by the year 1999. Invited to explain how Virgin had achieved such an extraordinarily attractive deal for itself, Trevor Abbott merely smiled. He pointed out that the cost of raising capital in Japan was only 2.5 per cent – far less than in Britain. 'If resources are available locally,' he said, 'it would be silly for us not to utilize them.'

Similar deals had been done in Europe and America. Virgin had teamed up with Blockbuster Entertainment Corporation, an American leisure conglomerate that had started as a chain of video rental stores, to develop its existing chain of megastores across continental Europe and in the United States. Once again, Blockbuster would be the majority investor in the partnership; but once again, Virgin would receive a valuable shareholding in a business to which it had been required to contribute only the very minimum of working capital.

By 1994, this method of expansion had become a pattern. Virgin struck an agreement with Wheelock, one of the territory's two or three largest industrial groups, to build megastores in Hong Kong and Taiwan, and eventually in the interior of China itself. A few days later, a similar agreement was announced in the notoriously hard to penetrate market of South Korea; this time Virgin's partner was to be Saehan Media, one of the world's leading makers of tapes and floppy discs, and a member of the Samsung group, South Korea's largest and by far its best-managed industrial conglomerate.

Interestingly, Virgin did not consider it necessary to impose a rigid management structure above the different joint-venture companies. While Simon Burke was left in charge of the British megastores, separate managers were given responsibility for the European, American and Japanese stores. Yet ideas were frequently interchanged between them; and it became a habit that whenever a new store was opened in one territory from which the others could benefit, those responsible for the other megastore territories would be invited to come and see it.

For all this expansion, however, Trevor Abbott's ambitions for the group's international retailing interests were carefully circumscribed. He was keen to make sure that Virgin was represented in the markets that would grow most quickly over the coming decade. But because retailing was by nature a low-margin business, Abbott insisted that the group should avoid investing in areas of high political or economic risk. He considered Israel in that category; and he was adamant that it would be dangerously premature for the group even to consider moving into Eastern Europe or Russia.

Despite this gap in the geographical spread, Virgin Retail could still boast that its sales were moving towards an equal split between Europe, the United States and the Pacific Rim. It had succeeded in achieving this with the very minimum of capital, and with the most aggressive possible use of the Virgin brand and Richard Branson's own personal reputation. For a company that by Branson's own admission had merely 'played' at shopkeeping during its first seventeen years in the business, Virgin Retail was an extraordinary success.

TWENTY-ONE

How John Thornton Earned His $3m

THORNTON'S FEE FOR bringing to a successful conclusion the sale of Virgin Music was between $3m and $4m, not counting telephone bills, first-class hotels and air tickets. True to Virgin form, it was not calculated on the standard straight percentage basis on which many such transactions are based. Branson was insistent that Goldman Sachs must have an incentive to achieve the best possible price for Virgin Music. Thornton would therefore receive a much higher percentage for selling the company dear than for selling it cheap.

Late in 1991, it had begun to look as though Thornton might receive no fee at all, for the sale seemed on the point of falling apart. MCA's Japanese bosses had remained utterly silent, which probably meant that they were not interested. Paramount had circled the body briefly, but then flown away. Michael Dornemann, the man in charge of the music division of the privately held Bertelsmann media group of Germany, had met Ken Berry in Connecticut for a discreet talk, principal to principal – and then, on discovering that Virgin Music's price was too high, had tried to go behind his back and buy Fujisankei's 25 per cent interest in the business. (This was another occasion on which the expensive legal advice Virgin had so often indulged in proved its worth: under the shareholding agreement, Fujisankei was powerless to sell to Bertelsmann, no matter how much it may have wanted to.) And most worrying of all, David Geffen had taken the highly unusual step of telephoning Sir Colin Southgate at Thorn-EMI to tell him that MCA was not going to buy Virgin Music. In doing so, Geffen was thwarting Thornton's attempts to play one seller off against the other.

Luckily, though, the momentum of the negotiations between

Berry and Thorn-EMI was now unstoppable. One day Thornton bumped into Southgate by chance in the departure lounge at Heathrow airport, where the two men were both waiting to board a Concorde for New York. Once aboard the cramped supersonic aircraft, they decided to sit together – and by the time they reached New York, less than four hours later, they had a deal agreed in principle. Thorn would buy Virgin Music for £510m, payable in Thorn shares, and would assume £50m of the company's debts.

The irony was that like any good poker player, Branson had never told even Thornton the minimum price for which he would sell the record division. But £560m was then worth very nearly $1bn. That, as Thornton was to remember later, 'had a certain magic ring to it'. In a recession that had persisted for longer than most businesses had expected, and in an international music market where the growing power of the big five companies would make the lives of independents harder, $1bn was an offer that Richard Branson could not refuse.

In fact, he very nearly did refuse it. Southgate offered Branson a choice between being paid in full in shares, or receiving a lesser sum in cash. Branson immediately chose the higher amount, but then began to have second thoughts about accepting another company's paper instead of real money. The sale of Virgin Vision to MCEG for $83m had taught him to be cautious: before Virgin had been able to dispose of the MCEG stock that made up the greater part of the sale price, the company's fortunes had declined and the shares had dropped in value to nil. No, Branson wanted cash for Virgin Music; but he also wanted to be paid the full price. Fortunately, Southgate, too, had been having second thoughts. The deal would have given Richard Branson control over the largest single shareholding in his business; and given Branson's history as a possible purchaser of Thorn-EMI, there was no telling what he might do with it. Surely, though, there should be some compromise that allowed them to agree on a cash price between the original cash alternative and the full price quoted in shares? There was not. Keeping his nerve to the last, Branson made Southgate blink. The deal went through on 6 March 1992, at the originally agreed price, in cash.

After lunch that day, the staff of the record company were asked to gather in the conference room behind the company's newly redecorated mansion at Harrow Road. The mood was almost funereal. Some of the two hundred people present had worked for Virgin Music for all of its nineteen-year history; many of the rest had been around for at least a decade. But even those who had only recently arrived knew that the sale meant the end of Virgin Music as they knew it. After all, the benefits to Thorn-EMI were not coming only from revenue enhancements. There must be cost savings, too.

Richard Branson gave a rambling, emotional speech, assuring the staff that their continued independence from the EMI side of the business was guaranteed, and promising a job at the airline to anyone made redundant after the takeover – hardly a practical suggestion. Simon Draper was at first more composed. 'I don't expect any of you to feel sorry for me,' he began. 'Today I'm very sad, but I have also become very rich. But . . .'

To their astonishment, the Virgin staff saw the words stick in Draper's throat and tears appear in his eyes. It was Ken Berry, controlled as ever, who took over, turning the discussion away from nostalgia and fears for the future, and back towards the details of the mega-deal that had just been struck. When Jon Webster, invited to ask the first question, instead proposed a vote of thanks for the past seventeen years, the happiest of his life, to 'Richard, Simon and Ken', Branson, too, began to weep. Finding all eyes on him, he rushed from the room, ran down to the bottom of Ladbroke Grove and turned right towards Holland Park. On the way, through the blur of his tears, he saw a placard for that afternoon's edition of the London *Evening Standard*: BRANSON SELLS FOR £560M.

It was a well-timed exit. More practical questions had followed Jon Webster's vote of thanks. The only difficult moment that Branson himself had witnessed occurred when Maria Forte, who had helped Steve Lewis build up the music publishing business, pointed out to Ken Berry that most of the press comment and his own words had referred only to the record company. What would happen to herself and her colleagues, she asked. The publishing business was as tightly run and profitable as any in the industry, but with 30,000 copyrights to administer it was a minnow by comparison with the EMI publishing and its 800,000 copyrights. Was it not likely to be swallowed up? Berry's answer was smooth and practised. 'As I said,' he replied, 'it's going to remain separate.' Branson had leaned forward and admitted that publishing was 'a bit more vulnerable'.

Vulnerable was putting it mildly. The deal was finalized on 1 June, after the competition authorities at the European Commission in Brussels decided not to prevent Thorn from buying Virgin Music. The following day there were eighty redundancies at the company that Branson had wept to sell. Of the thirty-three staff of Virgin Music Publishing, only nine were offered full-time jobs at EMI Music. Five accepted; the balance were made redundant, either on three months' notice or leaving the building that afternoon with a redundancy cheque and three months' pay in their pockets.

Among those who left was Steve Lewis, the managing director of the international music publishing company. Lewis had been with Virgin longer than anyone else. He had answered enquiries and packed records for the mail-order business before the record label was even set up; he had also worked for the Students' Advisory Centre, administering pregnancy tests for terrified teenage girls. But it was his nine years at the helm of music publishing that had been most important. When he walked into the publishing company in 1983, it had employed six people and dealt with all its overseas interests through sub-agents. When he left in 1992, there were fourteen overseas offices as well as the thirty-three people in London, and the company's turnover had risen from under £7m to over £35m. While accounting for only ten per cent of the group's turnover, it contributed twenty per cent of its profits. On the day that Lewis packed the contents of his desk into black bags, the company had eight songs in the top forty, including the number one, 'Game Boy' by KWS. A few months later, he went to a music industry awards ceremony at which he witnessed two EMI managing directors pick up prizes for acts that he himself had signed.

Although Lewis received generous compensation from EMI, found another job six months later starting a new record label in partnership with Chris Wright of Chrysalis and later became chief executive of the Chrysalis music division, he still felt aggrieved at the way he had been treated by Branson. Lewis had turned down offers of more money to work in other record companies, and had signed artists not on the terms that would maximize his own salary under the profit-sharing arrangements, but on those that would bring the highest long-run profits to the company. Yet the only equity he had been given was in Virgin's long-defunct artists' management company, which never made significant profits because it was squeezed between the interests of the artists it represented and the Virgin record labels they were signed to. Ken Berry was now worth significantly more than £10m, because he had asked Branson for equity. Like many others, Lewis had just taken it for granted that Virgin's employees would all share in the benefits from the company that they had helped Richard, Ken and Simon to build. When Island Records had been sold to Polygram in 1989, even the cleaning staff had received a pay-off. David Geffen had been less democratic when MCA bought Geffen Records from him in 1990. But his secretary was among those who benefited from the transaction; he gave her $5m.

Early in 1993, not having heard from Branson for a year, Lewis went to Holland Park to talk over the parting that had so hurt him. The man who had been tongue-tied and tearful the previous March was now a model of clarity. His answers were as smooth and detached as if he were talking to a television studio audience; but there was an unmistakable gloss on his comments. Lewis had thought the circumstances of the sale were a personal matter. For Branson, it seemed, they were politics.

Others felt similarly strongly. Jeremy Lascelles, who had joined Virgin in 1972, had worked for the record label from 1980 onwards, and had risen to become the company's head of A&R, observed that even in England, a number of independent record company owners had rewarded their secretaries with £100,000 when their companies were sold. 'I'd have settled for half that,' said Lascelles later with a wry smile. But what did he get? 'Not a single fucking dime, not a phone call,' recalled Lascelles, 'but a letter on everyone's desk which he [Branson] had had his secretary distribute. "Dear All," it said. I said to Simon the next day: tell him my name's Jeremy, not Al.'

Some days later, Lascelles succeeded in persuading Penni Pike, Branson's assistant, to give him an appointment. 'He knew what I'd come for; it was pretty damn obvious.'

'I think you'll find I'm not here heading a delegation,' began Lascelles, 'but my feelings are like those of many others. I feel disgusted and insulted about the way you've gone about selling the company. People like me who've worked for you for years in a moderately senior position . . . we feel shat on that you've just sold us down the river.'

Branson was clearly expecting the speech. His answers, Lascelles recalled, were like those of a politician on 'Newsnight': 'very slick, very evasive, a lot of sweet answers'. But it was the details of Branson's response that offended Lascelles most of all. 'He told me, well of course the music division was draining money, the group would have gone belly up if we hadn't sold, Simon wasn't paying attention any more since he'd made his money, the US company was running at too big a loss, the Virgin megastore . . . It was all spoken for. He said, "You might find this hard to believe, but none of this money's coming to me." He [even] implied that he was struggling financially.'

A few weeks after the sale, one of the more senior women who had been employed at Virgin Music overheard her husband explaining to a friend over the telephone that her redundancy from Virgin was in fact the best thing that had ever happened to her. Her worries at work had been so great that she had sufferered from stomach cramps, he confided; yet she had carried on working long hours and weekends because she believed in Richard Branson, and because she thought Virgin was in some indefinable sense a co-operative in which everyone would benefit. 'I've never told her this,' her husband continued, 'but all that co-operative stuff is just a load of crap.'

The eavesdropped conversation, at first so shocking, set her thinking. On reflection, she concluded, her husband was right. She had been misled; she had mistaken an atmosphere for the reality. In the end, the company had belonged not to the people who worked for it but to Branson, Draper and Berry. And it was they who had benefited when it was sold.

It was only a minority of the staff, however, who left promptly after the sale. Barbara Jeffries, in charge of Virgin's recording studios, was asked by EMI to stay on to look at ways of integrating the studio operations of the two companies. Over the coming three months, she gained an extraordinary insight into the differences in corporate culture that had allowed Virgin to grow so fast while Thorn-EMI had stood still. Virgin's studio businesses were making a 33 per cent return on sales, while those of EMI were making a return of only 14 per cent, and her new bosses wanted to know about the accounting differences that were responsible for this surely misleading disparity in performance. In the event, they were wrong; Virgin's studios were more than twice as profitable as those of EMI, and the reason was not hard to see. At EMI, there was an elaborate system of incentives, with managers setting targets and receiving salaries at the end of the year that reflected how well they had performed against them. At Virgin, there had been no formal system at all. Yet Virgin was managed more aggressively, and with more concern for the pennies, while at EMI the managers had simply set themselves targets that were low enough to be easily beaten.

Virgin was also far less bureaucratic. Except when times were hard, it had imposed no formal spending limits on its managing directors. Their habit was to check with Branson, sometimes out of courtesy, when they wanted to acquire a particularly expensive piece of equipment or sign a large contract; but they would do this by telephone, and would expect an answer either instantly or, if the matter was less urgent, at least within a few days. When Jeffries first proposed refurbishing the studios at the Manor, Richard Branson had wanted to be consulted on the details; some years later, he had approved her decision to buy a building for £1.5m to turn into a new set of studios, without even asking to come and see the site.

At EMI, the procedure was quite different. All items above £10,000 had to have prior approval from head office; and that approval could only given after a telephone conversation which sometimes had to be booked three weeks in advance. While working on the joint project with her opposite number from EMI, Jeffries once brought up the matter of recording assistants. How should the two managers decide who to appoint to this lowly paid studio job, which often demanded eighty hours of painstaking work a week? For her part, said Jeffries, she looked for someone with enthusiasm, with a real love of music, who probably had some kit at home and would kill to do the job. And the EMI man? 'Oh,' he said. 'We normally take people who have university degrees.'

Given the startling difference in the financial performance of the business she ran and its EMI equivalent, Barbara Jeffries looked forward with some confidence to the big meeting at which their joint future would be decided. Unfortunately, the Saturday night before the Monday on which the meeting was to be held, her two-year-old son suffered a fit of convulsions and had to be taken to hospital. Jeffries telephoned one of her superiors with the news, and was told to her relief that it would be no problem at all to reschedule the meeting because she was under such stress – and that she should not hurry back to work until her son was quite well. When the new date of the meeting came up, however, Jeffries was stopped on her way in at the EMI reception desk, diverted from the meeting, and sent directly into the boardroom. There she was told briskly that there was no longer a job for her. 'After all,' said the EMI executive with barely disguised triumph, 'you must, as a single mother, put the interests of your child first.'

For Simon Draper, the sale of Virgin Music to Thorn-EMI marked his final break with Branson. The two remained friends and tennis partners, but Draper decided that he would now retire from even the limited managerial role that he had performed at Virgin Music, and would also resist Branson's entreaties to put some of the sale proceeds back into the Virgin businesses that did not pass to Thorn-EMI's control. This was the conclusion of a gradual extrication of his interests from those of Richard Branson. When Branson had bought the airline group from Virgin before the listing for £5m, Draper had bought £2m-worth of preference shares, which represented less than ten per cent of the total funding required. He had sold half the shares back to Branson a year later; in the middle of the 1991 Gulf crisis, when the airline business was at the beginning of its long recession, he had liquidated the rest of his holdings. Draper knew that he was selling back to Branson at a very low price. But the transaction was not at Branson's own suggestion; against his partner's advice, Draper had decided firmly that he wanted to separate his affairs from those of the Virgin chairman.

Simon Draper had discovered the hard way five years earlier that the listing of Virgin's shares on the stock exchange had only given him half the freedom that he had hoped it would. Although in theory he had been free to sell his shareholding since 1987, Draper knew that its value was highly dependent on what Branson did with his own life or with the rest of the company: an ill-judged acquisition or even the rumour of another balloon trip could knock £1m off Draper's net worth. With the company once again private after 1989, he had taken comfort from his share of the $150m that Fujisankei paid for a quarter of the record company; but once again, he had found himself under irresistible pressure to put his money back in to secure group borrowings. It was in order to place himself beyond such pressure that Draper decided he must make a clean break.

An underlying difference of approach had also developed between himself and Branson. Behind the detailed discussions of new Virgin businesses – Draper had opposed the establishment of the airline, had warned Branson not to go into the property business, and had been sceptical of the growing ambitions of Robert Devereux – was a matter of principle. For Branson, running the business was not a way to make money for his own personal use, but an end in itself. He would often talk about giving it all up and retiring to Necker Island; but after two weeks, like Napoleon on Elba, Branson would once again be restless and unable to resist the lure of the fax and the telephone. Draper was different. His first response to the listing of Virgin's shares had been to go out and buy a new Aston Martin sports car; later, his collection was to grow to 37 or 38 Astons (he could never quite remember which). He had also acquired four more expensive tastes. One was wine: like Ken Berry, he had an extensive cellar, and he belonged to an informal group of well-heeled gastronomes with whom he would eat lavish meals washed down with old clarets. Another was architecture: not content with ordering an expensive and very dramatic refit of the reception area at the Harrow Road offices, he had engaged David Chipperfield, a fashionable British architect, to build a large structure housing his car collection in the country and to redesign the double-fronted stucco house that he acquired, only a short walk from the less grand parts of Notting Hill Gate that Branson and his friends had always frequented. A third was contemporary art, of which Draper had a respectable collection. And as if those were not enough to occupy him, he took to breeding rare pheasants, some of them imported from all over the world.

It was no surprise to his friends when Draper announced that he would set up a small private publishing house, to be known as Palawan Press (after the Philippine island home of one of his favourite pheasants). Its first project would be a lavish photographic history of Aston Martin, including pictures of many of his own cars; its second would be a pictorial guide to the world's pheasants. A century earlier, millionaire businessmen would retire to the country and become gentleman farmers. Simon Draper's new lifestyle was the 1990s equivalent.

Ken Berry, though barely younger than Draper, saw the sale as a beginning rather than an end. So well had he sold Virgin Music to Southgate and Fifield that it was already clear months before the sale that if the record company went, Berry would go with it. The responsibility of maintaining Virgin's independence from the other EMI record labels was therefore his; so, less happily, was the job of deciding which employees should be the victims of the immediate round of redundancies that followed the sale, and which bands should be dropped from the roster. For Berry, the move was a chance to detach himself from the skirts of Richard Branson and Simon Draper. Even in the past few years, as his power had grown beyond question, Berry had always been sensitive to the accusation that he was 'just' an accountant. Now the management of the entire Virgin Music empire was in his hands alone.

Not quite alone, though. Along with Ken Berry came his former girlfriend and now wife Nancy. The savings and the prunings that the Berry double-act put into effect were impossible to argue with. Just as Thornton had promised, the profit stream from Virgin Music rose sharply in the first year under its new owners. Its ten-month earnings came to some £53m. UB40, a vintage Virgin group, reached the top of the British charts in 1993. Even the last two big acts that Berry had signed before the sale – Janet Jackson for £27m and the Rolling Stones for £20m – seemed to be coming good. Both signings were a sharp departure from the Virgin style of preferring to nurture talent internally than to buy in megastars at corresponding prices from outside. Yet heavy promotion helped

Janet Jackson's first Virgin album to sell almost four million copies worldwide, after the release of only one track from it as a single. That was more than half the sales that her biggest ever album had achieved, with the help of no fewer than seven tracks released separately as singles.

The fortunes of the wider Thorn-EMI group continued to fluctuate. Confounding the accusations that Southgate had paid Branson too much, the company's share price performed dazzlingly in the year following the acquisition, topping £10 in August 1993. Yet despite the successful execution of its chairman's strategy of focusing the group on a pair of activities, music and television rentals, institutional investors still seemed uneasy. The group's stock market standing was damaged by accusations that Rent-A-Center, the company's American TV rental division, had used Hell's Angels and other unsavoury characters to prevent its poorer clients from falling behind on their payments or resisting repossession. There were also some difficulties in disposing of a loss-making defence contracting division. Was it proof of poetic justice that by late 1993, investors were asking whether Thorn-EMI should be broken up, demerged into its constituent parts?

At the press conference announcing the sale, Richard Branson revealed that Thorn-EMI had made him Virgin Music's president for life. He was being paid an 'enormous salary', he confided to the journalists present, 'but I won't tell you what it is.' It was only later, when they duly printed his words, that the reporters discovered that Branson had been pulling their leg. He was not in fact being paid anything for his services; he was to be no more than a figurehead.

Could he be blamed for the feeling of betrayal that overcame so many of the Virgin Music staff after the sale? From Steve Lewis downwards, the staff were unanimously agreed that Branson had made them feel that they were all working together in a co-operative enterprise from whose progress they would all benefit in the long term. In doing this, he had imbued them with a positive spirit, transmitting as if by telepathy his blind faith that every problem could be surmounted. Behind the jeans and T-shirts, Virgin Music had a clear corporate culture: it could be summed up in the view that it was idle to ask whether something could be done. Virgin people would assume that it could, and confine themselves to asking how. Branson had not only commanded great loyalty; by promoting quickly and from inside, he had also given many of the Virgin Music staff – particularly women – opportunities that they would never otherwise have had. And his confidence, his breezy sureness that he could do something even if he had no experience to back him up, had spread to them. Meeting for the many reunions that they called, many of Branson's ex-employees would muse that he had made them achieve things of which they had never imagined themselves capable.

Never, they had to admit, had Richard Branson made any promises about how the profits of any future sale would be divided. If there was anything they could accuse Branson of, it was only of allowing them to have the dreams and forget the underlying commercial realities. Richard Branson was a brilliant leader, and an instinctive motivator of people. But the aftermath of the sale of Virgin Music proved that he could be too good a motivator of others for his own good.

TWENTY-TWO

The BA Bonus

RICHARD BRANSON'S SKILL in dealing with the press was one of the reasons behind the success of his businesses – not just because it gave the Virgin Group more coverage than comparable companies of its size, but also because the coverage that appeared was generally more positive. Branson had even managed to stay on reasonably good terms with *Private Eye*: when the satirical magazine asked its readers to send in stories about him, Branson himself wrote in, asking how much the *Eye* was willing to pay per word and adding in a cheeky postscript that he was pleased to observe that the magazine had been forced to advertise in order to dredge up stories about him.

There was no secret to this media success. While other companies would send their directors on training courses to learn techniques for dealing with aggressive television interviewers, Branson was self-taught. He had the benefit of practice, for as the 1980s progressed his appearances in print and on the radio and television became more frequent. He was also unusually willing to talk to journalists. Where other executives would hide behind press officers or public relations consultancies, Branson would take press calls himself. As he became busier, Will Whitehorn and other minders were forced to become more protective of him; but even if the answering of mundane queries was left to others, Branson himself always remained accessible if the issue or the questioner was important enough. Editors of national newspapers liked the fact that they could talk to him whenever they wanted; and subconsciously or otherwise, they rewarded him for his availability.

Branson was also unusual in the way he treated visiting interviewers. He would smile. He would see them promptly rather than keep them waiting. He would offer refreshments, but not with the ostentation of those who would open a fresh bottle of champagne every time an interviewer arrived. His answers would be direct and straightforward; and if it was not in his nature to be pithy, he was rarely deliberately evasive. He was refreshingly unpompous, and often willing to admit his own failings. He would pre-empt any journalistic attempt to find a flaw behind his apparent perfection by delivering one on a plate: unprompted, he would tell the story of his attempted purchase tax fraud. He would even take an interest in the opinions of his questioner; showing genuine enthusiasm, he would sometimes lean forward and take notes in his day book of what he heard. Reporters who visited him for the first time would come away surprised that someone so successful and so busy could also be so nice and so normal. As they made their way back to White City or to Docklands, they would shake their heads and reflect to themselves how sad it was that this kind of unremarkable human behaviour should be sufficiently rare among businessmen, celebrities and politicians to be remarkable. But it was remarkable, and it helped to explain why television stations and newspapers reported Virgin and its chairman's activities with such benevolence.

Of course there was artifice behind this apparently natural façade. Journalists would sometimes realize only afterwards that Branson had planned his encounter with them carefully, dropping a choice morsel of information as if by accident, delivering an apparently spontaneous funny line, or appearing in a bizarre outfit or against an attractive backdrop that guaranteed a good picture. One even remarked that he felt 'conned' by Branson's very openness, for it had made him less suspicious than he would have been with a less polite adversary.

Early in his career, Branson had discovered with glee that some journalists could be hoodwinked because they were too busy to check details. It would never occur to a reporter who saw him having to interrupt an interview to answer a constantly ringing telephone that the incoming calls were actually being placed by a friend in a public callbox around the corner, who was under orders from Branson to make the business look busy. Nor did the makers of a BBC documentary smell a rat when Rob Gold, the husband of Branson's secretary, posed as a musician and gave a solemn interview on the subject of why he had decided to sign up with the fledgling

Virgin Records rather than with a major label. Richard Branson had told them that he had started a record company; it never occurred to the makers of the television programme to wonder whether he might not yet have signed up any artists at all. It was equally natural for guests at the press launch of Virgin Atlantic Airways in 1984 to assume that Richard Branson or his companies owned a substantial stake in the new business – even though they did not.

As Branson became better known, however, some of his advisers began to feel that Virgin ought to be more careful to make sure that every statement it made to the press was accurate and complete. One senior employee who left the company reported his disbelief at the 'whoppers' that were appearing in the press at a time when the airline was going through a rough financial patch. Another employee recalled being told by Branson to make an announcement about a new cheap promotional fare that the airline was offering, but to avoid making the fare sound less attractive to the newspapers by giving the full details of the conditions that customers had to fulfil before they could buy a ticket at the low price. When the announcement was duly made, a troublesome reporter telephoned Branson and accused him of misleading the public by failing to explain how restricted was the availability of the discounted ticket. Shamelessly, Branson disclaimed responsibility. 'My PR person must have forgotten,' he said.

When good manners and hospitality failed to turn hostile coverage friendly, Branson was willing to use more robust methods. He was always quick to respond to critical articles about his businesses, usually by telephoning newspaper editors direct or by firing off a faxed response in a style suitable for publication. In extreme cases, as with the unsympathetic analysis in the *Guardian* in 1991 of Virgin's cash flow and its ability to repay its debts, he would be willing to devote entire days of work to the attempt to have what he considered an unfair impression corrected. When he received advance warning that a damaging story was about to appear – as when the *Sunday Times* published details of the arrangements by which he had used offshore trusts to avoid the payment of millions of pounds of capital gains tax, or when the *News of the World* was preparing to print the kiss-and-tell stories of a former Virgin Atlantic stewardess – Branson would not hesitate to use the lawyers. Blood-curdling threats of litigation or injunction from Harbottle & Lewis could prompt even the most muck-raking editor to think twice before sending his front page to press.

There were some sins, however, which Richard Branson would never be caught committing. He was willing to talk his own business up a little; but it was not in his nature to denigrate his rivals. That was perhaps why it took Branson and his colleagues at Virgin so long to realize that a campaign was being pursued to discredit him and his airline in the columns of the British national press.

Clues had begun to appear in 1991, when Virgin employees began to receive a series of anonymous calls claiming that the company and its chairman were being investigated by private detectives. The cars of a suspiciously large number of senior Virgin executives were broken into. But it was only when Richard Branson was contacted by Chris Hutchins, a reporter from the *Today* newspaper, that he began to connect these strange incidents with the fact that Virgin was suffering a worse press than it had for some time. Hutchins was hardly one of Branson's favourite journalists; in 1989, he had infuriated the Virgin chairman by publishing, without troubling to check the facts with Virgin, a story claiming that Branson was to be given a knighthood. What Hutchins had to say, however, turned Branson's blood cold.

Hutchins explained that he had received a call from Brian Basham, a leading financial public relations man who was working for British Airways. The two men knew each other well, for Basham's wife had worked for Hutchins on his *Today* gossip column. Basham admitted, when Hutchins called him back, that he was working for Virgin's rival; he told the reporter that he had been investigating Branson and his business on behalf of BA; and he suggested that, if he was in search of a good muck-raking story, Hutchins should look into the goings-on at Heaven, Branson's gay nightclub, and should look at the *Guardian* article on Virgin's finances.

'There's a huge heap of rubbish outside the British Aerospace office in the Strand which backs on to Heaven,' Basham had said. 'When Admiral Sir Ray Lygo wanted it cleared, his office manager called Westminster Council. They said their people wouldn't touch it because of all the needles.' The PR man said that Virgin was in financial difficulties, suggesting that Branson must be 'bleeding with all these fare cuts' since the outbreak of the Gulf War; he ended by saying that he would be interested to see how Hutchins's inquiries got on.

At a meeting in Holland Park, Hutchins explained that he was due to meet Basham at the Savoy Hotel a week later. Branson, horrified at the idea that someone should be trying to harm his reputation in such a way, persuaded Hutchins secretly to tape record the meeting; and he confirmed with Martin Dunn, the editor of the newspaper, what was to be done. In the event, Hutchins and Basham met at the PR man's home in West Hampstead. Basham opened by saying that he had compiled a report on Branson and Virgin for British Airways, and then proceeded to give a gloss on the report's contents.

Some of what Basham told Hutchins was broadly correct. He said that Branson 'runs his cashflow close to the wire all the time'. He pointed out that ballooning was a 'very, very dangerous occupation'. He raised the hypothetical situation that Virgin might be prosecuted as a result of a scandal to do with drugs or male prostitution at Heaven just at the time when Salomon Brothers, the New York investment bank, was grooming Virgin Atlantic to attract a minority investor. (Listening afterwards to a cleaned-up version of the tape at Virgin's Town House studios in Shepherd's Bush, Branson knew how close this had once been to the truth: his own managing director had warned him five years earlier that scandal at Heaven might prejudice the Virgin Group's flotation.)

But Basham also added for good measure a number of points that were wholly wrong and damaging. He told Hutchins that Branson 'runs a dicky business . . . Bits of it are good, but . . . I wouldn't care to invest in that business with my money.' He also claimed that Mike Batt, the BA senior manager who had briefly defected to Virgin before returning to his former employer, had given a hair-raising account of mismanagement inside Virgin Atlantic. 'Without doubt,' Basham claimed Batt had reported, 'an aircraft is going to fall out of the sky.'

Neither Branson nor his friendly journalistic contact knew it at the time, but that conversation was only a tiny part of a far wider campaign by BA against its smaller rival. Rattled by Virgin Atlantic's political success in persuading the government to make space for its flights at Heathrow, and by the awards for quality that the smaller airline was winning year after year, the top management of British Airways had decided that it needed to fight back more aggressively against the Branson challenge. As well as setting in train a number of improvements to its service – ranging from more comfortable seats to a spanking new lounge for arriving long-haul passengers at Heathrow airport – the airline's chief executive, Sir Colin Marshall, had commissioned Basham to carry out a detailed investigation of what made Branson tick.

The report, for which BA paid Basham's company a fee of £46,000 after its delivery in October 1991, was a flimsy piece of research. Notwithstanding Basham's claim that it was the result of a great deal of work, the report consisted partly of half-digested information that was already available from three sources: the copious press cuttings on Richard Branson and his businesses that sat in half a dozen different newspaper libraries in London; the accounts of Virgin companies that were open to public inspection for a modest fee at Companies House in London; and *Richard Branson: The Inside Story*, a biography written five years earlier by Mick Brown with the Virgin chairman's help and approval.

Those parts of it that were unique to Basham and his researchers were a drab mixture of platitudes, misconceptions and pop psychology. Branson was hero-worshipped in Japan, it said. He had a 'Houdini-like' ability to escape from tight corners. He was 'extremely adept at handling publicity'. His strategy was 'experimental'. He was 'sensitive to criticism'. He took 'a close interest in the businesses, but more at a strategic level'.

Without troubling to cite any evidence, the report asserted that any loss of confidence in Branson or his businesses by Fujisankei and Seibu-Saison, the Japanese companies that owned minority shareholdings in Virgin Music and the holding company for Virgin Atlantic respectively, 'could and probably would cut off his cash lifeline and could lead to disaster'. In a section containing what purported to be profiles of Branson's closest advisers and business associates, the report spelled incorrectly the names of Terry

Baughan, Randolph Fields, Syd Pennington, Anthony Salz and Nik Powell. It described the Tokyo route, on which both Virgin Atlantic and BA were by then losing thousands of pounds a week, as 'highly lucrative'. It gave Branson's home address incorrectly as 'Holland Road'. It suggested wrongly that Frank Dobson had been retained as an adviser.

For six months before his conversation with Hutchins, Brian Basham had been touting the contents of this report around Britain's most influential newspapers, if necessary showing the report itself, under a cover marked 'Highly Confidential', to journalists who could use it to write suitably hostile stories about Richard Branson. Basham's most conspicuous success had been with the *Sunday Telegraph*, which ran an article on 31 March under the headline VIRGIN HEADED FOR STORMY SKIES.

But the writing of the report alone was not enough for British Airways. Basham would later claim that both Lord King, the BA chairman, and Sir Colin Marshall put him under pressure to take more drastic steps to harm Virgin's reputation. According to Basham's subsequent account, Marshall complained that the report was not hard-hitting enough; Robert Ayling, head of BA's legal department, teased Basham and David Burnside, BA's head of corporate affairs, for being unable to place an anti-Branson story in the papers. Lord King, Basham said, wanted him to get into print the unsubstantiated claim that Westminster City Council had refused to remove rubbish from the back door of Virgin's Heaven nightclub for fear that the rubbish might contain used HIV-infected syringes and needles.

British Airways was not relying on the efforts of Basham alone, however. As Branson was later to discover, negative public relations was only one of a number of BA activities in its campaign against Virgin. The firm was taking advantage of the fact that both airlines shared the same computer reservations system, and was gaining illicit access to information on Virgin Atlantic customers. With the help of the contact details it found there, BA set staff to mislead the Upper Class passengers from whom Virgin made the bulk of its profits into switching to BA flights. Some passengers were told that Virgin could not provide the seat assignments they wanted; others were told that the Virgin flight they had hoped to travel on would be delayed or had been cancelled – and were offered seats on BA.

Employees of the bigger airline also spread the damaging rumour that Virgin was being forced to pay for its fuel in cash. Branson's company was facing enough difficulty as it was delivering the cash flow necessary to cover its debts; this claim, had it gained wide currency, might have provoked a collapse in confidence of the kind that put both Air Europe and Laker Airways out of business.

There were also a number of less significant, but also clearly malicious, activities. By going directly into Virgin computer data, and by impersonating members of its own staff or its ground handling agent's staff, BA employees obtained confidential information on the number of paying passengers that Virgin had in each class on each of its flights. This information gave British Airways a more accurate impression of Virgin's profitability on each route than it could have obtained from public sources, and allowed it to target the smaller airline's most profitable routes. Along with this information, however, BA staff also obtained details of Virgin's punctuality record which were later passed to Brian Basham. When Basham tried to persuade a newspaper to run a report claiming that Virgin Atlantic was unreliable, however, the newspaper's reporter replied that Will Whitehorn had insisted that Virgin was no more prone to delays at Heathrow than any other airline. Forbidden by British Airways to produce the detailed evidence to support his case, Basham was forced to back down. In any case, the figures were misleading; although they showed correctly that Virgin Atlantic was slower than some other airlines in closing the door of its aircraft, its record in taking off late – which mattered a great deal more – was no worse than the average.

The final prong of BA's campaign was an aggressive operation to find Upper Class passengers inside airports as they prepared to board Virgin Atlantic flights, and persuade them to change to BA. There were a variety of incentives that could be offered: upgrades from business to first class; free flights (one woman was offered a pair of tickets to Paris in return for flying BA rather than Virgin back from Tokyo to London); and on the New York run, transfers from conventional Boeing 747s to seats on the Concorde supersonic jet. A favourite place for recruiting Virgin passengers was at the place just outside the terminal at JFK airport where Upper Class passengers disembarked from their limousines. When the limousine company informed Virgin that its passengers were being poached by BA, the larger airline's response was swift: it banned the limousine company from picking up passengers outside the terminal, which BA owned, and forced it instead to meet them in the car park.

Branson became aware of some of these activities because of the loyalty of his customers and suppliers. When offered such attractive inducements as Concorde flights or free upgrades, customers of a less popular airline might simply have accepted, and switched permanently from Virgin to BA. It was the fact that customers chose to write about their experiences in the visitors' books kept aboard Virgin's aircraft that proved Branson's salvation. Equally important, however, was a very British sense of fair play. More than one of the BA employees who were ordered to participate in the anti-Virgin operation went directly to Branson with their stories. More information also came through the legal process of 'discovery', by which Branson was able to force BA to produce documents that might be relevant to his case against BA and Lord King's counter-suit.

As evidence piled up of the war that was being waged against him, Richard Branson wrote to Sir Michael Angus, the most senior non-executive director on the British Airways board, with a list of allegations and asked him to order an independent investigation of them. Angus replied with a crushing letter telling Branson that it would be quite inappropriate to undertake an investigation on behalf of a third party, and advising him to address his complaints to BA's executive top management. Branson had no more luck in that quarter; when he wrote to Lord King complaining about a personal attack that had been made on him in a BA press release, King quoted to him a remark that he had earlier made for public consumption: 'I run my airline, Richard Branson runs his. Best of luck to him.' The airline did, however, order a discreet investigation by its lawyers into Branson's allegations – which failed to find any evidence to substantiate them, partly because some of the most important documents on the campaign had already been shredded by terrified BA staff. Convinced that a paid mole inside the company was feeding information to Branson, BA hired teams of private detectives in order to find the source of the leak. One of the agencies that it later hired sent a man to steal domestic rubbish from the bin of Roger Eglin, a business journalist at the *Sunday Times*. When the man had the bad luck to be caught red-handed, BA merely found itself in further difficulties.

So bizarre was this catalogue of corporate misdemeanours – and so implausible the idea that a respectable business like British Airways would become embroiled in it – that Branson was unable to get the press to take it seriously. At last, however, he struck lucky: Martyn Gregory, a documentary film-maker who had returned recently from the Middle East, took from Branson a list of his allegations against BA, and started to investigate it independently. The result of his investigation was *Violating Virgin?*, a hard-hitting ITV programme which provided corroborative evidence of the 'dirty-tricks' campaign. When Gregory asked BA to put up a spokesman to comment on his findings, however, the company responded with a letter from Mervyn Walker, the head of its legal department. Walker told Gregory that he had 'fallen into the trap of being used as a vehicle for Richard Branson's propaganda, which sets out to contrive controversy with British Airways to create publicity for himself and his company and to inflict serious damage on the reputation of BA.' In an attempt to reassure its own employees, the company then published the letter in its in-house newspaper, *BA News*. Walker also drafted a letter for Lord King to send to those who had written to complain after seeing Gregory's documentary. The letter accused Branson of continuing 'to mount a campaign against us through the media. It appears that Mr Branson's motivation is to create publicity for himself and his airline.'

Those two letters ended up costing BA over £5m. Citing the letters, the incensed Branson issued a writ for libel against both the airline and its chairman. As the case moved to court, Virgin's lawyers forced BA to produce a growing number of internal documents about the campaign, which corroborated rather than refuted the allegations that Branson had made. In December 1992, BA's board was warned by its lawyers that it no longer had any hope of winning the case. It must either settle with Branson, or expect to pay a higher bill still after losing in the High Court.

Branson's price was £610,000, the highest sum ever paid in Britain as a libel settlement – and the payment of costs estimated at £1.5m. (BA's own costs were believed to have topped £3m for the case.) He demanded that BA should read out a statement in open court accepting the truth of his allegations and apologizing for its disreputable behaviour against Virgin Atlantic. The only shred of comfort for Lord King and Sir Colin Marshall was that the statement insisted that BA's 'directors were not party to any concerted campaign against Richard Branson and Virgin Atlantic'. A later statement amplified this by saying that the 'regrettable conduct was confined to a relatively small number of unconnected incidents involving a small number of employees.'

But there were recriminations inside the BA boardroom. Sir Michael Angus wanted to know why, if the allegations were now proved true, he had been misled into rebutting Branson's approach so firmly. He also wanted, consistent with his position as chairman of the CBI and his links with Sir Adrian Cadbury's report on corporate governance, to be reassured that the executive directors had had nothing to do with the campaign against Virgin. At a tense board meeting, he and his fellow non-executives ordered Lord King, Sir Colin Marshall, Robert Ayling and another director to sign a confirmation that they had 'not implemented or authorized any of the disreputable business acts complained of by Mr Branson and Virgin Atlantic or any press campaign or other improper action against Virgin Atlantic Airways or Mr Branson.'

The executive directors signed as they were asked to. Their official position was that the campaign was all the fault of David Burnside, BA's head of corporate affairs, and of Brian Basham. Burnside was relieved of his post, but compensated generously; Basham was paid to the end of his contract, but then received no further work from British Airways. In one sense, this solution was successful: when Lord King retired from the company chairmanship a few months later, it was Sir Colin who took his place as chairman and chief executive, and Robert Ayling who was promoted to the job of group managing director. But Brian Basham was not to be so easily beaten. Stung by the accusation that he had exceeded his brief, Basham changed sides and told his story to Martyn Gregory, the maker of the television documentary that had lost BA its libel action. It was not long before a second film appeared, alleging closer links between BA's top management and the anti-Virgin campaign than Sir Colin and Lord King had admitted.

By the middle of 1994, the dispute was still not yet concluded. BA had settled a claim connected with its maintenance of Virgin Atlantic aircraft after the takeover of British Caledonian. But three legal cases were still outstanding. Virgin was suing BA for breach of copyright, citing the unauthorized use of Virgin Atlantic computer data when BA staff telephoned Branson's customers to persuade them to change their flights to the larger airline. It had a complaint outstanding at the European Commission in Brussels, alleging that BA had broken the competition rules of the European Union. And, potentially most significant of all, Virgin was also suing British Airways in the United States. In a complaint filed in the New York district court, Virgin alleged in October 1993 that British Airways had broken American anti-trust laws in its campaign. The complaint, broken down into eight different allegations of wrongdoing, accused British Airways of a broad variety of anti-competitive and unfair activities prohibited under American law. British Airways tried to have the complaint struck out as 'a quintessentially English dispute, misguidedly brought before this United States District Court'. But Virgin had on its side the precedent of Sir Freddie Laker's anti-trust claim in the United States against British Airways and other airlines. In this court case, Richard Branson's price was higher. The damages he was asking from BA were $325m; under US law, a jury might punish an unsuccessful defendant in an anti-trust case by requiring it to pay triple damages.

While the American litigation remained in doubt, however, Richard Branson was content to put the damages he received from British Airways to good use. Some £110,000 was put into a fighting fund for future Virgin Atlantic court actions against predators; the rest, the £500,000 that had been awarded to him personally, was distributed equally to every one of Virgin Atlantic's employees. 'Thank you all for your help in our defence,' he wrote to them. 'After all, a Virgin's honour is her most prized possession.' The money, which amounted to £166 for each employee, became known as the BA Bonus.

TWENTY-THREE

Heathrow Airport and the Slot Machine

RICHARD BRANSON was rich enough not to notice £500,000 here or there. But the act of dividing equally between his employees the libel settlement which he had received personally from British Airways provided further evidence of why he was so popular not only with his employees, but also with the public at large. The gesture may have been instinctive; but no public relations consultant, no matter how highly paid, could have come up with a better way of casting Branson in a good light.

The tale of the 'dirty tricks', however, reveals a great deal more about British Airways than about Virgin. The low standards of moral behaviour inside the company – from the lowliest operatives who were lying to Virgin passengers over the telephone, to the board members who authorized Basham to write and disseminate his damaging report, and ordered their own employees to break into Virgin's computer data – were only the most obvious sign that something was wrong in BA. The campaign against Virgin also showed a worrying commercial arrogance: only a company that dominated its home market as comprehensively as British Airways did could have believed that it could behave so disreputably and get away with it. The bureaucratic mentality that had plagued BA during its years as a public corporation had disappeared; but it had been replaced by an even less attractive swagger that bore an alarming resemblance to the anti-trust complaints made in the United States against such companies as IBM and Microsoft.

More embarrassing still was the degree to which the affair simply made British Airways look foolish. The Basham report was hardly worth the £46,000 that Sir Colin Marshall paid for it. Had BA's top management really wanted to know what made Branson tick, they would have done better to spend a weekend reading the authorized biography of him that had been published five years earlier. Similar observations apply to the use by British Airways of bungling private detectives and investigators. The company's willingness to believe that Branson was spending £400,000 a week to bug British Airways was proof of an alarmingly paranoid mentality. Even the aftermath of the affair made the company look no better. Notwithstanding Sir Michael Angus's concerns about good corporate governance, and the flood of editorials that appeared in the national press calling for the resignation of Sir Colin Marshall, British Airways had appointed to its chairmanship a man who was far too closely linked to the wrongdoing for which it had been forced to pay so highly.

For much of the 1980s, British Airways had advertised itself as 'The World's Favourite Airline'. Virgin had a good riposte to that advertising slogan; it was able to point out that BA was no more entitled to award itself that title on the basis of mere brute numbers of passengers than the M25, London's notorious orbital road, was entitled to call itself the world's favourite motorway. But the threat from BA's mammoth advertising budgets receded sharply in the fuss that followed Richard Branson's libel victory in January 1993. Newspaper and television commentators were so hot in their condemnation of the activities for which BA had been forced to apologize in the High Court that the airline's senior management decided that it would be prudent to back away from spending money on advertising at the moment. At considerable cost, it therefore cancelled a series of posters that it had been planning to run on billboards in prominent sites all around London. Once again, Virgin stepped in to capitalize on the larger airline's humiliation. Taking advantage of the coincidence of the libel settlement and a recent announcement that Virgin Atlantic had been awarded another industry prize for the quality of its service, the company's advertising agency scooped up at a heavy discount the spaces that had suddenly become vacant. Its new slogan was elegant in its simplicity: EVEN THE TOUGHEST JUDGES GIVE US AWARDS.

There was one important question, though, that had not been asked during the preceding months. BA's campaign against Virgin and Branson had certainly been shocking and dishonest. But how much harm had the 'dirty tricks' really done to the smaller airline?

For Branson, the campaign had become an obsession; the frustration of seeing his allegations dismissed as no more than an attempt to win publicity had provoked him into leaving the management of his businesses to others for almost a year and a half, and concentrating on the forthcoming court case to the exclusion of almost everything else. (One senior Virgin Atlantic employee estimated that Branson had spent two-thirds of his entire time over that period on the investigation and the ensuing court case.) Trying to calculate precisely the damage caused to Virgin by BA's campaign, however, would be an impossible exercise. Without scouring Virgin Atlantic's Upper Class passenger lists over a period of more than a year, and telephoning the customers one by one to discover how many had defected as a result of the high-pressure selling operation carried out by the larger airline, it would be hard to tell how much business had been directly stolen. And since Virgin Atlantic managed to survive the recession in the airline industry that followed the Gulf War, the attempt to provoke a public crisis of confidence in the company's financial stability had evidently failed.

Nobody will ever know how close BA came to achieving the destruction of its smaller rival. All Richard Branson knew was that he had received a visit from a senior manager at Lloyds Bank on the day after Air Europe went under – but had managed to reassure the banker by giving him evidence that Virgin Atlantic was still very much solvent; and that his attempts to restructure the Virgin Atlantic fleet by introducing new equipment in place of current aircraft that were expensive to maintain had been unsuccessful while the libel case remained outstanding. No sooner had British Airways admitted wrongdoing, however, than the presidents of both Airbus and Boeing had called him with clear messages that they were now willing once again to do business with Virgin Atlantic.

In fact, there are good grounds for believing that the real damage that British Airways did to Virgin Atlantic was not done clandestinely through disinformation, negative public relations and illicit passenger-poaching. More significant than any of these activities were the competitive tactics that BA was able to pursue quite openly and with the knowledge and approval of the British authorities.

The starting-point of any analysis of the struggle between the two companies must lie in the difference between their cost structures and their power in the marketplace. All told, Virgin's costs were probably 25 per cent lower than those of British Airways – an astonishing gap, given the fact that under conventional business analysis, increased scale is supposed to bring economies. The cost gap between the two was not due merely to BA's expenditure on private detectives and public relations men, absurd though that may have been; nor had it much to do with the difference in scale between Virgin Atlantic's modest head office in a suburban building in Crawley, near Gatwick airport, and the vastly grander corporate offices to which BA treated itself. The underlying reason that Richard Branson could fly passengers more cheaply than BA could was straightforward: he was paying his staff less.

BA had grown fat and lazy in its days as a publicly owned flag carrier. Without shareholders demanding dividends, there had been little incentive to cut costs; and reducing redundant staff from the company's headcount had been a source of embarrassment for the government rather than satisfaction at BA's rising efficiency. After its privatization, BA undertook the painful exercise of shedding many of the unnecessary workers that it had taken on during the fat years of the 1970s, but by the 1990s it was still overweight. Old habits were not yet dead. Branson, by contrast, ran a very tight ship. It had long been a principle of his that if staff were not loyal and hardworking, offering them extravagant salaries would not make them so. Virgin Atlantic's staff were therefore chosen for their enthusiasm, and expected to work harder and for lower salaries than their equivalents at BA or foreign state-owned airlines. When BA conceded defeat in the High Court, the gap between labour costs in the two companies was startling. On average, pilots were costing British Airways £61,000 per annum apiece; Virgin Atlantic was paying only £40,800. Cabin crew at BA cost £17,200; at Virgin, their price was £11,000. The salary gap was especially startling for Japanese-speaking cabin crew on the Tokyo run: those who worked for Virgin Atlantic knew that they could have earned three times as much or more had they been willing to sign up with Japan Airlines. It was no wonder that Virgin Atlantic was Europe's lowest-cost airline.

There were two reasons why Branson did not convert these lower costs into lower prices for the consumer. One was that, by tradition, air fares were set by international treaties between the country of departure and the country of destination; so even if the British government were willing for Virgin to undercut BA's fares, the government at the other end would be unlikely to allow its own airline to lose money. A vivid demonstration of this was given in Japan, when the authorities in Tokyo demanded that Branson, far from undercutting, should actually charge £5 more than BA or the Japanese airlines flying the same route to take account of the extra legroom and better facilities he offered on board his aircraft. The other reason for not cutting prices was that Branson did not want to start a price war with his competitors. With the help of Nick Alexander, he had realized early on that his competitors' pockets were deep enough to drive him out of business if he were to try to compete on price alone. That was the mistake that Freddie Laker had made. To survive in the long term, Virgin must offer a better quality of service. Independent surveys of passenger satisfaction and industry awards showed that he was succeeding.

But BA's power in the market was immense. At the time of its privatization in 1987, the company accounted for 79 per cent of all British-originating international passenger traffic. By the time of the libel case, after British Caledonian, Air Europe and Dan-Air had disappeared from the scene, BA's market share had risen to 87 per cent. Far from diminishing, its dominant position in the industry had merely increased as a result of privatization. This looked all the more surprising when BA was compared with British Telecom, another state-owned business that was sold off to private shareholders in the 1980s. There was a respectable case for arguing that BT was a *natural monopoly*, because it owned millions of miles of copper cables connecting households all over the country to the telephone system. But the regulator responsible for keeping BT in check had made sure that fair access was given to Mercury and other long-distance telephone companies. Independent long-distance carriers owned their own trunk lines between big cities, but they were forced to use BT's local networks to connect their trunk lines with individual customers. Although the system was a matter of constant dispute, the regulators in Oftel, the Office of Telecommunications, at least made an effort to ensure that the prices BT charged the independent telephone companies for access to its local network were not so high as to give BT a cost advantage in long-distance calls. The larger company was also forbidden to use profits from local calls to subsidize its long-distance business and thus harm the new companies that were trying to compete with it.

The situation with British Airways was quite different. There was no airline regulator; instead, there was a Civil Aviation Authority, set up by an Act of Parliament in 1972, whose job was defined in terms not so much of protecting the consumer or promoting competition but making air travel safe and preventing airlines from going bust. The word 'compete' appeared only once in the Act's 60,000 words; the word 'competition' did not appear at all. And there was no legal reason why British Airways should not use the profits from routes on which it had a domestic monopoly to subsidize the routes where it had to face competition from Virgin Atlantic. The routes that Branson had chosen were busy routes, on which airlines could hope to have a good chance of filling an aircraft daily and therefore operate an efficient, low-cost service; so it was reasonable to expect the general level of prices on routes he flew to be lower than on the more obscure long-haul routes. But the price gap was a great deal larger than this difference would imply. While the lowest published fare to Los Angeles worked out at 4.5 pence a mile, the equivalent fare for the similar distance to Lagos, the Nigerian capital, was an astonishing 16 pence a mile. The gap was greater still when discounts were taken into account. This difference was common across scores of routes. The conclusion was inescapable: quite legally, and with the knowledge of the CAA, British Airways was accepting much lower profits on the routes where it had to compete with other carriers than on the routes it had to itself. In hard times, it might even be able to sell tickets on Branson's routes at below cost in order to contain the challenge from Virgin Atlantic. The legality of such a strategy would be doubtful; but without a formal separation in the company's accounts between one group of routes and another, it would be hard for an outside analyst to identify whether this predatory pricing was in fact taking place.

But there was a second set of obstacles which served conveniently to curtail Virgin's expansion: slots. Winning permission from two governments to fly a new international route was at first hard enough. Not only was the entry of an extra airline the subject of delicate bilateral negotiation; on top of that, the bureaucrats at the Civil Aviation Authority demanded hard evidence that the airline had sufficient cash reserves to satisfy their own assessment of the commercial risks of flying the route. Even when an airline such as Virgin Atlantic had won theoretical permission to fly a route, however, it had to arrange for take-off and landing times for its aircraft at both ends. It was not governments that controlled allocation of the 'slots', as these times were known. It was the airlines themselves. Slot allocation committees at each airport, whose membership was made up in large part by the airlines that already flew from that airport, had the sole right to decide who should fly in and out, and when.

At first British Airways succeeded in excluding Virgin Atlantic from the most attractive slots at Heathrow by a simple device: Virgin Atlantic was banned from Heathrow altogether, under a 1977 rule laying down that only airlines that were already operating services through Heathrow airport would be allowed to do so in future. Virgin was allowed only to fly aircraft to and from Gatwick. He complained long and bitterly over this restriction, and with good reason. The original rationale for the blanket exclusion from Heathrow was that with 275,000 flight movements each year, the airport simply could not handle any further traffic; since Heathrow now handles more than 500,000 movements a year, the assertion that it was full up in 1977 was clearly false. But matters did not begin to change until Branson gave the government's secretary of state for transport a vivid example of how much the exclusion from Heathrow was hurting his airline. He pointed out that because Gatwick's main runway was exactly 2,000 metres shorter than the equivalent runway at Heathrow, Virgin Atlantic's aircraft could not take off from Gatwick fully loaded. On each departure, some eight tonnes of potentially profitable freight was having to be left behind. By 1991 the CAA had changed its tune: it recommended that the old 1977 restriction on Heathrow be rescinded; and Malcolm Rifkind, the transport secretary at the time, turned down BA's appeal against the decision. Proof of how valuable the old rule had been to British Airways was quick in coming: Lord King, who had authorized donations from company funds to the Conservative Party of £80,000 during the previous two years, announced that BA would give no more money to Tory funds.

Even after the Heathrow ban was removed, though, there was a second line of defence. Every Virgin slot had to be negotiated individually with the allocation committee, which was chaired by a British Airways employee; and the principle on which the committee worked was that once an airline had operated a slot for a year, it then acquired so-called 'grandfather rights', under which it could continue operating that slot if it wished in perpetuity. This made it extremely hard for new entrants to set up in business. Branson applied for 86 slots from Heathrow; the committee countered with an offer of 28. To make matters worse, the timing of the slots offered was clearly unviable: the committee was offering slots to allow Virgin to fly four aircraft out to Newark each week, but none back. It was a reminder of the row between the two airlines ten years earlier when Virgin Atlantic had first flown from Gatwick. The Gatwick committee, similarly influenced by BA, had at first told the fledgling airline that no slots were available, and had then offered an absurd set of times which would have required Virgin's passengers to turn up for their departing flights in the early hours of the morning. In that earlier row, Virgin Atlantic had been forced to threaten legal action in order to make the committee see sense; once admitted to Heathrow, it took time before Branson was given competitive departure and arrival times for his aircraft. Even then, he was still unable to win suitable slots to operate flights to Chicago, Las Vegas, Singapore, Sydney, Melbourne and Bangkok for which his airline already had formal permission to fly.

Virgin Atlantic was still at a disadvantage, though, even after it had wrestled a fair set of slots from British Airways. The larger carrier had 75 slots for every one of Branson's; and under the long-standing informal principle that had governed slot allocation at British airports, BA had the right to hold on to all the slots it already possessed. Yet this immensely valuable right was balanced by no obligation to maintain the services for which the slot had originally been allocated. When British Airways decided to suspend services occupying 5,000 slots each year from Heathrow Airport to

Ireland, therefore, it was quite free to use the departure and arrival slots that became vacant as a result to put more pressure on its smaller rivals. Its flight frequency to Glasgow went up from ten flights a day to fourteen, at a time when British Midland, a short-haul British operator, was setting up a Glasgow service for the first time; and BA established extra frequencies to Newark and Los Angeles, routes on which Virgin was already flying, and to San Francisco, Chicago and Washington – routes on which it expected to face competition from Branson.

It was this move by British Airways that alerted Branson to the unfairness of the 'grandfather rights' principle. In a number of speeches – to passengers' representatives in London, to a conference celebrating the Chicago air convention signed at the end of the Second World War, even to a committee of 'wise men' convened by the European Community to decide what to do about airline policy – Branson complained bitterly that the principle was anti-competitive and unfair. Slots at busy airports were a scarce resource comparable to the frequencies used by radio and television broadcasts, he pointed out; yet nobody suggested that a private company which had operated a radio or television station on a given frequency for a year should have a monopoly over that frequency for ever. If the rules were to be operated to the benefit of the consumer, Branson suggested, it would be better to allocate the slots at airports not according to some backward-looking historical principle, but instead in accordance with the number of passengers that an airline could expect to get through the slot in its allocated time. For if this principle were followed, then the number of passengers able to travel through each airport would be maximized.

This idea was of course self-interested. The average number of passengers aboard each aircraft departing and arriving at Heathrow was only about 150. Because Virgin Atlantic operated a fleet entirely made up of Boeing 747s, its average throughput was nearer to 400 passengers per slot. This principle would therefore strongly favour Virgin Atlantic not only over British Airways, but also over all the short-haul carriers who operated frequent services on smaller planes between the airport and European or domestic destinations. If there was to be radical reform, a more rational principle might have been simply to auction slots every year, and to allow the airline willing to pay most for each slot to have it. That would have allowed customers of high-value services such as Concorde flights to fly at times whose convenience matched the price they were willing to pay. But such a principle might not have been to Virgin's advantage, so Branson never pressed for it.

It was probably because of the shock of being allowed into Heathrow, and the work that was involved in rearranging Virgin Atlantic's operations so that it could operate simultaneously from two hubs at Gatwick and Heathrow airports, that Branson failed to discover in time that moves were afoot to enshrine into European law the unfair and exclusionary system of allocating slots. Until 1992, there was no formal legal basis for the 'grandfather rights': in fact the system was probably open to challenge under the European Community's competition laws. But in 1992, the EC's transport ministers looked at the subject of slots as part of a wider review of how airlines were regulated in the Community's twelve countries. The outcome was a decision in late 1992 that promised a slow and gradual opening up of the European airline business to competition from other European carriers (but not from carriers in the United States or elsewhere). Among its provisions was a plan to allow airlines that were registered in one EC country to fly between two others – whereas previously, any two countries had the right to ban any airlines except their own from flying between them. But the British government, which used its position as holder of the Community's six-month rotating presidency to broker the agreement, gave a concession in return to the countries that were opposed to liberalization. The principle that an airline which had occupied slots in the past should have a right to occupy them indefinitely was adopted by the transport ministers and given their formal blessing. Virgin's ability to lobby at Westminster against the massed ranks of British Airways representatives may well have improved. But the company had been slow to discover what was being plotted in Brussels, and had entered the fray far too late to prevent it.

Branson therefore faced a dilemma. Preparations were already under way to add Hong Kong and San Francisco to Virgin Atlantic's expanding list of destinations. But by the end of 1994, the Virgin chairman expected to be operating services on six out of the ten busiest international routes out of the United Kingdom. If the airline was to resume its expansion, it needed to find a way out of the artificial constraints imposed on capacity at Heathrow airport.

Once again, Richard Branson prepared to gamble. Refusing to stand still and manage the business he had created, he resolved to turn Virgin Atlantic upside down over the course of the coming two years. He would change most of his fleet of aircraft. He would fundamentally restructure the shareholding of the airline and establish a new strategic alliance. He would shake up the management system that had been established. And he would begin to experiment with an idea that might just, in the long term, give Virgin the chance to operate scores of new routes.

TWENTY-FOUR

A Matter of Timing

IN THE SPRING of 1992, when the airline industry was only just beginning to recover from its deepest recession ever, and when the propaganda war with British Airways was at its height, Richard Branson had plenty to worry about. So the news that Trevor Abbott had for him was particularly unwelcome. Seibu-Saison, the Japanese leisure conglomerate that had invested £36m in his airline holding company back in 1989, had indicated that it no longer wanted to be one of his shareholders. Never mind the corporate traditions of long-termism: less than three years after cementing what the two sides had agreed would be a strategic alliance, the Japanese-based company had decided that it wanted to sell. Branson faced an unpalatable choice: either to find another shareholder willing to take over from Seibu-Saison, or to find enough money to buy back the shares himself.

Three years earlier the two companies had seemed a good match. Both businesses spanned a number of different industrial sectors: Seibu-Saison's interests ranged from Japan's most fashionable department store chain to its third biggest supermarket group, and from travel agencies to a luxury hotel in Tokyo and a stake in the Club Med holiday village business. Like Branson, its chairman had a knack for appealing to young and upwardly mobile consumers. Both groups had ambitions to expand beyond their home bases. Branson wanted to raise Virgin's profile in Japan; he had opened his first megastore in Shinjuku, and had just begun flying between London and Tokyo. Seiji Tsutsumi, Seibu-Saison's chairman, had just completed a gigantic foreign acquisition. In 1988, the company had spent $2.15 billion to buy a chain of over a hundred Intercontinental hotels. Its presence abroad was thus established with a vengeance; and its chairman, who was a friend of the Japanese prime minister and had written under a pseudonym twenty novels, a play and a collection of poems, was wondering whether to step aside from executive management and to devote himself entirely to literary and political pursuits.

Yuji Tsutsumi, the chairman's brother who had been put in charge of the group's overseas expansion, had hired a representative in England to keep an eye out for European business opportunities for Seibu-Saison. His name was Sir Francis Nicholas Fraser Pearson; he was a baronet, a product of a fine English public school, a soldier and an entrepreneur. Having failed to be elected as a Conservative MP in the 1979 election that swept Margaret Thatcher to power, he returned to business as the chairman of the Turner Group. By 1989 he had sold his business and was working from a light-flooded office at the top of a house in Holland Park, five minutes' walk from Branson's looking for an exciting new business opportunity.

Pearson's first idea, since Virgin was preparing to fly to Tokyo, was that Seibu-Saison should provide ground handling services for the airline in Japan, and perhaps sell Virgin tickets through its travel agencies. But both sides were interested in a more intimate relationship. A deal soon took shape; Seibu-Saison would buy a 10 per cent stake in the airline holding company for £6m, and would lend the company a further £30m; if it wanted to, the Japanese firm would be allowed to convert that loan into another 10 per cent of the company's shares on agreed terms in 1992.

The principle was easy enough; the details took months of tiresome negotiations to pin down. Although Pearson had been given a power of attorney by Seibu-Saison, his Japanese employers had retained two different firms of lawyers: one in London and another in Tokyo. Every point had to be cleared through both sets, and there were often weeks of silence before Pearson could come back to Virgin with the answer to even the smallest point. The terms under which the loan could be turned into shares were enshrined in a formula based on the average of the previous two years' pre-tax profits, from which agreed marketing expenses would be deducted. To acquire a fifth of the airline, Seibu-Saison would have to pay twelve times that figure. There was only one sticking-point. Because its loan to the company was convertible into shares, Seibu-Saison would have to accept that its claim on the company's assets must be subordinated to some of the company's other debtors. The final agreement, which gave the Japanese firm the right to claim Virgin Atlantic's pool of spare aircraft parts as security for the £30m loan, and gave it a 'floating charge' over whatever assets were left after debtors with a higher priority had been paid, ran to two fat volumes. As an added protection, Seibu-Saison had the right to appoint two representatives to the company board. These representatives would have the right to approve changes to the company's budget; so Virgin would be have to win their approval before undertaking any item of unbudgeted expenditure above £25,000.

At first the dealings between the two sides were amicable. Pearson and another Seibu-Saison representative enjoyed their visits to the board, and pronounced themselves quite satisfied with the company's management. Then came the Gulf War. Not only did the airline's fortunes begin to go rapidly downhill; worse still, Seibu-Saison found itself in difficulties with its expensive new Inter-Continental hotel chain. The group had paid far too much for the deal – over $2bn for a set of hotels that were turning in only $80m in profits every year – and it had been obliged to buy out SAS, the Scandinavian airline with which it had hoped to share some of the risk. By 1991, with no sign that the airline industry's fortunes were improving, Seibu-Saison had learned its lesson. The Inter-Continental deal was simply too big to be unwound; but the Virgin deal was not. Tokyo decided to sell.

When Nick Pearson first told his fellow members of the airline company board that Seibu-Saison might be willing to sell, there was no feeling of panic. But the negotiations over selling back the stake to Virgin took longer than he had hoped. Eventually, a deal was struck whereby Virgin would buy back Seibu-Saison's equity stake for £10m, giving it a comfortable profit on the £6m it had paid three years earlier; and the outstanding capital of the eight-year £30m loan would also be repaid. But the successful completion of the deal was conditional on two events: first, Virgin had to sell its music interests; second, the consortium of banks to whose claims Seibu-Saison was subordinated had to agree to the deal. The first condition was met when EMI agreed to pay £560m for Virgin Music. The second was a little harder, for the banks tried to use their veto over Seibu-Saison's exit as a lever with which to extract extra security for their money from Branson.

But Pearson was told that the difficulties were not insuperable; Virgin would find a way around the problem. And he then terminated his contract with Seibu-Saison, having negotiated for the Japanese firm what he sincerely believed to be an honourable and not unprofitable exit route. Pearson thought that he was leaving both sides on good terms; Seibu-Saison because he had done a good deal for them; and Virgin, because he had shown himself to be a co-operative and valuable member of the holding company's board. Proof of this goodwill came in a discreet word from Trevor Abbott, who told Pearson that he would be delighted if Pearson would return to the board once the dust had settled, not as a Seibu-Saison representative but as a valued adviser in his own right.

Meanwhile the deal had been put into escrow and Pearson had been assured that it would be completed in a matter of weeks. But the weeks dragged on into months, and nothing happened. Seibu-Saison demanded to see verbatim transcripts of all conversations between Virgin and the consortium about the matter, and nothing happened. The Japanese company called board meetings and showed its dissatisfaction by taking a little longer than necessary to approve the airline's budgets. Still nothing happened. Gradually, it dawned on Pearson and on his former employers in Japan that Virgin would never complete the deal. 'It would have been possible,' he remembered. 'If the entire might of Richard's empire had been put behind the problem, it could have been solved. But it wasn't solved.'

There was a good reason why it was not solved. As business conditions continued to deteriorate, the price at which Branson had agreed to buy back Seibu-Saison's stake in his airline began to look highly favourable to the Japanese firm. It soon became clear that it was no longer in Virgin's interests to persuade the consortium of banks to drop their objections to the deal. For if the deal was not completed by 31 December 1992, it would lapse; and Virgin would then be free to reopen negotiations with Seibu-Saison, this time offering a much lower price at which to buy out the Japanese company's interest. In any case, the airline was by then losing money heavily. No other investor could remotely be persuaded to come in and take over the minority shareholding. It was only to be nearer the end of 1993 that a second deal was put together, significantly less favourable to Seibu-Saison, and the 10 per cent stake was bought back, to Pearson's intense embarrassment, for an undisclosed but significantly lower price.

The attempt to find another minority shareholder had by then been abandoned. Several companies had been approached, including Royal Brunei, Singapore Airways, Malaysian Air Services, Lufthansa, Air France and an American airline or two for good measure, but none had proved seriously interested. Branson had no option but to buy back the shareholding himself. The money was found from the offshore trusts into which he had transferred ownership of many of his Virgin shares more than five years earlier. Although Branson was not a beneficiary of the trusts, and was not himself one of the trustees, it was a simple matter for him to suggest to the trustees that it would be a wise use of their funds to make a substantial investment in his travel group. A sum of over £35m therefore made its way quickly back to Britain, and the Japanese minority shareholder was bought out without difficulty. A few weeks later, the London *Evening Standard* reported that Branson had put on the market the two neighbouring houses that he owned in Holland Park. The asking price for the pair, said the newspaper, was around £15m. Challenged to explain his going back on a decision to stay with his family at the Holland Park house for the rest of his life, Branson himself merely laughed that he had always wanted to return to a houseboat on the canal at Little Venice. That, he said, was what he was now proposing to do.

Abbott, who negotiated the exit of Seibu-Saison in his capacity as group managing director, defended himself against the allegation of sharp practice. 'They could have suggested that we didn't try hard enough [to overcome the banks' objections to the buy-back],' he said. 'I do not vehemently deny it. I'm a businessman. As far as I'm concerned, I will look at a deal, I will honour to the letter any binding agreement. But if there is uncertainty or there is room to renegotiate, particularly on exits ... When you are exiting from something then ... provided it is done in a reasonably gentlemanly fashion, you respect the other side to the degree they deserve. That is variable depending on who they are. The cut and thrust is all part of the game ... We could have accepted the conditions that the syndicate put to us ... We chose not to; they were unacceptable to us.'

Abbott also admitted that it was he, and not Richard Branson, who had second thoughts about appointing Pearson to the board of the Virgin Atlantic holding company. 'To be honest, until the dust had settled with Seibu-Saison, I thought it was inappropriate. Since then, life's moved on.'

It was not until six months later, in April 1994, that Virgin was able to put in place a new strategic alliance to replace the link with Seibu-Saison. This time there was no minority shareholding. Instead, Virgin announced a deal with Delta Air Lines, the third largest carrier in the United States, that promised to bring in extra revenues of £150m a year for Virgin. Assuming that the authorities on both sides of the Atlantic gave their blessing, Delta agreed to buy just under a fifth of all the available seats on Virgin flights between London and the airline's seven US destinations. In return, Delta would have the right to sell on those seats to its American customers at prices of its own choosing – and to identify the Virgin flights with its own flight numbers, so that it could appear to offer through services into London from scores of US cities. This system, known as code-sharing, had been pioneered in agreements between British Airways and US Air, and between Lufthansa and United.

The rationale behind the deal from Delta's point of view was simple. Until 1994 it had failed to gain permission to serve Heathrow; only American Airlines and United Airlines had the right to fly their own aircraft into London's main airport. The absence of London Heathrow from Delta's flight schedules was a significant disincentive to its customers. So the Virgin deal was the next best thing; while Delta continued to press the US government to demand 'open skies' between America and Britain, it had at least second-hand access to Heathrow.

For Virgin, the attractivenesss of the deal was different. Rather than pretend that Delta's vast domestic US network was merely an extension of Virgin's own international network – which would not only have seemed implausible to its customers but might also have given rise to some complaints from irate passengers who had expected to fly all the way to their eventual US destination on a Virgin aircraft, and discovered instead that they were required to get off and change on to a Delta jet for the second and onward legs – Virgin would simply sell to its customers old-fashioned through tickets that showed first a Virgin flight and then a Delta flight. But Virgin would have a guaranteed buyer for a sizeable chunk of its available seats; and its customers would be allowed to accumulate points on the Virgin frequent-flyer programme whenever they flew Delta. Since Delta had 563 aircraft, and flew 83 million passengers a year (compared with Virgin's 1.5 million passengers and 15 aircraft) – and was the airline which served the largest number of destinations from New York's JFK airport – this was clearly a valuable advantage.

The agreement with Delta provoked some raised eyebrows at British Airways. For in its anti-trust complaint against BA in the New York District Court, Virgin had complained that the similar code-sharing agreement between BA and US Air was anticompetitive. Virgin had argued that the deal between BA and US Air 'eliminates one of the limited number of United States carriers serving the markets for airline passenger service between the United States and the United Kingdom'; had said that the agreement 'creates strong economic incentives for passengers travelling to London or the United Kingdom from non-gateway United States cities served by US Air to travel through gateways where BA And US Air have a code-sharing arrangemnet and to fly with BA on the transatlantic portion of their trip'; claimed the deal 'effectively transforms BA and US Air into a single airline on these routes'; and finally, most damagingly, claimed that the deal 'forecloses competitors, like Virgin, from access to consumers in an effort to force such competitors from the relevant markets'. Virgin could claim with reason that BA, unlike itself, was in a dominant position in the market. But the new message from Branson, as the *Economist* pointed out, was unmistakable: if you can't beat them, join them.

The agreement with Delta was only one of a number of dramatic changes taking place inside Virgin. The most significant of these was Branson's decision immediately after his High Court victory over British Airways to restructure the Virgin Atlantic fleet. The airline had discovered in the course of the recession that while some of its current and proposed routes were busy enough to justify buying the new Boeing 747–400 aircraft, with a longer top deck than previous models, other routes were not. Flights to Tokyo, San Francisco and Hong Kong, for instance, might not bring in enough traffic to justify flying even a less capacious Boeing 747–200 every day. Although there were enough customers to guarantee filling half or more of the seats, the high running costs of elderly jumbos also meant that Virgin could nevertheless find itself doomed to make losses on these routes.

The answer was obvious, but elusive until the libel case was settled. Virgin needed to acquire some 747–400s, and to replace some of its 747–200s with smaller Airbus A340s. With more than fifty fewer seats than a 747, the A340s were ideal for the routes that Virgin Atlantic was serving; and because they were of a more modern design, their fuel and maintenance costs were sharply lower than those of the older Boeings. (It would cost £70,000 less to fly an Airbus than a 747–200 to Tokyo and back.) Here Branson was very astute. Because the airline recession had not yet lifted, nobody wanted to buy aircraft. Consequently, prices in the highly cyclical aircraft market were lower than they had been for years. By placing a judicious $1.5 billion order which would be delivered in 1994 and 1995, Richard Branson succeeded in getting himself a fleet of new aircraft that were not only more up-to-date but also cheaper to finance and to maintain than the machines his airline had operated before. He also managed to wring an unexpected extra concession from Jean Pierson, the president of Airbus. At a dinner after a long day of negotiations over the contribution that Airbus would make to the promotion of its new airliners in Virgin's fleet, Branson told his counterpart: 'If I can hypnotize you, I want four times what you've offered us.' Towards the end of the meal, he asked the Airbus president for the time.

'Ah,' said the president. 'I seem to have lost my watch.'

'I know,' Branson replied. 'That's because I have it.' He rolled up his sleeve and there it was, on his wrist.

Chris Moss, who was marketing director of the airline at the time, did not know whether Branson had used hypnosis or merely sleight of hand to get the watch. It was only in May 1994, when a documentary on the service quality of Virgin Atlantic was shown on the BBC, that Branson's secret was revealed. With the cameras running, Branson had given one of his passengers a long and friendly shake of the hand. Repeating the trick he had played on the Airbus president, the Virgin chairman gently removed the man's wristwatch with his other hand, and fastened it on his own wrist unnoticed during the conversation. The surprise and delight on his passenger's face when he discovered the prank was unmistakable; but not even the lifelong loyalty of one passenger was as valuable as the extra concession Branson had won from Airbus.

With a new fleet, and a new route to Hong Kong just open, the airline could hope to benefit from the much quicker growth in demand for air travel in Asia than in Europe or America. But work also needed to be done inside the airline itself. As it had grown bigger, the succession of new ideas for services to the Upper Class passenger allowed Virgin Atlantic to keep abreast of the competition, even as other airlines upgraded their film and sound systems and increased the size and spacing of their business class seats. But the transatlantic passenger surveys were beginning to show an alarming shrinkage in the gap between Virgin Atlantic and other airlines in the economy cabin. This was partly because of the cramped conditions there, for along with other airlines Virgin had crammed as many seats as it could into the back of the aircraft. (On the run between London and New York in 1993, airlines could afford to spend roughly £9 per customer extra on food, entertainment and presents for every inch saved in the pitch between seat rows.) Virgin needed to do something radical in order to rediscover the friendly spirit that had marked its early days.

When they looked at what had happened, Branson and his colleagues realized that the greater size of Virgin Atlantic – its staff roster now ran into the thousands, rather than the hundreds – meant that the cabin crews no longer knew each other as they had done when the airline first started flying. Instead of seeing one another weekly, the crews were finding that they met colleagues on average only once every three months. Branson therefore decided on a radical but simple solution. After an experiment on the Boston route, he would split up the cabin crews into fifteen teams of 150 people each, in the hope of recreating the small-company spirit that might otherwise have disappeared.

One aspect of his management style, however, would remain unchanged. For several years, Branson had been stating a radical view in the speeches he was asked to make with increasing frequency. Rather than putting shareholders first, he would say, Virgin believed in reversing the order of priorities. For him, employees came first; customers second; and shareholders third. To Branson's mind, a business that depended on people as much as the airline business did must make motivating its employees the very highest priority. And if after that it kept its mind on keeping its customers happy, he reasoned, the company would not need to worry too much about its shareholders – for the business would be a success, and the shareholders could be guaranteed a steady increase in the value of their equity.

As Branson was all too aware, this view was less radical in some circles than in others. Among Japanese companies, for instance, the obsession with motivating staff would not have seemed even slightly surprising. But this was more than just idle theorizing. The practical consequence of Branson's view could be seen in the arrangement of incoming mail that Penni Pike, his assistant, made for him every morning. Letters and messages would be sorted for Branson in different sheaves, each with a summary sheet on top listing the contents and held together with a bulldog clip. The sheaf he would read first – and thus the letters that received top priority from Richard Branson – was the one marked with the word STAFF.

These changes seemed set to transform Virgin Atlantic once again. They would turn it once again into a lean, low-cost airline whose aircraft fleet was exactly suited to the traffic on its routes; an airline that could guarantee in advance, thanks to its deal with Delta, to sell a substantial proportion of its tickets each year; and an airline that had grown large while managing to retain some of the virtues of a small business. But the old problem of slots remained. While Virgin remained a long-haul airline, it could continue to expand into new markets with only a dribble of new arrival and departure slots at Heathrow each year. (One competitor estimated that this strategy alone would allow Virgin Atlantic to double its turnover every three years into the late 1990s.) But that amounted to an upper limit on Richard Branson's ambitions – and he had never been willing to accept upper limits imposed by others.

As so often in the past, many of Branson's senior managers thought that 1994 was a good time to stand still and take stock. There was plenty to do in building up the new routes to Hong Kong and San Francisco, and in smoothing the arrival of the new Airbuses and 747–400s and the departure of the old 747–200s. Later on, pursuing a firm strategy of flying only routes on which it could hope to achieve a reasonable market share, the airline could look again at flying to Johannesburg and Australia. But Richard Branson did not want to stand still. Virgin had received two pro-posals from other companies that wanted to co-operate in opening up new short-haul routes: one from a Greek company, which wanted to run flights primarily intended for holiday-makers between London and Greece; another from City Jet, a fast-growing Irish firm that wanted Virgin's help in competing with British Air-ways and Aer Lingus between Britain and the Republic of Ireland – by flying British Aerospace 146 'whisper jets' in and out of the London City airport in the docklands to the east of the city.

Roy Gardner, the airline's joint managing director, thought Branson was mad. In both cases, he argued, Virgin would be expos-ing itself to great risk if something went wrong. If either of the two services failed to make money, it would be on Virgin and Richard Branson that the television cameras would focus. If an aircraft should fall out of the sky, it would be the wider Virgin Atlantic route system that would suffer the consequences. But Syd Pennington, the joint managing director responsible for marketing, took a more sanguine view. Both of the two small companies were willing to allow Virgin to monitor their financial health. Both were paying Virgin not only for the rights to its name but also for the management help they needed to set up the new services. Both were able to take advantage of a loophole in European Union rules that guaranteed slots to newly established airlines.

And in the case of City Jet's proposed service, there was a great opportunity. Hitherto, London City airport had failed to capture the imagination of the business community. Despite its advantages of proximity to the capital's financial centre and swift check-in, and despite the hundreds of thousands that were poured into marketing it, the airport felt ghostly and empty. Sir Michael Bishop, the head of British Midland, had tried to make the airport work; he used to say that he had 'been there, done that, and lost a lot of money'. Yet Richard Branson thought that it might – just might – be possible that London City had come of age. British Aerospace, keen to sell more of the compact jets that served the airport, had offered a launch budget of £800,000 with which to market the new service; as a result, City Jet was able to spend more on advertising it than Aer Lingus could afford for its entire route network out of Ireland. And if by some chance the route should become successful, Virgin would suddenly find itself with the ability to operate effectively unlimited numbers of short-haul flights out of London. That would bring it into clear conflict with British Midland, which would be a pity; every time he saw Bishop, Branson would joke that it was time the two companies 'got married'. But such an expansion would clearly be impossible otherwise. Establishing a new short-haul European route would require laying on eight or ten flights a day in each direction; and if Virgin had been able to get hold of so many slots at Heathrow, it would have used them for more lucrative long-haul business.

It had little material effect on Branson whether the two new services succeeded at all, let alone whether they provided a change in strategic direction for his airline. Not only did they bring free advertising for Virgin's conventional long-haul services: more important, they brought back the excitement of the old days. Once again, Virgin was busily training new staff, buying new equipment, checking up on quality control, deciding how to operate duty free. And once again, new staff were being taken on who reported back to a small company in their own country. What did Virgin, or Branson, have to lose?

TWENTY-FIVE

The £40m Wager

RICHARD BRANSON was an infrequent smoker, usually cadging cigarettes from other people on occasions when he had drunk too much. So he had mixed feelings when Anita Roddick, the Body Shop founder who had joined him on the board of the Healthcare Foundation, telephoned to ask him to give £100,000 of the Foundation's money towards an anti-smoking campaign. Would his involvement not lay him open to charges of hypocrisy? And was the campaign itself right? After all, Branson believed broadly that people ought to be allowed to make their own mistakes. He had always been in favour of the legalization of marijuana; he had 'tripped' on acid in his twenties, and tried cocaine too. So the Virgin chairman hardly thought of himself as puritanical in such matters. But Roddick made him promise to ask Des Wilson, the man in charge of the campaign, for some more details before making a decision.

It was early on a Saturday morning, and Branson was driving in the Range Rover down the M40 towards his home in Oxford, when he made the telephone call. Wilson, who had made his name campaigning for the homeless and against lead in petrol, was a fluent and persuasive advocate. He began by explaining that this was an anti-smoking campaign with a particular focus – on children. Under current law, he reminded Branson, it was illegal for shopkeepers to sell cigarettes to people under sixteen. But the law was not being enforced: only 29 retailers had been prosecuted under its provisions the previous year, yet surveys showed that 250,000 British children were buying cigarettes *each week*. About a quarter of fifteen-year-olds smoked; on average, boys smoked 56 cigarettes a week, and girls 49. A recent survey had shown that only five per cent of under-age smokers reported any difficulty in finding supplies of cigarettes. Despite the clear intention of Parliament to protect children from the blandishments of tobacco companies – and despite the proven fact that the majority of smokers became addicted at an age when it was still illegal for them to buy cigarettes – the tobacco companies still relied on under-sixteens for some £70m of their sales each year.

The object of the campaign was straightforward: to cut off the link between the tobacco companies and the young people who would become their future customers. An organization called Parents Against Tobacco had been set up, and it was intending to lobby Parliament in an attempt to have the law tightened up. But the campaign would cost well over a quarter of a million pounds. Godfrey Bradman, the maverick property millionaire who had participated in some of Wilson's most recent campaigns, had agreed to put up £60,000. Could the Foundation be counted on for another £100,000?

Branson knew full well that this was far from the only call on the Foundation's funds. As soon as the Mates condom brand had been launched in 1987, and the news was made public that all profits from it would be remitted to charity, the Foundation had received a flood of applications for help. They had spent money on AIDS prevention and on the care of patients with HIV; they had sponsored a plan to encourage the wider use of organ donor cards; and they had backed a new product called a Virotherm which was intended as a treatment for asthma and the common cold. But Parents Against Tobacco would be a very big and very public project to take on. It would also require Branson to contribute a commodity that was scarcer than mere money: his time. As well as giving his approval to the donation from the Foundation, he was to spend two dozen or more working days over the next two years on the affairs of Parents Against Tobacco.

The campaign commissioned a MORI poll which suggested that 95 per cent of the adult public wanted the existing rules to be strictly enforced. Only slightly fewer also wanted tougher controls on machines. Armed with this evidence of public support, Wilson and his colleagues set to work drafting a new piece of legislation: they called it the Children and Young Persons (Protection from Tobacco) Bill. The bill proposed a number of changes to the law.

Under the 1908 Act that had been intended to ban tobacco sales to minors, a shopkeeper could successfully defend himself against a prosecution simply by proving that the child had 'appeared' to be over sixteen. In future, this line of defence would be cut off; if the child actually was under sixteen, the shopkeeper would be guilty.

Another problem with the status quo was that the tiny number of shopkeepers who were actually prosecuted were often getting away with only token fines of £25 or £50. So the bill raised the maximum fine for an illegal sale from £400 to £2,500. In the past, there had also been confusion between the police and local councils as to who was responsible for enforcing the under-sixteen rule, with the result that neither did. So the bill imposed a legal obligation on councils to enforce the rules; any local authority that failed to meet this obligation could be hauled before the High Court and made to do its duty. The bill also made it compulsory for shops and vending machines to carry prominent notices advertising the under-sixteen rule, and banned shopkeepers from selling single cigarettes. Particularly in poor areas, where children could not afford a full pack of ten or twenty cigarettes, many smaller shops had adopted the policy of breaking open packets and selling the cigarettes for 10p or 15p each. This had the advantage of bringing higher margins to the shopkeeper; it had the disadvantage of encouraging tobacco addiction particularly among younger and poorer children. A survey in Bristol had shown that 80 per cent of all child smokers had bought cigarettes singly. Accordingly, the bill imposed a separate £1,000 fine on any shopkeeper who continued this practice. Even the rules on vending machines were to be tightened up; instead of the old rule that a court could order a machine to be removed if there was evidence that it was being 'extensively used by persons apparently under the age of sixteen', the bill made things more straightforward. If it believed that just one under-age smoker had bought cigarettes from a machine, a court would in future have the power to order its removal.

With the bill drafted, the next step was to get it through Parliament. Jane Dunmore, the campaign's director, wrote to more than 200 MPs to enlist their support; but it was only at a lobby reception at the House of Commons itself that Des Wilson discovered that Andrew Faulds, a Labour MP who had promised to back the campaign, had won the private member's bill ballot. Under the standard procedures of the House of Commons, the vast majority of debating time is taken up with measures proposed either by the government or by the opposition parties. Individual MPs who want to introduce a bill have to enter a ballot; only the winners have time set aside for the discussion of their proposed measure. So Wilson knew that he would never have a better opportunity to get the bill into Parliament. Leaving the reception, he talked his way into Faulds's office in the Palace of Westminster, and persuaded the MP that this bill was the one he should introduce. The wording was already drafted, he urged; the measure would clearly be popular; and it had such support on both sides of the House that it would have a good chance of success. The MP who backed it would undoubtedly earn reflected glory.

Under such overwhelming pressure, Faulds agreed. The bill was presented – the Duke of Gloucester, the Queen's cousin, making a rare appearance in the House of Lords to speak in its favour – and the process of haggling began. Only two substantive points had to be conceded. An attempt to restrict the use of cigarette brand names in shop windows was abandoned in the face of concerted lobbying from the tobacco industry. And the government had cold feet about imposing a formal obligation on local councils, for it knew that if it did so national taxpayers would have to pick up the bill for more frequent inspections of shops and for the wave of prosecutions that would certainly be required. So instead of an obligation to enforce, local councils were merely obliged to consider once a year what their policy on enforcing the law would be. Councils would be free to decide to do nothing at all unless they received complaints; but, in principle, the added public pressure would make most councils morally obliged to be more active.

The bill became law in 1991, and came into force in 1992. But although the campaign had been addressed entirely to this one issue, there was still much to do. Wilson wrote, and the government's Health Education Authority published, a book on the new legislation, explaining to local councils and lobby groups how to make sure of its enforcement. The book contained pages of useful details, even going so far as to include a draft press release for local Parents Against Tobacco (PaT) groups to use in order to win publicity when they tried to put pressure on local authorities. A system of 'PaT on the back' awards was set up to give credit to the retailers who took the new law seriously – and a hundred sympathetic celebrities, ranging from Branson himself to footballers and teenage pop-stars, made themselves available to give them out at public ceremonies.

But even with these efforts, there were difficulties. Some councils were happy in principle to prosecute shopkeepers who broke the law, but unhappy in practice about the use of children as *agents provocateurs* to prove that the under-sixteen sales rule had been broken. Magistrates proved reluctant to use the full weight of the law in the fines they imposed. The highest fine ever meted out was still only £1,000 by 1994; a few hundred pounds was more usual. And, for all the efforts of the lobby group, there was still a hard core of retailers who remained willing and able to supply children with cigarettes. Opinion polls showed that more child smokers were reporting that they were having difficulty in finding shopkeepers who would sell them cigarettes; but since the word on which shops would sell soon got around, it required only a small proportion of shops to carry on selling tobacco to children for consumption patterns to continue unchanged. By mid-1994, there was not yet any evidence that smoking by children had begun to decline at all.

Reflecting on the bitter-sweet mixture of success and failure in the activities of Parents Against Tobacco, Richard Branson was faced with a clear conclusion. Although the campaign had been run entirely privately as an independent organization, it had once again come up against the inertia of government and politics in achieving its goal. Not only had the stricter provisions that Wilson and Dunmore wanted incorporated into the bill been struck out by the government; more important, the limits even of the power of government to change private behaviour had been demonstrated. It would take a great deal more than a new law to eradicate smoking among children – just as it would take more than his association with Parents Against Tobacco to persuade Branson himself to give up smoking.

The easiest way to change society for the good was not from Westminster. For a businessman like Richard Branson, quicker and surer results could be obtained by by-passing the political process altogether, raising money using his own talents, and then giving it to others to spend directly in the community. Branson may not have known it at the time he was working on Parents Against Tobacco, but that would be the guiding principle behind his 1994 bid for Britain's new National Lottery.

Running lotteries is a highly profitable business. So profitable, in fact, that the governments of most countries in the industrialized world have deemed it too profitable to be left to business alone. They have forbidden private operators to run lotteries above a certain size, and have instead awarded themselves a monopoly right to operate a single lottery, either at a state or at a national level.

Britain was one of the very first countries to operate a national lottery. During the reign of Queen Elizabeth I, Parliament established the running of 'a verie rich Lotterie Generall, without any blancks, contayning a great number of good prizes, as well of redy money as of plate'. Its purpose was straightforward: 'such commoditie as may chaunce to arise thereof . . . may be converted towardes the reparation of the havens [ports] and the strengthe of the realme.'

But in the twentieth century, the British had held back where other countries had not. This was partly because of the misgivings of the Church, which had successfully resisted for many years the spread of gambling from race courses to high-street bookmakers. Partly, too, it was because the government thought it already had a perfectly adequate public betting system – the 'premium bonds', which were first sold in 1956. The idea behind the bonds was straightforward: every bond bought had its number entered into a monthly draw, and prizes were given out. But it was only the interest on their money that 'investors' in the premium bonds were gambling; for at any time after six months, they had the right to return the bond and receive back the original sum they had paid. Because of this principle, ministers were able to raise money for the Exchequer without subjecting themselves to the accusation that they were encouraging the sin of gambling. Premium bonds also had an alluring modernity about them: the winning numbers were picked randomly by an early sort of computer, which had been given the name ERNIE – Electronic Random Number Indicator Equipment.

By the 1980s, however, the situation had changed. Although Britain had no national lottery, the football pools that had been started before the Second World War had grown into enormous private gambling businesses, taking in and paying out millions of pounds a week. The two leading pools companies, Littlewoods and Vernons, had become a powerful vested interest supporting the status quo. So too had the hundreds and thousands of much smaller raffles and tombolas operated by charities up and down the country. These charities feared that a national lottery, whatever sums it might raise, would probably reduce their own revenues.

It was only the arrival of the single European market in 1992 that forced the government to act. Until then, it had always been theoretically open to the authorities to forbid British citizens to enter foreign lotteries. Once the European Community became a single market, such a policy became a restraint of trade which could, at least in theory, leave the government open to legal challenge in the European Court of Justice. As a Private Member's Bill was prepared in Parliament for the establishment of a national lottery in 1992, ministers began to think that a British lottery might not necessarily be such a bad idea after all. The word was therefore put out to Conservative MPs to oppose the bill; for the government was going to introduce a lottery bill of its own in the coming session.

Richard Branson, always quick to spot a market opportunity, had seen the possibilities of a lottery four years earlier. In 1988, he had been staying with Irish friends in County Kildare, and had passed an attractive new building – which he was told to his astonishment had been built with part of the proceeds of Ireland's national lottery.

He wasted no time. A few weeks later, he sent a letter to Margaret Thatcher.

> Dear Prime Minister
> As you may know, I am attempting to persuade various businessmen and women to use their business skills to underwrite and set up new businesses which would pledge 100% of their profits to charities. This is going very well.
> With this hat on, I recently visited Ireland to study their

National Lottery. I was enormously impressed with the way it was run and with the tremendously beneficial impact it has had on charities there. (In Ireland alone, £100m was raised in year one.)

I – and a group of British business leaders – would be willing to underwrite, set up, and run a National Lottery in this country, 100% of whose profits would be ploughed back in to good causes. (For instance a good percentage of the money raised could be used to help tackle the Inner Cities problems.) I believe that a well run National Lottery could earn between one and two billion pounds a year.

I also believe that if an organization like the Healthcare Foundation was to run this Lottery, any misgivings politicians might have would quickly be dispelled, and that it could become a great force for good in Britain as it has become in Ireland.

I am taking this matter up with the Rt Hon Douglas Hurd [the Home Secretary at the time] but thought you might also like to consider this approach to the lottery issue.

Yours sincerely, Richard Branson.

Margaret Thatcher was an admirer of Branson's; she had travelled down the Thames on his boat after the successful attempt on the Atlantic sea speed record. But her reply was noncommittal. The Treasury civil servants whom Branson later invited to lunch explained in more detail. The time, they thought, was not ripe.

By 1993, it was. But the government was not willing to hand the lottery on a plate to Branson and his friends, no matter how much they might protest that they were in it for solely altruistic motives. When the lotteries bill received its royal assent in October, an entirely different framework had been established. Rather than merely appoint a lottery operator, the government would be true to its principles and encourage the workings of a competitive market to maximize the amount of money raised by the lottery for good causes. An Office of the National Lottery (Oflot) would be established; and Oflot's director-general would be given the job of putting the licence to operate the national lottery until March 2001 out to tender. The company that won the contract to operate the lottery would be the company that offered to charge the lowest operating fee and to bring in the largest amount of revenue.

Many people, having had a selfless attempt to do something for the community rebuffed in such a way, would have retired in a sulk. Branson did not. Whatever his private feelings on the matter, the Virgin chairman felt that the idea of allowing an operator to make profits from the lottery was misconceived. Business, to his mind, was about taking risks and earning profits; but the long hours he had spent in conversation with John Fitzpatrick, the man who had run Ireland's national lottery for almost five years, had convinced him that there was remarkably little risk in running a lottery. It was a monopoly, after all; to make a success of it, the operator merely had to arrange matters in a half-competent way and wait for the money to flow in. As soon as he got wind of the government's plans, therefore, Branson started to consider how he might put in a winning bid.

His first move was to call upon John Jackson, the man who had set up the Healthcare Foundation. After spending a year establishing the foundation's new brand of Mates condoms, Jackson had been recruited by Anita Roddick to serve as the managing director for her Body Shop business, responsible directly to her and her husband Gordon. After more than five years, however, Jackson was ready to move on. Differences of opinion had begun to open up between him and the Roddicks; he felt that the couple were too concerned with social issues, and reluctant to recognize that their business had moved so much into the British retailing mainstream that it was now competing with the likes of Boots and Marks & Spencer. Jackson felt that his employers were not paying enough attention to the fact that the growth of their business was coming more from opening new shops than from rising sales in existing shops. So when Richard Branson, a man he knew he could get on with, suggested that Jackson should work for him as a consultant for a while, and do a feasibility study into a bid for the national lottery, Jackson had no hesitation. He jumped at the idea.

In September 1993, Jackson returned from a month-long trip to the United States with two firm conclusions to report: first, that the idea of putting together a bid for the lottery in which the operator's profits would go to charity was perfectly feasible; and second, that the figures that the government had talked of while the lottery act was proceeding through Parliament were highly favourable to the operator.

The estimates from which bidders were to start their calculations were as follows. Half of all the lottery's receipts would be repaid to the punters in prizes. About 12 per cent would be paid into the Exchequer in the form of a special lottery duty. About 23 per cent would go into a public fund for good causes, to be divided equally between sport, arts, charities, national heritage, and a new Millennium Fund. That left about 15 per cent of the receipts for the lottery operator itself. Yet Jackson's investigation of the accounts of the various companies who had contracts to operate lotteries around the world suggested that it was possible to run a lottery on the scale that would be necessary for a great deal less than 15 per cent of the total proceeds. According to his calculations, the lottery could be operated for a cost of only 9 per cent of its receipts. Every percentage point that the operator charged above that would be pure profit.

In September 1993, Branson and Jackson had lunch with Guy Snowden, the chief executive of GTech Corporation, the world's largest lottery operating company. When he heard Branson raise the idea that GTech might co-operate with a lottery bid whose profits would be remitted to charity, Snowden appeared pessimistic; he said that he did not believe it possible for an operator to make money on less than 13 per cent of the total receipts. 'He tried to persuade us not to enter the arena,' recalled Jackson. 'He wanted to frighten me off.' But Branson and Jackson had done their homework, and believed that they knew better. They drew the lunch to a speedy conclusion, and decided as soon as Snowden had left Branson's house in Holland Park that they would go for it. The UK Lottery Foundation set to work.

The division of labour between Richard Branson and John Jackson was clear. Branson's job was to open doors. He telephoned Lord Young of Graffham, with whom he had struck up a friendship while running the UK 2000 project, and won the former cabinet minister's immediate promise to serve as co-chairman of the project. It required only a few more meetings to balance the party weighting of the ticket by bringing in Lord Whitelaw, a former Conservative deputy prime minister, and Lord Callaghan, a former

Labour prime minister, as trustees. Branson was also able to drum up support for the project among small charities. As the organizations that would suffer most from the creation of a national lottery, Branson realized, the charities would be likely at first to oppose the entire idea; but a well-judged commitment to donate a proportion of the lottery operating company's profits to small charities was enough to turn scores of charities and voluntary organizations into backers of the scheme. Branson also approached John Fitzpatrick, and won his provisional acceptance of the position of chief executive of the operating company if the bid should succeed.

Jackson's job was to work on the details of the bid itself. After he had written a 200-page business plan, there were four elements to consider: the machinery and telephone lines that would be needed to connect lottery machines across the country with a central computer; the marketing of the lottery; the arrangements for as broad a distribution of lottery tickets as possible; and the financing of the operating company. Every Sunday for two months, Jackson flew across to Ireland and fired questions about lotteries at Fitzpatrick, working hard to achieve a detailed understanding of exactly what would be involved. Armed with this information, he started approaching potential partners. Everyone he discussed the bid with was required to sign a draconian confidentiality agreement, promising to keep secret and in a safe place the information on the bid that Jackson provided, and agreeing to pay costs and damages if it were inadvertently released.

The logistics department was straightforward. With Fitzpatrick's help, Jackson wrote a specification for the computer and communications system he wanted, and put it out to tender with half a dozen big computer and telephone companies. The winner was IBM. Not only did the US giant have proven expertise in building large, widely distributed systems; it also controlled the second largest telecommunications network in Britain – larger than that of Mercury, the country's biggest competitor to British Telecom. And, conveniently, its bid was lower than that of NCR, ICL or AT&T.

For their marketing strategy, Jackson and Branson went to most of the top advertising agencies in London. They did not see Saatchi

& Saatchi; the country's biggest agency had already signed up with Camelot, the consortium that GTech Corp had established. After long meetings with Grey Communications and Abbott, Mead, Vickers, they chose J. Walter Thompson. In its favour, JWT, like Branson, had been thinking about the lottery for some years. But in the case of the advertising agency, the motivation was more economic: whatever the risks of becoming involved in the lottery, the operating company's advertising agency was almost certain to make millions of pounds. For their public relations consultancy, the two picked Burson-Marsteller, the company to which Des Wilson, Branson's old friend from Parents Against Tobacco, had decamped after decades of impoverished political correctness.

Much of the success of the lottery would depend on its ability to persuade newspaper kiosks and small shops across the country to stock tickets. Unfortunately, Cadbury-Schweppes, Britain's leading confectionery company, was already signed up with GTech in the Camelot bid. But Mars UK, its most bitter competitor, was not; and after a brief meeting and a stroll around his back garden with some of their directors on a cold January morning, Branson was able to sign the company up to handle his bid's distribution. The company was interested because it knew that lottery tickets and sweets were both bought on impulse; being involved in the lottery would help it to place its Mars Bars and other products in advantageous locations in supermarkets and shops. So it was willing to put its powerful database of information on the country's chocolate retailers at Branson's disposal.

Arranging finance proved a little more difficult. Jackson's plan showed that the lottery would require over £200m in start-up costs. For a lottery consortium intending to pocket the proceeds, this posed no obstacle; shareholders would put up the start-up capital in return for the profits they expected to receive in future. But Branson's bid had no shareholders to call on. Instead, it would have to raise bank finance. The first port of call was the Hong Kong and Shanghai Bank, because Lord Young knew its chief executive. In principle, the bank was interested; but as a matter of good practice, it wanted Midland Bank, its British subsidiary, to sort out the details. When Jackson sat down with the lending officers from Midland, however, his heart sank. Although their questions were intelligent and to the point – and they were offering to charge an interest rate of only a percentage point and a half above base rates – it soon became clear that the bank viewed itself as a surrogate shareholder. It would be willing to provide funds; but it wanted at least half of the money it lent to be backed by a personal guarantee from Richard Branson.

Branson, on holiday in Thailand for Christmas, hardly paused for thought when Jackson broke the news to him over the telephone. Could he put £40m of his own money at risk? Certainly he could. But if a better deal could be struck elsewhere, he would rather avoid giving such a guarantee. Over the next few days, Jackson worked frantically to arrange meetings with other banks. By early January, he had a more attractive suggestion. IBM itself would provide credit to cover the upfront costs of the £150m of equipment it would provide. And J. P. Morgan, an American investment bank which sent most of its executives across the Atlantic aboard Virgin jets, announced within a matter of days its willingness to lend £50m to the foundation at an even lower interest rate – and without a personal guarantee. With a guaranteed overdraft facility from Lloyds of £15m, the UK Lottery Foundation had overcome its highest hurdle. By the time Branson returned from his holiday, the financing of his bid was in place.

The bid was announced at the Roof Gardens, Branson's Kensington nightclub, on 20 January. Des Wilson had done a superb job. To put public pressure on Peter Davis and his colleagues at Oflot, he unveiled the results of an opinion poll which showed that 72 per cent of the British public wanted the lottery to be awarded to a company that would give all its profits to good causes, and 64 per cent had actually said that they would be more likely to play if they knew that all profits were going to charity. Wilson claimed the support of the Bishop of Liverpool, who had reversed the Church of England's initial hostility to the idea of a lottery at all, but had said firmly that the franchise ought to be awarded to the company that promised to give the highest proportion of its profits back to charity. (Given the ill-feeling between the lords of the church and the ministers of the Crown, however, this was of dubious benefit in convincing the government of the merits of Branson's campaign.)

Wilson had also drummed up an early day motion from the House of Commons, signed by 54 MPs of all parties, urging 'Her Majesty's Government to give preference in awarding the licence ... to those companies or foundations which ... will ... donate all their profits ... to worthwhile causes, as happens in other countries.'

There was also a careful script for Richard Branson himself to read, though its inept phrasing bore his own personal stamp. 'If together we can achieve this, there is no one action any of us on our own, or collectively, could take in our lifetime that could achieve more.'

But this was no oratory competition. The challenge was to show that the bid made sense in business terms. Here Lord Young stepped in. 'Let me make one thing clear,' he said. 'This is not, as some describe it, a non-profitmaking bid. On the contrary, we are determined to make more money than anybody else. We intend to be leaner, more efficient more dynamic, and in the end more profitable. The difference between us and the other bidders for the licence is what we will do with the profits; they will keep them and we will return them to the community.'

For all the publicity and hoopla, however, there was an angle that neither Branson nor his colleagues had addressed: scale. In trying to maximize the returns to good causes, Branson and his team were offering to pay all their operating profits to charity (though there was some doubt about whether a non-governmental foundation could officially be the arbiter of a 'good cause'). But to Peter Davis and the Oflot committee this seemingly faultless altruistic pledge may not, of itself, have amounted to the best deal for the charities. Once corporation tax has been paid, this profit – the bonus after all prizes have been distributed and the lion's share has been given to the government's National Lottery Fund – this profit for which Branson had such high hopes, would amount to only one or two per cent of the total lottery turnover. If another operator could achieve total lottery sales just a few per cent higher than Branson could, then Oflot would still be justified in giving the franchise to the rival. For even after taking its profits – even after enriching its shareholders in what Branson so dismissively believed to be a monopoly requiring little entrepreneurial imagination – the rival company would be bringing in a larger total sum for good causes. The good bishop who had argued for awarding the lottery to the company that gave the largest share of its profits to charity, therefore, was talking through his mitre.

As the 14 February deadline for submission of applications approached, Branson's became the bookies' clear favourite. Since the UK Lottery Foundation bid was being funded entirely out of Branson's own pocket, the various subcontractors were required to cover their own costs. That was flattering enough, since the bid had been prepared on a shoestring. While other bodies were believed to have spent £10m or more in producing the 3,500 pages of documentation demanded by Oflot, the UK Lottery Foundation's bill, which was to be paid by Richard Branson personally, had been kept well under £1m.

Matters began to look more promising still on the day when bids were actually submitted. All the contenders had made an effort to attract some publicity of their bids. Faceless men in suits and women in bright T-shirts braved the February drizzle for the sake of the photo-opportunity. The Branson bid did better. Simon Burridge, the man at J. Walter Thompson who was in charge of the lottery project, was a member of the family that owned Desert Orchid, arguably the most famous horse in British racing history. In an apparently pointless gesture, Richard Branson and Lord Young posed with the horse in front of the Oflot headquarters to commemorate the submission of their bid. Relevant or no, however, their gesture stole the lion's share of the publicity. With the space to print only one photograph from among the eight consortiums that had submitted bids, the following morning's papers did not hesitate in choosing the Branson pictures. The moral seemed clear: if the UK Lottery Foundation could attract coverage in such a small matter as this, it would surely outclass the others effortlessly in running the lottery itself.

Peter Davis, the director-general of the lottery, decided that his committee's decision would be communicated simultaneously by fax to the eight bidding consortiums. On the appointed day in May 1994, a small crowd of photographers and television cameramen gathered outside Branson's house in Holland Park in anticipation of the announcement. A huge banner across the front of the house bore the legend UK LOTTERY FOUNDATION: A NEW MILLIONAIRE A WEEK. Indoors, Branson, Jackson, Young and a number of others involved in the bid waited anxiously by the fax machine. As the appointed moment approached, Branson found himself unable to bear the tension. He left the room to wait alone next door.

It was his friend Simon Draper, invited from his office in the mews around the corner, who brought the news. 'It's Camelot,' he said.

Richard Branson had lost.

His first reaction was a mixture of anger and disappointment. The UK Lottery Foundation was keeping no profits for itself; Branson had used all his negotiating wiles to secure the lowest possible prices from the various subcontractors and suppliers. So how could it be that another bidder had undercut him? Interviewed for the lunch-time news, the crestfallen Virgin chairman declared his intention to seek a judicial review of the decision. Radio Four's current-affairs programme 'The World at One' expatiated on the iniquity of Oflot's failure to choose Branson's bid, and subjected Davis to a searching interrogation on the matter.

It was only in the succeeding weeks that the real story emerged. Davis had ignored the Foundation's claim, based on its opinion poll, that more people would play the lottery if they knew the profits were going to good causes. He had also ignored the plan to donate the Foundation's profits to a private charitable foundation, rather than to throw them into the public pot of the National Lottery Development Fund. So the two great strengths of Branson's bid had been effectively ruled out of the decision-making process. Once that had been done, the UK Lottery Foundation's figures looked less exciting. Davis's decision to award the lottery to the Camelot consortium could therefore be justified on the grounds that its bid would raise more money for the National Lottery Development Fund than any other.

Although the information was never formally made public, John Jackson tried to piece together afterwards the figures that showed why the UK Lottery Foundation had lost. His table looked something like this:

BRITAIN'S NATIONAL LOTTERY: WHY BRANSON LOST
Breakdown of how two different bids would have spent the lottery proceeds

	UKL	Camelot
Prize money	50%	50%
Duty payable to government	12%	12%
National Lottery Development Fund (including unclaimed prizes)	28.1%	28.1%
Operating costs	8.3%	8.8%
Corporation tax payable on profits	–	0.3%
Profit after tax	1.6%	0.8%
TOTAL	100%	100%

Source: UK Lottery Foundation estimates. The full statistics have not been made public.

Clearly the Foundation had surpassed its rivals by finding a cheaper way of running the lottery, with operating costs at 8.3 per cent, and they were surprised to discover how low the after-tax profit amongst the competition had been. In one way, this calculation made Branson more miserable than ever. There was only one consolation: by entering the bidding, it was Branson who had forced the others to cut their profit margins to the bone. Instead of paying the operator 13 per cent of the lottery's turnover to run it, taxpayers would instead be paying only 10 per cent. The gap between the two was more than merely an academic measure of efficiency: in practice, it meant hundreds of millions of pounds extra into the National Lottery Development Fund, for which Branson could take personal credit.

Branson had already come in for public criticism because he had intemperately described Davis's decision as 'crass'. The *Daily Mail* told him that he 'really ought to be big enough and philosophical enough to take this setback on the chin'. The *Daily Telegraph* observed dryly that 'British sports managers have institutionalized the disagreeable custom of proclaiming after their defeats: "We wuz robbed!" It was sad to see Mr Richard Branson on Wednesday outdo all of them in his lamentations ... Mr Branson is not St Francis of Assisi. He is an astute businessman who has made a large fortune, and goes out of his way ruthlessly to promote his own virtues. He cannot expect that his drive for beatification will necessarily be received by the world on his own terms.' The *Scotsman* was more pithy still: 'Poor Richard Branson. Now there's a comment we never expected to write in these columns.'

Given a day or two to think matters over, Branson decided that he would not after all seek a judicial review of the decision. There was a practical reason for not doing so: to have a hope of winning, he would have to show that Davis had acted negligently or had performed a gross act of maladministration, which would not be easy to do since he had clearly carried the intentions of Parliament as well as he and his panel of experts knew how. The newspaper editorials offered a further reason for giving up the idea of asking for a judicial review. Since the lottery would be in limbo until the review was concluded, Branson would inevitably be blamed for delaying the lottery and thus for denying millions (and possibly tens or even hundreds of millions) of pounds to the good causes he had so publicly espoused. His good name was now too valuable a commodity to put at risk in such an enterprise.

EPILOGUE: UP, UP AND AWAY

ONE RAINY DAY in May 1994, Richard Branson looked out of the window of his house in Holland Park and decided to compile a list of all the outstanding business projects for which he was awaiting approval from the authorities in different countries. The list, scrawled in his confident ballpoint hand, started with his bid for the National Lottery and his attempt to persuade the Radio Authority to transfer his Virgin 1215 station from its medium-wave slot to a more lucrative frequency that would allow broadcast in stereo – both of which were later to be turned down. But there were fifteen other items on the list, ranging from the opening of a Virgin megastore in New York's Times Square to the building of a new hotel on the Greek island of Hydra, and from a plan to run Virgin trains through the Channel Tunnel to a secret deal to sell a 10 to 20 per cent stake in the airline to a Hong Kong investment group.

Branson's life had changed dramatically over the past twenty-five years. Instead of living on a houseboat and envying the well-to-do inhabitants of the stucco mansions in Holland Park, he was now rich beyond his dreams, living in a mansion and considering a return to the simpler life of a houseboat. Instead of having to spend two hours on the telephone every day pleading for advertisements for his student magazine, he now had to employ three secretaries to protect him from those who wished to call him. Instead of cutting corners and indulging in petty deceits to keep his tiny business in profit, he was now the proprietor of a billion-pound business that could run itself adequately if he decided to take a six-month holiday. The 'battle for survival' that had been the defining characteristic of his early business career had been won.

The year 1994 had other resonances, too. It marked the twenty-

357

first birthday of Virgin Records – an occasion which was celebrated with a number of lavish parties and with a 90-minute television programme which was broadcast in the main evening slot on the May Bank Holiday. Branson was a willing participant, but he had sold the company five years earlier. More important to him was the other anniversary that summer: the tenth birthday of Virgin Atlantic Airways. With many great commercial successes behind him, Branson had still not yet attained his forty-fourth birthday. Judging by his grandmother, who had won herself a place in the *Guinness Book of Records* in 1989 as the only 90-year-old ever to achieve a hole in one at golf, Branson still had half his life ahead of him. And he was as popular and as good at public relations as ever. In the middle of the parties, *Newsweek* magazine put his face on its cover. UP, UP & AWAY, said its story. 'The hair is shorter and the beard greying, but the irrepressible Richard Branson still just wants to have fun expanding his Virgin Group worldwide.'

The car crash took place while the magazine was on the news-stands. After attending a Friday night awards ceremony, Branson was driving his family down the M40 motorway from London to their home in Oxfordshire just after midnight. Swerving to avoid another driver who had cut in on his Range Rover, Branson drove a few inches too far towards the central verge of the motorway. One of the wheels of the heavy vehicle caught in a gully and exploded – and before Branson or any of his passengers knew what had hit them, the Range Rover had flipped over and was skidding downhill on an unlit stretch of motorway. Trailing sparks and smoke, it came to rest on its roof in the outside lane.

Branson, his wife and his two children may have survived the crash. But they were now trapped upside down inside the car, unable to open doors or to break the windows, helpless before the oncoming cars. Fortunately, a woman police officer was waiting in her car on the other carriageway of the motorway almost exactly opposite. It was almost eight minutes before the brave officer was able to run across the road and smash the windows open with a metal cosh she had confiscated from a thief caught earlier that day. During those eight minutes, there was no time for the sort of meditation in which Branson had indulged when he was trapped aboard a runaway balloon high above the Irish Sea. The children were screaming, and the shocked Branson and his wife were drawn into a terrified argument about whether it would be safer to stay in the car and risk being driven into by an oncoming car or to get out and risk being mown down as they ran across the lanes to safety.

Twenty-four hours later, it was all over. Branson had recovered from the shock; his wife Joan and 12-year-old daughter Holly had sustained minor bruising from the action of their seat belts, but were now fine; and Sam, his son of nine, had been discharged from hospital after spending the night there under observation.

The Virgin chairman cancelled all his appointments for the following day – including the scheduled final interview for this book. But he threw himself back to work immediately afterwards, and his first task was to deal with some mail. Not only did he receive many messages of sympathy from old friends who had heard about the accident on the news. Also, considerate police officers had retrieved a sheaf of two hundred unanswered letters which had been thrown out of the back of the Range Rover by the accident on to a road below. 'There was obviously a temptation to say that's settled that lot of mail,' he told me as we perched on sofas in his Holland Park sitting-room at eight o'clock on the following Wednesday morning, trays of coffee and toast in front of us. 'But you have a responsibility in life, you know ... I've answered all the letters.' That night, he was off to County Hall for another Virgin Atlantic birthday party; the following morning, he had to be up early to catch a flight to Edinburgh so that he could be present at the opening of the latest Virgin megastore. Less than a month later, he decided to reorganize the airline's entire top management, moving both his joint managing directors out of their posts.

To most people, a man who can answer two hundred letters within a few days of nearly losing his life in a car accident has an unusual dedication to his work. Branson does not see it that way. He feels a responsibility to his employees, and to his customers; and he feels a obligation to put the money he has made to good use. 'I've never ever seen it as personal money; always seen it as a means to achieve things,' he said. 'Money's there to be invested and used to its full. It gives one an element of freedom but at the same time gives one such a big responsibility.' He cites his cleaning lady's reaction to the family's brush with death: 'It's too early for you to go up there,' she told him. 'You're needed down here.'

In a sense, these sentiments are richly ironic. Many entrepreneurs set out to make themselves wealthy with the aim of retiring, but then find themselves unable to stop because they have grown fond of the work habits they have acquired rich. In feeling a moral obligation to his own offshore bank accounts which requires him to keep on working, Branson has gone one better.

The truth is of course that Richard Branson loves his work for its own sake, and finds the principal fulfilment of his life in it. He no longer seeks to justify it to his wife in any other terms. 'Joan knows that I've got work to do; I suspect she knows that our relationship would be more difficult rather than easier if I gave everything up.' Nor is he working for his children; although Branson can fairly boast that he spends more time with them than most fathers do, he does not want them to think they will never have to work. He sees his own childhood of impoverished gentility as perfectly happy – and he believes that his parents' lack of money (which made them unable to supply puddings after dinner or to afford any better form of transport than a 'bumpety-bump' car) was entirely healthy and beneficial to him and his sisters. Although Sam and Holly will be billionaires by the time they reach adulthood, Branson does not want his children's lives to be empty of purpose merely because of the existence of the offshore trusts he has set up.

The future of their father must remain hard to predict. A few weeks before the accident, he was expecting to devote the bulk of his time over the next two years to running the National Lottery. Once his bid failed, Branson took it for granted that he would return to the airline, his principal interest among his businesses, and continue looking after it from day to day. There is clearly a job there for him to do, serving as a figurehead both for employees and for customers, and as a magnet for ideas and for potential new employees. But the rate of change of his life so far makes it unlikely that Branson will still be launching new airline routes and opening new megastores in the year 2004. He may well have sold the retail businesses or the airline or both, and moved into a new business; or he may have parlayed the public prominence that his business career has given him into something wider.

When he is asked whether he has political ambitions, Richard Branson's first reaction is to laugh. He has always tried to stay aloof from supporting one political party rather than another, and he denies the newspaper reports that quoted him in the 1980s as having said that if Virgin were to give money to a political party, it would be to the Tories. Trevor Abbott, his group managing director, describes Branson as 'more apolitical than most people I know'.

There is a more serious hurdle. In order to fit in to the current structure of British politics, Branson's first step would have to be to serve as a backbench member of Parliament. Yet that life, glamorous though it must seem to most people, would be a distinct step down for Branson. His day would be wasted in unnecessary meetings and interminable debates. His outspoken frankness would wither under the gimlet eye of the party whips. His opinions would be his party's, not his own. Denied the opportunity to launch a new business venture every six months, he would be less in the public eye – and less influential – than at present.

Yet it is easy to see how Branson's skills could be put to use at the top of politics. His supreme ability is to deal with people: to motivate those who work for him; to enthuse those who watch him from afar; and to disarm those who dislike him. His lack of interest in detail, and his instinctive feel for the big picture, are assets. And even if it may be true, as his own managing director jokes, that Branson cannot read a balance sheet, the same has been true of numerous Conservative Chancellors of the Exchequer.

Undoubtedly, British methods of governance would have to change before an outsider in the Branson mould could become a political force. The nature of political parties would have to reform; the rhetoric of discourse would have to become more technocratic and less ideological; and proportionality would have to play a greater part in the electoral system. None of these things are impossibilities. The prospect of Branson becoming a British prime minister may seem highly remote; but it was what his mother wished for when he was a child. Underneath the guile that lies underneath the frankness, that may just be Richard Branson's most private ambition.

ACKNOWLEDGMENTS

This is not an authorized book. When I first wrote to Richard Branson to let him know that I was working on it, he replied that he was too busy to participate; it was only later on, as news filtered back to him of the research that I was doing, that he changed his mind. We agreed to meet once, and then again. By the time the project was finished, we had completed eight long sessions: some of them over breakfast or in the garden of his house in Holland Park, and others running from morning until early evening during weekends at his estate in Oxfordshire. Branson also encouraged his friends, his family, his business partners and his employees to talk to me.

I am therefore very grateful to him for his time and his hospitality, and for that of his wife, Joan. Branson was careful to tell me, however, that his principal reason for talking to me was in order to correct what he feared might be the negative impressions I would receive from other people. As the research drew to a close, and I began to put to him in detail the less flattering things that I had been told, he came to the conclusion that the book was deliberately biased against him.

I was in two minds on the question of whether to offer to let him read the manuscript. On the one hand, doing so would allow him to correct any mistakes or misinterpretations that had not been picked up by the four other participants in the story who checked it for accuracy. On the other, I had concluded from my research that Branson is sensitive about the way he is portrayed almost to the point of paranoia – and I feared that he might use his lawyers to bully me into removing from the book anecdotes or incidents that he would prefer to remain secret, even though they were fair and accurate. In the end, I offered Branson a deal: he would read the book, and I would agree to correct anything that he could show was wrong; but he would not be allowed to send in his lawyers afterwards.

On the advice on Gerrard Tyrrell, his solicitor at Harbottle &

Lewis, Branson declined this proposal. Despite his attempts to gain access to the manuscript by other routes, and his increasingly strident demands to read it on his own terms, he has not read the book.

Gill Coleridge and Michael Fishwick can each fairly claim to have thought of the idea for this book, and both of them have been supportive and consummately professional as it has progressed. I am also particularly grateful to Richard Wheaton for his patience and his advice on editorial and other matters.

It would have been impossible to write this book without the cooperation of scores of people who have known or dealt with Richard Branson, or who have been employed by him. I owe thanks above all to Trevor Abbott, Don Cruickshank, Simon Draper and Steve Lewis for the many hours they spent telling me stories and answering questions. Kristen and Axel Ball were hospitable when I visited them in Mallorca.

Some of those I spoke to or who gave me documents preferred not to be identified. Among those who were willing to be named are Nick Alexander, Freda Angus, Moto Arizumi, Mike Batt, David Benson, Ken Berry, Sir Michael Bishop, Tony Bland, Chay Blyth, Eve Branson, John Brown, Mick Brown, Simon Burke, David Campbell, Tim Chaney, Eiko Cho, Ray Colegate, Roger Cowe, Chris Craib, Robert Devereux, Jane Dunmore, Tony Elliot, Sir Malcolm Field, Randolph Fields, Christian Flood, Maria Forte, Simon Foster, Andrew Galloway, Roy Gardner, Caroline Gold, Rob Gold, Mike Herriot, Colin Howes, John Jackson, Barbara Jeffries, Mike Kendrick, Jeremy Lascelles, Ann Leach, Charles Levison, Per Lindstrand, Bronwen Maddox, Malcolm McLaren, Jonathan Meades, Fiona Miller, Chris Moss, Stephen Navin, Tom Newman, Clifford Paice, Sir Nicholas Pearson, Syd Pennington, Penni Pike, Nik Powell, Peter Preston, Nigel Primrose, Anthony Salz, Roger Seelig, Rob Shreeve, Victor Smart, Cob Stenham, David Tait, John Thornton, John Varnom, Arthur Viccary, Rod Vickery, Lord Wakeham, James Ware, Tessa Watts, Michael Watts, Jon Webster, Hugh Welburn, Will Whitehorn, Sir Graham Wilkins, Richard Williams, Des Wilson, Carol Wilson, Chris Witty and Lord Young of Graffham.

I would also like to thank the library staff at the *Independent*, the *Evening Standard*, *The Times*, and the *Financial Times*; and the picture desk and picture libraries of the *Independent*, the *Daily Mirror* and News International. Andreas Whittam Smith was particularly generous in agreeing to allow me access to *Independent* photographs printed in this book. My thanks also to Pictorial Press, London, and Channel Four Television for kind permission to reproduce their photographs. My colleagues Roger Berthoud and John O'Sullivan were understanding of the demands that writing placed on my time, and cooperative with my efforts to meet my responsibilities to the paper while the book was progressing.

The manuscript was read, either in whole or in part, by Trevor Abbott, Ruth Benjamin, Simon Draper, Don Cruickshank, Judy Jackson, Steve Lewis and Yehuda Najman. I am grateful to all of them for their comments. I would also like to thank David Blackburn and Judy and Michael Jackson for the many hours of advice they gave during the course of the project. Above all, however, I owe a debt to Emily Marbach for her patience, her inspiration, her good humour, her moral support and her weekday lunches. This book could never have been written without her.

CHRONOLOGY AND INDEX

CHRONOLOGY

1950   Richard Charles Nicholas Branson born, first child of
Edward (Ted), barrister, and Eve Branson, former
dancer and air stewardess

1956   Early education at Scaitcliffe Preparatory School

1963   Moves to Cliff View House to be crammed for
Common Entrance Examination

1964   Admitted to Stowe School, Buckinghamshire

1966   Founds *Student* magazine with a schoolfriend

1967   Leaves Stowe after O Levels, moves to London to work
full-time on magazine

1968   First issue of *Student*
Branson's first appearance on television
Founds non-profit Student Advisory Centre to help
with young people's problems
Opens nurses' employment agency

1969   Takes out High Court writ to force the Beatles to
provide recording for *Student*'s front cover
Opens mail-order record business to take advantage of
abolition of retail price maintenance; first
advertisement appears in last issue of *Student*

1970   Fined £7 for using words 'venereal disease' in publicity
materials for Student Advisory Centre; defended by
John Mortimer
Gives boyhood friend and partner Nik Powell 40 per
cent stake in Virgin

1971 Postal strike. Opens first record shop
Simon Draper, Branson's South African cousin, joins
Virgin
Buys Shipton Manor, Oxfordshire for £30,000. Tom
Newman supervises building of recording studio
there
Raided by HM Customs & Excise, and arrested for
purchase-tax fraud. Agrees to pay £53,000 in tax, duties
and charges over coming three years. Prosecution is
dropped
Mike Oldfield arrives at Manor, starts working on
Tubular Bells

1972 Marries Kristen Tomassi
Mail-order record business continues to grow

1973 Registers first Virgin logo as property of offshore trust
Virgin Records releases first four albums. *Tubular Bells*
shoots to top of charts in UK
Establishes music publishing operation

1974 Virgin releases Tangerine Dream's *Phaedra*
Tubular Bells chosen as theme music to *The Exorcist*
Kristen meets Kevin Ayers; marriage to Branson begins
to crumble

1975 Branson fails to sign 10cc and Rolling Stones

1976 Sex Pistols swear at Bill Grundy on TV; Branson fails
to sign them when dropped by EMI
Tom Newman leaves Virgin, forfeiting his shareholding
in the studio business
Meets Joan Templeman, then married to pianist Ronnie
Leahy

1977 Branson signs Pistols after they are dropped by A&M
Records
Mike Oldfield contract renegotiated to increase his
royalties

1978   Buys Necker, private island in British Virgin Islands
Opens The Venue, first Virgin nightclub
Human League signs to Virgin Records

1979   Sid Vicious dies; Pistols fall apart amid litigation
Margaret Thatcher becomes Prime Minister; recession
    continues until 1981

1980   Virgin closes loss-making US office
Phil Collins, former Genesis drummer, signs to Virgin
    record label
Expansion of Virgin Records overseas begins with
    licensing deal in France

1981   Branson buys Roof Gardens nightclub in Kensington,
    and Heaven gay disco in Charing Cross
Powell leaves Virgin with £1m settlement and other
    assets
Branson proposes partnership with Tony Elliot to
    revive his strike-hit magazine *Time Out*. Elliot
    refuses.
Branson launches *Event* in competition to *Time Out*
Mike Oldfield contract renegotiated again
Event closes after heavy losses

1982   Demise of Sir Freddie Laker's airline
Virgin talent scout discovers Boy George

1983   Randolph Fields applies for airline licence to fly Atlantic
Culture Club's hit record 'Do You Really Want to Hurt
    Me' revives Virgin's musical fortunes
Vanson Developments founded to develop residential
    and commercial property
Virgin Games, publisher of computer games software,
    launched

1984   Branson goes into equal partnership with Fields on
    airline, then renegotiates to win majority control
Maiden Voyager, Boeing 747-200, opens New York
    route

Fields resigns as airline chairman

Don Cruickshank hired as Virgin's new group managing
director; Trevor Abbott hired as finance director

Virgin buys into Majorca hotel run by ex-wife Kristen

1985 Fields's airline shares bought out for £1m

Virgin raises £25m by private stockmarket placing

Branson transfers bulk of Virgin shareholding to
offshore trusts

Virgin Holidays formed

Joins unsuccessful *Challenger* attempt on Atlantic sea
speed record, financing Virgin's sponsorship of the
boat by arranging sub-sponsorships and equipment
loans

1986 Branson breaks Atlantic sea speed record in *Challenger
II*, winning huge publicity after success

Branson and Prime Minister Margaret Thatcher
perform lap of honour in speedboat up Thames;
boat later sold for £1m and delivered shortly before
record broken again by Americans

Virgin Group goes public at 140p per share, valuing
company at £240m

Branson becomes chairman of UK2000 environmental
group

1987 Stockmarket crashes, knocking Virgin share price back
below 90p

Forced to abandon attempt at hostile takeover of EMI

Launches Mates condoms, with proceeds to go to
Healthcare Foundation. Virgin directors veto use of
company name in condom venture

Crosses Atlantic in hot-air balloon with Per Lindstrand,
crash-landing in the sea off the coast of Northern
Ireland

Founds Virgin Airship & Balloon Company

Virgin shares listed on NASDAQ over-the-counter
exchange in US

1988 Virgin Atlantic wins right to fly to JFK New York, Los
Angeles, and Tokyo; services start over next two
years
Publication of Mick Brown's *Richard Branson: The Inside
Story*, written at Branson's invitation
Virgin sells smaller record shops to W. H. Smith
Virgin board prepares for withdrawal from stockmarket
Property market reaches peak
Branson and other directors buy company from other
shareholders with loan of £182.5m

1989 Cruickshank resigns as Virgin group managing director;
Abbott takes over
Branson marries Joan Templeman after 12 years'
cohabitation
Vanson Developments loses money heavily on Crawley
property venture, eventually writing off £12m
Fujisankei, Japanese media group, buys 25 per cent of
music businesses for £115m

1990 Lindstrand and Branson fly Pacific in hot-air balloon
Gulf war breaks out during flight; airline recession
begins
Seibu-Saison, Japanese travel and leisure group, buys
10 per cent of airline in £36m deal
Virgin and Marui, Japanese department store chain,
establish 50–50 joint venture company to open
megastores in Japan. First store opens in Shinjuku
district of Tokyo
Virgin Atlantic sends 747 to Iraq to pick up hostages

1991 Virgin operates first Heathrow services
Virgin sells 50 per cent of megastores business to
W. H. Smith
Branson decides to sell Virgin Music Group, the 'jewel
in the crown'
Publishing interests of Virgin Books and W. H. Allen
integrated into Virgin Publishing

1992   Virgin Music Group sold to Thorn-EMI for £560m;
Simon Draper retires and Ken Berry becomes new
chief executive
Blockbuster buys controlling stake in US megastore
business, half of European megastores
Branson threatens libel action against British Airways
for dismissing his allegations of 'dirty tricks'
campaign as publicity-seeking

1993   BA settles libel action for £610,000; total costs of case
believed to be over £4.5m
Virgin Atlantic signs deal with Airbus to acquire new
fleet of A340 aircraft, offering cheaper maintenance
Airline opens business-class lounge at Heathrow
Branson launches Virgin 1215 radio station
Prepares to bid for franchise to operate long-distance
train service in competition with British Rail
Enters deal with Greek airline running London–Athens
service under Virgin colours
Buys back Seibu-Saison's stake in airline

1994   Bids for franchise to run Britain's National Lottery,
promising to give profits to charitable foundation
Airline franchises City Jet to operate Dublin service
from London City Airport
Lottery awarded to rival Camelot consortium; Branson
threatens judicial review, then decides to focus
energies on setting up lottery in South Africa
Airline enters code-sharing agreement with Delta
Airlines
Branson fails to persuade Radio Authority to transfer
Virgin 1215 from medium wave to more lucrative FM
slot
Virgin Atlantic takes $325m anti-trust case against
British Airways to US court
Branson family narrowly escapes death in car accident
on M40 motorway

INDEX